ALL OF THE ABOVE

VOLUME II

With Supplement

ALL OF THE ABOVE
VOLUME II
GENEALOGY AND HISTORY
LINEAL ANCESTORS OF
CECIL VIRGIL COOK, JR (1913-1970)

COOK, FARMER, DORLAND, GOODE, FLOOD, BONDURANT, JONES, KEINADT (KAINADT, KOINER, KOYNER, COINERT AND COINER), DILLER, DORRIS, IRELAND, FELLOWS, SLAGLE, GRADELESS (GRAYLESS GRAYLEY), VAN ARSDALEN, MOORE, COTTON, CHENEY, CARMEAN (CREMEEN), CHEATHAM, HAWKINS, CROCKETT (CROSKETAGNE), DE SAIX, VAN METER (VAN METEREN), BODINE, DUBOIS, RENTFRO, RANDOLPH, BAILLET, PAYNE, AKIN, GRIFFIN, ROPER, BLACKBORNE, HALEY, RICKETTS, NICHOLSON, POWELL, TRIPPET, MACE, CURTIS, BEAUCHAMP, ADAMS, DILLON, BROWN, PEARSON, CROCHERON, STOFF, AISTER, ROBERTSON, DAVIS

Richard Baldwin Cook

NATIVABOOKS.COM

Nativa Books
Cockeysville, MD

Cook is a graduate of the University of Richmond, VA, Union Theological Seminary, New York and Loyola Law School, New Orleans.

ALL OF THE ABOVE
VOLUME II
GENEALOGY AND HISTORY
LINEAL ANCESTORS OF
CECIL VIRGIL COOK, JR (1913-1970)

2ND EDITION, REVISED
With Supplement

COOK, FARMER, DORLAND, GOODE, FLOOD, BONDURANT, JONES, KEINADT (KAINADT), KOINER, KOYNER, COINERT AND COINER), DILLER, DORRIS, IRELAND, FELLOWS, SLAGLE, GRADELESS (GRAYLESS GRAYLEY), VAN ARSDALEN, MOORE, COTTON, CHENEY, CARMEAN (CREMEEN), CHEATHAM, HAWKINS, CROCKETT (CROSKETAGNE), DE SAIX, VAN METER (VAN METEREN), BODINE, DUBOIS, RENTFRO, RANDOLPH, BAILLET, PAYNE, AKIN, GRIFFIN, ROPER, BLACKBORNE, HALEY, RICKETTS, NICHOLSON, POWELL, TRIPPET, MACE, CURTIS, BEAUCHAMP, ADAMS, DILLON, BROWN PEARSON, CROCHERON, STOFF, AISTER, ROBERTSON, DAVIS

Richard Baldwin Cook

NATIVABOOKS.COM

Nativa Books
Nativa LLC
Cockeysville, MD

Copyright 2008 Richard B. Cook

ISBN: 978-0-9791257-2-0

This book and its companion volume are available at on-line sellers, such as Amazon.com, and at bookstores.

CONTENTS

Introduction	Page 5
Cecil V Cook, Jr (1913-1970)	Page 9
Blanche Jeannette Dorland (1873-1967)	Page 21
Cecil Virgil Cook, Sr (1871-1948)	Page 41
James Emory Dorland (1844-1915) Arabelle America Ireland (1850-1895)	Page 55
Sarah Fellows (1829-1921) Martin Ireland (1821-1904)	Page 79
Susan Farmer Cook (1838-1890)	Page 97
Katherine Hawkins (1814-1851) John Goode Farmer (1808-1871)	Page 111
Mary Crockett (1781-1856) William B. Hawkins (1781-1845)	Page 123
Joshua Flood Cook (1834-1912)	Page 131
William F Cook (1802-1850/55) Lucy Flood (1802-1865)	Page 163
Susan Goode Farmer (1783-1864) Her father John Goode (1739-1792)	Page 169
Joshua Flood (1772-1850) Mary Bondurant (1782-1863)	Page 175
Abraham Cook (1774-1854) Sarah Jones (1777-1857)	Page 179

William Cook (abt 1730-abt 1790/91)
Margaret (Jones?) (1734-1797)   Page 223

John Van Meter (1683-1745)
Sara Bodine (1687-1709)   Page 249

Michael Keinath (1720-1796)
Margaret Dillar (1734/44-1813)   Page 263

Anna Barbara Dornis (1703-bef 1766)
Caspar Diller (1696-1787)   Page 269

John Flood (1695-1782)
Agnes Payne (?-?)   Page 279

Thomas Farmer (1586/94-?)
and Virginia Colony   Page 281

Appendix A
"Death of a Husband"
by Betty Cook (1982)   Page 297

Appendix B
"A Short Account of My life and travels"
By William Hickman (1829)   Page 305

Roster of Illustrations   Page 341

Index   Page 343

Supplement   Page 363

Introduction to 2nd Edition

This is the second of two volumes of family history. The first book is devoted to the ancestors of my mother, Elizabeth Huey Taylor Cook. This second book is focused on Dad's ancestry. Cecil Virgil Cook Jr.

The context of our family's personal doings includes the sweep of U.S. history during its first four hundred years. Every life is a story. Every genealogist is a historian and every historian is an editor, selecting facts and arranging them into the story. Hopefully, the finished product is accurate – whatever that means. The four hundred year period, beginning in North America in 1607, is a saga of remarkable incidents, many of them astonishing for their bizarre violence and religious fervor.

Our ancestors played parts in Revolutionary and Civil Wars, in the early settlement of Massachusetts, Virginia, Maryland, New Amsterdam (New York), New Jersey, Pennsylvania and then westward into Ohio, Indiana, Kentucky, and Missouri. These colonists, settlers, frontier folk, militiamen, judges, sheriffs, farmers, professionals, house keepers, and preachers were actors in a number of mythic happenings. Many of the recorded events were legal proceedings: Witch Trials, Boston Massacre trials, the murder of a three year old girl and the trial of her enslaved mother, the murder of a Kentucky Klansman by a cousin. These incidents, many of them heavy with irony, reflected and also contributed to the character and self-understanding of the people of the United States.

Some of our ancestors, from earliest colonial days, made decisions which allowed them to *own* other human beings. These choices were a moral catastrophe and could have and should have been seen in that way at the time. There were those, including some in the family, who saw the horror of race slavery for what it was and said so. Slaves owned by our ancestors were among the first slaves recorded in Massachusetts and possibly also Virginia Colony. Those who owned slaves bore family surnames (treated in this and the companion volume): Cotton (?), Stone, Maverick, Winston, Gaines, Moore, Dwight, Mayo, Bodine, Van Meter, Grayless, Keinath, Flood, Farmer and Cook. There were others.

A different choice could have been made; a different choice *was* made by some of our ancestors, whose names were Putnam, Scott, Baldwin, Carmean, Slagle, Ireland, and Dorland. At the critical moment – usually in the early 19th century - these families settled in Ohio or Indiana, not in Kentucky. The repellant fact of slave-holding requires a treatment which does not overlook racist pretensions and self-interest. These themes leap out from the writings of some of our ancestors.

An easy argument is that slavery was imposed in North America by another country. Therefore, the individual was constrained at that time, and excused today, by a necessary, pragmatic subservience owed to systemic, overwhelming and lawful colonial policy. A corrupted context may excuse misconceptions but not misconduct. Some behavior – rape, the murder of children, the imposition of inherited and lifelong race slavery – cannot be justified. Today, our family is a racially rainbowed mélange, with a notable percentage of us at present, residents or citizens of other nations. If your family included slave-holders, you ought to have the details. Some are provided here; a fuller picture will require a fuller investigation.

So far as is known, our ancestors fought on only one side in the genocidal warfare against those people, who were already resident on the land. This warfare raged for more than three hundred years, from the 1500s until the close of the nineteenth century. Our ancestors and English and European immigrants generally, simply insisted on taking possession of the land. Their adversaries, clans of hunter-gatherers, rejected the notion of land as *property*. This fundamental European concept was imported and imposed upon the aboriginal peoples, who had been at home in North America for thousands of years – long before any of the British Isles were home to anyone. (Which, then, was the "new" world?)

Against our advance, the residents had no chance. That is the long view, expressed in stark terms by none other than George Washington: *"the gradual extension of our Settlements will as certainly cause the Savage as the Wolf to retire, both being beasts of prey tho' they differ in shape."* Doubtless, Washington put into words the sentiments of the majority of European settlers, the lonely farmer in his field, startled by movement in nearby underbrush; a mother and child, terrified in a rough little cabin, wondering if the puncheon door will hold. This was the experience of our 17th and 18th century ancestors in their outpost clearings in Massachusetts, Connecticut, Pennsylvania, Maryland, Virginia, Ohio and Kentucky. Abject terror was also the experience of families in the Indian towns and forts, frightened to distraction for themselves and their babes, as an armed and furious militia rushed upon them - *beasts of prey tho' they differ in shape.*

The Originals were in the way. Plus, their gods were different. These were the twin rationales invoked to justify their extermination. They were destroyed, by Hathornes, Swaynes, Morrells, Crocketts, Moores, Harrisons, Dawsons, Van Meters, Cooks and others of our kin, who killed and who were killed, often in the chaotic and enterprising violence of hand to hand combat. These struggles gave the nation its central idea about who is the Innocent Victim (virtuous WE), and who is the Depraved Enemy (godless THEY).

It is not necessary to idealize the Originals to speak of the catastrophe that was the beginning and the end of their encounter with European settlers. For uncounted thousands of years, the Originals seem to have conducted warfare among themselves. There are remnant traces, a residue of human activity from early eons, which suggest the American continents had been occupied by peoples from ancient Asia, the Pacific Rim and, yes, from Europe, all of whom had arrived haphazardly over millennia. By 1600, bewildered European adventurers, sailors and Pilgrims peered into the faces of Siberians, who may have come last, in greater numbers, or with better organization and weapons and wiped out all the others.

wiped out all the others? - Perhaps not. There is mounting recent evidence that an extraterrestrial object, a giant meteor, say, crashed into the ice-covered Canadian land mass 13,000 years ago. This cataclysm is thought to have caused supersonic winds and continent-wide firestorms, which made life impossible for enormous mammals and the human beings who hunted them. Widespread genocide may not have occurred in the Americas until the Europeans arrived (again) five hundred years ago.

In many of our direct lines (not all) the history of our family, in both Taylor and Cook branches, could be described as an examination of the fortunes of certain Huguenot immigrants and their descendents in North America. In general, these French people moved outward and upward so rapidly in America that all memory of France quickly became a positive but vague abstraction. The widespread nature of Huguenot immigrant origins has required much space to be given to the Huguenot genesis and fate in medieval France. Both volumes outline the twists and turns. On the Cook side, there are more Dutch ancestors than I had thought.

A surprising number of our ancestors were devout. Their zeal on behalf of deep, evangelical convictions is a theme that rhymes down the generations. Overemphasis is possible here as well as in the display of legal matters. But churchly and judicial actions tend to be better documented than, say, farming or daily trade or business activities, before eighteenth century hamlets grew into nineteenth century towns.

Too little is said of the women whose lives were risked, and often lost, in giving issue generation upon generation. Our women are almost completely invisible until the nineteenth century. We want to know much more of our ancient Mothers, but cannot, it seems.

An apology is offered for the factual errors which this data-laden document (and its companion) certainly must contain. The writer is grateful to cousin Charlie L Cook and his wife Billye who have suggested corrections to the first edition. Any others with better evidence are invited to offer corrections. Please write to me at **cookrb1@gmail.com**.

LEAH FANNING MEBANE THE ARTIST - www.fanningart.com

These volumes gain immeasurably from the rare gifts of a remarkable artist, Leah Fanning Mebane. Leah has taken many of our family's photos, portraits, and the occasional poorly preserved daguerreotype, and has found and expressed the deep character of our beloved ancestors. Applying the genius of eye and hand to a moment in time, Leah has created an individual mood, an attitude, and has captured their truth.

ELIZABETH HUEY TAYLOR COOK – BETTY COOK

With its companion volume, this book is my attempt to honor the memory and the labor of my mother, Elizabeth Huey Taylor Cook (1918-2000). Betty Cook worked on a family genealogy for half a century. She did all the necessary tasks. She preserved documents handed down to her, asked questions, wrote letters, called siblings, uncles and aunts, cousins near and distant. Betty organized and preserved everything and passed it along. It arrived in the hands of this writer as a grand genealogical chart book in which Mother collected the facts and made the connections. Her life-long effort is the basis of this set of family narratives. It is hoped that Betty's gentle, thoughtful presence may be felt on every page.

"NOBODY WAS SPARED, LIVING OR DEAD"

Cecil V Cook, Jr

Cecil Virgil Cook, Jr was born May 11, 1913 in Danville KY. He grew up in Charlottesville and Farmville, VA, and graduated from Hampden-Sydney College, Farmville, VA in 1937.

Cecil's wife Betty Cook, with obvious pride, wrote in her **Family Tree**, that Cecil also attended the University of Virginia summer program. In 1941 Cecil obtained a B.D. from Southern Baptist Seminary in Louisville. He took seven years to complete the three-year curriculum. Cecil said he stretched it out because he was enjoying his student pastorates. But Cecil also stated - and Betty confirmed after his death - that Cecil's career goal in college was to become a doctor.

Cecil's father, **Cecil Virgil Cook, Sr** (1871-1948), his grandfather **Joshua Flood Cook** (1834-1912) and Joshua's grandfather, **Abraham Cook** (1774-1854) were Baptist ministers. There were other preachers, too, notably **John Ernest Cook** (1860-1926), Cecil's paternal uncle, as well as Cecil's paternal double great uncle, the notable and exquisitely named Missouri preacher **Noah Flood** (1809-1873). There was also the excitable **John Goode** (1739-1792) of Chesterfield County, VA, Cecil's triple great grandfather. John Goode would speak of his conversion with such emotion that he could hardly remain in his saddle. All of these preachers were spoken about from time to time by Cecil and Betty. There were others.

Cecil V Cook, Jr and **Elizabeth Huey Taylor** (1918-2000) were married by Cecil's father on December 30, 1941, in his parents' home in Charlottesville, VA. The couple eloped, an event which created consternation in the Taylor family and which was conspired in by Cecil's parents. The fact of their elopement was kept from Betty and Cecil's children until after Cecil's death.

Cecil Virgil Cook, Jr

A Baptist minister for some eighteen years, Cecil was, for the last thirteen years of his life, a campaign director and then vice-president of Ward Dreshman and Rheinhardt (New York City, Worthington, Ohio), a firm of philanthropic fund raising consultants. Even after his active ministerial days were behind him by 1958, Cecil stayed in touch with the broader theological scene. Cecil often expressed admiration for Martin Marty at the University of Chicago Divinity School. When Cecil's second son, this narrator, decided to attend Union Theological Seminary in New York, Cecil said, in 1968, "Reinhold Niebuhr is there but between the two of them, his brother Richard at Yale was the smarter." He also expressed the view, later proved correct, that his son, with a degree from Union Seminary, NYC, would never have a Southern Baptist pastorate.

Cecil was known among his friends for his entertaining sense of humor and frequent hilarity. These traits Cecil inherited from his father. Cecil's university and seminary pals called him "Cookie." Cecil could break into song, fake a limp in order to cross traffic on a busy street (in, say, Mexico City) and sit down at a piano to play hymns or Sousa. In 2004 at Chautauqua, NY, this writer encountered ninety-year-old Herbert Gabhart, Baptist preacher and retired President of Belmont University, Nashville, TN, and was greeted with: "Are you really Cookie's boy?" The old gentleman then described how comical it could be simply to watch Cookie stroll the long sidewalks on the seminary campus behind Norton Hall. While a pastor in Bluefield, WV, Cecil once put a press card in his hat to attend a news conference by the president of the United Mine Workers, John L. Lewis. Cecil's press credential was his editorship of the church newsletter. On one occasion, Cecil lay down on the basement floor of his home for two hours with a twenty-two caliber rifle locked and loaded, "hunting" an illusive rat. The ricochet of a spent bullet sent the rat back into the darkness and Cecil upstairs, both unharmed. "That's enough of that."

Cecil Cook, Jr at Hampden-Sydney College

Cecil often wrote jaunty letters to his wife and other family members. Rarely did he write with such joy to his sons, whom he may have considered too young or too much in need of a disciplinarian, to benefit from a light touch. In 1962, Cecil wrote to his older brother, about a reunion with cousins in Evanston, IL. To Dorland, he wrote, "What a ball Paul, Helen, Mary and I had last weekend! More than once we wished for you to get in on it with us . . . . That night we went to a good restaurant and put on a show for ourselves which nearby tables enjoyed also. Nobody was spared, living or dead."

At home, Cecil would put on an apron and chef's hat when preparing Saturday breakfast. A grand event for his young sons was to march through the house while Cecil played *Onward Christian Soldiers* at the upright piano in the living room. He would often head for the piano without taking off his hat and coat. Cecil could create an outing for his little boys by announcing a "trip" to the post office. Other "outings" were an afternoon ride up East River Mountain to see the fall foliage, a drive downtown to meet a train or a ride out to the new airport after Piedmont Air Lines began to provide service to Bluefield. Cecil would pay an eight year-old son a nickel for a good backrub and, six or seven years later, play ping pong for two hours or more. Best of five? Best of seven? He never conceded a game or a point.

Cecil was fond of tossing a German word or two into casual conversation. Never to be forgotten by his towheaded little boys is *kartoffel*, the German word for *potato*. Cecil had studied German at the male-only Hampden-Sydney, in Farmville, Virginia, a college none of his own sons expressed the slightest interest in attending. In the sacrosanct chambers of his library at home, Cecil had a copy of the Bible in German and several Greek New Testaments. These books survived the holocaust Cecil created in a wire mesh frame in the back yard in 1957, to which he consigned all of his sermons after resigning his thirteen-year pastorate. Not a single sermon survived the flames.

Cecil Virgil Cook, Jr

The First Baptist Church of Bluefield voted against a raise, even after Cecil put the congregation into a new building, debt free. He allowed himself to be a candidate at one or two other Baptist churches but (this observer believes, in imagination if not quite in memory) Cecil's heart was not in it. Relying on references from pastor friends and colleagues, off Cecil went in 1958 to organize fund raising campaigns for hospitals and universities, who paid up front for professional services, and well enough for Cecil to plan for the higher education of his five sons.

Except for the summer months, Dad never lived at home with Mother again, until his final illness from lung cancer in 1968, when he came home to stay. Earlier in that same year, in an irony that sent him careening from exultation to bitterness like the ping pong he loved, Cecil was made a vice president of the firm.

After Cecil left the pastorate and began his fund raising work away from home, he and Betty moved the family, in 1959 to Betty's hometown, Louisville, KY. They joined Crescent Hill Baptist Church, the church in which she had grown up. Betty and Cecil had five sons: Bill (b. 1943), Richard (1944), Cecil III (1946), David (1948) and Charles (1953). For "the boys" moving from Bluefield, WV to Louisville was like stepping out of the shadows into the high noon sun. Bluefield was (and is) a market and railhead town on the southern edge of the West Virginia coalfields. The charms of this small town and its austere, surrounding mountains began to fade for the Cook boys, as soon as their parents talked about Louisville. Louisville! On the great falls of the Ohio River; Betty's childhood home town; location of the renowned Southern Baptist Theological Seminary; scene each spring of the world famous Kentucky Derby. We could not wait to get there!

Cecil, whose only sibling was his older brother, Dorland (1904-1966), was the second son of **Blanche Jeannette Dorland** (1873-1867) (page 21) and **Cecil Virgil Cook, Sr** (1871-1948) (page 41). The reader will note that Cecil Jr and Betty resisted until the third baby boy before naming a son Cecil III. Hoping always for a

15

baby girl, Betty recalled, by the time the third baby boy arrived, the pressure from Cecil's father was overpowering.

As mentioned, Cecil worked as a fund raising professional from 1958 until his death from lung cancer in 1970. In the spring of 1968, he was informed by the other officers of his firm that he was to be made a vice-president. Cecil arranged for his sons to join him and Betty in New York City for a company banquet. He withheld from his sons the news of the promotion until it was announced publicly at the big event. Cecil was ecstatic. Betty was as proud for him as he was for himself.

As the firm was moving out of New York City (big mistake!), Cecil needed to relocate to the new headquarters on the outskirts of Columbus, Ohio. Cecil and Betty, with Charles and Betty's mother, **Nan Elizabeth Taylor** (1883-1993), moved that summer (1968). Later that fall he made an appointment to be seen by a doctor, who might tell him why he was having a persistent cough.

On Christmas Day, 1968, Cecil was operated on in Columbus and his right lung, some vocal cords and lymphatic nodes were removed. He then underwent a program of chemotherapy.

Cecil fought hard against his dying. He continued to work as a company executive but tried to conceal the seriousness of his condition from colleagues. He took a speed reading course so that he might work more efficiently from home in the little time he could function each day before getting tired. In 1969, as he grew weaker, Cecil became bedridden at home; he responded by refusing to let any of his colleagues visit him. Everything had to go through Betty, who was instructed to tell the world he was getting along pretty well. He rarely discussed the course of his illness with Betty or Charles or his mother-in-law, Nan Elizabeth. His sorrow and anguish expressed itself as denial. Cecil's disavowal of the mortal illness he was battling added greatly to Betty's burdens. She was much more inclined than he to be candid about personal matters, which would have allowed their friends to offer her needed support.

In the spring of 1970, a family friend and missionary physician, William Gaventa, made a long car trip to Columbus OH, with his wife, Alice, Betty's close friend. Bill examined Cecil and, after a time, told Betty he had detected cancer in Cecil's liver. This diagnosis was confirmed some days later by Cecil's doctors. Cecil never discussed this new peril with Betty. In July, at fifty-seven years of age, Cecil died in the hospital in Columbus.

In 1999, Betty allowed herself to be video taped by her son David. She spoke of the eventful years that had passed since Cecil's death. Betty spoke of her daughters-in-law, her grandchildren and even a great grandchild, **Isabella Henderson Cook** (born: 1998), whom Betty had come to know. She wept with David, and repeated, "Cecil missed so much, so much."

Betty has written about how hard Cecil's death was for her. (See her *Death of a Husband,* below, page 297.) As terrible as it was to be widowed, Betty told David, in the 1999 video, the worst time of her life was in 1957, after Cecil had been informed by his church that a modest raise in salary had been denied. Betty said this unexpected turn put Cecil in a severely depressed state, which lead to his resignation and a search for a new job. He just could not go on in the pastorate, Betty said. Working from home, Cecil never moved his office into the new church building. He believed he could no longer preach, having nothing to say.

After Cecil's death, Betty often spoke with great pride of Cecil's successful real estate venture in Bluefield, WV. Betty came to believe that this gambit may have contributed to the refusal of the church to raise Cecil's salary. This rejection propelled him, in turn, out of the pastorate and out of the pastoral ministry altogether. But Betty concluded that Cecil's investment in Bluefield, on the edge of the Appalachian coal fields, saved his mother and her parents from likely economic ruin.

By 1950, shortly after his father's death (1948), it became clear to Cecil that **Blanche** (see page 21, below), Cecil's by-now bedridden mother would require continuing and probably increased financial support from him for the rest of her life. On a pastor's salary, but with hope to college-educate all of his sons, what to do? Additionally, Betty's parents, **Nan Elizabeth Huey** (1893-1993) and **John Oliver Taylor** (1891-1962) were in severe financial straits, owing to two factors. John's Depression-era sales careers had not qualified him for the then-new federal Social Security program. Nor was John able to continue working because of a debilitating (horrifying, to young grandsons) case of emphysema, which had settled into his lungs in middle age. His grandchildren never knew John to take a healthy breath. By age fifty-five, he could hardly walk ten paces without coming to a full stop, panting and heaving. In this condition, worsening from month to month, John Taylor could not work at all. (Sketches of the lives of Nan Elizabeth and John Oliver Taylor are found in **All of the Above I**.)

The plan Cecil and Betty devised was to take the remaining money Blanche had inherited from her father **James E. Dorland** (1844-1915) and buy a business of some kind, which John Oliver and Nan Elizabeth Taylor could operate together. This would provide investment income for Blanche as well as employment income for Betty's parents. (For more on James Dorland, see page 55.)

With money from his mother, Cecil bought a small building in Bluefield, converted it into space for a bookstore and invited Betty's parents, Elizabeth and John Taylor, to move from their home in Raleigh to operate *the Bluefield Bookshop*.

The plan worked. Blanche Cook had income from this business for the final sixteen years of her life. And Betty's parents were able to operate the bookshop for a few years, until John qualified for Social Security. At that point, and on the death of Nan's mother **Sara Crouch Huey** (1861-1956), John and Nan Taylor moved back to her ancestral home in Union, KY. There in Union, Nan could care for not only John but also her ancient, widowed father, **James Addison Huey** (1862-1961). After the Taylors moved to Union, the bookshop was entrusted to other employees and Blanche's modest investment income continued until her death in 1967.

Well done, Father.

Cecil and grandson Matthew Mitchell Cook, 1969

Cecil's life was marked by his courtly acceptance of responsibility towards those who depended upon him. He was full of fun and was creative with whatever resources that came under his control. With Betty, he raised and saw to the education of his five sons. His good planning provided for Betty after his death. Cecil may have let his sense of duty to his demanding father get in the way of his own good judgment; perhaps he had become a preacher just to please his "Pop."

Cecil was too quick to hide his feelings and his disappointments from his sons, who wanted to share more of his life. But Cecil saw the tragic-comic aspects of existence. He indulged and magnified these aspects to the merriment of others. But at the end, to the grief and distress especially of Betty and youngest son, Charles, Cecil took his eye off the farcical features of life. He stopped kidding around. Too much was being taken from him, too soon.

Dad is owed an appraisal of his life of self-giving, that does not focus on his early death – a death he certainly helped bring upon himself by smoking his ever present *Kools*. The assessment due Cecil Cook Jr includes an acknowledgement of his love for those around him, a love reciprocated by those who knew him best, who were grateful for his having lived and given so much care and happiness to so many. May we meet Dad in the Elysium invoked by his ministerial progenitors, and longed for by their dutiful spouses, where Cecil will greet one and all with a fake limp, a chef's apron and a ping pong paddle, ready for whatever.

> Dear Rich,   Jan 30 1962
> Wish I could be on hand for your Uncle Dorland's birthday. I think he said Aunt Carrie was to fix a roast beef dinner for him. I'd go for that, too. [. . .] We had a big crowd (for Presbyterians) at the Rally yesterday – somewhere between eight and nine hundred. It will help the campaign to get going, to develop this good spirit and response. Now to get them to w-o-r-k! [. . .] Think I'll have an apartment by tomorrow. Tired of the hotel and eating out!   Love, Dad [Schenectady, NY]

"MY ALWAYS BRIDE"

Blanche Jeannette Dorland
Mother of Cecil V. Cook, Jr

Blanche Jeannette Dorland was born Oct 12 1873, in Columbia City, Indiana and died in her home in Charlottesville, VA in 1967. Blanche and her sister Ethyl grew up in Louisville, in the stately home of her parents, **James E. Dorland** (1844-1915) and **Arabelle ("Belle") America Ireland** (1850-1895). It was in Louisville that the tall, blonde, curly haired Presbyterian met and married the dashing and impressive Baptist seminarian, **Cecil Virgil Cook Sr** (1871-1948). Little is recalled of their late 1890's courtship in Louisville, which occurred while Cecil was a student of theology. Her church, Warren Memorial Presbyterian, shared the same city block with Norton Hall, home of the seminary Cecil attended. They might have met on the sidewalk on a Sunday morning.

By their early twenties, both Blanche and Cecil had lost their mothers. Cecil's mother **Susan Goode Farmer Cook** (1838-1890) died May 10, 1890, when Cecil was nineteen. Blanche's mother, **Arabelle America Ireland Dorland** died of cancer on Feb. 9, 1895, when Blanche was twenty-two. A common mother-loss might well have created strong attachments between two young people planning their lives for an exciting new century. Sixty-seven years after Arabelle died, Blanche, addressing a grandson, spoke tearfully of the death of her mother.

Blanche and Cecil were married on June 20, 1900 in Louisville, KY and made a wedding trip to New Orleans. Their first home was in Webb City, Missouri, where Cecil had his first pastorate. No doubt, the way to Webb City had been opened by Cecil's father, **Joshua Flood Cook** (1834-1912), who had moved to Webb City in 1896 to be president of a fledgling Baptist college. By 1901, Cecil and Blanche had moved to St. Louis, where Cecil had accepted a call to pastor a mission church, which he led to become West Park Baptist Church. They attended the 1904

Blanche Jeannette Dorland

Louisiana Purchase Exposition, popularly known as the St. Louis World Fair.

Blanche and Cecil were the parents of two sons, James Dorland (1904-1966) and **Cecil Virgil Jr** (1913-1970), born in St Louis and Danville KY, respectively. That their sons were born 9 years apart is suggestive of Blanche's unfixed and almost nomadic life with Cecil. Like a Romany wanderer, he moved her from one Baptist pastorate to another in half a dozen states over the next forty-five years. From St. Louis to Birmingham, AL, to Danville, KY to Charlottesville and Farmville VA, Gaffney, SC, Albany, GA, and back again to Charlottesville. During these changes, Blanche cut out and saved newspaper clippings, letters, church bulletins and other ephemera that mentioned Cecil. In her enthusiasm for saving family memorabilia, Blanche Dorland Cook proved a match for her daughter-in-law **Betty Taylor Cook** (1918-2000) and Betty's ancestors, whose instinct for saving the slightest snippet was worthy of a monograph by Darwin.

To commemorate their twenty-fifth wedding anniversary in 1925, Cecil gave Blanche a framed poem: *All the world I've sorted out into classes two, Folks that I can do without - and - You.* Blanche, of course, saved this poem and also a letter Cecil wrote to her from New Orleans in 1922, in which he told her he missed "my always Bride" as he re-visited the city where they had spent their honeymoon.

Raised a Presbyterian as befitted her Dorland heritage, Blanche conducted Sunday School classes in the Baptist churches pastored by her husband. She was active in many other ways as well, typically directing her energies to leading the women's groups that were thought needed as a compliment to the various male organizations in Cecil's congregations.

"AFTER WHILE HAS COME. NOW STOP IT!"

Likely, Blanche was present on Sunday evening, January 17, 1904, when Cecil delivered a sermon at West Park Baptist Church in St Louis, MO. For some reason, the sermon was transcribed by "M A Maaher stenographer." Cecil's text was Ezekiel 18:21.

"But the children rebelled against me; they walked not in my statutes, neither kept mine ordinances to do them, which if a man do he shall live in them; they profaned my Sabbaths. Then I said I would pour out my wrath upon them, to accomplish my anger against them in the wilderness."

Cecil's theme was the inevitable coming Judgment. "Certain laws are laid down," Cecil announced, "if we break those laws we have to be punished." But "this verse shows us our way out," the thirty-three-year old pastor declares. *"God wants people saved"* and has given *"his only son that the world might be saved. . . . I sometimes feel a sort of terror when I talk to people about giving up sin . . . how many times has the human heart said, I can toy with this sin and give it up after while . . . well, after while has come, now stop it! . . . Suppose a man has yielded his heart and says I am going to give up all my sins but one. Let me illustrate by morphine . . . he will not give it up because it will gradually get hold upon him and fasten itself upon his soul until he is as helpless in its grasp as a little feather in a cyclone. . . . and liquor . . . . that hell fire that has drowned natural affections. . . . How is this all going to end men and women? You do not want to live as you are living now, some of you . . . You do not want to die as you are now. Oh change it, turn from evil. . . . put your hand in His and go out into the world trying to obey him in everything. Will you do it?"*

In admitting to "a sort of terror" in confronting the "sin" of liquor, was Cecil giving voice to a prescient sense of foreboding? (Both of Cecil's sons would take up vices he condemned; Cecil Jr would become addicted to cigarettes and Dorland, to drink.) Both his mother's and his father's families, as Cecil Sr would know, had felt the devastating power of alcoholism. His mother, **Sue Farmer Cook** (1838-1890), wrote letters to him and certainly also would have spoken frankly to him about the destructive effects of strong drink among her siblings. His father, **Joshua Flood Cook** (1834-1912), was probably equally candid.

Joshua's own father, **William F Cook** (1802-1850/55), on his Kentucky farm, had combined alcohol with gunfire. (See the Lucy and "Billy Dick" Cook sketch, page 163.)

Cecil's and Blanche's eldest son, James Dorland Cook (1904-1966), would be born later in 1904, the year of this sermon. Within twenty-five years, Dorland would become a life-long alcoholic, only intermittently employed and employable. From time to time, Dorland would check himself in or be checked in to a "sanitarium," when his drinking became too much for his doting wife and parents. Dorland would dissipate his father's income and his mother's inheritance in pursuit of profitless real estate schemes. With borrowed and family funds he would found a business he could not operate. All of this the result, as his nineteenth century relatives might have said, of Dorland having "looked too long down the whiskey glass." A thoroughly charming man, a stylish dresser and avid golfer, Dorland was much loved by his indulgent parents and his younger brother, **Cecil Cook, Jr** and was well liked, even admired, by all who knew him, including his five nephews.

In October, 1941, Dorland married Carrie Mayes (1904-2001), a country girl from Nelson County VA. Carrie's father was a Confederate war veteran. Her parents may have been Old South but she was born in a new century and embraced it fully, serving in uniform herself during WW II and then becoming a well trained nurse-anesthetist and an enthusiastic golfer, like her beloved Dorland. Their highest times were road trips to Augusta, GA, to watch Ben Hogan and Sammy Snead. Carrie worked some forty years at UVA hospital in Charlottesville. Childless, Carrie cared for Dorland throughout their marriage. She, like all the primary people in his world, indulged Dorland and suffered with him. In his last decades, Dorland became as dependent upon support from Carrie, as his mother was on her younger son, Cecil Jr.

Without doubt, Blanche and Cecil Sr were much grieved by Dorland's libational disease but they also accommodated themselves to it. In 1904, it is unlikely that Cecil and Blanche looked into their infant's crib and saw misfortune magnified with the coming years; but it was there just the same. The "terror" Cecil warned against in his youthful sermon the year of Dorland's birth must have visited Cecil and Blanche repeatedly through the trials the inebriate Dorland inflicted upon his parents for the rest of their lives.

Those who knew him were charmed by the attractive and sweet-tempered Dorland, though none loved him so much as his congenial Carrie. Carrie Mayes Cook was Dorland's companion for 26 years and outlived him by 36. Though charming and affable on all occasions, Dorland was a devourer of the wealth and happiness of others. In death, in 1966, he was loved and missed in equal parts - loved for what he was and missed for what he never was.

In July 1947, Blanche broke her hip. A *broken hip* in mid-20th century was a decree of permanent incapacity. Blanche was severely hobbled and was soon virtually bedridden for the final two decades of her life. Her grandsons never remembered Blanche to be free from her cane or "walker."

During these final two decades Blanche enjoyed the gentle, faithful attentions of Dorland and Carrie. They had taken Blanche into their home after Cecil Sr died in 1948. Dorland's conviviality continued to be helped along too often by alcohol. But the three lived more or less contentedly under the same roof for almost twenty years.

Dorland died in 1966 and Blanche in '67. For more than thirty years Carrie Mayes Cook lived on at 701 Lyons Avenue in Charlottesville, reaching ninety-seven years of age. The aged Carrie was always in generous and amiable remembrance of Dorland, Blanche, and the singular family she had married into seventy years before.

In the early 1960's, confined to her Charlottesville, VA home, Blanche impressed at least one of her grandsons as a stately, even an austere woman. She always spoke in august tones of her late husband, sometimes referring to him as Cecil, but often as *Dr. Cook*. This formality was probably the result of protective habits developed over 48 years as a pastor's wife. Blanche's great reserve and dignity

Blanche Dorland Cook

did not restrain the old lady from poking a hole in every last chocolate in the box until she found just the right one.

THE HUGUENOT PHENOMENON

We have indicated that Blanche had been raised a Presbyterian but upon her marriage to Cecil had become a Baptist. This was of course a change for her but the marriage also marked a kind of reunion of Protestant traditions, a blending of several unique American religious strains, which shared a dramatic and wrenching medieval history: the Huguenot phenomenon. Because Huguenots appear so prominently in so many of the family's ascendant lines, a closer look might be of value.

The derivation of the term *Huguenot* (like the word *Christian*) can only be guessed at, but probably resulted from multiple originating influences. In general, a Huguenot was a French Protestant of the 16th and 17th centuries, whose doctrines were close to those of John Calvin. Besançon Hugues (c. 1491–1532?), a Swiss political operative may have contributed his surname to its conflation with the German, *Eidgenosse* (comrade), as in *those allied with Hugues*. Hugues is remembered as the leader in Geneva of the Confederate Party, which favored closer cooperation between Geneva and the Swiss Confederation, in opposition to capitulation to the Duke of Savoy.

Huguenot may have been at first a name given and taken as an insult. Until the term assumed a nostalgic and positive aura as an identification of principled and persecuted true believers, French Protestants themselves preferred to be known as *réformée*. The Catholic Church, in its official pronouncements has preferred to call them *prétendue réformée:* pseudo-reformed.

The first Huguenot Synod (national convention) was held in 1559. This assembly led to the founding of a French national church on a Presbyterian model. A Huguenot political party was formed in 1573. The powerful anti-Huguenot Holy League was formed in 1576.

The great inspirations for the Huguenots were Geneva and its preeminent religious and civil ruler, John Calvin, himself a Frenchman. Calvin's magnum opus, *Institutio Christianae Religionis* (*Institutes of the Christian Religion*), provided the fundamental doctrinal content of Huguenot belief. Never just a theologian but always also an organizer, Calvin's 1535 Preface to *The Institutes* was addressed to the King of France. In it Calvin rallied French Protestants into the conviction that they were not and could never again be Roman Catholic.

The Huguenots, whose existence pre-dated Calvin and his *Institutes*, warmed to his fierce critique of Catholic ritual and priesthood and embraced with him the notion that individual salvation, like all of creation, is the work of God alone. Reformed Protestantism, despite Calvin's constraining rhetoric, contains at its heart a sprouting seed of anarchy, which is matched in Rome by a venerable, blooming authoritarianism. These two fundamental and contradictory tendencies may account for the inability in late medieval France for either faction to accept for long a workable civil compromise. The adversaries looked into one another's hearts, saw therein a truly demonic enemy, and hated each other to death.

An interesting perspective on Huguenot origins is found in the *Catholic Encyclopedia* (1914). This source candidly maintains that the sixteenth century French context truly did call for churchly reforms. But, the official narrative continues, any legitimate reform was aborted after popular reformist energies were placed in the hands of – the usual Catholic villain - Renaissance humanists. Here is the official 1914 description of the state of French Catholicism:

"That the ideas of these two Reformers [Luther and Calvin] were to a certain degree successful in France was due in that country, as elsewhere, to the prevailing mental attitude. The Great Western Schism, the progress of Gallican ideas, the Pragmatic Sanction of Bourges, and the war of Louis XII against Julius II had considerably weakened the prestige and authority of the papacy. The

French clergy, owing to the conduct of many of its members, inspired but little respect. After the Pragmatic Sanction (1438) the episcopal sees became the object of ceaseless rivalry and contention, while too many of the bishops ignored their obligation of residence. In spite of some attempts at reform, the regular clergy languished in inactivity, ignorance, and relaxation of discipline, and all their attendant imperfections. The humanism of the Renaissance had created a distaste for the verbose, formalistic scholasticism, still dominant in the schools, and had turned men back to the cult of pagan antiquity to naturalism, and in some cases to unbelief. Other minds, it is true, were led by the Renaissance itself to the study of Christian antiquity, but, under the influence of the mysticism which had shortly before this become current as a reaction from the system of the schools and the philosophy of the literati, they ended by exaggerating the power of faith and the authority of Holy Scripture. It was this class of thinkers, affected at once by humanism and mysticism, that took the initiative, more or less consciously, in the reform for which public opinion clamoured."

Misguided humanist intellectuals exaggerated "the power of faith and the authority of Holy Scripture." Isn't that an odd way to put it? Isn't that just another sounding of an anti-intellectual theme, heard in official Catholic pronouncements to this today? Wasn't the true focus of the religious conflict in France not the content of belief but the control of institutional levers in the larger society? Yes. Yes and Yes.

It was not until the Huguenots turned toward a consolidation of their power in an institutional form (the 1559 Synod) that they posed an immense risk to the Catholic hierarchy. A century later, after the Huguenots turned away from institution building, their influence in France dissipated and they found themselves in great personal peril. This point is driven home by the observation that the actual threat posed by the Huguenots surfaces around their attempts to control the forms of worship in the towns. The *Catholic Encyclopedia* again:

"Since 1530 there had existed at Paris a vigorous group of heretics, recruited principally from the literary men and the lower classes, and numbering from 300 to 400 persons. Some others were to be found in the Universities of Orléans and Bourges; in the Duchy of Alencon where Margaret of Navarre, the suzerain, gave them licence to preach, and whence the heresy spread in Normandy; at Lyons, where the Reformation made an early appearance owing to the advent of foreigners from Switzerland and Germany; and at Toulouse, where the Parliament caused the arrest of several suspects and the burning of John of Cahors, a professor in the faculty of law."

A new, dangerously progressive rector was appointed at the Sorbonne, which is where a very young John Calvin makes a first appearance.

. . . *"the Sorbonne witnessed the banishment of Beda and the appointment of Cop to the rectorship of the University of Paris, although he was already suspected of sympathizing with Lutheranism. At the opening of the academic year, 1 November, 1533, he delivered an address filled with the new ideas. This address had been prepared for him by a young student then scarcely known, whose influence however upon the French Reformation was to be considerable; this was John Calvin. . . This address called forth repressive measures against the two friends. Cop fled to Switzerland, Calvin to Saintonge."*

It all seems to be a matter of grave individual errors and mounting civil disobedience, fomented in France by the Lutherans and humanists.

"[Calvin] soon broke with Catholicism, surrendered his benefices, for which he received compensation, and towards the end of 1534 betook himself to Basle in consequence of the affair of the 'placards' — i.e. the violent

manifestos against the Mass which, by the contrivance of the Lutherans, had been placarded in Paris (18 October, 1534), in the provinces, and even on the door to the king's apartments."

The civil disobedience has the opposite of its intended effect upon the king, who in January 1535, "took part in a solemn procession during the course of which six heretics were burned; he let the Parliament arrest seventy-four of them a Meaux, of whom eighteen were also burned; he himself ordered by edict the extermination of the heretics and of those who should harbour them, and promised rewards to those who should inform against them... In 1539 and 1540 the old edicts of toleration were replaced by others which invested the tribunals and the magistrates with inquisitorial powers against the heretics and those who shielded them. At the instance of the king the Sorbonne drew up first a formula of faith in twenty-six articles, and then an index of prohibited books, in which the works of Dolet, Luther, Melanchthon, and Calvin appeared; the parliaments received orders to prosecute anyone who should preach a doctrine contrary to these articles, or circulate any of the books enumerated in the index. This unanimity of king, Sorbonne, and Parliament, it may be said, was what prevented the Reformation from gaining in France the easy success which it won in Germany and England... At Aix the Parliament passed a decree ordering a general massacre of the descendants of the Waldenses grouped around Mérindol and de Cabrieres, its enforcement to be suspended for five months to give them time for conversion. After withholding his consent to this decree for five years the king allowed an authorization for its execution to be wrung from him, and about eight hundred Waldenses were massacred — an odious deed which Francis I regretted bitterly until his death. His successor, Henry II, vigorously maintained the struggle against Protestantism. In 1547 a commission — the famous Chambre Ardente — was created in the Parliament of Paris for the special purpose of trying heretics; then in

June, 1551, the Châteaubriant Edict codified all the measures which had previously been enacted for the defence of the Faith. This legislation was enforced by the parliaments in all its rigour. It resulted in the execution of many Protestants at Paris, Bordeaux, Lyons, Rouen, and Chambéry, and drove the rest to exasperation."

How did things get so out of hand?

"The Protestants were aided by a certain number of apostate priests and monks, by preachers from Geneva and Strasburg, by schoolmasters who disseminated the literature of the sect; they were favoured at times by bishops — such as those of Chartres, of Uzès, of Nîmes, of Troyes, of Valence of Oloron, of Lescar, of Aix, of Montauban, of Beauvais; they were supported and guided by Calvin, who from Geneva — where he was persecuting his adversaryies (e.g. Cartellion), or having them burnt (e.g. Servetus) — kept up an active correspondence with his party. With these helps the Reformers penetrated little by little into every part of France. Between 1547 and 1555 some of their circles began to organize themselves into churches at Rouen, Troyes, and elsewhere, but it was at Paris that the first Reformed church was definitely organized in 1555. Other followed — at Meaux, Poitiers, Lyons, Angers, Orléans, Bourges, and La Rochelle. All of these took as their model that of Geneva, which Calvin governed; for from him proceeded the impulse which stimulated them, the faith that inspired them; from him, too, came nearly all the ministers, who put the churches into communication with that of Geneva and its supreme head. It lacked only a confession of faith to ensure the union of the churches and uniformity of belief. In 1559 there was held at Paris the first national synod, composed of ministers and elders, assembled from all parts of France; it formulated a confession of faith, drawing inspiration from the writings of Calvin. From this moment the French Reformation was established; it had its creed, its discipline, its organization."

The encyclopedia researcher-writer is so taken with the importance of church organization that he returns to describe it in painstaking detail.

"The discipline established by the Synod of 1559 was also contained in forty articles, to which others were very soon added. The primary organization with its successive developments may be reduced substantially to this: Wherever a sufficient number of the faithful were found, they were to organize in the form of a Church, i.e. appoint a consistory, call a minister, establish the regular celebration of the sacraments and the practice of discipline. A church provided with all the elements of organization was an église dressée; one which had only a part of these requisites was an église plantée. The former had one or more pastors, with elders and deacons, who composed the consistory. This consistory was in the first instance elected by the common voice of the people; after that, it co-opted its own members; but these had to receive the approbation of the people. Pastors were elected by the provincial synod or the conference after an inquiry into their lives and beliefs, and a profession of faith; imposition of hands followed. The people were notified of the election, and the newly elected pastor preached before the congregation on three consecutive Sundays; the silence of the people was taken as an expression of consent. The elders, elected by those members of the Church who were admitted to the Supper, were charged with the duty of watching over the flock, jointly with the pastor, and of paying attention to all that concerned ecclesiastical order and government. The deacons were elected like the elders; it was their office to administer, under the consistory, the alms collected for the poor, to visit the sick, those in prison, and so on.

A certain number of churches went to form a conference. The conferences assembled at least twice a year. Each church was represented by a pastor and an elder; the function of the conference was to settle such differences as might arise among church officers, and to provide generally for all that might be deemed necessary *for the maintenance and the common good of those within their jurisdiction. Over the conferences were the provincial synods, which were in like manner composed of a pastor and one or two elders from each church chosen by the consistory, and met at least once a year. The number of these provincial synods in the whole of France was at times fifteen, at other times sixteen. Doctrines, discipline, schools, the appointment of pastors, erection and delimitation of parishes fell within their jurisdiction. At the head of the hierarchy stood the national synod, which, in so far as possible, was to meet once a year. (As a matter of fact, there were only twenty-nine between 1559 and 1660 — on an average, one every three years and a half). It was made up of two ministers and two elders sent by each provincial synod, and, when fully attended, it had (sixty or) sixty-four members. To the national synod it belonged to pronounce definitively upon all important matters, internal or external, disciplinary or political, which concerned religion.*

. . . The organization of their discipline and worship gave the Huguenots a new power of expansion. Little by little they penetrated into the ranks of the nobility. One of the principal families of the kingdom, the Coligny, allied to the Montmorency, furnished them their most distinguished recruits in d'Andelot, Admiral Coligny, and Cardinal Odet de Chatillon. Soon the Queen of Navarre, Jeanne d'Albret, daughter of Margaret of Navarre, professed Calvinism and introduced it into her dominions by force. Her husband, Antoine de Bourbon, the first prince of the blood, appeared at times to have gone over to the Huguenots with his brother the Prince de Condé, who, for his part, never wavered in his allegiance to the new sect. Even the Parliament of Paris, which had so energetically carried on the struggle against the heresy, allowed itself to become tainted, many of its members embracing the new doctrine. It was necessary to deal severely with these . . . it is evident that the Huguenots could no longer be regarded as a few scattered handfuls of individuals, whose case could be satisfactorily dealt

with by a few judicial prosecutions. Organized into churches linked together by synods, reinforced by the support of great lords of whom some had access to the councils of the Crown, the Calvinists thenceforward constituted a political power which exerted its activity in national affairs and had a history of its own."

Thus came into being the Holy League, whose purpose was to combat the *réformée*. The face off between the Huguenots and the Holy League lead to the Wars of Religion (1562-1598).

There were five civil wars, which were stimulated as much by powerful and ambitious clans (the Bourbons and the Guises) as by religious devotion. The wars saw the employment of such tactics as the destruction of churches (both Huguenot and Catholic), the burning of heretics, political plots and assassinations on both sides and the raising on a national scale of private armies who laid siege to fortressed cities. Each war was ended by the issuance of a royal edict, decree or accord, which always seemed to leave one party much aggrieved, and intent upon further violence designed to humiliate and crush the other.

The worst of many horrifying events was the so called "St. Bartholomew's Day Massacre," August 24 to Sept 17, 1572, when Catholics killed thousands of Huguenots in Paris and other towns. The well orchestrated attacks are believed to have caused the deaths of 110,000 people. Afterwards, Pope Gregory XIII held a service of thanksgiving and had a medal struck, which he sent with a congratulatory note to the French King. In 1573, an amnesty was extended to the perpetrators. The *Catholic Encyclopedia* states, "There is no proof that the Catholic clergy were in the slightest degree connected with the massacre." Good to know.

In 1598, Henry IV (with Huguenot parents) promulgated the Edict of Nantes, ending (for the time being) the Huguenot insurgency, which by then had spread across France. This Edict recognized in the Huguenots certain rights and privileges in their religious practices, their qualification to hold and receive government appointments, and official funding for churches and schools. The Edict gave Huguenots control of specified French walled cities and towns, within which they appear to have persecuted Catholics in their turn, destroying alters, icons and churches and depriving the Catholic minority of its civil protections and privileges.

Apparently, the first Huguenots, as a group, to leave France, did so in 1562. They went to the banks of the St. John's River near present day Jacksonville, Florida. Their settlement, Fort Caroline, would have been the first permanent foothold by Europeans on the territory of the present-day United States - *would have been permanent* - had it not been for a Spanish settlement, established shortly thereafter at St. Augustine. In 1565, the Spaniards came around not to exchange recipes but to wipe out the Huguenot pioneers. Not a single one was left alive.

Meantime in France, tensions increased and soon the bloodshed of the 1500s was replicated in the 1600s. Vicious outbursts of violence were renewed in the 1620's, culminating, by the end of the century, in the absolute decline of Huguenot prospects within France. This reversal of momentum led to the revocation, in 1685, of the never more than half-heartedly enforced 1598 Edict of Nantes. With its revocation, Huguenot parents were subject to civil penalties if they did not see to the instruction of their children in Catholic doctrine. Catholic French soldiers, often no more than the ill-trained and brutal muscle brought in to intimidate, were quartered in Huguenot households. The French state would not protect its Protestant citizens from robbery, murder and mayhem perpetrated by thugs acting under the pretext of Catholic zealotry.

The complete civil defeat of French Protestantism in 1685 caused a massive out-migration of Huguenot families. To the apparent surprise of the King of France, these subjects constituted large portions of the French artisan and educated classes as well as thousands of business owners and entrepreneurs. In vast numbers, these productive and creative French citizens, having lost all hope for life in France, sought out more hospitable countries: Holland, Switzerland, Norway, Denmark, South Africa, England, the north German Protestant states of the Palatine ("Paltz"), and in America: New Netherland (New York and New Jersey), Virginia Colony (mainly Chesterfield and Powhatan Counties) and South Carolina (mainly around Charleston). Some 400,000 men, women and children are said to have left France in a few short decades after 1685. The exodus crippled France as a world power. Continuing to inflict its destructive anti-Huguenot program upon itself, France barred the Huguenots from settling in population-starved New France (Canada), and thus crippled French Canada as well.

French Protestants did not enjoy restored civil liberties at home until the Revolution of 1789. Full religious freedom did not come to France until Church was separated from State in 1905. The current state-church arrangement in France is described as *laïcité*, which understands religious practices to inhabit a category separate from conduct open to all French citizens, who are not obligated to show an allegiance to any religious tradition. Nevertheless, present day France remains (like all other nations?) a *pastiche* of ethnic groupings, remaining together from shared notions about who they are not, rather than who they are.

Meanwhile in America, Huguenot immigrants and their descendents were becoming successful and even well known. Paul Revere, Jr, son of *Apollos Rivoire,* would ride his ride; John Jay would write his **Federalist** Essays; Alexandre Hamilton would partner up with Jay in this writing project and then set up a national bank; Henry David Thoreau would camp out at Walden Pond; Marlon Brando would pine for Stella and make offers that could not be refused. Fully one third of all US Presidents are said to enjoy Huguenot heritage, which, it may be hoped, does not reflect to the disadvantage of the *réformée*.

An important and positive feature of the bitter Huguenot experience in France was the undermining of royal rule by divine right. After the mass murders of Huguenots in August-Sept, 1572, the French King and the very idea of royal rule were denounced by reformer pamphleteers across Europe. *Rule by divine right? Nonsense!* How can you blame God for putting an idiot in charge, when the idiot depends upon a sectarian rabble to hold his place? The arguments of the pamphleteers would resonate for centuries: a government that oppresses its citizens in the name of God must be resisted.

The history of the Huguenots in France reminds us that Europe has passed through its own periods of warlord-dominance and bloody religious strife. This knowledge may be of some value as we try better to understand why our emigrant (departing) ancestors immigrated (entered) in the first place. Some of them were asylum seekers.

Historian Fernand Braudel called attention (1979) to the habit of early Huguenot exiles to live and conduct business in "a compact group" in London and elsewhere in Europe. Braudel sees evidence of this "still today." Not so in America, where all sharp distinctions are buffed until a smooth, bland veneer becomes the norm for most European comers. From the histories of the Cecil Cook and Betty Taylor Cook families, we discover Huguenot descendents in North America, either as individuals or couples, who have retained a proud and respectful but faded awareness of their French Protestant origins.

The French language soon disappeared from the lips of the immigrants. Indeed, most Huguenots, stopping for a generation in Amsterdam or London or the German Palatine, had left off speaking French before they reached America. In the colonies, many of the heirs of the *réformée* affiliated with Protestant denominations, which espoused Calvinist principles, mixed with other doctrines.

This trend is well expressed in the lineage of **Blanche Dorland Cook**, whose mother's family in America was Reformed Lutheran, whose father's family was Dutch Reformed and Presbyterian, and whose several early ancestral lines on both sides were largely French Protestant. Not to be overlooked is Blanche's choice for a husband, **Cecil Cook Sr**, a Baptist preacher, whose *new light* (Welch & Dutch) ancestors mixed Calvinist and Anabaptist themes. Cecil did the same, himself, in half a century of sermons.

SOURCES:

Genealogical information generally, and documents from Betty Taylor Cook's unpublished book, plus reminiscences of the writer.

For the History of the Huguenots: See the American Heritage® Dictionary of the English Language, Fourth Edition. Houghton Mifflin Company, 2004 and the **Catholic Encyclopedia,** on CD-ROM. Both the American Heritage item, "Huguenots," as well as the Catholic Encyclopedia on CD-ROM, were found on the web at Answers.com 12 Oct. 2006. There are also many and various internet links to "Huguenot."

An excellent 3-volume treatment of pre-industrial life, including a few snippets about the Huguenots: **Civilization & Capitalism 15th 18th Century**, Fernand Braudel (New York: Harper & Row, 1979)

> EULOGY FOR CECIL VIRGIL COOK SR
> *[. . .] He seems to have been rather frail as a young child but developed a physical toughness that lasted to his final illness. In temperament he was rather artistic and high strung and possessed considerable talent for music, which was to have been his life work. Early in life he possessed a strong sense of justice, for which he would fight regardless of the odds, and his moral courage in maturity was specifically used in his ministry. [. . .] As far back as the records go, the Cooks were Baptists. Family records also indicate that these hardy people knew the meaning of Indian warfare and several of them lost their lives in these struggles. [. . .] On his mother's side he was a Farmer. [. . .] Of great amusement to him was the comment of an ancient servant who had been raised with the Farmer family, "Them Cooks were rough folks!" [See page 116, 149, below]*
> Cecil V. Cook Jr, 1948

"YOU HAVE KEPT THE VISION SPLENDID"

Cecil Virgil Cook, Sr
Father of Cecil V. Cook, Jr

Cecil Virgil Cook, Sr was born on Dec 10 1871, in LaGrange, Missouri and died in September, 1948 in Charlottesville, VA. Cecil's parents were **Joshua Flood Cook** (1834-1912) and **Susan Goode Farmer** (1838-1890). As an adolescent, Cecil attended a conservatory where he studied piano and learned to play well enough to be paid as a church pianist while a seminary student in Louisville, KY. Cecil's accomplishments in music were so impressive to his son, that Cecil Jr, in a eulogy to his father (see page 40), wrote that music "was to have been his life's work." Cecil Jr described his father as "rather artistic and high strung."

Cecil was a graduate (BA, MA) of LaGrange College (where his father was President) and then attended the Southern Baptist Theological Seminary in Louisville, receiving a Masters and a Doctorate (Th.M., Th.D.). Cecil later served as a member of the Board of Trustees of the Seminary. Cecil was awarded honorary doctorates from Georgetown College in Kentucky and Howard College in Birmingham, Alabama.

At the Louisville Seminary and probably also at LaGrange College, Cecil studied Greek and learned it well. While a seminary student he made a notebook entitled "Exegesis of Luke" and filled it with Greek words and phrases and references to specific sentences and verses. A second notebook entitled "S.B.T.S. 1897, Theological Words in Luke," is also full of handwritten notes and comments. His Greek New Testament (1891, Westcott and Hort), bought in Louisville on Oct. 3 1893, has underlining and marginal notes on virtually every page. Cecil kept in his library and therefore must have moved with him a dozen times, a volume of the Septuagint, an ancient translation into Greek of the Hebrew Scriptures. The edition Cecil owned was the **Vetus Testamentum Graecum**, published in Leipzig in 1894. All of the publishing data, editorial notes and comments are in Latin. This hardbound book runs to over a thousand pages. On the cover page is inscribed, "Cecil V Cook, Oct 1 - 95." In the books of Isaiah and First Maccabaeus there are underlinings and notes in the margins.

Probably the first document Cecil Cook wrote was a journal he kept as a child. On Saturday March 27, 1886, the devout fifteen-year old Cecil recorded, "I was baptized this morning. I joined the church Wednesday night and was baptized today by Prof. Weber."

An 1898 research paper of Cecil's is entitled "Hymnology Before the Reformation." The draft of this 119 page document is full of handwritten corrections, comments and suggestions to a typist. Among the conclusions Cecil reached are the following: "the Hebrews had little or no time or inclination to cultivate [sacred music] until the peaceful reign of David allowed them not only to mold what they had adopted from others, but to enlarge upon and develop these ideas" (page 4); "portions [of hymns] are quoted by Paul in several places; in the Greek these have a distinct rhythm" (page 9); "the Roman, Lutheran and Reformed Churches each may appeal to primitive authority for its practices" (page 110); "at present much hymnody is like that of the Eastern Church, dwelling on the facts of Christ's life, and like the early Latin church, devoting itself to the ethical side of the Gospel and the practical duties of life" (page 112).

Some of Cecil's sources in this paper were used by his great-granddaughter, **Sarah Taylor Cook Guzmán** (1970-) in her research in obtaining a Masters degree (2000) at the *Universidad Autónoma Nacional de México*, Mexico City. The subject of Sarah's research was the transformation of *canciones profanas* (secular songs) into sacred music, through a process of composition and adaptation known as *divinización*.

On June 20 1900, Cecil married **Blanche Jeannette Dorland** (1873-1967) of Louisville, KY. After a honeymoon in New Orleans, Blanche and Cecil lived in Webb City, Missouri, where Cecil had his first Baptist pastorate. By 1901, they were in St Louis, where Cecil had become pastor of West Park Baptist Church. Blanche and Cecil were the parents of two sons, born 9 years apart, James Dorland (1904-1966) and **Cecil Virgil Jr** (1913-1970), born in St Louis and Danville, KY, respectively.

Cecil Cook's preaching style and theological formulations were occasionally noted publicly. Some of these published comments have been saved and passed along. In St Louis, probably in 1901, as he was under consideration that year for a call by the West Park Baptist Church, Cecil preached at North Baptist Church. The event was preserved in a clipping from an undated and unidentified newspaper. The paper's sub-headline announced that on Sunday morning, young Dr. Cook "preached to Christians and at the evening hour to the unconverted." The paper stated that "Rev. Cook is a young and eloquent speaker. He possesses a well-modulated voice of rare excellence and his persuasive notes last evening as he pleaded with argument and exhortation were indeed effective. Speaking without seeming effort, with excellent enunciation; at times in tones sonorous yet without a tinge of harshness, and again in softer tones, low yet penetratingly clear and distinct."

The newspaper reproduced Cecil's definition of the Kingdom of God, as he preached from Mark 12:34:

> *"Many vague ideas are entertained as to what is the Kingdom of God. The New Testament in describing it says nothing about territory or form of government, or display of power. The church is not the kingdom of God though the Kingdom of God is in nearly all churches. The Kingdom of God has more reference to the idea of King-ship than Kingdom. The Kingdom of God is the rule or reign of God in the souls of those who, by His election and their obedience become the willing subjects of His sway."*

Cecil Virgil Cook, Sr

Cecil Cook Sr was, for fifty-four years (1894-1948), a well known and widely admired Baptist minister, serving churches in Missouri, Alabama, Kentucky, Georgia, South Carolina and Virginia. In Charlottesville, VA, Cecil Sr was pastor of both the First Baptist Church (1914-24) and the University Baptist Church (1938-48), which he saved from financial ruin during the Great Depression (1929-1942). The mortgaged church building was the subject of a bank repossession, just before he began his pastorate there. Cecil raised the funds needed to save the edifice from creditors.

A skilled piano player and also possessed of an affable personality, Cecil Sr did not limit his gregarious reach to members of his congregation. In April 1924, soon after beginning his pastorate in Gaffney, South Carolina, Cecil Sr was crossing the courthouse square and encountered a "colored" couple (as the local paper reported) who had acquired a marriage license and were looking for a judge or minister to marry them. Cecil performed the ceremony on the spot. In the '30s, back in Charlottesville, VA during the Great Depression, Cecil would stop people on the streets and ask for loose change to forestall a foreclosure on the University Baptist Church.

Jovial and engaged though he was, Cecil would not tolerate public ridicule directed at himself. In May, 1927, he promptly resigned a pastorate, when made the butt of a joke about getting drunk. In the run up to the 1928 presidential election, Cecil refused to support Al Smith, popular governor of New York and the likely Democratic candidate. But Governor Al Smith supported the ending of Prohibition; in other words, he favored rescinding the Constitutional Amendment which outlawed alcoholic drink. Because Al Smith was "wet," Cecil denounced him from the pulpit of the First Baptist Church in Gaffney, SC. This was close to political treason for many White Southerners, who had voted Democratic since the Civil War and could not stomach any Republican or support for any. With help from the local newspaper editor, someone made fun of the "dry" local pastor, Dr. Cecil Cook.

On March 22, 1927, the following article appeared in the Gaffney *Ledger*:

> ### Baptist Pastor Seen With Quart of Corn
> *Dr. Cook Misses Sunday Services Following Visit to "Bob" Johnson.*
>
> Last Sunday Dr Cecil V. Cook, pastor of the First Baptist Church, was presented with a quart of pure corn, which R.E. Johnson, local coal dealer, gave as a premium with a ton purchase of coal.
>
> The member of the pastor's congregation, who reports this incident, says that the pastor was last seen going in the direction of home, carrying the quart with him. Said member also states that the pastor was missing on the following Sunday morning, both from his Sunday school class and the pulpit.
>
> Now whether the corn (which by the way was pure seed corn) had anything to do with the pastor's absence, the brother is not in position to say.

A bare five weeks later, on May 3rd, 1927, Cecil announced his resignation to the startled congregation. He stated he would become pastor of the First Baptist Church of Albany, Georgia, the first Sunday of June.

Firm protection of his public persona did not mean that Granddad lacked a sense of fun. This he shared with friends and within his family, including very small grandsons. After one Sunday dinner in the West Virginia home of Betty and Cecil Jr, Granddad speculated to the assembled tiny people around the dining room table, whether there might not be enough dessert to share with them. Worried looks were followed by adult laughter.

Having grown up the youngest boy in a household with at least one servant, Granddad was unaccustomed to looking after children. Daughter-in-law Betty Cook was left speechless, she recalled years later, when Grandfather Cook discovered an infant of hers in urgent need of a change of diapers. His solution was not to shoulder the task or even to summon competent help. Instead, in a state of alarm, he picked up the baby, holding it hygienically away from himself, and carried it, dripping kaka onto every floor, until he found Betty. Without one word, Granddad handed off the diminutive defecator to its astonished mother.

The year 1944 was the fiftieth anniversary of Cecil's ministerial ordination. The event had to be commemorated and it was, in grand style by Cecil Jr. This dutiful son solicited letters of appreciation from dozens of friends and colleagues and presented these to "Pop" in a bound book, at a surprise celebration at University Baptist Church, Charlottesville, VA on Dec 3, 1944. Apart from the many perfunctory congrats, this letter-book is a trove of anecdotes and personal commentary offered by people (99.9% elderly White men), who responded to an invitation to reminisce. Among the written remarks made to Cecil Sr in 1944 are some from ancient Baptist gladiators, many of whom, like Cecil himself, had been born well back in the nineteenth century. The oldest correspondent was born in 1843. Here are a few of the accolades.

"I greet you for I knew your beloved father . . . for the years of fellowship we have had in Old Virginia . . . for I knew your brother Ernest so well. He and I fought over nearly every section of Old Missouri for years." P.T. Harmon (West Lynchburg Baptist Church, Lynchburg, VA)

"I am not forgetting the lovely girl with curling blond locks, who has kept you so young." Everett Gill (Wake Forest, NC)

"You came into my life with the pointedness and emphasis of a staccato note." Ellis A. Fuller, President, Southern Baptist Theological Seminary, Louisville, KY)

"Even longer than [fifty years] I have claimed you as one of my 'seminary boys.' Your sweet voice led the choir in my Louisville church. You so inspired the ordination of my brother Howard Lee. When you entered the state of matrimony with beautiful Blanche Dorland, you, as I, were 'saved by Grace'." Carter Helm Jones (Lynchburg, VA)

"By way of identification, I can say that I am the Jones that roomed with W.L Hayes, diagonally across the corridor on the second floor of New York hall. Those were the best days of the seminary, when the most of the faculty were outstanding scholars. The student body rated high in scholarship and natural exuberance of animal spirits." W.M Jones (Barnwell, SC)

"Let me imagine I am bursting into your room again in old New York Hall, yelling in song, 'Did you ever see my Susan Ann Melindy Jane Brown? She's my honey! She's my sweet thing! She's my baby!' And let me slip my card into the box of chrysanthemums which you were taking to Katherine Gaines." Jim Franklin (Richmond, VA)

"I knew your honored father and your brother Ernest was a member of the first class I ever taught in the seminary. What a brilliant and lovely soul he was! In more recent years it was my privilege to know your son as he studied with us here in Louisville." John Sampey (Southern Baptist Theological Seminary, Louisville, KY)

"When I resigned from West Park Mission in St Louis to go to Seminary, you led the group in the transition from the status of a mission to that of a church." W.O. Lewis (General Secretary, Baptist World Alliance)

"I have known you in denominational life, in your local church life and in your home life and have always found you true blue." A. Paul Bagby (Louisburg Baptist Church, Louisburg, NC)

"I regard you as my father in the ministry." H.L. Banister (First Baptist Church, Oxford, NC)

"I have admired you ever since I was a student and heard you speak at chapel at LaGrange." Wallace Bassett (Cliff Temple Baptist Church, Dallas, TX)

"Since my retirement from the Home Mission Board Jan 1 1943, I have spent most of my time in my room in this hotel, thinking and living my life over, thanking and praising God for the many men that crossed my pathway and left rich and gracious experiences that *enriched my life and strengthened my faith.*" J. W. Beagle (Hotel Harrison, Cynthiana, KY)

"*I have thought a great deal of you since I first came to know you through your brother, Ernest, who was my good friend and helper during my student days at William Jewel College. I think much also of your son and his wife who was one of our finest girls at Crescent Hill.*" W.C. Boone (Crescent Hill Baptist Church, Louisville, KY)

"*You have been a soul winner and master builder. The first fifty years are the most difficult. After that period a fellow gets the hang of it. After a like period I feel we can work without friction.*" John E. Briggs (Temple Baptist Church, Washington, DC)

"*I remember happy days in the Seminary. I remember when you took two of us to call on Blanche Dorland and we were so solemn and pious.*" Ryland Knight (Second-Ponce de Leon Baptist Church, Atlanta GA)

"*When this century was yet young, you were with me in a meeting in Somerset KY, where I was then pastor. During that meeting one of our deacons came to me and confessed that he had been studying* Pastor *Russell's books and stated that if you were preaching Baptist doctrine, he was no longer a Baptist. I persuaded him to have a conference with you. He came with his Russelite books and met you with the Bible. Before the conference closed he had seen his error, and agreed to bring his books and help start a bonfire with them.*" O.M Huey (Supt. Emeritus, Louisville Baptist Orphans Home, KY).

NOTE: Oscar Myrix Huey was "Uncle Oscar" to Cecil's daughter-in-law **Betty Taylor Cook** (1918-2000). Oscar was Betty's first cousin twice removed - the son of George Washington Huey, who was brother to her mother's father, **James Addison Huey** (1862-1961). Cecil Cook and Oscar Huey's meeting in Somerset KY took place before Betty or Cecil were born and of course before Betty grew up in Crescent Hill Church in Louisville, where Oscar had been pastor, 1913-1918.

"*May I reminisce a few seconds and take you back to one of your first churches in the '90's, 'the little one* room frame church' at Okalona, KY." N.S. Norton (Louisville KY)

"Your teaching and leading of the music will always be held in grateful remembrance by this missionary. Our picture of our graduating class at the Seminary is now with our other things, left in China, in the hands of the Japanese." Margaret and John Lowe (Richmond, VA)

"You have brightened and sweetened and blessed every life you have ever touched, I think!" E. D. Poe (Belmont Baptist Church, Roanoke, VA)

"I remember that I felt rather lonely when I saw you walk away with your doctor's degree. It meant that you would not be there at the Seminary when I returned in October but would be away in the wilds of Missouri." James M. Shilburne (First Baptist Church, Danville, VA)

"This is from 'Obese.' More than fifty years ago, you walked into my heart and your place there has grown larger and sweeter with every passing year." Bernard Washington Spilman (Field Secretary, the Sunday School Board, Nashville, TN)

"You will possibly not remember when you were pastor of Rhuhama Baptist Church in Birmingham and delivered to me at commencement in May, 1911, on the stage of Howard College, the medal for winning the junior oratorical contest." Jerome O Williams (Nashville, TN)

"How vividly do I remember that night fifty one years ago when your father performed that difficult service of coming to tell my mother of her husband's death. I remember how valiantly your brother Ernest came to our assistance and arranged the details of the funeral, and then took over the management of the paper and was our unfailing tower of strength during those trying years." Harry (W. Harrison) Williams (Pritchard Memorial Baptist Church, Charlotte NC)

"You have maintained a happy outlook on life and have kept the vision splendid." (E. J. Wright)

"I had not made my appearance in the world at the hour of your ordination in LaGrange Missouri, but in some way you were able to be ordained without my being *there."* (Kyle M. Yates, Walnut Street Baptist Church, Louisville, KY)

"I have my helper for both spring and fall meetings, but will remember you in case someone asks me about an evangelist. Have been here nearly ten years. Mighty good people. Doing very well. Should do better. Membership 1450. Gave only $24,600 last year. 129 additions. We are capable of doing better." James L. Baggott (First Baptist Church, College Park, GA)

"R.T. Bryan, a servant of God and a citizen of the Kingdom of Heaven and a child of God and a missionary for fifty nine years and a minister of God for sixty seven years unto Dr. Cecil V. Cook, my brother in Faith's Family: Grace Mercy and Peace from our Father-Mother God and Jesus Christ our Lord. I bring you greetings from my three kingdoms. U.S. A. for eighty nine years and the Kingdom of God for seventy eight years and the kingdom of China for fifty nine years." R.T. Bryan (Dallas TX)

"God be thanked for what he has wrought in and through you. And may a soft light fall upon the way as it winds on and up." Solon Cousins (Dept of Bible, University of Richmond)

"May I say it has been a high personal privilege to know you for the past several years. Naturally my regard increased when you were adopted into our family as 'Little Willie'." Jerry Lambkin (Baptist Training Union Department, Southern Baptist Convention, Nashville, TN)

"Beloved, Oh how discouraged I was this morning when I discovered I was too late to get in a word of congratulations to your noble father . . . I was sick in bed . . . I was found by loved ones in a dead faint on the floor. I had taken no medicine of any kind, ever, or used tobacco or liquor and am careful about my diet. Haven't even drunk tea or coffee for many years but I'm seventy four and a half years old next Monday. Have never been strong and have, since 1904, spent most of my time preaching and working in lands too hot for most. And the leper work described in the enclosed Bulletin was just a sideline - my golf and tennis! It's a wonder I'm alive." John Lake ("John Lake Leper Work," Tai-Kam Island

Leper Hospital and Colony, South China Sea and Kansas City Missouri)

"It has been forty six years since we left the Seminary. You graduated with the degree of Th.D. and I with Th.G. I was told by someone that the seminary course was like a bridge on which to cross over to better things, but we were not expected to take the bridge with us. I have left the bridge. . . . It is hard to realize that forty six years have rolled by since that memorable night when you were tried for criminal neglect of bringing a fruitcake given you by your sister. I am sure you have not forgotten how dear old Dr. Kerfoot cleared you on the plea of insanity on the subject of fruit cake and how you fell upon the floor screaming 'Fruit cake!' Fruit cake!' in the most dramatical way until all laughed until they cried." P. H. Cowherd (Norway, SC)

"I am reminded that you were ordained by a council of which I was a member at LaGrange December 3, 1894. . . . I was a guest in your father's home when I came to LaGrange in 1869. Graduated from the College in 1870, took my theological course in Chicago, accepted first regular pastorate with Kirkwood church in St Louis. In 1875, I accepted a professorship at LaGrange College and during about five years had your brother Ernest and sister Lula in some of my classes. Willie and you were of the younger set, who came on to guarantee an illustrious family devoted to the highest attainments of life." Elbert H. Sawyer [age 101] (Honorary Associate Pastor, First Baptist Church, Chickasha, OK)

Cecil was pastor of University Baptist Church, Charlottesville, VA from July 1, 1938, until July 1, 1948, when he retired at age 76. Cecil had gone to this pastorate at 66 years of age, after the church had been evicted from its building. (See note, page 53.) Suffering with cancer, Cecil died four months after he retired.

Cecil and Blanche, daughter-in-law Carrie and son Dorland Cook, are buried in Monticello Memory Gardens, on state hwy 53 (670 Thomas Jefferson Pkwy). The famous Mitchie Tavern is just across the road from the cemetery entrance. Grab a bite where Carrie enjoyed taking her visiting Cooks, and then spend a gentle hour with the folks.

JOHN ERNEST COOK, 1860-1926

A note about Cecil's older brother, Ernest, is not out of place. The ancient Elbert Sawyer, and several others, who wrote congratulatory letters to Cecil, made very positive mention of John Ernest Cook (1860-1926). Uncle Ernest was born on July 17, 1860 in Shelby County, KY and died on Dec 2, 1926 in Richmond, VA. Ernest married Julia West (Aug 28, 1865-Nov. 6, 1937) in Richmond, VA on Dec 20, 1888. Ernest was a lawyer (1881) and was also ordained (1887) a Baptist minister. Seminary Professor John Sampey remarked in his letter to Cecil Sr that Ernest was a "brilliant" student. Ernest held pastorates in Missouri and engaged in denominational work in Missouri, South Dakota and Virginia and served as a Red Cross Director in World War I at Camp Funston, KS, and at Camp Pike, AR. He and Julia were the parents of five children: Helen, Ernest, John, Sue, and Paul. Ernest and Julia West Cook are buried in Richmond, VA. (See p. 108.)

> *On Dec 8, 1937, the University Baptist Church building was sold at public auction to satisfy its creditors . . . permission to remove the communion table was denied. In May, 1938, the church extended its call to Dr Cook . . . Nov 1938, the bank . . . offered to sell the building to the church . . . the money was raised in dimes and quarters through gifts, sale of candy, collection of soap coupons . . . [at weekly meetings of the Kiwanis Club, Dr Cook] offers to sell his salad or dessert for a 10 cent or 25 cent contribution . . . members walked to church in order to contribute bus fare . . . almost daily, Dr Cook emptied his pockets of change representing the day's gifts.* "Exile & Return," Howard Newlon Jr, Univ. Baptist Church bulletin, Charlottesville, VA, Oct 19. 1975.

SOURCES:

Cook genealogical information: the unpublished genealogical book of Betty Taylor Cook, his daughter-in-law. See also Ellery Farmer's **A Farmer Book**, www.geocities.com/ Heartland/Flats/ 7314/Farmer/elam.html.

Incidents within the family are taken from conversations with Betty and Cecil Cook Jr.

Quotations celebrating the pastorates of Cecil Cook Sr are taken from honorific letters in a bound book presented to Cecil Cook by his son, Cecil Jr. This book is in the possession of the writer.

Newspaper description of Cecil Cook's 1901 preaching style was generously provided by David Huey Cook, a grandson.

Text of 1904 Sermon by Cecil V. Cook: preserved by Betty Taylor Cook, in the possession of the writer.

You have kept the vision splendid – E.J. Wright, above, page 50.

"About my retiring"

Do not think for a moment that I have forgotten the importance of this Sunday to you. When you stand up to speak your peace, remember that all who have known you and loved you through the years are unspeakably proud of your ministry, and that if you think it means you are through, you are the only one who thinks so. It was never meant for us to see very far ahead at any time, anyway, and besides, we belong to Something much bigger than ourselves. "He who began a good work . . ." My own expectation is that when the die is cast, you will feel more content about it than you ever dreamed and that some of your happiest times lie straight ahead.

Cecil Jr to Cecil Sr, June 27, 1947

"I FIND IT VERY HARD TO PART WITH BLANCHE"

James Emory Dorland
Arabelle America Ireland

Blanche Dorland Cook (1873-1967)
Cecil V Cook, Jr (1913-1970)

    James E. Dorland (1844-1915) was born in the village of Holmesville, Ohio, on March 15, 1844. James' father **Ezekiel Dorland** (1812-1846) died when James was two years old. James' mother was **Lucinda Haley Dorland** (Lash) (1818-1893). James brother, Richard (1839-1871), was older than James by five years. The 1860 federal census records Lucinda Dorland and sons Richard, 21 and James, 16, living in Salt River Township, Wayne County Ohio. James Dorland's middle name, *Emory*, has not yet been accounted for. Was James given his father's name as a middle name but somehow *Ezekiel* became *Emory*?

    On March 6, 1893 Lucinda Lash purchased Lot 16, Square 3 in East Union Cemetery, East Union Township, from the Wayne County clerk (Deed Book page 348). Lucinda must have known she was dying. Ezekiel Dorland had died 46 years earlier, on April 23, 1846 at age 32. Although Lucinda had remarried twenty-five years after Ezekiel died, Lucinda buried herself beside him. Also buried here is "Mary E. Dorland, Jan 1842-24 Aug 1855."

    The early deaths of James' father and his thirteen year old sister, Mary Ellen, when James was but 11, may have prompted strong family feelings in young James. Such sentiments are on display in letters written to his mother during James' Civil War service.

James Emory Dorland, USA, 1862-1865

In August, 1862, James, 17, enlisted as a Private, Company C, 41st Ohio Infantry Volunteers. He served to the close of the war. Betty Cook, whose husband, Cecil Cook, Jr, was James Dorland's grandson, has recorded in her unpublished family genealogy that young James was present at thirteen named battles: Missionary Ridge, Lookout Mountain, Orchard Knob, Resaca, Adairsville, Ricetto Mills, Dallas, Kenesaw Mountain, Chattahoochee, Atlanta, Jonesboro GA, Nashville and Franklin TN. To these battles certainly must be added many skirmishes and disorganized, unplanned encounters with the enemy. So far as is known, James was never seriously wounded.

On March 15, 1863, James was in a convalescent camp near Nashville, TN, for a respiratory problem. "I have a bad cold," James wrote to his mother. "I can hardly speak out loud. I was on guard last night and it made my cold worse." James' main concern on that occasion (which was also his nineteenth birthday) was that his brother Richard be stopped from trying to bring James home.

"You know how I would feel if he would come down here and have to go home without me and I know or almost know that he would. There would be ten chances to one for him to for I have seen too many cases like that. Some brings their children citizens clothes and take them home but I would sooner stay my two years than to go home that way. Tell him to stay at home until I send for him."

In all of James' surviving letters to his mother he tries to follow a fine line. These letters are vaguely descriptive of warfare and the fighting he was in, as he means to adopt a youthful bravado without terrifying his mother about the dangers. On June 1, 1864, James wrote, "We were ordered to make a charge, which we did, with great slaughter." The letter was penned "near Pumpkin Vine Creek." (See page 78.) Three months later, James, by then one of Sherman's seasoned veterans, wrote again to his mother, reporting with slight drama and no embellishment, "We marched about 50 miles to get the rebels out of Atlanta and we took possession and are now laying in camp."

After the war, James moved to Louisville KY, where he conducted a profitable career as the managing representative for the American Book Company. He provided textbooks to the public schools of Louisville and the near region. The 1911 Louisville City Directory ("Carson's 1911 Directory"), page 353, lists James E Dorland's residence at 1307 S First St. It was in this stately residence that James and Belle raised their two daughters, **Blanche** and Ethyl, during the closing decades of the nineteenth century. James may have lived in Illinois prior to settling in Louisville. This is suggested by the federal census of 1900, which recorded that his second daughter, Ethyl, 23, had been born in Illinois in 1876-77.

In Louisville, James was known as a gregarious and popular man. In keeping with his Dorland heritage, James was an active Presbyterian. This Calvinist legacy extended back to James' grandfather, for whom he was named. The first **James Dorland** (Aug 1, 1781-Feb 2, 1858) was himself a Presbyterian lay reader. This first James was the great grandson (pages 66-70, below) of **Gerret (Garret) Dorlandt (Dorland)** (1707-1774), who was an original subscriber of the first Dutch Reformed Church in Harlingen, NJ and served the congregation as both deacon and elder.

The Lutheran heritage of **Arabelle America Ireland** (1850-1895), wife of James E. Dorland, vied with the Calvinist/Presbyterian traditions of the Dorlands, until their daughter Blanche brought to a halt all Protestant high church inducements, by her marriage to a zealous Southern Baptist minister, **Cecil V Cook Sr** (1871-1948). For a couple of generations after that, everyone is Baptist. At this writing (107 years after the marriage of Blanche Dorland and Cecil Sr) the Baptist consensus has diminished, with one or another descendent having adopted an affiliation that is (or has been) Baptist, Methodist, Catholic, Presbyterian, Pentecostal, Buddhist, agnostic, atheist, and none-of-the-above. Welcome to 21st century devotion in America, and elsewhere.

James died in New York City on January 14, 1915, while visiting his daughter Ethyl Barnes Qualey and her husband, Joe. At his death, James Emory Dorland was a member of the Warren Memorial Presbyterian Church (4th and Broadway) in Louisville, where he was eulogized as "one of the best loved men in the city."

"AFFECTIONATE ADVICE" GIVEN IN 1871

It is not known how James Dorland met Belle Ireland, but we can guess it had to do with the relocation of relatives from Wayne County Ohio to Whitley County Indiana. The 1860 federal census lists a William Dorland, age 26, living in Columbia City, IN, working as a dry goods salesman. Awaiting confirmation is the identify of this William. Cremer's book (see page 75, below) does not show a William Dorland, born in the mid 1830s, who could have been in Columbia City in 1860. But Cremer (footnote, pp. 208-9) does have Luke Dorland (uncle of James E.) in Columbia City; public records confirm this. On April 25, 1861, in Columbia City, the Rev. Luke Dorland, pastor of the Presbyterian Church, presided at the wedding of Simon H. Wonderlich and Elizabeth Edwards. This Luke Dorland (1815-1897) is a younger brother of James' late father **Ezekiel Dorland**. In 1853, Luke Dorland was the founding pastor of the Presbyterian Church in Ontario, Ohio, but Luke did not remain in Ohio. By the late 1850s he appears in the minutes of the Presbyterian Synod as a pastor in the Indiana Presbytery. Cremer states that Luke moved back to Ohio, to pastor churches in Belleville and Northfield Center. By 1867, Luke and Juliette Dorland were Presbyterian missionaries in North Carolina. They are enrolled in the 1870 census, in Concord, NC. (Additional information about Ezekiel and Lucinda: pages 66 and 73 below; for Luke and Juliette Dorland, see page 70.)

Besides William and Luke, there were other Dorlands linked to both central Ohio and Columbia City, Indiana. James' mother **Lucinda Dorland** married her second husband, Henry Lash (1801-1882) in Columbia City. The wedding took place on Sept 25, 1872. Lucinda and her son Richard had moved from Ohio to Indiana during the Civil War. [NOTE: See Supplement, page 363, James Dorland met Belle Ireland after moving to Columbia City in 1865, to rejoin his mother there after his military service.] James Dorland and Belle Ireland were married the year *before* Lucinda married Henry Lash. It is possible Lucinda and Henry met each other at the wedding of Belle and James and married the following year. Lucinda and Henry did not stay long in Columbia City. The 1880 census has Henry Lash, age 79, and Lucinda Lash, 62, in Wayne County Ohio, in Paint Township. As stated, Lucinda was buried in a cemetery in East Union Township, Wayne County Ohio, beside her first husband, Ezekiel.

Arabelle and James were married in her parents' home in Columbia City, Indiana, on October 11, 1871. The date is recorded in a formal certificate of marriage in the handwriting and signature of the minister, Hugh Wells, the pastor of Grace Lutheran Church in Columbia City. Wells served this church for 16 years (Oct. 1862-1878).

The Oct 11, 1871 marriage certificate for Arabelle America Ireland and James Emory Dorland is found in a small book passed down through the family, entitled *The Christian Minister's Affectionate Advice to a Married Couple*, written by James Bean (New York: American Tract Society, no date). The book is in pristine condition and may never have been consulted by the newlyweds, who found reason enough to preserve it for the marriage certificate within.

Among the tidbits of "affectionate advice" offered, James Bean included:

"A woman must guard against the tormenting disappointments to which childish expectations render her liable." What might be such "childish" disappointments? Well, "always expecting to be caressed" is one. And a serious risk indeed, this expectation of a caress: "if she do not become more rational in her expectations, this folly will occasion its own punishment" (page 10). Mr. Bean neglects to specify the punishment.

Arabelle America Ireland

Mr. James Bean also advises the wife against confusing "indifference" with "the agitations of mind to which men are particularly liable, from their having more to do with the world then women have" (page 11).

"There should be some allowance made for what is natural to men, especially Englishmen: namely a certain bluntness, through which they seem indifferent when they are not really so" (page 11).

A husband's "attention" is more likely to be won by a "gentile and submissive spirit" (page 16).

It is a "monstrous perversion of character" (page 14) in a woman to make herself "tormentingly busy in her husband's immediate province" (page 15), when she ought to "confine herself" to "her sex, her situation in the family and her vows" (page 15). "Family worship" should occur "before breakfast" and "before supper" and there should also be "a stated time for retirement" (page 83). One longs to hear from Ms. James Bean on all these matters.

After their wedding, Belle Ireland and James E. Dorland may have settled for a brief time in Indiana or perhaps Belle returned to her parent's home in 1873, for the birth of their baby girl **Blanche**. Though born in Indiana, Blanche Dorland grew up in Louisville, KY and it was there that **Blanche Jeannette Dorland** (1873-1967), met **Cecil Virgil Cook** (1871-1948) and on June 20, 1900, married him.

To the lasting grief of James and his daughters, Belle Ireland Dorland died in 1895. Belle probably never met Cecil Cook, who courted Blanche while he was a student at the Southern Baptist Theological Seminary, a training school for Baptist ministers, which had recently been relocated from South Carolina to Louisville.

With Blanche's marriage to the young Baptist minister, a family's ancestral Lutheran affiliation came to an end. It probably ended in her girlhood as Blanche's father James (and probably her mother Belle, following James) was an active Presbyterian in Louisville.

Shortly before her marriage to **Cecil V. Cook Sr** in 1900, James sent a direct letter to his prospective son-in-law. This was in response to a (now lost) letter from Cecil.

> *Your favor of recent date has been rec'd. I am very glad to hear from you.*
>
> *Yes. Blanche and I had a full and free talk over the matters in which you & she are most concerned. My position has always been in these matters to allow the girls to make their own choice. I have invariably kept aloof from creating an impression that I was favorably inclined to one more than another of their callers. Hence the impression on your part that I did not favor attentions. Had I not favored your attentions you would certainly have known of it. I find it very hard to part with Blanche but as it will occur sooner or later and that you seem to be her choice for a companion I am sure that you both have my hearty sanction and to her happiness I most unreservedly entrust to your care.*
>
> *As to the time, you and she will decide as to that.*
>
> *I wish it were so that you could locate in Louisville so that the little home could remain in tact and that I could live with you. But I have said to Blanche not worry about me. I would take care of myself and be happy too. Wishing you both a most happy and prosperous journey through life,*
>
> *Yours truly,*
> *J.E. Dorland*

The wedding would have been a poignant event as the much-loved mothers of both bride and groom were absent in death. We presume that the fathers of both the bride and groom were present at the wedding.

At the reception for their children, what would James E. Dorland and Cecil's father, **Joshua Flood Cook** have talked about? We have no record or family recollection which might guide our speculation. James Dorland had settled in Louisville. After the Civil War, Louisville was decidedly tilted toward Old South mythologies and politics. But James had reached manhood in the uniform of the federal army. By age twenty, he was a battle-hardened veteran with two or more years' service, much of it under the command of General William T. Sherman. By his 21st birthday, on March 15, 1865, James had seen death and destruction and had caused some of it. During the war he had written to his mother that he had participated in "great slaughter." No doubt James had buried many a young Ohio boy like himself, to say nothing of Rebel boys as well.

Joshua Flood Cook, father of the groom, was of a slave-owning family. At age 27 in 1861, Joshua had resigned the presidency of a female educational institution in Kentucky, moved to Mississippi, and had become a Baptist chaplain in the Southern cause. J.F. Cook had buried more than one Confederate soldier, including his young brother-in-law, Willie Farmer, who died in 1862 from a shattered hip, shortly after the battle of Shiloh. (See page 100, below.) In his memoir, **Old Kentucky** (1908), Joshua records with pride that his brothers "rode with Morgan" on rebel raids into James Dorland's home state of Ohio. The deepest penetration into Ohio by John Hunt Morgan and his irregular "Raiders" was to Lisbon, in July 1863. Lisbon was the first Ohio hometown of James Dorland's grandparents **Mary Moore** (1785-1869) and the first **James Dorland** (1781-1858). A monument five miles south of Lisbon commemorates the capture of Morgan and the horsemen who rode with him. (For more on Morgan's Raiders, see pages 166-67, below.)

On their children's wedding day, did James Dorland and Joshua Cook speak to each other of the Civil War? Would they have felt the veterans' rapport, a mutual affinity, which the calenture of their youthful allegiances entitled them? Did they speak in candor of their common survival? Or, were they guarded with each other? Would they have been guided by their life-long, mutually successful stratagems of decorum and polite allusion? They had, in their own ways, pursued very successful careers as sales agents, earning above average livings by making themselves pleasant in the company of people whose opinions and resources they aimed to win. They had each, undoubtedly, fine-tuned their natural gifts of *politesse*

James Emory Dorland

during their thirty-year careers in the border states of Missouri and Kentucky. Did their wartime experiences bind them close, as forthright old soldiers and now as affectionate fathers-in-law? Or did they merely exchange affable comments, as they observed together their much loved and promising newlywed children, embarking into the adventures of a new century? Such questions prod the imagination but remain unanswerable in this life.

JAMES DORLAND'S PATERNAL ANCESTRY

James' father was **Ezekiel Dorland** (Sept. 14, 1812-April 23, 1846) dead at age 34. His mother was **Lucinda Haley Dorland** Lash (1818/20-1893). Although father-orphaned at age two, James knew both his paternal grandparents. He had been named for his father's father, the first **James Dorland** (Aug 1, 1781-Feb 2 1858). Grandfather James married **Mary Moore** (Nov 22, 1785-Feb. 16, 1869) in southwestern Pennsylvania on Dec 11, 1804. James and Mary Dorland made their home in Lisbon (called at first, New Lisbon Village) Ohio. The couple subsequently moved to nearby Fredericksburg. Mary Dorland is listed in the 1860 Fredericksburg census, where she and James had raised thirteen children, eleven of whom reached maturity. Mary Moore Dorland was buried in Crestline, Ohio.

The Moores, James Emory Dorland's great-grandparents, were Ohio pioneers. They moved from Pennsylvania to Lisbon, OH, not long after their daughter Mary's PA wedding in 1804. The move to Ohio is certain because Mary's father **John Moore** (?-?) was a reader in the Presbyterian Church in Lisbon, Aug 7, 1807-Sept 19, 1812. To function as a lay reader usually meant a person conducted the regular weekly service in the absence of an ordained minister. Congregational leadership and public reading by her father, infer that Mary came from an educated background. Mary Moore's Presbyterian principles imply *Borderer* ancestry (page 83). The Moore influence caused the Dorlands to exchange their ancestral Dutch Reformed traditions for a Presbyterian affiliation.

DORLANDS - FROM *BRUEKELEN* TO BROOKLYN

The word *dorlandt* appears to be a Dutch compound, *dor* (sterile, barren) and *landt*, and therefore can be taken to mean *unproductive soil*. There is no clear reason how *Dorlandt* came to be a proper last name. Absence of certain etymology is a characteristic of many names. A reasonable speculation suggests that last names were a convenience, developing out of the circumstance that sir-names became both needed and common as Europeans, whether peasants or privileged, became more mobile during the fifteenth and sixteenth centuries. You could call yourself or were called by whatever moniker identified you most conveniently to your original place or people. The Dorlandts were Dutch people from, it seems, barren farmland.

In checking bound registries of *feoffs and rents* housed in Utrecht, Dutch researchers Robert and Eric Van Dorland identified the early use of *Dorland* as a proper name. In a register for the castle Nijendode, Bruekelen, Holland, a notation dated April 8, 1434 records a grant by Jan van Nijendode to two half-brothers, *Claes* and *Dorlant* who are identified as the bastard sons of the lord of the castle. But something more is known about the ancestry of James E. Dorland. Jan's supposed naming of his own children, legitimate or not, was not the earliest appearance of *Dorlandt*. Jan van Nijendode had a younger brother, *Claes Dorlandt* (?-?). This was a generation before a Dorlandt ancestor was named for the barren land given a bastard boy by the philandering son of the master of the castle. The use of *Dorlandt* as a proper name occurred in this family even earlier than with Jan's brother, Claes. More ancient ancestors, the details and dates now lost in medieval mists, also may have inherited inferior lands.

Claes Dorlandt's and Jan van Nijendode's father was **Ghysbrecht Van Nyjenrode** (?-1396) and his mother was Ghysbrecht's first wife **Bella Van Lejenburg** (?-?). Their oldest son, brother of Claes and Jan, was **Ghysbrecht Dorlandt Van Nyjenrode** (1391-1454). Ghysbrecht Dorlandt and Bella Van Lejenburg are the lineal ancestors of James E. Dorland, as traced in **The Dorland Family in Holland** (1965) by Grant Dorland. (See Sources, below.).

On April 16, 1663, **Lambert Janse Dorlandt** (1639-1720) arrived in New Amsterdam on the ship *Bomekoe* (Spotted Cow). Lambert, six generations after Ghysbrecht Dorlandt Van Nyjenrode, was the first of James E. Dorland's ancestors to travel an angry sea from Bruekelen, Holland to Brooklyn, New York. In about 1710, Lambert Dorlandt built a farm house along Sunset Road, Montgomery Township, New Jersey. An historical marker was placed on the farm north of Sunset Road, to locate Lambert's grave after the headstone was lost. Recent reports suggest the farm house still stands. Road trip.

In his book, **The Dorland Family in America** (1898), John Dorland Crener has traced forward the Dorlands and their collateral lines from this Lambert Janse Dorlandt. Betty Cook's research seems to have picked up some of the data found in Crener. John D. Crener's and more recent research indicates that Lambert Janse Dorlandt and his cousin Jan Gerretse Dorlandt, who arrived in New Amsterdam in 1652, are the progenitors in the United States of the families Dorland, Dorlon, Dorlan, Durland, and Durling.

Lambert Janse Dorlandt married **Hermina Janse Peters** (Hermptje Janse Pieterse) in 1665. Lambert and Hermina had eight children, the oldest son (and third child) being **Gerret Janse Dorlandt** (abt 1666-1736). Gerret was born in Brooklyn, NY, and died in Somerset, NJ. Gerret married Jannetje Jansen Schenck (abt 1673-bf 1695) on May 20, 1692 in Brooklyn. He then married **Marytje** _____ (abt 1665-abt 1751). Gerret and Marytje had four children, including **Gerret (Garret) Dorlandt (Dorland)** (1707-1774), who married **Hilitie (Matilda) Van Arsdalen** (1712-1774) on March 13, 1730/31 in Harlingen, Somerset County, NJ. Garret Dorland was an original subscriber of the Dutch Reformed Church in Harlingen and served as both deacon and elder of the church. Garret's body was reportedly moved from a family cemetery to the Harlingen Reformed Church Cemetery.

Garret and Hilitie Dorlandt were the parents of ten or eleven children, including **Lucas (Luke) Dorland** (1748/9-1787/90), who married **Eleanor (Aulche)** _____ (1752-Oct 16, 1835) c. 1773 in New York. Eleanor then married David McKinley Sr., double great grandfather of President William McKinley. Lucas Dorland has been confused with his namesake grandson, the founder of Warren Wilson College in Ashville, NC. (Pp 70-71, below.)

The youngest of the four children of Lucas and Eleanor Dorland was the first **James Dorland** (1781-1858), who was born in Harlingen, NJ on August 1, 1781 and died on Feb 4, 1858 in Fredricksburg, Ohio. As stated, James Dorland married **Mary Moore** on Dec 11, 1804.

This Dorland line, traced forward from Lambert[1], Garrett[2], Lucas[3], and James[4], remained for generations in New Jersey and then migrated from New Jersey to Ohio. Theirs was not the route of the so-called *Low Dutch*, from NJ to south central PA and on to KY in the late 1700's. The eighteenth century term *Low Dutch* seems to have been adopted to distinguish Dutch from German (*Deutsch*) immigrants; Germans were called *High Dutch*. While we are grazing in the linguistic gardens, we may as well point out that *Pennsylvania Dutch* is a misnomer. These German-speaking immigrants of pietistic, Anabaptist (re-baptizing) persuasion, including their present day Amish and Mennonite descendents, would more accurately be called *Pennsylvania German.* But don't bother to tell that to the tourism commissions or the owners of the Dutch Markets that have sprung up all over everywhere.

The seventeenth and eighteenth centuries *Low Dutch* NJ-PA-KY migration is well documented and did include Dorlands – but not the direct line under present consideration. These folks left New Jersey in distinct family groups, heading for Conewago (Conowago) in York Co (now, Adams Co) PA. Conewago was a detour and a delay for these Dutch migrants, whose objective was to settle their extensive families on equally extensive lands in Kentucky. The larger goal was delayed because of the chaotic state of land sales in KY after the Revolution. Many eventually did reach Kentucky. Settlements of Dutch immigrants were established in Mercer, Jefferson and Shelby Counties. Among these Dutch settlers there were Dorlands (including at least one Lucas) and Van Arsdalens. But our particular Lucas and Eleanor Dorland were content to remain in New Jersey while friends and relatives moved west. Their son, the first James, did leave New Jersey but, as stated, found his way into Pennsylvania and then Ohio, marrying (in PA) the nineteen year-old Mary Moore. The Presbyterian loyalties of Mary Moore Dorland displaced her husband's Dutch Reformed ties and resonated down the Dorland family for three generations.

Betty Taylor Cook's research expands upon the Dorland lineage proposed in John Dorland Crener's influential 1898 history of the Dorland family in America (see above, and sources, below). Some researchers do not list all of the children of Mary Moore and the first James Dorland. Missing Ezekiel, they have only Luke Dorland (1815-1897), and his wife Juliette E. Goodfellow (1824-1897) and their son, Charles Johnson Dorland (?-?).

LUKE DORLAND: "COLOR, CASTE, OR CLASS DISTINCTIONS ARE AN EVIL THING"

Although not lineal ancestors of James E. Dorland, there is good reason to remember uncle Luke and aunt Juliette Dorland, who left an impressive historic legacy. They were Presbyterian missionaries, employed by the Presbyterian Board of Home Missions. In 1867, working in central North Carolina, they founded, in Concord NC, Scotia Seminary for Negro Women. Luke Dorland was the school's first president. (In 1932, the name of Scotia Seminary was changed to Barber-Scotia College.) Historian Glenda Elizabeth Gilmore has written (see Sources, below) that Scotia Seminary's "biracial faculty oversaw a curriculum calculated to give students the knowledge, social consciousness, and sensibilities of New England ladies, with a strong dose of Boston egalitarianism sprinkled in." Seminary President Luke Dorland declared that "skilled hands must be directed by a sound mind in a sound body, motivated by a zeal to serve others." An early

Scotia student, Mary McLeod, recalled her northern white teachers' insistence that "the color of a person's skin has nothing to do with his brains, and that color, caste, or class distinctions are an evil thing."

In 1867, Luke Dorland led in the organization of the Bellefonte Presbyterian Church, Concord, NC. In 1869, and '72, he was pastor of the Second Presbyterian Church in Concord, NC and, in 1884, was pastor of the African Presbyterian Church, also in Concord. Luke and Juliette Dorland remained active even in retirement. In 1887, they secured financial backing from northern Presbyterians and founded yet another school, further west, in the NC mountains. This was the Dorland Institute in Hot Springs, Madison County NC. Luke and Juliette Dorland provided the early instruction in their home and erected the first buildings at their own expense. In 1914, the school was described as worth $40,000, and was providing instruction, room and board for 70 girls as well as 30 boys, who were also taught farming practices. In addition to the boarders, there were 60 non-residential students. The Dorland Institute merged in 1918 with the Bell Institute to form the Dorland-Bell School which merged in 1942 with the Asheville Farm School, which was the predecessor of Warren Wilson College in Asheville, NC.

DORLANDS: JAMES[1] EZEKIEL[2] JAMES[3] BLANCHE[4]

Luke Dorland was not the only son of James and Mary Moore Dorland. Relying on information obtained from her mother-in-law, Blanche Dorland Cook, Betty Cook lists Mary and the first James Dorland as the parents of Luke and also of **Ezekiel Dorland** (1812-1846), who with his wife **Lucinda Haley Dorland** (1818/20-1893) were the parents of **James Emory Dorland** (1844-1915). James E., the primary subject of this sketch, was the father of **Blanche Dorland Cook** (1873-1967). In addition to Luke and Ezekiel, the children of Mary and James Dorland included: Eleanor (1806-1845), wife of John R Bell; John Moore (1807-1808); Cornelius (1809-1879), who married Margaret Griffin (?-?) and infant James (1811-1811).

Ezekiel Dorland died at 34. The cause of the death of this young husband and father is unremembered. Ezekiel appears in the 1840 Census for Prairie Township, Holmes County Ohio (p. 222). His widow, Lucinda, and their sons, Richard and James E Dorland, are recorded in the 1860 census in Wayne County Ohio. Civil War letters, written by James to his mother, mention his brother Richard. The previously referenced cemetery deed, for Lot 16, Square 3 in what was then called the East Union Cemetery, in East Union Township, was purchased by Lucinda Dorland (Lash) and is recorded in the Wayne County Ohio Deed Book at page 348. According to genealogist Patricia Watts, in a communication with the writer, the Wayne Co. Ohio Burial Book, at page 277, lists Ezekiel M. Dorland, Mary Dorland and Lucinda Dorland (Lash), buried together in Apple Creek Cemetery (formerly the East Union Cemetery). My guess is that James E. Dorland gave money to his mother, Lucinda, for her to purchase the cemetery plot. After her second husband had died, James would have wanted Lucinda buried where James' father and sister were already buried.

Just as the first James Dorland, at the close of the eighteenth century, left behind his Dutch reformed traditions and family in New Jersey to settle in Ohio, the nineteenth century found some of the Ohio-based Dorlands striking out on adventures of their own. Some of these seem to have been stimulated more by wanderlust than from any well designed plan.

In March, 1852, a certain Garret Dorland of Perry Township, Ohio led a one-hundred member company of men to the California gold fields. The party included a Cornelius Dorland as well as Garret. The company traveled by boat down the Ohio River, up the Mississippi to Independence, MO and then overland to California. As far as is known, they found no gold but may have managed to establish Dorland progeny in the far West.

JAMES DORLAND'S MATERNAL ANCESTRY: HALEY, COTTON, RICKETTS, CHENEY, NICHOLSON, POWELL, JONES

James Dorland's mother, Lucinda Haley (1818/20-1893) was the daughter of **Richard Healy** (1786-1824) and **Rachael Cotton** (1785-?). They were married April 16, 1807, possibly in Wayne County Ohio. Richard died in Salt Creek Township, Holmes (formerly Wayne) County OH. Richard's parents were **John Healy** (?-?) and **Sarah Wilson** (?-?).

Rachael was one of eleven children born to **John Cotton** (1748-July 15, 1818) and **Mary Ricketts** (July 15, 1755-Nov 29, 1833). They were married June 2, 1774, probably in Anne Arundel County, MD. In 1810, John Cotton appears in the Beaver County, PA census. By 1814, he is the owner of 160 acres of land in Holmes County, OH. Both John and Mary died in Salt Creek Township, Holmes County OH. John Cotton is known to have been buried in the Wolgamot Cemetery in Salt Creek Township.

Mary Ricketts Cotton, grandmother of Lucinda Haley Dorland, was the daughter of **Cheney Ricketts** (1732-May 15, 1814) and **Ann Cheney** (1734-Sept 13, 1813). Cheney Ricketts was born in Maryland Colony and died in Fairfield County, Ohio. Ann was born in Prince George's County, Maryland and probably died in Fairfield County, Ohio. Cheney Ricketts was the son of **Edward Ricketts** (1706-1786) and **Mary Ann Cheney** (?-?).

Edward's parents were **Thomas Ricketts** (Sept 20, 1685-?) and **Rebecca Nicklisson (Nicholson)** (April 19 1681-?). Both Thomas and Rebecca were born in South River, Anne Arundel County, Maryland. Rebecca's parents were **John Nicklisson** (1651-?) and **Rebeckath** _____ (1655-?). Both John and Rebeckath were born in South River as well.

Lucinda Haley Dorland (Lash)

Mary Ann Cheney (wife of Edward Rickets) was the daughter of **Charles Cheney Jr** (1703-?) and **Mary Powell**(?-?). Charles Jr was the son of **Charles Cheney Sr** (June 6, 1673/77-1745) and **Anne Jones** (1677/81-?). Both Charles Cheney Sr and Anne Jones were born in Anne Arundel County, Maryland. They were married July 15, 1701. Therefore, we reach the conclusion that James Emory Dorland, father of Blanche, was, through Lucinda, his mother, two generations removed from Anne Arundel County, Maryland, where his Haley, Cotton, Ricketts, and Cheney ancestors and allied families, had lived for close to two hundred years, prior to the arrival into central Ohio of James' maternal grandparents.

James and Belle Ireland Dorland are buried in Cave Hill Cemetery in Louisville, KY in a perpetual care plot, which James bought at the time of Belle's death. They lie beneath a large granite monument James selected for them and located among the Ballards, Fields, Galts, Speeds, and other Louisville notables of the nineteenth century. **Cecil Virgil Cook, Jr** (1913-1970), grandson of James and Belle and Cecil's wife **Betty Taylor Cook** (1918-2000) are also buried in the Dorland plot at Cave Hill.

SOURCES:

Dorland and Ireland genealogy, generally: Betty Taylor Cook's unpublished genealogy book, and her notes, which include information provided to her by Belle Ireland's daughter, Blanche Dorland Cook and Harriet W. Ireland, wife of Homer A. Ireland, of Media PA, in letters written to Betty in 1945.

For location of graves of Ezekiel Dorland, Mary Dorland and Lucinda Dorland (Lash): Patricia Watts, Wayne Co Ohio genealogist, sewannsew45@yahoo.com

Additional Dorland genealogical information: **The Dorland Family in America**, by John Dorland Crener (Washington DC, 1898); see also the excellent presentations on the web by Judy Cassidy and Jacqueline

Wells Lubinski (and others?) at: familytreemaker.genealogy.com/us/users/1/u/b/Jacqueline-Lubinski, where informative PDF files are located as well as the valuable document: "Descendents of Gerard Splinter Van Ruwiel."

The above mentioned Cassidy/Wells website, which reproduces much information found in the Crener book, also cites an important Dorland archive: Records of William Edward Durling (RIN 5132), in the possession of Carl L. Durling and provided by Judy (Smith), RIN 6228, Cassidy, 117 Evergreen Court, Blue Bell, Pennsylvania.

Information about Luke and Juliette Dorland in Western North Carolina: Presbyofcharlotte/concordance. The quotations and data concerning the Scotia Institute: **Gender and Jim Crow: Women and the Politics of White Supremacy in North Carolina, 1896-1920**, Glenda Elizabeth Gilmore (Chapel Hill: University of North Carolina Press (1996). See also: **History of Western North Carolina - Chapter XVII - Schools and Colleges,** By John Preston Arthur (1914), on the web at newrivernotes.com/nc (HTML by Jeffrey C. Weaver (Oct 1998)

For the Dorlandt family prior to their arrival in New Amsterdam: **The Dorland Family in Holland** by Grant Dorland (1965), used by web-based researchers.

For the 1852 Dorland-led expedition to the California Gold Fields: material found in the Genealogy Department of the Wayne County Ohio Public Library, which was consulted in June, 2006.

The 1911 Louisville City Directory ("Carson's 1911 Directory"): on the web at distantcousin.com/Directories/KY/Louisville/1911/Pages.asp?Page=0353)

For the etymology of "Dorland:" **An Etymological Dictionary of Family and Christian Names With an Essay on their Derivation and Import** by William Arthur (New York, NY: Sheldon, Blake, Bleeker & Co., 1857), cited by Ancestor Search: http://www.searchforancestors.com/surnames/origin/d/dorland.php

For Dorland research in Holland, conducted by Henk, Robert and Eric van Dorland: see vandorland.nl

> ## "THE MIXTURE RAN IN THE WOODS"
>
> The following New Jersey note is added as a caution, to set against the idea that we have something certain, after we figure out our documented genealogy. This item was written by William Carlos Williams (*Patterson*, [1946-58] page 12). Can a poet be trusted with the facts?
>
> *Violence broke out in Tennessee [abt 1712], a massacre by the Indians - hangings and exiles – standing there on the scaffold waiting, sixty of them. The Tuscaroras, forced to leave their country, were invited by the Six Nations to join them in Upper New York. The bucks went on ahead but some of the women and the stragglers got no further than the valley cleft near Suffern. They took to the mountains there, where they were joined by Hessian deserters from the British army, a number of albinos among them, escaped negro slaves and a lot of women and their brats released in New York City after the British had been forced to leave [abt 1783]. They had them in a pen there – picked up in Liverpool and elsewhere by a man named Jackson under contract with the British government to provide women for the soldiers in America.*
>
> *The mixture ran in the woods and took the name Jackson's Whites. (There had been some blacks also, mixed in, some West Indian negresses, a ship-load, to replace the whites lost when their ship, one of six coming from England, had foundered in a storm at sea, He had to make it up somehow and that was the quickest and cheapest way.)*
>
> *New Barbadoes Neck, the region was called.*

*On the Battlefield near pumpkin Vine Creek,
Wednesday June 1, 1864*

Dear Mother,

Once more I am spared to write to you. On the evening of the 27th we were ordered to make a charge which we did with great slaughter. We had an awful place to go up. Nothing but rocks and shrubs and when we got up the rebs let us have it & we them for about a half an hour when something knocked me down and the first thing I knew I was in the hospital. We lost out of the regiment in killed and wounded and missing 108 and when we went in we had 263 and that leaves 155 men. Our company lost 13 killed and wounded – three killed and ten wounded. The killed were Corporal Edward Lensinger, Pvt. Jacob Jackson and William Harley and the wounded were: Sgt. F.W. Eckiman, Corp. S. Graybill, R.R. Jamison, Bos Payl, S. Saulzenhesser, Tho. Cully, Wm. Erison, Jno Homan, Jno Axe & myself as one. And yesterday we had another one killed, Solomon Miller. The rebels made a charge on us yesterday and we drove them back. . . . I only wish this campaign was over so we could get time to wash and clean up. It was just a month yesterday since this campaign opened and the Lord only knows where it will end. We can see the rebels plain from where we are and every time they see a man they shoot. . . . I hope this will soon be over and we can all return to our sweet homes once more.

*I still remain your dear son.
James* [James Emory Dorland]

*Write to: Company C 41 CVVG, Chattanooga Tenn.
(in haste)*

"FRIENDS IN ALL RANKS"

Sarah Fellows/Fellers
Martin Ireland

Arabelle America Ireland (1850-1895)
Blanche Dorland Cook (1873-1967)
Cecil V Cook, Jr (1913-1970)

Arabelle (Belle) Ireland (1850-1895), wife of **James E. Dorland** (1844-1915) was born December 3, 1850 in Columbia City, Indiana. Belle was the second child of eight belonging to **Sarah Fellows/Fellers** (1829-1921) and **Martin Ireland** M.D. (1821-1904). Sarah and Martin were married in Whitley County, Indiana on September 22, 1847. The marriage was recorded in the county marriage book.

An 1882 book of prominent Columbia City and Whitley County Indiana residents contains the following note about Martin and Sarah Ireland. It may be presumed that the subjects were interviewed and that they provided the published details:

__MARTIN IRELAND, M. D.__ is a native of Ross County, Ohio, where he was born November 29, 1821; son of __Stephen__ and __Elizabeth (Carmean) Ireland__, both natives of Maryland, and the parents of twelve children, eight of whom are yet living. They came to Ross County, Ohio, about 1805; were identified with the early settlement of the county. Mr. Ireland followed the occupation of farming during life. The mother passed away in Ross County, and the father, in 1848, moved to McLean County, Ill., and from there went to Missouri to look after some property in 1857, where he died April 3 of that year.

Martin Ireland

Martin remained on the home farm until twenty-one years of age, receiving such education as the schools of that day afforded. After leaving home, he engaged in teaching winters, and was variously employed during the summer months. He was married, September 23, 1847, to **Sarah Fellers**, a native of Virginia. She came to Ohio at the age of four years, and to Whitley County when thirteen.

Dr. Ireland came to Whitley County, Ind., the fall of 1846, and taught the first school in the first school building erected in Columbia City. The next year he decided to perfect himself in the study of medicine, to which he had paid some attention previously; and, in 1849, attended medical lectures in Cincinnati. He located for the practice of his profession in Fayette County, Ohio, remaining six years, after which he returned to Columbia City, practicing here for over seventeen years, when he removed to Nokomis, Ill., remaining there seven years; but, in April, 1880, Dr. Ireland and family returned to Columbia City, where they have since resided. Their family consists of nine children-Augusta V., **Arabella A.**, Clara V., Wooster M., Franklin S., John M., Sarah J., Merritta [Merritte] W. and Homer A. Dr. I. is a Republican; a member of the A. F. & A. M., of Columbia City, and a graduate of the Wooster Medical University of Cleveland.

Martin Ireland may have returned to Columbia City in 1880 to oversee his investment in a new business. In April 1881, investors erected a two-story brick building to be used as a woolen mill. Martin Ireland was President of the joint-stock company. It is also recorded that Martin Ireland was a Mason, serving on occasion as an officer of the Columbia City Lodge, No. 189, A. F. & A. M.

Belle's younger brother Merritt (Merritte) Webster Ireland (1855-1954) (erroneously listed as *Merrita* in the above hometown bio) became a physician, like their father. Merritte told an interviewer that his father, Martin, disappointed in his other children, refused to pay for Merritte's education but gave him a job in his woolen mill.

Merritte Ireland spent his life as an army doctor, culminating his career in service with General Pershing during World War I and then in Washington, D.C. At the close of the war, Pershing arranged for Merritte to become surgeon general of the Army. In this capacity, Merritte Ireland presided over the planning and the construction of Walter Reed Army Hospital in Washington.

On May 23, 1899, Martin Ireland made a will, in which he left property to his wife, to their children and also to his two granddaughters, **Blanche Jeannette Dorland** (1873-1967) and Ethel Barnes Dorland, the daughters of his own deceased daughter **Arabelle America**.

Martin Ireland died at 82 on February 11, 1904 in Columbia City, IN. His funeral was conducted at the Grace Lutheran Church by Rev. Porch whose sermon was based on Job 5:26. *"Thou shall come to thy grave in a full age, like as a shock of corn cometh in in his season."* The three hymns selected and sung by a quartet, were *I Would not Live Always*, *Nearer My God to Thee*, and Cardinal Newman's *Lead Kindly Light*. Martin was buried in Columbia City in the Masonic cemetery (now, the Masonic section of Greenhill Cemetery, GH-Masonic Sec 2-6-27). Sarah Fellers Ireland died in 1921 in Chicago at 92. She was buried beside Martin (GH-Masonic 2-6-27-2). The well-kept graves of Martin and Sarah Ireland, under a large IRELAND headstone, were visited in June 2006 by great-great grandsons, David H. Cook, and the writer.

Martin was a son of **Stephen Ireland** (Sept 20 1799 - April 3 1857) and **Elizabeth Carmean** (1798-1848). Stephen Ireland was a son of **John (George?) Ireland** (March 4 1772 - June 18, 1843) and **Elizabeth Dillon** (?-?) who became John's wife in 1815, after the death of his first wife, Esther Johnson (?-abt 1814). John (or George) Ireland was a son of the first **John Ireland** (1747-?) and _____ (?-?). The first John, with two brothers, emigrated from Scotland to Westmoreland County Maryland. Stephen and Elizabeth Carmean Ireland moved from Maryland to Ross County Ohio, where Martin was born.

SCOTTSH, ENGLISH AND IRISH "BORDERERS"

It seems the first John Ireland and his two brothers were part of the wave of Scots-Irish pioneers, sometimes called "borderers," who sailed from one or another English port and arrived, often at Philadelphia, in the 1700s. From the British countryside, finding themselves in a noisy, bustling, crowded American port city, these immigrants quickly headed out of town, south or west to get on their own land. The Scots-Irish migration to America was a voluntary one. This means these new Americans were not, as many other English-speaking immigrants before them had been, abject and poor, compelled to indenture themselves in a foreign and savage wilderness to escape crushing debt back home. Nor were they convicted criminals, forced onto ocean-crossing ships to avoid prison or execution. Criminals would continue to arrive until the success of the American Revolution left only Australia as a destination for deported English delinquents.

From the point of view of Londoners and perhaps English townspeople generally, Scots-Irish country folk were semi-civilized rustics. Any people from outlying regions of the realm were called "border people" or "borderers," whether from the north of England, Scotland or Ireland. This distinction was made even if some heartland English shared with the border denizens a militant Presbyterian outlook. Few of the English-speaking immigrants to America in the 18th century, even those from Ireland, would have been Catholic.

The border immigrants tended to come as family groups and, as stated, were not indentured. These two factors distinguished them from the general run of English immigrants, arriving in the mid-Atlantic or southern colonies in the century before. These earlier heartland English, like the later arriving borderers, were looking to acquire land, but the indentured immigrants were delayed in their plans by their obligatory terms of service.

The left-behind "border people" grieved at first and then learned to celebrate the departure of their own for the colonies. James Boswell, taking a holiday break from his biography of Samuel Johnson, reported from the west coast of Scotland in October, 1773:

"Mrs. Mackinnon told me that last year when the ship sailed from Portree for America, the people on shore were almost distracted when they saw their relations go off; they lay down on the ground and tumbled, and tore the grass with their teeth. This year there was not a tear shed. The people on shore seemed to think they would soon follow."

The arriving border lasses seem to have delivered quite a shock to Quaker Philadelphia. They came ashore with "bare legs and skirts as scandalously short as an English undershift." Their mothers appeared "in long dresses of a curious cut. Some buried their faces in full side bonnets; others folded handkerchiefs over their heads in quaint and foreign patterns. The speech of these people was English, but they spoke with a lilting cadence that rang strangely in the ear." The men "wore felt hats, loose sackcloth shirts close-belted at the waist, baggy trousers, thick yarn stockings and wooden shoes." To everyone's relief, the borderers left town as soon as they could.

THE IRELANDS' GRAYLESS ANCESTRY

Merritte Ireland, a bit of a curmudgeon (see the note on page 96), once said that his grandmother **Elizabeth Carmean Ireland** (1798-1848), would not permit criticism of anyone not present to answer for themselves. This trait was so strong with her, Merritte reported, that a grandchild, wanting to test her principles, once asked her, "Aunt Zilpha, what do you think of the devil?" She allegedly responded, "He's powerful industrious. Has friends in all ranks."

This vignette could not have applied to Elizabeth, who died before any of her grandchildren were born. But what about her mother? Elizabeth was the sixth of ten children born to **Philadelphia Grayless** (1760-1854) and **Curtis Carmean** (1760-1819) of Caroline County

Maryland. Curtis and Filley Grayless lived for a time (1801-04) in Baltimore County MD and then moved, probably with some of their grown and married children, to Ross County Ohio. They are believed to have been buried in the Wilson cemetery on Wilson Lane in Ross County. The parents of Philadelphia Grayless were **Jesse Grayless (Grailey?)** (1733/37-1799) and **Trephina Johnson** (?-by 1789) of Dorchester (now, Caroline) County Maryland.

Jesse Grayless was credited with "patriotic service" in the form of wheat delivered to the revolutionary army in 1782 – a curious date, since the war had ended the year before. (The date could refer to the date of the crediting deposition, not the date the wheat was delivered.) Jesse was stated to be either 47 or 52 at the date of the deposition.) Anyway, Jesse's patriotism cannot be questioned; he was a second lieutenant in 1777 and a first lieutenant the year following, in different companies of the 14th Battalion, Maryland militia, enrolled under the name "Greyless" or "Guyless." Jesse was assessed taxes on property in Caroline (Dorchester b/f 1773) County MD in 1783. He was the owner of "Todds Venture," 74 acres, lower Caroline County, in the Choptank District Hundred. His wife Trephina had died by 1789, for on May 2 of that year Jesse married Sarah Andrew. He was recorded in the 1790 census for Caroline County MD, as the owner of a slave.

Who were Jesse Grayless' parents? In 1784, Mary Bishop, in her Caroline County MD will, identified Jesse Grayless as her "son." In 1769, Mary Bishop is executrix on the will of Robert Bishop, with Jesse Grayless and Robert Bishop (Jr?) as sureties. On June 10, 1733, "Mary Grayley" was ordered "whipped at the bublick whiping post" with "ten lashes on her bare back" for she "did commit fornication" and "begat then and there a bastard child." Proceedings were also brought against one Joseph Pearson for the pregnancy of "Mary Gralyless." From this record it appears the mother of Jesse Grayless was **Mary Grayley Bishop** (?-1784), who gave Jesse her own maiden name as his surname; Jesse Grayless' father appears to have been **Joseph Pearson** (?-?).

He loved her up and he loved her down
O lilly and lonelee,
He loved her till he filled her arms
Down by the greenwood sidee.

Some genealogies identify Jesse's father as Owen Grayless (?-?) or Timothy Greyless (?-aft 1742) but without accounting for the documentation, which pinpoints Mary, wife of Robert Bishop, as Jesse Grayless' mother, apparently by Joseph Pearson.

THE IRELAND'S CARMEAN ANCESTRY

The Carmean line has been documented quite well. **Curtis Carmean** (husband of Philadelphia Grayless, father of Elizabeth Carmean Ireland) was enrolled in 1777 as a soldier during the Revolution, serving, as did his father-in-law Jesse Grayless, with the 14th Battalion of Militia of Caroline County, Maryland. Curtis was a son of **Alice Trippet** (?-?) and **Jacob Cremeen** (1731-1790) of Wicomico County MD. Jacob was the fourth child of the five children of **John Cremeen III** (1720-1754) and **Mary Adams** (?-?). John, who died young, was the tenth child of twelve born to **Elizabeth Beauchamp** (?-?) and **John Cremeen Jr** (1691-1749) of Dorchester (now, Caroline) County MD. Elizabeth was a child of **John Beauchamp Jr** (?-?) and **Mary Curtis** (?-?). John Cremeen Jr was the fourth of six children of immigrant **John Cremeen Sr** (1656-1713) and his second wife **Susanna Mace** (1656-1734). Susanna was the daughter of **Nicholas Mace** (?-?) and **Anne** _____ (?-?)

John Cremeen Sr was from County Cork, Ireland. "John Crimine" was certified by ship's captain Thomas Taylor as arriving into Maryland Province in October 1677, having been transported on the ship *Crown Maligo*. He was listed subsequently as an indentured servant. From his surname, it is plausible to assume that immigrant John Cremeen was Irish; however, this may not be correct. Many English people had moved to Ireland during the sixteenth and seventeenth centuries, and earlier. By 1677, the Calvert's efforts to bring large numbers of well connected Catholics into Maryland was long over. That plan, hardly more than a dream of the Lords Baltimore, was destroyed by Oliver Cromwell after the English Civil Wars.

A big push to encourage English Catholic immigration to Maryland was never again attempted, even after the restoration of the monarchy in 1660. In 1676, a violent Protestant (Puritan) rebellion in Maryland attempted to take over the government. This was put down. But in 1688, with the overthrow of Catholic James II in England, the Calvert's proprietary charter was rescinded by the newly installed Protestant monarchs, William II and Mary III. Maryland became a Crown colony, with the governor appointed by the King of England.

It appears unlikely that immigrant **John Cremeen Sr**, living in Maryland in a state of indenture, was a Catholic Irishman. Why would a Catholic from Ireland, in 1677, break for America under conditions which would enslave him to an Englishman? He could remain in Ireland and be a slave, just as well. Starving Irish (not English) Catholics would come in numbers to America but not until the nineteenth century.

PLYMOUTH COLONY: "CONTENTIOUS, CRUEL AND HARD HEARTED"

As noted, the wife of John Cremeen Jr was Elizabeth Beauchamp. Elizabeth's grandfather, **John Beauchamp Sr** (1585-1655), was a financial backer of the ship *Mayflower*, which came to Plymouth MA in 1620. John was one of about 50 stockholders who backed the founding of Plymouth Plantation. Beauchamp and the other investors were willing to risk their wealth for a chance at a large return. But the investors were not happy about the Pilgrims' fixation on coerced uniformity of religious thought and practice. In 1624, hearing about court ordered beatings of Anglicans and even of Pilgrim dissenters in Plymouth Colony, the "Adventurers" (as the financial backers in London were called) expressed their displeasure at the Pilgrims for being "contentious, cruel and hard hearted, among your neighbors and towards such as in all points both civil and religious, jump not with you." In 1628, the stock company was reorganized as a result of severe financial problems. Beauchamp was one of only four of the earlier investors to join with some of the colonists to buy out the original investors. He may never have made any profit from Plymouth Colony, or recovered his money. The settlers had picked a stretch of poor coastline for settlement. Within a generation, Plymouth would become a backwater to the better led Massachusetts Bay Colony.

THE IRELAND'S AMERICAN LUTHERAN HERITAGE: DILLER[1] KEINATH[2] SLAGLE[3]

The Lutheran affiliation of the Irelands in Indiana can be traced five generations back to Belle Ireland's triple great grandparents, **Anna Barbara Dornis** (1703-bef 1766) and **Caspar Diller** (1696-1787). In Europe, this venturesome couple emigrated from Amsterdam to Philadelphia on the ship *Samuel* in 1733. As the children of Huguenot refugees, they likely inherited a Calvinist-tinged Protestantism from Caspar's parents, **Adam Elias (Johnsses?) Diller** (?-?) and **Marie (Maria) Balliet** (?-?). (Additional details are found in a separate sketch devoted to Caspar and Anna Barbara Diller, page 269.)

There is speculation among genealogists that Anna Barbara was English. However, Caspar (and probably also Anna Barbara) was German-speaking, as may be judged from the German language inscription on his well maintained gravestone in the Hill Cemetery, Hill Lutheran Church, above North Annville Township, just west of Lebanon, PA.

Prior to their departure for America, Anna Barbara and Caspar had lived in the German Palatinate, where their four oldest children were born. The Palatinate or Palatine (*Platz*) was that collection of northern German states, where French Protestants were invited to live after riot, persecution and death were visited upon thousands of them in Catholic France in the seventeenth century. It would have been in the Palatine, that the Dillers, perhaps a touch more laid back as second generation Huguenot exiles, adopted Lutheranism in lieu of the Calvinism of Caspar's parents.

Settling in Lancaster County, PA, Anna Barbara and Caspar helped found the Hill Lutheran Church, where Caspar (and probably also Barbara) are buried. Among their several children was daughter **Margaret Diller** (1734/44-1813), who married **Michael Keinath** (1720-1796). (See page 263 f.)

Late in life, Margaret and Michael Keinath moved to the Shenandoah Valley, VA, where they helped found Trinity Lutheran Church (the old "Keinadt's Church") in Crimora, near Waynesboro VA. They are buried there, beneath a large monument that was erected over their graves at the end of the nineteenth century.

Margaret and Michael's daughter **Catherine Keinath (Coiner)** (1766-1855) married **George Slagle** (1761-1828/29) in Cumberland County, PA in 1789. George was born in York, PA on January 30, 1761. During the War of independence, young George served as a drummer. His Crimora, VA gravestone reads "George Slagle Drummer Forman's PA. Troops, Revolutionary War." The date of his death is given as "21 April 1828." The Pennsylvania digital archives confirms that a George Slagle served with the York County Militia.

Not long after their marriage in 1789, George and Catherine also moved to the Shenandoah Valley of Virginia. The migration to Virginia coincided generally or perhaps even precisely with that of Catherine's parents, Margaret and Michael Keinath. Like his in-laws, George Slagle's grave and the above noted Revolutionary War inscription are in the Trinity Lutheran Church Cemetery, Route 865, Crimora, Virginia.

George's parents were **Jacob Slagle** (1723-1790) and **Mary Catherine Klein (Kelin?)** (1729-1775). Jacob Slagle was born on June 10, 1723 in Hanover, Lancaster County PA and died on April 9, 1790 in Berwick, York County, PA.

Sarah Fellers Ireland

Jacob's father was the long-lived **Christoph Friedrich Slagle** (1676-1772), who was born on October 24, 1676 in Grimma, Germany, Saxony. Christoph died in York, PA. Christoph's wife (Jacob's mother) was the equally long-lived **Anna Maria Aister** (1698-1793), born on January 10, 1698 in Stuttgart, Neckar, Wuerttemberg, Germany dying 95 years later in Berwick, York County PA. George and Catherine's daughter (one of twelve children) was **Margaret Slagle** (1794-aft 1843), born in Augusta County, Virginia and named for Catherine's mother. Margaret and her husband **Jonathan Fellows** (abt 1795- aft 1843), were **Belle Ireland**'s grandparents.

We are left to speculate whether Jonathan Fellows (or Fellers), a denizen of Augusta County, VA, might have been English, or Irish, or possibly of an immigrant, German-speaking family. If German, then Jonathan was probably of Lutheran affiliation, like his wife's paternal grandparents (the Keinath/Coiners) or perhaps reformed Lutheran (Lutheran cum Huguenot), like her Huguenot great grandparents, Caspar and Anna Barbara Diller.

Jonathan Fellows' parents or grandparents may well have migrated from Lancaster County PA to Augusta County VA, as did the Slagles, Keinaths and so many other German-speaking families, beginning in the mid 1700s.

Jonathan and Margaret Fellows were married in Augusta County Virginia on January 8, 1822. In May of that same year they sold 60 acres along the South River to "Amunuel Fellers," land belonging to the deceased **John G. Fellers** (?-?) who was probably Jonathan's father, as Jonathan received this land by will. In 1833, Jonathan sold 84 acres on the Little North Mountain (Shenandoah County). He and Margaret moved to Ohio that year and to Whitley County Indiana ten years later.

The second child of Margaret and Jonathan was **Sarah Fellows (Fellers)** (1829-1921), who would live beyond ninety years and die in Chicago, a "*mighty inland city yet unsurvey'd and unsuspected*" (Whitman) in the year of Sarah's birth.

Sarah Fellers Ireland

Sarah married **Martin Ireland M.D.** (1821-1904) in Columbia City, Whitley County, Indiana on Sept 23, 1847. As stated (page 79, above), Martin and Sarah Fellers Ireland were Belle's parents; Belle Ireland became the wife of **James Dorland** (1844-1915) and the mother of **Blanche Dorland Cook** (1873-1967). (See page 21.)

> A brief review: **Sarah Fellows Ireland** (1829-1921), the great grandmother of **Cecil V Cook, Jr** (1913-1970) and mother of **Belle Ireland** (1850-1895), was born in Waynesboro, VA in 1829 and died, aged 92, in Chicago, IL in 1921. Sarah was the daughter of **Jonathan Fellows** (abt 1795-aft 1843) and **Margaret Slagle** (1794-aft 1843). Margaret was the twelfth child of **George Slagle** (?-April 21, 1829) & **Catherine Keinath** (Sept 1766-Oct. 11, 1855). Catherine was born in Lancaster, PA. George and Catherine were married in 1789 in Cumberland County PA. Catherine Keinath was the daughter of immigrant **Michael Keinath** (Jan 29 1720-July 11, 1896) and **Margaret Diller** (1744-Nov 18, 1813) Michael and Margaret were married in 1751, in Millertown (Annville), Cumberland Co (formerly Lancaster County) PA. In attendance at the wedding would have been the bride's parents, Huguenot immigrants, **Anna Barbara Dornis** (1703-bef 1766) and **Caspar Diller** (1696-1787).

SOURCES:

Ireland genealogy, generally: Betty Taylor Cook's unpublished genealogy book, and her notes, which include information provided to her by Belle Ireland's daughter, Blanch Dorland Cook and Harriet W. Ireland, wife of Homer A. Ireland, of Media PA, in letters written to Betty in 1945.

A large amount of information about Ireland, Fellows, Carmean and collateral families may be found at the website(s) established by Donald E. Gradeless at gradeless.com. Grayless eighteenth century Maryland property records and judicial proceedings and Jesse Grayless' service during the American Revolution: "Bishop Family Notes" at family.gradeless.com/bishop.htm

Carmean (Cremeen) genealogy and interesting biographical details, found in the Maryland State archives, have been posted by Dr. Gradeless (see above) and also as "Descendants of John Cremeen" at: familytreemaker.genealogy.com/users/c/a/r/Gordon-Carmean-OH/FILE This information appears to be research conducted by Gordon Carmean of Delphos OH and also John E. Cremean, who copied documents at the Maryland Hall of Records in 1986. Gordon Carmean has also posted this material at rootsweb.com/~mdcaroli/JohnCremeenDesc.htm

The displeasure expressed by the financial backers of the *Mayflower* is taken from **Mayflower**, Nathaniel Philbrick (Penguin Books, 2006, page 162). A Beauchamp genealogy was found on the web at flemingmultimedia.com/Genealogy/JohnBeauchamp

Whitley County Indiana Marriage Abstracts by Nellie Riley Raber have been placed very helpfully on the web by Donald Gradeless (Dr G); see also Whitley County Indiana Marriages 1838-1910, at kinexxions.com/marriages1/grooms.

For details of Caspar Diller's French origins and PA gravesite: **The Diller Family**, By JL Ringwalt (1877, Released February 2003) on the web at various sites, incl accessgenealogy.com/scripts/data/database.

For the passenger list of the *Samuel*, which brought Caspar and Anna Barbara Diller to America in 1733: The Palatine Project, on the web at progenealogists.com/palproject/pa/1733sam

For information concerning the church and burial records of the Keinadt/Coiner family in Augusta County, Virginia: Bethany Lutheran Church History, on the web at: Bethany-trinity-va.org/history.

For George Slagle's Revolutionary War service: Pennsylvania digital archives on the web as "Archives Records Information Access System (ARIAS)" at digital archives.state.pa.us/ariasfaq.asp. A listing of the graves at the Trinity (Bethany) Lutheran Church, on the web at geocities.com/augcem/index

For George Slagle's ancestry: Ancestry.com

For Jonathan Fellows/Fellers: generally: Betty Taylor Cook's unpublished genealogy book; see also Martin Ireland bio (noted below).

Much Fellers information available on the web seems to have been taken from **FELLERS / FELLOWS Families of the Shenandoah Valley**, posted by Gordon. A great deal of research has been conducted by many in the records of Augusta County. See Augusta Co., VA Deed Book 46 p310-11.

For Martin Ireland's bio and information related to his business activities in Columbia City: **History of Whitley and Noble Counties, Indiana**, by Weston A. Goodspeed and Charles Blanchard (F. A. Battey & Co. Chicago, 1882)

on the web at: whitley/kneller/com/book1882/sketch/247 256

bare legs and skirts as scandalously short as an English undershift - The description of seventeenth century English and Scots- Irish immigrants as "borderers" and the quote from Boswell confirming this description: **Albion's Seed** by David Hacket Fischer, Oxford University Press (1989) pages 605, and ff. and 608.

He loved her up and he loved her down: The stanza from "Down by the Greenwood Sidee," or "The Cruel Mother" is #20 in Francis James Child's **English and Scottish Popular Ballads** (1882-1898), transcribed in West Virginia 1924-54 by Patrick W. Gainer, **Folk Songs from the West Virginia Hills** (Grantsville, W V: Seneca Books, 1975, page 26).

mighty inland city yet unsurvey'd and unsuspected – Walt Whitman's *Thoughts*, from *Songs of Parting,* **Leaves of Grass**

"No Truck With Pacifists"
[Gen. Merritte Ireland] *was deeply religious and said publicly, "I never want to see another war." But even though feeling that way, he was "all for the army" and his hackles rose quickly when the so-called religious people were passing anti-war resolutions. In fact, he quit cold the church of his ancestors in which he grew up from infancy, the church in which he was married and to which his wife held membership, because right after World War I, it passed a pacifist resolution. Not one time since did he darken its doors. [. . .] Maybe. Uncle Merritte supposedly also said, "My top sergeant in the Philippines was a gentleman. One day I said to my wife, 'That boy lies better than we do.' He's a captain in the Army now." The Bulletin,* Whitely County Historical Society (April, 1968).

"I WISH TO BE REMEMBERED BY ALL LOVED ONES"

Susan Goode Farmer Cook

Cecil V Cook Sr (1871-1948)
Cecil V Cook Jr (1913-1970)

Susan Goode Farmer Cook was born August 8, 1838 in Kentucky and died in Missouri on May 10, 1890. She was the daughter of **Katherine Spencer Hawkins** (1814-1851) and **John Goode Farmer** (1808-1871).

Sue was named for her grandmother, **Susan Goode** (1783-1864), who was born in the Skinquarter section of Chesterfield County, Virginia, the daughter of a locally well known dissenting Baptist preacher, **John Goode** (1739-1792). (See page 169.) Katherine, Sue's mother, died when Susan was thirteen. As Susan's published obituary states, young Susie was left with the care of four brothers, one of whom, John, (later a professor at LaGrange College, Missouri) was but one year old.

> *Oh hush, my little baby brother*
> *Sleep, my love, upon my knee*
> *What, though, dear child, we've lost our mother*
> *That can never trouble thee.*

Another brother, Willie Farmer, would die in agony from wounds received on the Shiloh battlefield in 1862.

> *My only solace, only joy*
> *Since the sad day I lost my mother,*
> *Is nursing her own Willy boy,*
> *My little orphan brother.*

Susan Goode Farmer Cook

Charles Lamb's effecting *Nursing* stanzas suggest the daunting burdens Susie took up, after her mother died in 1851. Sue's own brave letters in the face of her losses indicate that she accepted her responsibilities with a steely devotion. But the burden of mothering her brothers was carried off with mixed results. Cadmus was recalled in his siblings' letters as a heavy drinker. About 1871, John Jr fled Kentucky to get away from Cadmus, going to live with Sue and her husband in Missouri.

As a young girl and throughout her life, Sue was loyal to her Baptist heritage. She was helped along in this by the forbidding, even morbid religiosity of her father, John Farmer (see page 111). Susan Farmer attended Georgetown KY Seminary, a finishing school for young women. Completing the school curriculum in 1858, Susan, age 20, promptly married the ambitious and promising **Joshua Flood Cook** (1834-1912). On her marriage, Susan was thrust into the role of wife of a college President. In 1859, Joshua was named president of New Liberty College, New Liberty, KY. Notably, young Susan herself took on a public role, as she "presided over New Liberty Female Seminary" (as her obituary stated) until the Civil War began in 1861.

In 1860, in Shelby County KY, Susan gave birth to John Ernest, the first of her four children. John was followed by Lula (1862-1943) born in Corinth, Mississippi August 27, 1862. Lula was followed by two more baby boys, both born in LaGrange Missouri: William Flood, born Feb 2, 1868 and **Cecil Virgil** (1871-1948), Dec. 10, 1871.

"VIRGIL... BUT HE DIED"

Betty Cook, Cecil's daughter-in-law, told this writer, her son, that Joshua and Sue Cook named their fourth child "Cecil Neale," but that Cecil did not like either the name or the person for whom he was named and, at about age 12, changed his middle name to *Virgil*, for the Roman poet. This is a curious statement.

In a Bible which was inherited by Lula Cook Stone, Sue's daughter, and shown or given by her to family historian, Ellery Farmer, it is stated that Sue Farmer had a younger brother, Virgil (1843-46). Virgil was recorded in the Bible as follows: "August 26, 1843 Virgil son of J.G and K.S. Farmer May 7th 1846 of measles 10:30-noon a more beautiful form & sympathetic [ ] never graced this earth, erect carriage, black hair and eyes but he died."

Sorrow is not hidden in this succinct eulogy to two year old Virgil Farmer. A single sentence in a family Bible may be the only record to note the passage of this child's brief time on earth. But it permits us to know that Sue Farmer Cook memorialized Virgil, her lost little brother, in the naming of her youngest son. This Bible record also permits us to know that Virgil's death was the first major grief to assail young Susan. It was not the last. As a child, she buried Virgil. As an adolescent she would grieve at her mother's grave. Then, to her horror, in a Mississippi churchyard, she would bury her killed little brother, Willie, slain at Shiloh. From her letters, we know that Sue took these traumas and turned them into a stout nurturing that made her children want to excel at life, to please her.

"AMONG THE MORTALLY WOUNDED WAS . . . HANDSOME WILLIE FARMER"

As we have noted, Virgil was not the only son of John Farmer to die too soon. In 1861, as the Civil War began, Joshua Cook moved Sue and baby, Ernest, from Kentucky to Mississippi. In Corinth, MS a second child, Lula, was born. During the war, Joshua served as a Baptist chaplain in the southern cause. He also bought property in Mississippi and taught school. These details suggest that Joshua's work as a military chaplain may have been informal. Unofficial or no, J.F. Cook conducted pastoral work among the soldiers. He reported on some of this activity in his 1908 memoir. After the 1862 battle of Shiloh, Joshua recalled:

"Among the mortally wounded was handsome Shelby County boy, Willie Farmer, who was scarcely grown. His thigh was shattered; he was laid upon a cot in

Corinth in the great room where the wounded were placed, and where, every day, soldiers were dying; he was so badly wounded that the physicians said nothing could be done for him. The morning before he died the physician came to me and said, "You ought to tell Willie, he does not know it, but gangrene has set in and he will not live to see the sunset." So I went and talked with the boy. He was calm, brave, and made various requests, one was that if it was possible he wanted his body taken care of, and after the war was over or when it was possible he wanted it laid in the old Christiansburg (Shelby Co., KY) graveyard by the side of his mother. After his death it seemed impossible, as things were, to get the body out. I prepared it for burial as well as I could, and had a great box made, and as Bragg was then commander of the post I spoke to him about it. He paid me scant courtesy. I consulted Breckinridge, and there was a private understanding between us that I was to do as I pleased, and should I get into trouble he would stay with me, whatever the cost might be. That day there was to be brought a train of box-cars to carry off the wounded; and I spoke to some of the Kentucky boys and told them of my plans. I was acting absolutely contrary to what General Bragg had said.

J.F. Cook's recollections of General Braxton Bragg are consistent with the testimony of many others, who considered Bragg dangerously unsuited for high military command. Bragg became one of the worst remembered generals in American history. He was fixated upon decorum and earned the hatred of his own men and inferior officers because of his indecision in battle. Although Bragg was a favorite of President Jefferson Davis, many Confederate Generals urged Davis to remove him. General John Breckenridge, became so enraged at Bragg, he is said to have challenged Bragg to a duel; Gen. Nathan Forrest refused to follow Bragg's orders. But Davis kept Bragg on, often transferring Bragg's critics.

J.F.'s memoir continues:

I intended to take that body out at whatever cost, for I had given my promise to a dying boy. When the train pulled in the box was sitting right on the platform. I made arrangements with the Kentucky boys immediately on the arrival of the train to shove that box into a car. I remember two boys more especially, from Shelby County, Kentucky - Henton and Thomas; it may be one of them is living to-day. As soon as the box was placed back in the end of the car wounded soldiers and all sat down upon it and covered it. It was carried to its destination, my home in Mississippi, put in a vault, and when the war was over all that remained of the young soldier was brought back and laid beside his mother. Without General Breckinridge I never could have done it."

Willie Farmer's gravestone in the Christiansburg Cemetery, like that of thousands of others markers across the nation, was memorialized in romantic sentiments then popular:

"William H. Farmer, of Breckinridge's brigade, C.S.A., born in Shelby County, September 26, 1840, died at Corinth, Mississippi, April 21, 1862, from the effect of a wound received at the Battle of Shilo, April 7, 1862. Dying among strangers, he said, 'Let me be buried by Ma, tell them good-bye at home.' Erected by brothers & sisters."

One wonders at first why J.F. Cook did not mention in his 1908 narrative that Willie Farmer was the brother of his wife, Susan Farmer. The answer is that by the time J.F. wrote of Willie's death, a half-century had passed and J.F. had twice re-married, being then married to Drucilla Herons. By the time Joshua Cook's memoir was published, his first wife, Sue, had been dead for eighteen years.

"AH! IF THERE IS RECOGNITION IN HEAVEN!"

On June 8, 1862, Sue Cook, Willie's stricken sister, wrote to John Farmer, her long-widowed father, in Shelby County KY. Sue hoped that John had already learned of

Will's death. Parts of her letter, in tiny script (no doubt to save scarce paper) are illegible:

> My dear dear Pa,
> It has been a long while since I had the pleasure of writing to you or of having a letter from you. Indeed we have not had a line from you since we left our Kentucky home and I fear it will be a long while before we do.
> Many harsh changes since we last met. Many have been called to their last long home and many have drunk sorrow's bitter dregs. The last two months have been to me months of deep anxiety and care. [. . .] I have been more cheerful than could be expected of me [. . .] until I heard of my dear brother's sufferings. Then and not till then, I gave up. My head has never known sorrow before. I had spent so many anxious hours and had done all I could for him - I prayed so earnestly that he might be spared to come and tell you of his many trials. . .
> Oh my dear Pa, I cannot <u>cannot</u> realize that my dear brother is dead, that he sleeps the sleep that knows no waking. Shall I not again see him or hear him tell his deep anxiety to get home to loved ones once more. And never no never in this life can I see him. Ah! If there is recognition in heaven! Is this thought filled my dear ma's head, when she sees her dear son free from his torments of earth and walking in God's glory [. . .] bearing a palm of victory. [. . .]
> Mr. Cook has written you several times since brother's death but I have no idea any of them reached you. He was with brother from Friday till Monday before he died. Poor fellow was wounded 11 days before we knew it. He made every effort to get home but the surgeon said he would have died on the road. I should have given anything in the world to have had him with me in his last moments but God's ways are not as ours. He expressed a great desire to be brought home after Mr. Cook got there but it was <u>impossible</u>. He could not be moved enough to change his clothes! And no father or sister near - is almost more than I can bear. We had a nice [. . .] vault made and

he is preserved so he will keep material 20 years. So the physicians say.

He sleeps in our church yard so I can visit his resting place every evening with little Ernest, who seems conscious that it is a sacred spot to me, for he comes and places his arms around my neck and says, "Bless Uncle Will in the sky". Brother appeared and I think he was perfectly resigned to death. He told Mr. Cook he wanted Gadmus to have his watch, D_____ his pistol and his books divided with all of us. I sent his picture to home by Mr. Cook. We looked at it a long while and wrapped it in $50 [for burial in KY]. [Sue did not return with Will's body to KY because] I could not think of leaving Ernest and had no one to leave him with. [Sue did not go to see Will in Corinth because] I felt I could not stand the scene of suffering that would be at the hospital. But I have regretted a thousand times not trying to get there. [. . .] He said he wanted to be laid beside our dear dear Mother. And if I live I intend it shall be.

He felt doubly dear to me since he came here, being the only one I could hear from. I sent him boxes of clothes and provisions. One he never got. Oh dear Pa I have much to say if I could see you but my heart is so full I can't write. I want you to try and get through and see us this fall and spend a month or so here. The climate delightful and I think you would have splendid health and would have pleasure with the piney woods.

[Sometimes I lose hope] of ever seeing you again. We can meet at the throne of grace and there supplicate "Our Father" for each other's welfare and happiness. I could ask many questions of all of you but when would they be answered?

I wish to be remembered by all loved ones. I always think of you when the 4th Sabbath comes. And in imagination see so many faces seated in the old church where I so often have met with them.

William Hawkins Farmer – "Willie"

I think of cousin F____ and his good wife often and hope he with many others will remember us in their prayers. These are times of sorrow and sadness to all. Few, very few are exempt. I wish Sis could be here. I would love to see her and her family. I wrote to her from Nashville but suppose the letter never reached her. Remember me to Mr. Cook's relations. Write when you have an opportunity. I hope you have your money from brother Garnett. I hear he collects slowly. I write so seldom I can hardly write a correct sentence. Remember us often Dear Pa in your prayers. [. . .] There is so much I would like to know of all my acquaintances but I must content myself with hoping all is right.

Your devoted daughter, Susie

After the Civil War, Joshua and Sue Cook moved their family to LaGrange, Missouri, where Joshua became president of a Baptist school, LaGrange College. J.F. Cook retained the presidency of LaGrange College for thirty years.

The relocation to Missouri caused Susan to influence her siblings to move to LaGrange from Shelby County Kentucky. She also took an active interest in the local Baptist Church in LaGrange, becoming a Sunday School teacher of the youngest class and raising funds for the completion of a new "church house."

Sue Cook was a candid writer of letters, several of which have been preserved. In 1885, during a visit to her Kentucky home, she wrote to *"My Darling Baby Boy,"* Cecil Virgil Cook (1870-1948) that *"Uncle Jim* [possibly, Sue's cousin, James DeJarnett Farmer (1834-?)] *got on the biggest drunk yet! Papa got after him."*

In this letter, Sue Cook admonished young Cecil to study hard: *"Papa says you are getting behind terribly in your Greek."* This appeal is suggestive of the high goals Sue had for her children. Judging from Cecil's later accomplishments, the effect of her exhortation was positive. On Oct 18, 1888, Sue wrote a letter to *"My Dear Children,"* which seems to have been addressed to Cecil, but to which of the others is not clear as her other three children, Ernest, Lula and Will, are mentioned by name. Once again, her affection and close emotional ties to her children are on display. *"I think you certainly are the most industrious people in the world as you can find no time to write. [. . .] Well were you surprised at Ernest news? I was not. Had a presentment last May that Miss West was to be the chosen one - though I never told him so. Will says it is too funny to hear Bro talk - he has really grown boyish again. She has Will sophisticated, too. Says her picture is beautiful. But he sees through <u>Bro's</u> eyes. I shall try to do my part to make her feel she is one of us. And you must fix your mouths to say <u>Sister</u>. Poor Jesse! I feel sorry for her. Yet I feel God overrules all things for our good."*

Sue Cook died in LaGrange at the relatively young age of fifty-two. She was remembered as confident, devout and devoted to her children and to her husband and his career.

Sue Cook's funeral was the first to take place in the completed building of the church she had attended and helped to lead. A lingering illness preceded Susan's death. She gave directions for her funeral, which included a request that her Sunday School class "attend the funeral in a body and the members of it throw into her open grave flowers of their own cutting and arranging." This was done. The LaGrange *Democrat* reported on the funeral and observed: "The class, made up of the youngest children, had reserved seats, each little one bearing flowers of his or her own gathering. Huddled in their select corner the tear-stained, motherless brood presented one of the most touching features of the funeral procession."

Susan left her eldest son Ernest with a strong impression of her ardent Baptist principles, which had been prefigured in her by her great-grandfather **John Goode** (1739-1792). In 1924, the minutes of the Middle River Baptist Association of Virginia preserved a letter from Ernest:

"Please find enclosed my check for $10.00 to help out on the memorial to Baptist Preachers at Chesterfield Court house. Besides my interest as a Baptist, I have a personal and family interest. My mother was Susan Goode Farmer. Her great grandfather was John Goode the first settled Baptist Pastor of the Skinquarter Church, where he died in the pastorate in 1790.

John Goode was the first Baptist among my mother's ancestors. In his early youth he lost respect for the established church, having been fined in Henrico County for fox hunting on Sunday and failing to support the church. He removed to Chesterfield, married Sarah Brown and settled near Skinquarter Springs.

"Now when they imprisoned Baptist preachers for preaching the Gospel a fellow feeling and curiosity took him to the court house to hear them preach. He fell under conviction, was baptized and later ordained by William Hickman. Since John Goode, there have been nothing but Baptists in my mother's family.

"Fraternally yours,
John Ernest Cook
(brother of Cecil V Cook)"

Dear Betty and Cecil,   25 March, 1945

It is a pleasure sending you this chart showing about all I know of your grandmother, my Aunt Sue Farmer Cook, who was one of the grandest women I ever knew. I remember her well although I was just ten years old when she died. She practically raised my father, as their mother [Katherine] died when he was one year old, and she was about twelve years older than he. All of us were devoted to her.

Ellery Farmer

SOURCES:

Susan Goode Framer genealogy, Betty Taylor Cook's unpublished genealogy book, and her notes.

For biographical information concerning J.F. Cook's activities in Missouri: Betty Taylor Cook's research notes. See also: **The Baptist Encyclopedia** (Philadelphia: Louis W. Everts, 1881, William Carthcart, Editor, p. 272) and "Hannibal-LaGrange College History" by J. Hurley & Roberta Hasgood, 1995, p. 130; both sources made available by the generosity of Charles L. Cook.

Additional biographical information: **History of Lewis, Clark, Knox and Scotland Counties, Missouri** (1887), Reprinted, Stevens Publishing Co, Astoria, Illinois 61501, pages 731-A to 732-AJ., and made available through the generosity of Farmer descendent, Carolyn Farmer Wickens.

The 1890 LaGrange *Democrat* obituary of Sue Farmer Cook, and her 1862 letter to her father, have been preserved and shared most generously by Farmer descendent Carolyn Farmer Wickens, who also provided photocopied pages from the Farmer/Cook Family Bible (1852), containing details of the brief life of Virgil Farmer.

For the inscription on Willie Farmer's grave: "Early and Present History, Christiansburg Baptist Church" Covering The Year 1799-1999, generously shared by genealogist Charlie L. Cook, ancestorstories.org

Farmer genealogy generally: Ellery Farmer's **A Farmer Book** Ellery Farmer (1955), which is on the web at: geocities.com/Heartland/Flats/7314/Farmer/ekam.html.

Dear Cecil and Betty,

I have just read Betty's letter telling of the little ceremony she had on opening the package containing our uncle Will Farmer's watch. I admit my eyes became a little moist that she should have thought of doing that.

Ellery Farmer
November 23, 1960

"MY HEART LIKE A MUFFLED DRUM IS BEATING MY FUNERAL MARCH TO THE TOMB"

John Goode Farmer
Katherine Spencer Hawkins

Susan Goode Farmer Cook (1838-1890)
Cecil V Cook (1871-1948)
Cecil V Cook, Jr (1913-1970)

  Susan Goode Farmer (1838-1890), wife of **Joshua Flood Cook** (1834-1912), mother of **Cecil** and grandmother of **Cecil V. Cook, Jr** (1913-1970), grew up in the intensely devout home of her parents, **John Goode Farmer** (1808-1871) and **Katherine Spencer Hawkins** (1814-1851), who died at 37. John G. Farmer and Katherine Hawkins were married on September 17, 1835. The wedding was performed in Franklin County KY by her brother-in-law, William C. Blanton. In June, 1842, Katherine was baptized into the Baptist Church in Christiansburg, Shelby County KY. Katherine and John Farmer were the parents of seven children, including **Susan Goode Farmer** (1838-1890), wife of **Joshua Flood Cook** (1834-1912). Katherine Hawkins was the daughter of **William B. Hawkins** (1781-1845) of Franklin County, KY and **Mary (Polly) Crockett** (1781-1856). (For Hawkins and Crockett family information, see Index and other sketches in this volume.)

  John Goode Farmer's parents were **Benjamin Farmer** (Sept 13, 1783-1837) and **Susan Goode** (Dec. 1, 1783-1864). The parents were from Chesterfield County, Virginia but had moved to Franklin County, Kentucky, before John was born. Prior to the relocation of Benjamin and Susan Farmer to Kentucky, his Farmer ancestors had lived in Virginia for two centuries.

  John Goode Farmer was born in Franklin County KY on July 11, 1808. He was named for his mother's father, the noted Virginia Baptist preacher **John Goode** (1739-1792), who has been remembered by his descendents as "the first Baptist." (See on page 108, a letter published in 1924 by the Rev. John Goode's double great-grandson, Ernest Cook (1860-1926).

Benjamin Farmer, John's father, was the son of **Hezekiah Farmer** (1769-1826) and **Elizabeth Cheatham** (?-?) of Chesterfield Co VA. Elizabeth was her husband's first cousin. Elizabeth and Hezekiah were married January 1780. The parents of Hezekiah Farmer were **Elam Farmer** (?-1782) and **Phoebe Cheatham** (?-aft May 1783).

Elizabeth Cheatham's parents were **Stephen Cheatham** (?-?) and **Elizabeth Akin** (?-?). Elizabeth was the daughter of **William Akin**, (?-abt 1757), whose Chesterfield County VA will is dated Aug 26, 1757. She was named for her mother, **Elizabeth _____** who's 1771 will mentions her (Elizabeth Cheatham).

Stephen Cheatham's parents were **Grace Williams** (?-?) of Amelia County, VA, and **Benjamin Cheatham** (?-abt 1765), who were also the parents of Phoebe Cheatham. Grace and Ben were married Nov 17 1747. Ben was a son of immigrant **Thomas Cheatham** (1645-1726).

Elam Farmer's parents were **Henry Farmer** (1686-1753) and **Sarah Ward** (?-?). Phoebe Cheatham's parents were **Benjamin Cheatham** (?-1765) and **Grace Williams** (?-?). Elizabeth Akin's father was **William Akin** (?-bef Aug 26, 1787?), whose August 26 1787 will mentions daughter Elizabeth (Chesterfield VA Book I 1795).

The Farmer line has been proved from **Thomas Farmer** (1586/1594-?) to living Farmer descendents and collateral lines by **Ellery Farmer**. Ellery conducted research and enlisted the aid of a professional genealogist during the 1940s & '50s, publishing his results in 1955. Ellery Farmer, a career Army officer and gifted researcher, was a friend and collaborator of **Betty Cook** (1918-2000), wife of his second cousin **Cecil V. Cook, Jr** (1913-1970). Betty and Ellery exchanged many letters and shared considerable genealogical materials. In 1955, Ellery Farmer published **A Farmer Book**, a copy of which has been placed generously on the web (See Sources, below).

Ellery Farmer's book is a well documented, detailed and literate volume, highly recommended both for its content and its clear and professional approach to genealogical research. Ellery documented the Farmer line from **Thomas Farmer** (1586/1594-?) to **Benjamin Farmer** (1783-1837) as follows: **Thomas Farmer**, born in England 1586/1594, **Henry Farmer** (circa 1657-? Henrico County Virginia), **Henry Farmer II**, (Henrico County, VA b/f 1696-1753), **Elam Farmer** (Henrico Co., Va, circa 1725-1784), **Hezekiah Farmer** (Chesterfield Co., Va. circa 1760-1826); **Benjamin Farmer** (Chesterfield Co., Va.1783-June 8, 1837 in Kentucky). Every Farmer mentioned from Henry to Benjamin was born in Henrico Co or Chesterfield Co Virginia (which had been part of Henrico County). Thomas immigrated to Virginia in about 1616, where his Farmer descendents resided until Benjamin moved to Kentucky some 192 years later. (See other Farmer sketches elsewhere in this volume.)

JOHN FARMER: "I KNOW I AM GOING DOWN RAPIDLY TO THE TOMB."

All of John and Katherine Farmer's children (Mary, **Susan**, William, Virgil, Cadmus, Lucian, John Jr) were born in Christiansburg, Shelby County KY. John Sr was postmaster and farmer and also the operator of a general store. He was recalled as faithful in attendance at the Baptist church and "austere." We shall see why.

In order to provision his general store, John Farmer visited wholesalers in Philadelphia. He made two such buying trips in February and March, 1845. In letters he wrote to his brother Thomas in Frankfort, KY and to his wife, Katharine, John Farmer demonstrated an active and precise understanding of the retail goods business he has begun in Christiansburg. His brother Thomas was in the same business in Frankfort KY. His letters are written in the archaic 18th century style, which produces a double s as fs.

From John's letters we learn the Farmer brothers made regular shopping trips back East for each other. In March, 1845, John wrote to Thomas from Philadelphia, ". . . Bonnets are the same [as last year] in price and style, leghorns and palms too are the same, I think. I am afraid, it seems, to touch them. The style of prints is good, the quality does not please me. [. . .] J. M. Morgan and Buck have the nicest goods I think that I find. Mellows house looks rather old somehow. I have not priced domestics yet, only by the bolt. I have not looked much yet in the silk houses - they have some fine goods for shew. They pretend to be (all of them nearly) selling at much reduced prices than last year, but I can't see it. [. . .] I have not yet been to Watkins or Stiniker yet. All the others claim to be especial friends of yours and say <u>they</u> could always please you and have no doubt if you were here they could sell you very promptly."

Transporting the purchased goods from Philadelphia to Kentucky posed a challenge of its own. "I am entirely stumped about sending my goods off," wrote John. "They say they won't take any more for Cumberland, that it is now full.- some are sending to Chambersburg at 65 cls and are going there to make their own time with the wagons and some are putting up in the warehouses to wait for the opening of the canal. They are now offering to deliver in Pittsburg at 2.12 in 15 days, subject to wagon dockage as settled by the Pittsburg board but what that is no one knows here. There are a great many Kentuckians here and coming in every day. They are not buying very heavily they tell me. I hear no news, only the pafsage of the Texas Resolution."

To his wife, Katherine (Catherine) in February, 1845, John wrote extensively about his journey from Christiansburg, KY to Philadelphia. He had the opportunity to play the tourist.

"I have to write in the midst of the crowd [at the hotel] it being too cold to write in my room and a fire would cost me fifty cents. [. . .] I left mother's [Franklin County, KY] at 7 o'clock on Thursday and Cincinnati at 10 on Friday. I got to Wheeling at 8 Sunday morning and took a Virginia diner at 1, being something finer than usual, toped of with fine venison - I then took stage for Cumberland 131 miles over hills, dales and mountains presenting some to me fine views of nature. I wanted you there that you might see some of the freaks of nature. I was shown Braddock's grave, Washington's first battle and the site of his fort, called "Necefsity." [. . .] From Harper's Ferry, 110 miles in five hours (think of this: 2 miles in lefs than three minutes).

John adds ominously to his wife, "*At this Ferry are some sights of which if I live to see you, I will tell you.*" It is impossible to even guess what John saw or what Katherine might have made of this sentence.

John then continues his travel narrative: *"From this to Baltimore by sundown. I now began to think I was entering the old world. Here was town in all directions with countlefs numbers of new things. Here I had a hard supper and left for Philadelphia but there being no vefsel, I came in cars, pafsing through the state of Delaware & City of Wilmington. I got here at three in the morning (yesterday) and plodding about an hour hunting my lodgings."*

In his letter to Katherine, John's sentimental and remarkably somber impulses vie with each other. One or two of this homesick shopkeeper's pen strokes are worthy of Poe himself.

"I will now go to my little cell. I try to remember you all in the right place. It might be well for you to think of me in the hour in 'audience with the deity.' For it lets down 'a stream of glory on the consecrated head of man.' I know I am going down rapidly to the tomb. O that Heaven's King may prepare me for the change for I cannot say that I am prepared. How is it nothing seems to effect my hard heart? Although I know my heart like a muffled drum is beating my funeral march to the tomb, I

cannot feel as I ought. May it please the Lord to blefs you abundantly that you may pofsefs your soul in patience and sanctify yourself to his service - be a means in his hands of turning the feet of our little ones to seek his favor. I feel that I shall be spared to see you all, so I close remaining your affectionate, John G Farmer."

"Kifs the children and tell them to be good babes. But Oh William G. and Mary L, I fear for you but you do not know, poor things, if you could only see and feel you would mind your ma."

CHARITY: "WORTH ABOUT FIVE CENTS HERE"

In a final postscript, John Farmer asks his wife Katherine about Charity, a slave in his house: *"I wonder if Charity has behaved herself - she would be worth about five cents here - I wish you could see one table set right."*

John Goode Farmer's exasperation at the conduct of his slave is expressed at the same moment that he fearfully commends his own soul to God. The amazing triviality of his complaint – which of course is serious and heart felt – gives a form in words to John's self-interested assumption that human bondage is all about the proper setting of his, the master's table. John was raised this way; the world is this way. John Farmer came of age just as the debate over Black slavery was running its Southern course and the powers in that region settled into its preposterous endorsement of permanent lifelong servitude for Africans and their descendents. We step back to a distance of centuries and are free to observe and make our own judgment upon this fact, which was at the center of John Farmer's way of life: the worth of a human being, entrusted with intimate matters under his own roof, can be calculated in currency. John's casual arithmetic determined that such a girl/woman is found to sell for cheap. John Farmer was capable of entering into this calculus at the same moment he was thinking of his unworthiness to stand before a wrathful Divinity.

A slave who was given the name, Charity - a person sharing the familiarity of John Farmer's home, setting his table, caring for his children, preparing his meals, cleaning his clothes, emptying his chamber pot. Charity is simultaneously an essential component in the daily workings of that home and demeaned as a commercially worthless commodity. The physical and emotional closeness of Charity's presence is taken for granted and yet denigrated by her master.

What of Charity's point of view? The casual routines of the Farmer household are for her, mandates. Charity fulfills them not by choice but as a result of her enslavement to the others in the home, including the children. The norms of this home are for her a set of chores played out in daily routines. They are obligations imposed upon Charity under sanction of custom and law. The failure to perform these tasks brings down upon Charity a greater or lesser degree of punishment.

What of Charity's own home? Was she permitted to have one? What of its routines? What of her children? What of her *husband* and any expectations he might have had about the setting of his table? In Kentucky in 1845, such questions are absurd. Charity is obliged to maintain the home and hearth of others, who claim her, own her, place a dollar value upon her. Charity's private doings and destiny are irrelevant to all her own choices because of her status as chattel in the home of John and Katherine Farmer.

After many patient or exasperated explanations to her, Charity continues to set incorrectly her master's table. Might this lapse have been her rebellion? Had she other means of withstanding the daily expectations of domestic duties? These labors were required to be performed to benefit others. In order to fulfill mandatory services imposed upon her, she could do no better than ignore her own duties to herself. That so, might not Charity have employed the quotidian weapons of ill-placed silver and china to conduct warfare against a world set against her? If there be heroic acts in Shelby County Kentucky in 1845, Charity's disorderly setting of the Farmer family table may be seen as such an act.

John Farmer's offhand comment is a summation of the condition of slaves in America: simultaneously indispensable and worthless. This contradiction was the essential aspect of race slavery in the nation; it was the quintessence of the rationale for the enslavement of the productive capacities of a Black person by a White person. The utterly irreconcilable notions of indispensability and worthlessness are the touchstones of what passed for moral principles in the lunatic world of the devout but brutish John Farmer.

Are we yet encumbered by the contradictions lived out by devout John and willful Charity? Brooding John and enslaved Charity rise up out of our past and into our present imagination. They mark for us a place beyond time. They call us back to old Christiansburg, inviting us to comprehend their world and understand them - the better to comprehend our world and understand ourselves. They inquire: *would you join us in our eternity of solace-seeking, for all things done and not done by us and to us*?

We are a people not yet broken free from a willful embrace of a vicious social system of incredible violence and degradation. This system, both fashioned and destroyed by our ancestors, has, for generations before and after the Civil War and even to this moment, defied the best ideals of our nation's founding and demeaned everyone within its reach. John and Charity are a secret presence within us. The riddle of Black and White may find a key in the coerced setting of John Farmer's table in 1845.

We know nothing more of Charity. But perhaps there is more that can be known. The LaGrange, Missouri household of Joshua and Susan Farmer Cook reported to the 1870 census the presence of Sarah Fisher, 16, Black, a "domestic servant," born in Kentucky. Perhaps Sarah, born a slave in 1854, and Charity, a slave in the Farmer household in 1845, are connected through two generations of service to Farmers and Cooks. For the moment – if not forever – Charity appears to us only in a sentence in her owner's letter and, without a word of her own, disappears from our view. (But see the note of eulogy, page 40.)

Katherine Farmer, mistress of the Farmer household in 1845, died on November 1, 1851. This event left a number of small boys (William, Cadmus, Lucian, John II) in the charge of their older sister, **Susie**, 13. On the death of their mother, was the slave Charity enlisted to aid in raising the Farmer children? In an obituary written from LaGrange, Missouri in May 1890, Sue Farmer was credited with managing the home of her father after her mother's death. Sue remained in this role until she left home to board at a female institute and then to become the bride of J. F. Cook.

There is no obituary for Charity. No report of her having a last name. No printed statement of gratitude for her labors in the Farmer household. Did Charity remain in the Farmer home for years to come? After Sue left home, did Charity take up some of the mothering of John Farmer's sons? Did she live to see the Civil War? to set her own table? in her own house? in her own way? in her own good time?

A decade after Katherine died, John Farmer married a young woman not much older than his daughter, Susie. Her name was Nannie Basket (Baskett) (1831-1915), the daughter of Thomas Basket, also of Shelby County. John's marriage to Nannie took place in 1863, 12 years after the death of his first wife, Katherine. The 1860 census records no wife in the Farmer home. Those listed in 1860 were John Farmer and his adolescent sons, William H, 20, Cadmus, 14, "Lucino" (Joseph Lucien) 11, and John, 10. His other children with first wife **Katherine Hawkins** were Mary (1836-1905), **Susie,** by then married to **Joshua Flood Cook** and a son, Virgil, who had died in 1846 of measles.

By the time John Farmer married Nannie, she was a widow, Mrs. Nannie Bondurant. Nannie and John Goode Farmer became the parents of three children: Frances, Edward, Thomas and a son born in 1864 who lived only three days. The tiny infant was buried in the cemetery in Christiansburg, KY in the Farmer plot under a stone, which is inscribed in the melancholy and romantic expressions of the day.

Infant Son of John G. and Nannie Farmer
Born Aug 3, 1864 / Died Aug 6, 1864.
Sweet bud of promise early gone
Torn from the parent stem
The casket mouldrs in the earth
But Heaven claims the gem.

Despite his 1845 premonitions of an early death, John Goode Farmer lived another twenty-five years, to age 63. He died on Feb. 1, 1871. John is buried beside his first wife Katharine Hawkins Farmer in Christiansburg, KY. His second wife, Nannie Basket(t) Bondurant Farmer lived 44 years after the death of John. Perhaps *she* is buried beside *her* first husband, William S. Bondurant. Perhaps she married again and was laid beside a third husband.

"DO NOT FEEL LIKE TAKING IT"

John Goode Farmer took a militant view toward preserving slavery. In 1860, addressing his son-in-law J.F. Cook as "Dear Son", John wrote that "two of my neighbors had rather give up all their negroes than go out of the union." John himself is of a different opinion: "feel we have borne the insults of the north long enough. Do not feel like taking it." The War soon came and John's son Willie, 21, promptly marched off and promptly was killed. William Goode Farmer died in agony in Mississippi from wounds suffered at the battle of Shiloh in the spring of 1862. Idling in camp before the battle, doomed Willie wrote spirited letters in which he declared he was going to take it to the Yankees right enough.

Sue Farmer Cook wrote to her father (p. 103) from her home in Summit, Mississippi, telling John of Willie's death. Sue's letter reveals her sense of terrible loss:

"Oh my dear Pa, I cannot <u>cannot</u> realize that my dear brother is dead, that he sleeps the sleep that knows no waking. Shall I not again see him or hear him tell his deep anxiety to get home to loved ones once more. And *never no never in this life can I see him. Ah! If there is recognition in heaven! Is this thought filled my dear ma's head, when she sees her dear son free from his torments of earth and walking in God's glory."*

Perhaps John Farmer's 1845 foreboding sense of his heart – *"like a muffled drum beating a funeral march to the tomb"* - was wrong only in a small way: the prophesy had to do not with John but with Willie.

Walt Whitman, poet of America and of the generation of John Goode Farmer, invites us to be understanding yet harsh with our John Farmer and his venerated daughter, whose rebellion cost them so dear. Addressing the state of Virginia in secession, the Republic of Whitman's poetic vision asks Virginia, how it is, *"you provided me Washington--and now these also."* In raising *"the insane knife,"* the rebellion will be met by *"the noble son . . . dressed in blue."* And so it was.

In 1871 John Farmer was eulogized by his pastor, T.M. Daniel, as *"a decided Baptist – uncompromising in his views and feelings on all points of doctrine and practice that distinguish us from others. He was rather Calvinistic in his idea of theology but believed strongly in human effort to do good and gave his money as freely as any member of his church, if not more so, to have the glorious gospel proclaimed at home and abroad. . . Brother Farmer died at his residence in Christiansburg, exercising strong confidence in the dear Redeemer, saying he 'had had a long and hard struggle against sin, was now through with the world and did not desire to return to it.'"*

SOURCES:

John Goode Farmer and Katherine Spencer Hawkins Farmer genealogy, generally: Betty Taylor Cook's unpublished genealogy book, and notes. Also **Old Kentucky**, by Joshua Flood Cook (New York and Washington: Neale Publishing, 1908)

Ernest Cook's 1924 letter concerning John Goode was published in the minutes of the Middle River Baptist Association of Virginia.

if you could only see and feel you would mind your ma: The letters of John Goode Farmer cited here are in the possession of descendent Carolyn Wickens, a Farmer descendent and family genealogist, who has generously shared photocopies.

Goode genealogy and additional Farmer genealogical records: **A Farmer Book** Ellery Farmer (1955). Ellery's book is an essential Farmer family resource: geocities.com/Heartland/Flats/7314/Farmer/ekam.html.

Walt Whitman's "Virginia – The West," **Leave of Grass** (New York: Airmont Publishing Company, 1965, page 211)

Travel in Kentucky, 1800

All land travel was over dirt roads, full of dust in the summer and deep in mud in the winter. . . Some of them followed lines originally marked out by the buffalo, time out of mind before, and were broad enough for highways of commerce; but most of them were mere traces and bridal paths, which no one but a woodsman or acquaintance could follow. Across the streams were no bridges, and people passed them at shallow places called fords, or in rude flatboats or in canoes used for ferries. The travel and trade upon the rivers were in canoes or in flatboats, and barges or keels propelled by oars or sails.

Reuben T. Durrett, from "Kentucky, Her History and Her People," his chapter in Joshua F. Cook's **Old Kentucky** 1908, pages 236-37

"HIS LAST DAYS WERE TRULY HIS BEST..."

Mary Crockett
William B. Hawkins

Katherine Spencer Hawkins Farmer (1814-51)
Susan Goode Farmer Cook (1838-1890)
Cecil V Cook (1871-1948)
Cecil V Cook, Jr (1913-1970)

John Goode Farmer (1808-1871) married **Katherine (Catherine) Spencer Hawkins** (1814-1851) on September 17, 1835. The wedding was performed in Franklin County KY by her brother-in-law, William C. Blanton. In June, 1842, Katherine was baptized into the Baptist Church in Christiansburg, Shelby County KY. Katherine and John Farmer were the parents of six children, including **Susan Goode Farmer** (1838-1890), wife of **Joshua Flood Cook** (1834-1912).

Katherine Hawkins was the daughter of **Mary ("Polly") Crockett** (1781-1856) and **William Benton Hawkins** (1781-1845) of Franklin County, KY. Mary Crockett was born Feb 9, 1781 and died Mar 31, 1856. Mary was the daughter of **Mary Robinson** (?-?) and **Anthony Crockett** (1756-1838).

The children of Polly and William Hawkins are:

1. Elizabeth (1802-1840)
2. Mary R Hawkins (1804-1852), married Rev. Wm C. Blanton
3. Rebecca (1806-?)
4. Anthony Crockett (1808-?)
5. Martha (1811- 1890)
6. Emily Head (1813-?)
7. **Katherine Spencer** (July, 1814-Nov 1 1851)

William Hawkins and Mary Crockett were married Jan 15, 1802. The research of genealogist Charlie L. Cook permits us to infer that the marriage took place at the

Forks of Elkhorn Baptist Church in Franklin County KY. This was very likely the church of the bride's parents, as other siblings and relations were married there. At Forks of Elkhorn in 1807, Elisha Hawkins married Sally Crockett, Mary's sister. Mary's brother Dandridge S. Crockett and Mary Ann Vaughan were married there in 1820.

WILLIAM HAWKINS AND THE HAWKINS FAMILY

Genealogist and Farmer descendent Carolyn Wickens has discovered that the Hawkins-Crockett marriage bonds were published without consent. As Mary (also known as Polly) was almost twenty-one, consent may have been unnecessary. On the other hand, William Benton Hawkins' nickname (reported by Carolyn Wickens and found in Will Book 2, p. 157, for Franklin Co KY) was "Black Head Billy." This proves only that Will Hawkins was given an odd nickname - not that Anthony Crockett, the distinguished father of the bride, objected to their marriage. But you gotta wonder. Black Head Billy? Another William Hawkins, perhaps an uncle of our Will, seems to have had the nickname, "Red Head Billy."

Billie was the oldest child of **Reuben Hawkins** (1747-1812) and **Rebecca Edwards** (1762-1840) of Orange County, VA. Their other children were:

2. Elisha Hawkins (1783/85-1859, in Caseyville, Union County KY)
3. Roddy (abt 1785 -1841, in Franklin County, KY)
4. Elizabeth (abt 1786- ?)
5. Arculus Hawkins (abt 1787-?)
6. Reuben Jr (abt 1789-?)
7. Lucy Hawkins (abt 1791- aft 1810, in Franklin CO KY) - married (1) William Anderson (1809 in Orange VA) and (2) Squire Jenkins
8. Moses Bartlett (1793-Sept 15, 1848)
9. Uriah Edwards (abt 1795-?)
10. Emily H. (Milly) (abt 1798-1875)
11. Benjamin S. Hawkins (abt 1800)
12. Sally (abt 1802-1840/41 in Mercer Co., KY)

Reuben Hawkins was born in Orange County VA, where he died 65 years later. His wife, Rebecca, was from Spotsylvania County VA. They were married in 1778, when Rebecca was 15. Rebecca died in Franklin County, KY in 1840 at age 78. Rebecca's parents were **Uriah Edwards** (?-?) and **Mildred Head** (?-?).

Reuben's parents are believed to be **William Hawkins Jr** (abt 1720-1799) and **Elizabeth Wall** (?-?). William Jr was born in Spotsylvania County and died in Orange County VA The parents of William Jr have been stated to be immigrant **William Hawkins** (abt 1699-abt 1776) and **Margaret Smith** (?-?). The first William Hawkins was born in England and died in Orange County VA. William and Margaret are thought to have been married after 1715. Notably, William is believed to have had a brother, John (1718-1778/9), husband of Mary Long, and father of Mary Hawkins, wife of Taliaferro Craig, ancestor of Cecil's wife, **Betty Taylor Cook** (1918-2000). (See **All Of The Above I** for details.) The parents of immigrant William Hawkins are not proven.

Attempts to connect the various Hawkins lines further back in Virginia and to (prominent) English Hawkins are ongoing but not yet persuasive. Well known English personalities include William Hawkins (b/f 1539-Oct 7, 1589) of Plymouth, Devon, England, where he was mayor. William Hawkins was the commander of the ship *Griffin* against the Spanish Armada. William's brother, Sir John Hawkins (?-1595), was an associate of Francis Drake, who may also have been a Hawkins relation. Sir John was a *privateer*, i.e. pirate. His voyages to transport slaves out of Africa to Spanish buyers in the West Indies and Mexico were sponsored by wealthy London backers including Queen Elizabeth I. Sir John is credited with establishing a naval blockade in the Azores, the better to rob Spanish ships returning from New Spain. Sir John became (1577) treasurer of the English navy and helped design faster and better armed vessels, which contributed to the English victory against the Spanish Armada in 1588. He was third in command in this engagement, for which he was knighted. Sir John died apparently of natural causes off the coast of Puerto Rico in 1589. A connection between these seamen and Black Head Billy Hawkins of Franklin County KY remains unproven.

ANTHONY CROCKETT (1756-1838)

Through alliance with the Hawkins family, Farmer and Cook descendents may claim connection to medieval France. This, in the person of **Antoine Crosketagne (Crocketagne)** (?-?). Billy Hawkins' wife, Mary Crockett (1781-1856) was the daughter of **Anthony Crockett** (1756-1838) of Virginia and Kentucky, and **Mary Robertson** (1760-1818) of Botetourt County VA.

Anthony Crockett was born in Prince Edward County, Virginia Colony and moved with his parents to Botetourt County, where he grew up. Betty Cook's research included a review of Crockett's petition for a Revolutionary War pension, made in Frankfort, KY in 1832. Betty recorded that Anthony Crockett enlisted as a Private in Capt. Posey's Company, 7th Virginia Regiment, serving Feb 1776-78. Crockett saw action in VA, PA, NJ, NY, and served under "tough" Daniel Morgan, perhaps the most gifted tactician of the Revolutionary War.

The most significant engagements of the youthful Anthony Crockett's Revolutionary War career were the savage battles, which lead to the defeat and surrender of British General John Burgoyne in New York in 1777. The defeat of Burgoyne turned the war in favor of the insurgents, who established their credibility as effective fighters against a professional British army. Crockett also saw service under General Washington in Pennsylvania, fighting near White Marsh, PA in December, 1777. In the White Marsh campaign, Washington successfully avoided the destruction of his army and went on to winter, famously, at Valley Forge, PA.

Crockett was with Washington in New Jersey against Hessian mercenaries and subsequently was commissioned a Lieutenant. He saw continued service in the west, under Colonels John Montgomery and George Rogers Clark, as far as the Mississippi River at Kaskaskia.

Clark became famous for decisiveness and the employment of frontier psychology, which gained him strategic victories, at times, without the firing of a shot. Crockett later participated in campaigns against the Shawnee and possibly other *originals* (as the British called them) whose towns, Crockett affirms in his pension petition, he "burnt."

After the war, Anthony Crockett moved to Kentucky, where he was "one of the earliest and most prominent of Kentucky pioneers," who "retired to the cultivation of his farm and the domestic quiet of private life." This source goes on to say that Crockett's "services were not forgotten by his countrymen" as he was "twice chosen as representative from the county of Kentucky to the Legislature of Virginia." Family historian Betty Cook recorded that Crockett was elected to the Virginia legislature from Mercer County KY in 1790 and (after Kentucky attained statehood in 1792) he was elected to the KY legislature from Franklin Co KY (1796-99).

During the so called second war with England (War of 1812-14) Crockett again saw military service with General Harrison at the Battle of the Thames in Ontario, Canada. Crockett was under arms until the end of the war, traveling as far west as Detroit.

For thirty years, Crockett was Sergeant at Arms of the Kentucky Senate, which published a memorial upon Crockett's death in 1838. In commenting on his death, the Senate stated, "it is worthy of remark that the brass field-piece, now in the arsenal at Frankfort, which was used at his burial, he twice assisted in taking from the British. He aided in taking it at Saratoga; it was afterward surrendered to the British at Detroit and retaken at the Thames, to which the personal bravery of Col. Crockett much contributed." An 1877 History of Kentucky, drawing on proclamations and resolutions passed when he died, records that for Anthony Crockett,

> "his last days were truly his best, for he had the rare felicity at an advanced age of seeing his numerous progeny settled around him, and raised to respectability and distinction. There was

mingled with his age much of the sprightliness and buoyancy of youth, and he had the rare faculty, seldom possessed by old men, of recollecting that he was once young. The varied events of his life, his personal difficulties and adventures, all tended to render his conversation interesting and delightful. Many are those who will recollect the venerable form that moved among them, adding to the gravity and wisdom of age the vivacity of younger years and rendering himself the center and delight of the circle in which he moved."

Betty Taylor Cook recorded that Anthony Crockett entertained Lafayette during his visit to KY in 1824. A review of reports of Lafayette's triumphal visit to KY has not substantiated a role by Anthony Crockett in the feting of the Marquis in Lexington or Louisville. We do learn, however, that the old General was tossed dangerously into the Ohio River, when the boat conducting him to Louisville ran aground. Whether the elderly veteran of the Revolution was on hand to fish out the even more elderly French General has not been thoroughly researched.

Anthony Crockett was buried in the Frankfort Cemetery, in the DAR section, reserved for veterans of the Revolutionary War.

Betty Cook lists Anthony as the son of **William Crockett** (Aug 10, 1709-?) of Prince Edward County VA. William was the son of **Mary Stewart** (?-?) and **Joseph Lewis Crockett** (1676-?). Joseph was the son of **Antoine Crocketagne** (?-?) and **Louise de Saix** (?-?). Antoine's father was **Gabriel Gustave Gaston de Crocketagne** (?-?). Gabriel or perhaps Antoine have been said to be well placed Versailles official (Versailles France, not Versailles, Kentucky). This suggestion seems to have made its way in the world without solid evidence. But to be fair, Farmer family historian Ellery Farmer is cited (below, page 130) as the authority for this genealogy, in a private communication he sent to Betty Cook.

SOURCES:

Hawkins and Crockett genealogy, generally: Betty Taylor Cook's unpublished genealogy book, and her notes, which include information provided by Ellery Farmer, author of **A Farmer Book**, posted on the web. geocities.com/Heartland/Flats/7314/Farmer/ekam.

Hawkins-Crockett wedding information: **Forks of Elkhorn Church** by Ermina Jett Darnell, (1946, esp. page 249, 293); additional information generously provided by Cook family genealogist Charles Cook and Farmer family genealogist Carolyn Wickens, who shared the inscription on the Farmer infant's grave in Christiansburg KY.

Several web sources have posted Hawkins genealogies including: Southern-style.com/Hawkins. A good summary of the results of current Hawkins research: "Descendants of William Hawkins and Sir John Hawkins at freepages/rootsweb.com posted by: "Mostly Southern - Mark Freeman & Carolyn Terrell's Family History"

John Hawkins' career in the Spanish Main is summarized in **American Slavery, American Freedom, The Ordeal of Colonial Virginia**, Edmund S. Morgan, (New York: Norton 1975, 2005 pages 9-11).

his last days were truly his best: For the quotations commemorating Anthony Crockett's war service: **Kentucky: A History of the State** "Franklin Co" (Battle, Perrin, & Kniffin, 5th ed., 1887).

NOTES OF CROCKETTS

Col. Anthony Crockett of Frankfort, Kentucky, my Great Great Grandfather on my father's side, was born in Prince Edward County Virginia. He enlisted in Captain Posey's company of the Seventh Virginia Regiment Feb. 1776 to 1778. He served in Virginia, Pennsylvania, New Jersey and New York in many skirmishes and battles and in the Burgoyne Campaign. From 1778 to the end of the revolution he was a 1st Lt. in the Illinois Regiment of Virginia, Col. George D. Clark commanding and served at Bryan and Gordon station in Kentucky, Kaskaskia, Illinois, Vincennes, Ind. and Piqua, Ohio. He returned to Virginia and married in 1780 and rejoined the army. After the Revolution he moved to Kentucky. He was in the Virginia legislature from Mercer County Kentucky in 1790 and in the Kentucky legislature from Franklin County, Kentucky from 1796 to 1799.

The family originated in France and there it was spelled Crocketagne. Antoine Crocketagne, the father of our immigrant ancestor, was an officer in Louis XIV household guard. He married a French woman of the nobility named DeSaix, who was a cousin of General Lafayette's mother. Antoine was converted to Protestantism, and when the Huguenots were expelled from France in 1672, he fled to England with his family for a short time and later to Ireland, where our immigrant ancestor (Joseph Lewis Crockett) was born in 1676. To escape persecution as a Huguenot and lose his French identity, he changed his name to Crockett.

Various books in the Congressional Library in Washington are the authority for the above records.

                    Signed: Ellery Farmer
                    Col. U.S. Army, Retd.

"SHOULD I GET TO HEAVEN I WILL BE PRAYING FOR YOU THERE"

Joshua Flood Cook

Cecil V Cook, Sr (1871-1948)
Cecil V Cook, Jr (1913-1970)

Joshua Flood Cook (1834-1912) was born near Bagdad, KY (some 40 miles east of Louisville) on Jan 14, 1834. He died in LaGrange, Missouri in May, 1912. Joshua was the son of **Lucy Flood** (1802-1865) and **William Fredrick ("Billy Dick") Cook** (1802-b/f 1855). William and Lucy Cook's other children were Joseph, Alexander, Mary and Abraham. At age 13, Joshua thought he would become a blacksmith and undertook a three-year apprenticeship (1847-50).

In 1850 young Joshua moved to Missouri and lived for four years with his uncle, the well known Baptist preacher, Noah Flood, which is a name combo that must always have had a tick of humor for the parents, who put it together. In Missouri Joshua went to Fayette High School in Howard County. While attending high school (1850-54), Joshua is said to have also been a school teacher. If true, this suggests that Joshua had been doing his own studying while an apprentice blacksmith in KY. It is also an early indication that Joshua benefited from personal connections in Missouri, connections which would be fruitful in the years to come.

In 1854, Joshua returned to Kentucky and became a student at Georgetown College, where he graduated in 1858. In a memoir (**Old Kentucky**, 1908) Joshua wrote that he was licensed to the Baptist ministry while a student at Georgetown. The licensing was promptly followed up by Joshua's ordination as a Baptist minister in 1858 at Campbellsburg, KY.

Joshua described himself as "homeless" when he went to Georgetown College in 1855. He had not lived at home with his parents since at least age 16 when he went to

Missouri. Joshua has also written that he spent his college vacations visiting in the homes of his classmates rather than with his own family. Joshua reported in his 1908 memoir that his childhood home broke up upon his father's death and his mother's subsequent 1855 marriage to Thomas Brewer. It is not known whether Joshua might have been unwelcome in Thomas Brewer's home or whether, already twenty-one in 1855, he had simply concluded he was old enough to manage without a home.

On Nov. 4, 1858, Joshua married **Susan Goode Farmer** (1838-1890). Sue Farmer was born August 8, 1838 in Kentucky and died in Missouri on May 10, 1890. She was the namesake of her grandmother, **Susan Goode** (1783-1864) who had been born in the Skinquarter section of Chesterfield County, Virginia, the daughter of a locally well known dissenting Baptist preacher, **John Goode** (1739-1792). Sue's mother, **Katherine Spencer Hawkins Farmer** (1814-1851) died when Sue was thirteen. As her published obituary stated, Susie was left with the care of four brothers, one of whom "Prof. J.G. Farmer," who grew up to follow a respected teaching career in Missouri, was but one year old when their mother Katherine died. Susan attended Georgetown KY Seminary, a kind of finishing school for young women. Joshua Cook and Susan Farmer no doubt courted while both of them attended school in Georgetown. They may have known each other as children, growing up in Shelby County KY.

Suzie's father, **John Goode Farmer** (1808-1871), was a devout Baptist layman. A farmer and owner of a general store in Christiansburg, KY, John Farmer must have been pleased when his daughter married the young Reverend Cook. In letters to her father, Sue Cook referred to her husband as "Mr. Cook" but within two years of the marriage, John was writing letters to Joshua, "my son."

In 1858, Joshua Cook, the newly married, newly minted college graduate and preacher became chaplain of New Liberty Female College (now defunct), New Liberty, KY. In 1859, at age twenty-five, Joshua was made president of this institution and held that post until the outbreak of the Civil War in 1861.

Susan Farmer Cook seems to have matched her young husband in self-confidence and decisiveness. When Joshua assumed the presidency of New Liberty Female College, she herself "presided over New Liberty Female Seminary" (as her obituary stated).

Susan and Joshua had four children: John Ernest (1860-1926), Lula (1862-1943), William Flood (1868-1947) and **Cecil Virgil** (1871-1948). The Rev. John Ernest Cook was born in Kentucky, July 17, 1860; Lula was born in Corinth, Mississippi August 27, 1862, William Flood, in LaGrange, Missouri, Feb 2, 1868; **Cecil Virgil** (1871-1948) was also born in LaGrange, Dec. 10, 1871.

In 1861, J.F. Cook left New Liberty College and moved his family to Summit, Mississippi, where he became a school teacher and chaplain to Confederate Army troops. During the war, Joshua bought farmland in Mississippi, about a hundred miles north of New Orleans. The disposition of this property has not yet been traced. Nor is it known how Joshua and Sue Cook financed this purchase or whether they conducted agricultural activities on this land. In 1865, Joshua and Susan returned to KY, where he assumed the pastorate of the Baptist church at Eminence, KY.

On Sept. 7, 1866, Joshua Cook once again was chosen to be president of a college, this being a co-educational school then known as the LaGrange Male and Female Seminary. The college was located in LaGrange, MO, a small town on the banks of the Mississippi River about 110 miles north of St. Louis. Joshua was thirty-two. In 1868, Joshua was awarded an honorary doctorate (LL.D.) from Baylor University, Waco, TX. He was ever after referred to as Dr. J.F. Cook.

In 1879, the name of the seminary was changed to LaGrange College. Joshua held the presidency of LaGrange College for thirty years. In the twentieth century, after Joshua had passed from the scene, the college relocated to nearby Hannibal, MO and became Hannibal-LaGrange College.

Early on Joshua developed a habit of reading and a love of books. In 1912 (the year of his death) Joshua reminisced about how difficult was his struggle to obtain an education. "I live in a dream from early boyhood," he wrote to his son Cecil, "Almost broke myself down trying to get an education. They [thought?] once they would have to send me to an asylum - but I rallied." This curious statement is unaccompanied by any clarifying facts, but suggests an early and overt anxiety to acquire what was not readily available to a farmer's son in the middle of the nineteenth century: schooling.

Somehow, Joshua pulled it off. In 1858 he not only graduated from college, but was invited to deliver a graduation speech. The original document, preserved and reproduced by proud descendents, reflects the florid oratorical style of its time and also indicates Joshua's solid command of the written and spoken word. Joshua took as his subject a well known Baptist Missionary. This choice probably reflects Joshua exposure to books in the Missouri home of his uncle, the Rev. Noah Flood, whose library no doubt included an emphasis upon Baptist history and traditions. A short excerpt from Joshua's 1858 graduation address:

> "Among the brave, the great, the good of our country, whose names are worthy to be transmitted to posterity, stately column or immortalizing song will never guard the memory of a nobler spirit than Adoniram Judson. For sublime, heroic action, for noble, pure Christian philanthropy, for devoted love to every human creature, he may justly challenge comparison with any that have lived. He knew not self, he felt not his own woes - he lived for others."

Joshua Cook's own library grew throughout his life and contained a number of volumes, which have made their way on to the shelves of his sons, grandsons and great grandchildren. J. F. Cook cherished his books. At age seventy, he acquired a copy of **Outlines of Medieval and Modern History**, by J.V.N. Myers (Boston: Gynn & Company 1903) which he loaned to someone and which he

Joshua Flood Cook

inscribed, "When done with this, return immediately to J.F. Cook, LaGrange, MO." J.F. got his book back.

Joshua Cook's 30-year tenure (1866-96) at LaGrange College was generally viewed as a success by contemporaries. He was said to have assumed charge and then saved the school, when it had but a single dilapidated building, no money in the bank and a debt burden of $10,000, a sum equivalent to many times that amount by the standards of today. Reflecting on his tenure in a letter to son Cecil, J.F. Cook recalled in 1912 how hard the task was. "The thirty years here [LaGrange] were too much. No living soul knows what I went through those years. Wonder I am living and that I have any mind."

The arrangement Joshua made with the trustees at the 1866 beginning was to lease the college from them for a ten-year term, raise the needed funds and conduct an educational program as specified by the charter and the policies adopted by the trustees. Joshua, as lessee of the college, could keep any amount raised above that needed for college expenses. This seems to have been the agreement for three consecutive ten-year leases, from 1866 to 1896.

The college trustees expected the enforcement of strict standards and President Cook delivered. Applicants were required to meet with an admissions committee. Parents as well as prospective students were advised of the behavioral standards required of the students.

An "Abstract of College Laws" dating from J.F. Cook's tenure, contained the following provisions:

Every student shall attend the daily devotional exercises in the college chapel, also, public worship on the Lord's day, at such churches as the parent or guardian may designate.

Students will not be permitted to be absent from their rooms after 7 o'clock at night without leave, except to attend religious service, or the literary societies connected with the college.

No student will be permitted to leave the city on any pretext whatever, during his or her connection with the college, without previous permission from the president or some member of the faculty.

No student shall carry deadly weapons, or attend any exhibition having an immoral tendency, nor frequent any bar-room or tippling house.

Students in the male and female departments are to have no communications, either verbal or written, further than true politeness requires.

An 1872 advertisement for the college in the LaGrange *Democrat* included the following statement: *"Moral and religious influences here are superior, students being unexposed to the vices and temptations of larger cities. One hundred and seventy-five dollars will pay the tuition for the college year. Our students are living with the best of families, not in mess halls. The graduates of this institution are as good as any other college in the state."*

Soon after moving to LaGrange, Joshua and Sue Cook built a 14-room brick mansion at the edge of the college campus. They moved into it in 1868. Their residence "on the hill" was the focal point of fund raising and social activities for the college. At graduation, an elaborate reception, a "levee," would be conducted at the President's home. J.F. Cook also organized an alumni association and encouraged alumni to support the school.

During all of the years at LaGrange, Sue Cook was helpfully at Joshua's side. The mother of four children, she nevertheless fulfilled the social requirements that fell to the spouse of a college president. Sue Farmer Cook also continued to look after her Farmer siblings in Kentucky, whom she had helped care for after their mother had died young. Following her move to Missouri, Sue influenced her brothers to join her and Joshua there. The 1870 Lewis County Missouri census reports the Cook household contained J F Cook, age 36, Sue G, 29, Ernest, 10, "Lulu"[Lula], 7, and Willie 2; there is Lucius Farmer, 21, Sue's brother and himself a student at the college. There is Brinkman Lewis 17, also a student. Finally, the household census included Sarah Fisher, 16, Black, a "domestic servant," born in Kentucky. Sue's youngest brother, Joseph, became a professor at LaGrange College. Ellery Farmer, the Farmer family genealogist, concluded that Sue influenced virtually all of her siblings to move from Kentucky to Missouri.

In 1887, J.F. Cook gave a twenty-year report to the trustees and announced he had raised and expended over $15,000 for debt retirement and building improvements. The college, he said, had assets greater than indebtedness. During the 1880's, college enrollment exceeded the University of Missouri and the college was widely acknowledged for its co-educational focus. One may surmise that Sue Cook was a stimulus and advocate for the education of women. Daughter Lula attended and graduated from LaGrange College.

While in charge of the college, J.F. Cook exercised his calling as a Baptist minister. For at least fourteen years he was pastor of Dover Baptist church in Pike County, Missouri. The church building, constructed in 1862, still stands: Route D, Calumet Township. In May, 1890, a delegation from this congregation attended the funeral of Susan Cook, who had died on LaGrange College commencement day.

Susan Cook was the subject of a lengthy obituary in the LaGrange *Democrat*, which pointed out her life-long active interest in the local Baptist Church, including her long incumbency as Sunday School teacher of the youngest class. She also raised funds for the completion of a new "church house." Sue's own funeral was the first to take place in the completed building.

An unspecified lingering, painful illness preceded Susan Cook's death. Near the end Sue gave directions for her funeral, which included a request that her Sunday School class "attend the funeral in a body and the members of it throw into her open grave flowers of their own cutting and arranging." This was done. The newspaper observed: "The class, made up of the youngest children, had reserved seats, each little one bearing flowers of his or her own gathering. Huddled in their select corner the tear-stained, motherless brood presented one of the most touching features of the funeral procession."

Sue Cook's death was a severe blow to the morale of her husband. President Joshua Flood Cook, the public man, acknowledged this. In August, 1890, two short months after Sue Cook's death, J.F. Cook, was observed to be "somewhat depressed" when he attended the Wyaconda Baptist Association's annual meeting; he mentioned that he might resign from the school. But the Association, as partners with him through the trustees of the college, offered Joshua a lifetime contract and over-pledged funds for needed improvements. He returned home, it was reported, "inspired, and determined to make renewal efforts and think no more of surrendering this charge until relieved by physical infirmity."

In 1893 a near tragedy at the college became an episode worthy of the Marx brothers. While J.F. was in New Orleans, flames spread by chimney sparks set fire to the roof of one of the main college buildings. Thanks to the quick action of neighbors, no lasting damage was done. But where was the LaGrange fire department? "The tardiness of the fire department was accounted for by the fact that a pair of very small mules hitched to the truck, in addition to the apparatus, had to haul about a dozen able-bodied men to the top of the hill." The newspaper, which reported the presence of the "very small mules," does not state whether in future, larger mules would be harnessed to the fire wagon or whether firemen would be asked to run to fires that were uphill from the firehouse.

J.F. Cook continued at LaGrange College for a full thirty years, resigning in 1896. He then promptly assumed the presidency of Webb City College, Webb City, MO, and continued there until his final retirement in 1900. In that year Joshua returned to LaGrange and lived there until his death in 1912.

Joshua was married three times: his first wife, as stated, was **Susan Goode Farmer** (1838-1890); they wed on Nov. 4, 1858. In May 1891, a year after Sue's death, Joshua married Bessie Hughes of Saline County, Missouri. They had no children. Bessie died of tuberculosis on May

8, 1894, almost four years to the day after the death of Joshua's first wife. In 1895, Joshua married Drucilla Hirons (?-Nov 12, 1962). They became the parents, in 1900, of Howard Elliott Cook; Joshua was then sixty-six years old. Howard Cook fought in World War II; he was captured on Wake Island in 1941 and spent three years as a Japanese prisoner of war, apparently held in Shanghai. Suffering from lingering traumatic stress after the war, Howard required care the rest of his days. He lived in Florida with his mother Drucilla until his death. Both Howard and Drucilla (known in the family as "Aunt Drucy") are buried beside J. F. Cook, in LaGrange.

"OLD KENTUCKY"

In 1908 J. F. Cook published a book of reminiscences which he titled **Old Kentucky**. Much of the information we have about Joshua and his immediate family has been taken from this book, which is a paean to the Kentucky of Joshua's youth, as J.F. recalled, in his eighth decade. Undoubtedly, Joshua intended his book, sprinkled with opinion and the occasional Baptist minister's joke or pun, to be received as a serious and valuable contribution to the annals of his home state. He dedicated his book to "Colonel Reuben T. Durrett, Scholar, Historian, Founder of the Filson Club," in Louisville, KY, The Filson Club continues to be a noted repository of Kentucky history and documentation. Durrett contributed a chapter to J.F.'s book, entitled *"Kentucky, Her History and Her People."* Joshua sought and received permission from President Theodore Roosevelt to include a selection of Roosevelt's writings in the volume, which appear in a chapter entitled *"Kentuckians and Bordermen."*

A third contributor to Joshua's volume was then Congressman and future Speaker of the House of Representatives, Champ Clark of Missouri. For three years J.F. Cook's oldest son, John Ernest Cook (July 7, 1860-Dec 2, 1926), had been Champ Clark's law partner in Bowling Green, MO.

Joshua has written in **Old Kentucky** (pages 135, 136, 137) that he grew up in Shelby County KY, surrounded by all of his grandparents and most of their children. Joshua remembered his boyhood with a nostalgic glow, notable even for a sentimental old man.

"Every house was near a fine spring, and around them grew magnificent forests. Such forests I have seen no where else between ocean and ocean . . . In those days there were trees standing with the marks made on them by the claws of bears, and grandfather has pointed out to me different trees where he had killed bears after he settled there. . . I see the old house as I saw it when a child. The first house or cabin had been turned into a hen house; the house that was new when I was born was of hewed logs, two rooms. The upstairs of the house was all one room, where we boys slept and we were well and happy. . . . Grandfather owned all the land and had enough to divide and give homes to a large family of children. We always had good gardens, abundance of milk, and butter and poultry. Nearly every home had its bees, and when the family desired more honey, they could go out in the woods and cut down a bee tree. . . . What more to be desired then these old time people had?"

The elderly Joshua recalled his childhood with an extravagant reverie that would do credit to the troubadours who touted Robin Hood and Jolly Old England. Joshua wrote (page 138) that hardly a boy in the neighborhood failed to grow up to less than six feet tall "rugged, hardy splendid men, and girls into beautiful women." Joshua, himself six feet tall, seems to have enjoyed good health, despite a bout with typhoid fever in 1844, when he was ten years old (page 133). Joshua lived to be seventy eight.

Devout from an early age, Joshua took his zeal in the Baptist, frontier style. "Before I was thirteen years old, I was lead to Christ and never, from that day to this [1846-1908] have I ever purposely done anything to dishonor my profession." By "profession" Joshua is taken to mean not his secular career as a college administrator or even his calling as a Baptist Minister, but his "profession" of faith in Jesus, to which he committed himself as a boy of twelve.

Joshua's paradoxical memories and musings are intriguing and illusive in equal measure. He was twenty-seven years old when the Civil War began. Joshua's mature memories and perspective cover three important epochs: ante-bellum Kentucky and Missouri, the Civil War in the western regions of the South (Mississippi, Kentucky, Tennessee) and the period of Reconstruction as observed by an energetic and admired educator in small-town Missouri.

Joshua takes care to infuse his memoir with a tranquil and positive aura of gentility. The larger social themes of the period – the national economic life, the transformative employment of steam power, a massive and bloody civil conflict and the subsequent establishment of a rigid race-conscious caste system, the settlement of the West; all are overlooked. Slavery and civil war, their causes and consequences, Joshua takes to be difficult episodes, which he had the good taste to survive.

Joshua's selective reminiscences transform his memories into soft-toned fancies. He writes (page 159, 162) that General John C. Breckinridge ("the ideal Kentuckian") came to Chaplain J F Cook at a Confederate Camp at Jackson, Mississippi "put his arms around me, and said, 'Cook, we shall never win. We shall all be a set of rag-a-muffins.' I was shocked and surprised and never breathed it to another human being."

Joshua writes (page 159, 158) that Lincoln was "the only man . . . called to the great and seemingly impossible task of leading the nation to the final settlement of the two questions which lead to the war: slavery" and "whether all the states were bound together by a rope of sand or whether they were bound in an indissoluble union." Joshua cites (page 163) his friend Green Clay Smith as "an intimate friend of Mr. Lincoln's, really his pet, and always had free access to him and to the White House. He has told me many incidents that I have never seen published in regard to Mr. Lincoln's private troubles, some of which I could tell but it would probably do no good."

THE RACE OF HAM

J.F. Cook's memoir is more than dreamy reminiscences found in the musings of a genial old man. Race and race-consciousness were longstanding obsessions with Joshua. Throughout his memoir, he often returns to these themes. Invoking phrenology, that nineteenth century pseudoscientific fad, Joshua writes (page 39) that official Civil War autopsies demonstrate "the negro brain is over five ounces less than that of the white;" moreover, "the percentage of exceptionally small brains is largest among the negroes having but a small percentage of white blood." These *facts* appear to prove to Joshua (page 40) "that the race of Ham has ever had some cloud hanging darkly over it."

Joshua does not speculate about the nature of the "cloud" or ruminate upon interactions required to introduce "white blood" among African slaves. A greater degree of candor on his part might have better enabled Joshua's readers to learn what he must have known to be true, that there occurred in the "Old Kentucky" of blessed memory the regular assault by white men upon female slaves, both girls and women, who had not the slightest means of protecting themselves.

The nexus between race and sex was The Forbidden Subject in the ante-bellum South. Joshua carried this prohibition forward into the twentieth century. Well aware of the taboo, Joshua speaks of racial matters only in terms of superior versus inferior peoples. Joshua invokes white racial superiority to clarify (page 40) the family's traditional interest in owning human beings.

"By way of explanation, I want to say that my ancestors, all of whom were from Virginia, owned slaves; that I inherited slaves, that I was reared among them; and from childhood I played with them and loved them, and in after years, when they came into my possession, I was as kind and tender to them as if they had been of my own race, and in my whole life never bought or sold one;

that I have contributed to their education after they were freed."

Following this defensive broadside, delivered forty years after the Civil War, Joshua retreats to the safe haven of abstract musings (page 41): *"Why God, in his providence, permitted this country to make the blunders it did, no human mind can comprehend."*

Joshua relates (page 46) that his grandfather once offered his slaves their freedom to go to Ohio. But they preferred "to remain in Kentucky--with him and live with him until some of them died, and others were kindly cared for after his death." Joshua does not specify which of his grandfathers is meant, whether **Abraham Cook** (1774-1854) or **Joshua Flood** (1772-1850). But the mention of the death of this grandfather suggests that Grandfather Flood is in mind; Abraham Cook moved to Missouri before he died.

According to Cook wills, slaves were owned and also bought and sold by family members. Seth, Joshua's great uncle - the son of Joshua's great grandfather **William Cook** (abt 1730-abt 1790/91) provided in his 1842 will for the sale of a black man, Sandy, who was valued at $100.00. Another of Joshua's great uncles, William Cook, stipulated in his 1816 will that a slave, "Peter should be free on the payment of Fifty Dollars; a balance of two-hundred and fifty dollars which Seth Cook and Abraham Bohannon as agents for Peter had undertaken to pay which is all paid but the aforesaid fifty dollars."

Believing the Civil War was fought to resolve the question of slavery, Joshua also believed (page 46) that the white citizens of Kentucky would have freed their slaves but for a single factor: "constant agitation awakened bad feelings, and the people of Kentucky did not feel like being driven to anything by falsehood and abuse." Joshua implies that the only abuse he knew of that might be connected with slavery was directed against "the [White] people of Kentucky" who were put upon by "constant agitation."

It is little wonder that, according to **Betty Cook**, wife of J F's grandson **Cecil V. Cook, Jr** (1913-1970),

Joshua's 1908 memoir was received with chagrin by his son, **Cecil Cook Sr** (1871-1948), and others of the family.

By 1908, Joshua was (page 47) an admirer of abolitionist John Brown. Joshua knew religious fervor when he saw it and so describes John Brown as "that poor old fanatic" who nonetheless "had courage to risk all to carry out his convictions." The compliment to John Brown becomes a segue into the subject of the collective insanity of slavery's opponents. Joshua now condemns Northern anti-slavery sentiment as "a pitch of madness," because "the Bible was not strong enough" for Northerners on the abolition question, the "madness" thus being Northern declarations for "an anti-slavery God, an anti-slavery Constitution, and an anti-slavery Bible."

For the elderly Joshua, looking back on the war from the distance of fifty years, old John Brown and the rest of those pesky Northerners had taken things too far. *"My opinion is that slavery was a dark shadow upon this country; that in nature it could not exist in a republic; and that Providence let this thing be developed so that it could be abolished; and that it has given to the American people a great problem which no man can solve, but which calls for the wisest and most conservative action."*

In all of his remarks about slavery and race, J. F. may be talking about the enslaved past but his eye is on the era of his successful career as an educator. This career coincided with Reconstruction and extended to the cusp of the new century, the so-called "Progressive" era. Joshua retired from the Presidency of LaGrange College in 1896, the year the Supreme Court announced the fiction in *Plessy v. Ferguson,* that demeaning and near worthless racially segregated services(public schools, transportation) provided to recently emancipated citizens were, in Constitutional terms, *separate but equal.* The precise purpose of *Plessy* was to placate the influential and widely held views expressed by Joshua Cook.

Joshua reminds his readers that he grew up in a time of human slavery but he does not then state clearly how he lived out the rest of his life in a time of apartheid. His ambiguity about slavery as both a family custom and a large historical motif permits Joshua to adopt a studied ambivalence towards severe post-Civil War White hostility directed against Negroes, which insisted upon the brutal re-segregation of the nation. Joshua claims this ambivalence in the afterglow of his reminiscence. He offers his readers a casual detachment as a substitute for what surely was, during his public career, an embrace of the retrenchment under way during the post Civil War generation. What might be said in Joshua defense?

The currents of reaction had to be taken into account by a college President trying to raise money and shoulder all the other tasks necessary for the survival of a segregated Baptist college in Missouri from 1866-1896. Had Joshua been so foolhardy as to distance himself from the retrenchment called "redemption" or "Jim Crow," he could not have had a career at all. Much of J.F. Cook's memoir reads like notes for the fund raising addresses he made to Baptist gatherings in the cities and towns of Missouri in the final four decades of the nineteenth century.

Slavery, Joshua announces in 1908, "developed so that it could be abolished." This is casuistry of the first water. Undeterred, Joshua continues. The presence, he says, in one society of freed Black slaves and defeated White slavers calls for "the wisest" but also the "most conservative action." Joshua's convoluted bromides are the opinions of a White, prestige-conscious stakeholder.

Nothing is said here of beatings, lynchings, or of voting rights prohibitions and the other legal restrictions that accompanied the retrenchment, just as Joshua wrote nothing about brutal slave conditions in Kentucky before the war. We find nothing from Joshua about the slave pens of Lexington and Louisville, or about runaways, or the "paterollers" (patrollers) who hunted them down. Nor does Joshua reminisce about Kentucky's reputation as a prime breeding state for Mississippi field hands and the "fancy girls" who were conceived and raised in Kentucky and sold off to the bordellos of New Orleans. Like his father-in-law, John Goode Farmer, Joshua's mind was on Heaven while so many around him were living in Hell.

JOHN MURPHY: OPPONENT OF SLAVERY

We have noted Joshua's remark: *"my ancestors, all of whom were from Virginia, owned slaves."* While this may be literally true, there were dissenting voices within the family and even among those members of the family who felt themselves called to a holy vocation. In Kentucky in the early decades of the nineteenth century and especially in the Baptist context (where *calling* is ratified by majority vote of the congregation) those who opposed slavery paid a severe price for their convictions. One of these was Joshua's great uncle, John Murphy (1752-1818). John Murphy was a Baptist preacher, the son of William Murphy (by 1726-1799) and his first wife, Martha Hodges (?-by 1767). John's father, William Murphy was himself an early Baptist preacher. In 1757, William was baptized in Orange (now Chatham) County, NC, by the notable Shubal Stearns, a "new light" (Baptist) from New England, who brought the principles of religious dissent into Virginia and NC as early as 1755. William Murphy soon became a Baptist preacher and traveled and lived for years the life of a farmer and an itinerant frontier preacher. (For more on the new light phenomenon, see the memoir of William Hickman, appended to this volume, see also page 216.)

John Murphy married Rachel Cook on Feb 8, 1774. Rachel was the daughter of **Margaret (Jones?)** and **William Cook**. No doubt John had met Rachel after William and Martha Murphy had re-located their family on the Pigg River in southside Virginia, near the home of William and Margaret Cook. Like his father, William, John, and Rachel followed a semi-nomadic career, notable ever for those times of frequent family moves. Various land tractions have John recorded as a resident of Virginia, North Carolina, Tennessee and Kentucky. Rachel and John Murphy were the aunt and uncle of William Fredrick ("Billy Dick") Cook, a son of Abraham Cook, who was a brother to Rachel. Rachel Cook and John Murphy were therefore the great aunt and uncle of Joshua Flood Cook.

John Murphy took an oath of allegiance to the United States of America on August 30, 1777 and was appointed Ensign of Captain Haile's militia company in March, 1779. In Feb 1782, he was a lieutenant in the Washington County NC militia.

John Murphy was baptized by his brother-in-law Isaac Barton on Dec 4, 1790 in NC or Tennessee and became a member of the Bent Creek Baptist Church in Green County, TN. By Nov 1798, John and Rachel Murphy are found living in Barren County, KY, where they were enrolled as founding members of the Mount Tabor Baptist Church. John was the first clerk of this congregation and was licensed to preach in 1801. Some time after that date, he took up preaching duties in Kentucky, along the Green River.

John's career as a Baptist minister in Kentucky was cut short because of his hostility to slavery. In 1808, John Murphy was "excluded" by the Mount Tabor (KY) Church "on account of his declaring non-fellowship" with the church "for tolerating slavery." Carter Tarrant, himself an anti-slavery Kentucky preacher and one-time pastor of Mount Tabor Church, said of John Murphy, "He was the first minister south of Green river, who publicly opposed slavery." These mutual denunciations appear to have ended John Murphy's career as a preacher. Spencer's **History of Kentucky Baptists From 1769-1885** (1886, vol I, page 387) which is our source for the Tarrant comment, states of John Murphy, "What became of him after his exclusion from the church, does not appear." Thanks to the careful research of family historians Elizabeth L Nichols (2004) and Alice Murphy Sturgess (1918) John Murphy's views on slavery have been preserved.

From Warren County, KY in 1810, John wrote a letter to "Brothers, friends and acquaintances" in what came to be St Francois County, Missouri (which John Murphy refers to as "Louisiana Territory"). In addition to family news, John made these comments:

"There is considerable dissention among the Baptists and some among other sects about slave holding. For my own part, I prefer to stand opposed to that

system, because I fully believe it to be contrary to the law of nature, contrary to sound reason, contrary to good policy, contrary to justice, contrary to republican principles, and above all, because it is in direct opposition to the Scripture directions. Neither does it accord with the principles of humanity."

The earliest publication of this letter seems to have been in 1918 (Alice M Sturgess' pamphlet), which was too late for Joshua Cook's 1908 memoir. The exclusion of any reference to John Murphy points to several other elements, which are also missing from Joshua's comments about slavery in his **Old Kentucky**. Joshua makes no mention of the turmoil among the early (White) Baptists of Kentucky about slave-holding. Did J.F. not know of the dissent within his own extended family from the slave-holding consensus? Did he not know that the system of slave ownership was not generally accepted among (White) Kentucky Baptists until principled people of conscience, such as John Murphy, were silenced or removed from the membership of the churches? The process of exclusion began in the first decade of the 1800s and continued until the 1820-30s, when a universally enforced, slave-sanctioning consensus carried the day.

"THEM COOKS WERE ROUGH FOLKS!"
(Farmer Family "Servant" – See page 40)

Just as Joshua's 1908 memoir neglects to remember anything about his great uncle, John Murphy, he passed without a word over the post-Civil War in Kentucky, and the human costs inflicted upon its victims, on the larger society and even upon his own extended family. In fairness, he was in Missouri, but J.F.'s many numerous relatives were yet Kentuckians. They were present and were players in some of the more sensational and violent local events of those times. His family members are found both as victims and as aggressors. On whatever side, they proved quick to resort to the weapons at hand. Joshua's father William Cook had a brother, Wesley (?-

1864), husband of Sarah King (?-1892). Wesley and Sarah were the parents of numerous children: Elizabeth, Amanda, Martin, Zerilda, Addison (1846-Aug 16, 1871), Alexander, Simeon, Cynthia, Smith, Thomas, and Ella.

Under the heading, "The Death of Cook and the Disorganization of the Ku Klux Klan was a Great Relief to Many," a narrative of the killing of Addison Cook was published in the *Shelbyville Record*, in 1917:

In 1870 and 1871 there was an organized band of lawless men in [Shelby] county, who operated principally in the northern and northeastern part of the county. The organization was known as the Ku Klux Klan, and members of it whose homes were in the vicinity of Bagdad, Consolation and Jacksonville, were suspected of being the parties who assaulted and beat a colored mail agent, in the early part of 1871, while in his mail car, that was then standing on the railroad track near Benson Station. The local authorities were helpless, for the reason that the people of the vicinity where the outrages occurred were afraid to give information that would lead to the arrest of the guilty parties, knowing that if they did so that the vengeance of the Ku Klux Klan would fall heavily upon them.

After the assault had been made on the negro mail agent, the Government officials took the matter in hand and a company of U.S. soldiers was sent to Bagdad in the spring of 1871. This company was Troop 1 of the Seventh Cavalry, Capt. Miles W. Keogh, commanding. The company was stationed at Bagdad for several months, when it moved to Shelbyville, into quarters in a brick livery stable that stood then, at 8th and Main streets, owned by Mr. James L. Long. By the way, this company remained in Shelbyville a couple of years and went from here to Lebanon, and from there out West. Out there it was a part of General Custer's command, that was massacred by the Indians, Capt. Keogh and all of his men, as well as Gen. Custer, and many others, being killed.

It was while the soldiers were at Bagdad that a tragedy occurred within a half-mile of that town, and the trial of the defendant, on a charge of murder, was one of the most interesting and hard-fought in the history of the county. The defendant in the case was Hiram Bohannon, a reputable citizen, and the man whom he killed was Addison Cook, a reckless dare-devil, and the alleged leader of the Ku Klux Klan. There had been hard feelings between the men for some time, for the reason that some one had told Cook that Bohannon had said that he (Cook) had proposed to the Government to give the Klan away for $20,000, and Cook had threatened to kill Bohannon, on numerous occasions. On the morning of August 15th, 1871, Bohannon went to a point about half-way between Bagdad and Consolation, with his shotgun, loaded with buckshot, and waited for Cook, whom he knew would go that morning from Consolation to Bagdad. There were no eye-witnesses to the killing, but the circumstantial evidence that Bohannon had killed Cook was strong, and he never denied it at any time. Both loads of buck-shot were fired and Cook was killed instantly, his head being nearly shot off. It is doubtful if he knew who shot him, as his death was instantaneous.

Mr. James White, who was less than a half-mile from the scene of the tragedy, heard the gunshots and a few minutes later met Bohannon, who told him he had just shot "a d--n thief." Mr. White went to where Cook's body was lying, beside the railroad track, with his head in the water of a ditch. Cook was dead, and a loaded revolver was in his pocket. Willie Connell, a small boy living in the neighborhood, saw Bohannon get out of his father's cornfield, with a gun, and a few minutes later, heard the gun-shots. He ran over to the place where the killing occurred, arriving there nearly as soon as Mr. White. They and a section hand who came along a few minutes later, took the body of the man out of the ditch and laid it on the bank, and then gave information of the tragedy. (The Willie Connell here mentioned is the well-known Shelbyville stock dealer.)

Squire G. W. Demaree, who lived at Christiansburg, about three miles away, was called, and after holding the inquest issued a warrant for the arrest of

Hiram Bohannon. The warrant was given to Deputy Sheriff H. T. Montfort, who arrested Bohannon and took him to his (Montfort's) home that night. During the night a crowd of men went to Montfort's house, to mob Bohannon, but they were frightened away before they could accomplish their purpose. The next day, fearing trouble for his prisoner, he took him to the soldiers' camp, where he was kept that night in safety from the gang of Ku Klux, who wanted to get hold of the man who had killed their leader. The next day, accompanied by a detail of soldiers, Montfort brought Bohannon to Shelbyville and turned him over to County Judge Erasmus Frazier. On August 17th, the examining trial was held before Judge Frazier, and Bohannon was committed to the custody of Jailer I. A. Payne, to be held until the following term of Circuit Court.

Bohannon was indicted on a charge of murder, by the grand jury, on the first day of the term, and his trial was set for a few days later, at that term. Five days were taken up by the trial, and all during it there was a fight for legal points by Robinson, Foree and Major, for the defendant, and Phil Lee, the Commonwealth's Attorney. On the fifth day (Oct. 12th) after hearing the evidence and arguments and devoting nearly two days to a consideration of the case the jury brought in a verdict of "guilty as charged in the indictment."

On the following day a motion for a new trial was made, but the motion was overruled, and an appeal to the Court of Appeals was asked and granted. On the following day Hon. H. W. Bruce, then the Circuit Judge of this district, in open court, asked Mr. Bohannon if he had anything to say as to why he should not be punished in accordance with the law and the verdict of the jury. The writer, who was present, remembers distinctly the appearance of the venerable looking, bearded old man, as he stood up to answer Judge Bruce. He did not seem to be the least excited and simply said: 'Judge, I have nothing to say, except there have been many lies told in this trial, and if I had not killed Addison Cook that day, he would have killed me before this.' He then sat down and Judge

Bruce sentenced him "to be hanged until he is dead" on Friday, Dec. 29th, 1871.

Bohannon's attorneys got busy immediately, and prepared an appeal to the Court of Appeals. On Dec. 23rd the higher court rendered a decision reversing the lower court and remanded the case for retrial. A copy of the decision was taken by Bohannon's attorneys to Judge Bruce, in Louisville, and an order was made that the defendant, who had been in jail four months, might be liberated from custody upon his giving a good and sufficient bond in the sum of $10,000 for his appearance at the next succeeding term of the Shelby Circuit Court. The bond was given with N. Flood, Leroy Kestler (sic) and Benjamin Scroggins as sureties, and Bohannon reached his own home in time to celebrate Christmas with his relatives and friends.

At the March term, 1872, the decision of the Court of Appeals was ordered to record, and the case of the Commonwealth vs. Bohannon was continued to the September term. At that time, upon a motion of the Commonwealth's Attorney, the case was dismissed. Mr. Bohannon lived many years, a respected and highly esteemed citizen. After the death of Addison Cook there was evidently an end to Ku Kluxism, for no more trouble came to the people of that vicinity. At the trial of several young men charged with the assault of the negro mail agent it was demonstrated that Addison Cook, then dead, was the guilty party and nothing further was done about it.

During the troublous times, good citizens of that vicinity suffered much by mistreatment at the hands of the Ku Klux and from threats that were made. Addison Cook, upon one occasion, ran a man by the name of "Chick" Johnson out of the town of Bagdad, threatening to kill him. His action did not meet with the approval of good citizens, and some of them did not hesitate to express their indignation at such proceedings. Among these was Mr. W. C. Baskett, a farmer who lived near Bagdad. A few days before Cook was killed, Mr. Baskett received note which read as follows:

> *Headquarters K. K. K.*
> *General Order No. 5*
> *Mr. W. C. Baskett:*
> *If it appears on examination that you and "Jim" White are connected with W. C. Johnson, in any shape, manner or form, whatever, you had better prepare for leaving this country forever.*
> *Respectfully, KU KLUX KLAN*
> *P.S. - Contempt of this notice is death. Respectfully, ETC.*

The death of Cook and the disorganization of the Ku Klux Klan was a great relief to many, who felt that their lives and property were in danger.

Hiram Bohannon (1846-1912), the man who shot and killed Addison Cook was the son of William (Henry?) Bohannon, Justice of the Peace of Shelby County, who was the son of John Bohannon (1755-?) and Helen Cook. Helen was the sister of Abraham Cook (Joshua's grandfather) and the aunt of Addison Cook's father; Helen was, then, Addison's great aunt as well as Hiram Bohannon's great grandmother. Addison Cook and his killer, Hiram Bohannon, were second cousins. Addison was a first cousin to **Joshua Flood Cook**.

FROM STRENGTH TO STRENGTH

From 1859 until his retirement in 1900, J.F. Cook went from strength to strength in a respectable career. His success was dependent upon intelligence, amiability and administrative skills but also upon a cool talent for putting at their ease other stakeholders in the society in which he thrived. His call for "wise" and "most conservative" action as to relations between the races was intended to dispel any faint anxiety that J. F. Cook, in his role as preacher and educator, might leverage his influence in the interests of some kind of dangerous racial or social reform.

The personal style Joshua discovered by his mid twenties, if not earlier, that worked well for him in his long public life, was to divide things between the abstract and the practical. In the abstract, slavery was of course wrong; but as a practical matter, the slaves, at least those in Kentucky and certainly those held by *his* family, were uniformly happy even while they were lamentably disadvantaged by their inherent low intelligence, that tragic mark upon the race of Ham.

The interplay between abstraction and actual life was revealed to Joshua in other ways. Strong drink was a moral danger, against which he energetically worked to protect his LaGrange College students. But in the romanticized Kentucky of Joshua's youth, whiskey needed to be plentiful. In old age, Joshua recalls such events as a corn shucking or a hog-killing, when home-brew was omnipresent. On these occasions, everything was done in good fun and, any way, it was just "the negroes," those poor creatures of low intelligence, who thought Joshua's dad was drunk when he shot a pig in the face, not to kill it but to hear it squeal. Everyone laughed at his father's pranks and jests, Joshua recalled seventy years later, even if the antics involved liquor, gunfire and the maiming of slaughter animals. *Them Cooks were rough folks!*

In actual fact, Joshua's idyllically-remembered boyhood home seems to have been destroyed when his father died and his mother re-married. In the last letter he wrote - to his son, Cecil - Joshua confessed (for the first time and only time?) that the anxieties he displayed in adolescence caused those close to him (his mother? his step-father?) to consider sending him to an asylum of some kind.

The youthful Joshua Cook, mired in the blacksmith shop for three years, was helpless to prevent the downward turn in his personal prospects. His father had died. This was an abandonment young Joshua could not repair. He could not ever again look to that source for counsel or support. My conclusion is that this circumstance caused a

Joshua Flood Cook

terror within Joshua, a terror of losing his one chance out of the smithy's shop: an education. Fear of becoming trapped in a harsh and limiting trade seems to have become the engine used by the self-confident and engaging J. F. Cook to launch himself into the wider world.

Returned from Missouri, finally in college, and apparently unwelcome in his step-father's home (or unwilling to live in it), young Joshua visited in the homes of his socially important college chums, whose fathers could help him into important connections. No doubt he made the most of his contacts in Missouri, forged when he was in high school, living in the home of uncle Noah Flood. How else could Joshua have been plucked from Kentucky by Missouri Baptists to operate a college?

J. F. Cook was a survivor and more than that. He was a career winner in a region devastated by enslavement, civil war, and economic and social turmoil. His memoir is testimony to his survival and, if read carefully, indicates how he was able to pull it off. Joshua's ambition, tenacity, and expressions of love to his children are admirable and positive traits of character, and may serve as examples to descendents, even if his narrow social theories cannot.

Knowing he was dying, Joshua, in 1912, wrote a loving, last letter to his youngest son, Cecil ("My precious Boy"), then 41 years old. Fortunate to have such an affectionate, affirmative statement from our ancestor, we give Joshua Flood Cook the last word.

"As a grandfather if possible I grow more affectionate. I love all my children as my own soul and D__ [wife, Drucilla] as a part of myself body and soul. I believe man and wife are one and in everything & praying for you and yours - Blanche & Dorland as one body. I think I pray for you one hundred times or more a week. Some nights I hear the clock strike every hour and 1/2 hour for ten hours. I just lie and try to sleep but fail. I always remember you at times you preach - earnestly <u>every</u> Sunday...

I have lain down & rested & I want to close this with every expression of love. I do <u>love you</u> and thank you *for your constant love and goodness to me. God bless you and yours always. My prayers to my dying hour will be for you and should I get to heaven and if it is possible I will be praying for you there. Dear little Howard and I have a prayer service every night. - he prays sweetly "for all our dear ones" often by name - "for forgiveness of sins - to be kept from sin and that in the 'sweet by and by' we may meet on the beautiful shore" - I am doing my best to direct him heavenward - sometimes, often he closes – 'may we light in that beautiful world at last.'*

> *Good bye*
> *Bushels of love to all,*
> *Daddy"*

SOURCES:

Joshua F. Cook, Cook family, and Susan G Framer genealogy, generally: Betty Taylor Cook's unpublished genealogy book, and her notes.

Joshua Cook's career in LaGrange Missouri: in addition to Betty Taylor Cook's materials, see **History of Lewis, Clark, Knox and Scotland Counties, Missouri** (1887), Reprinted, Stevens Publishing Co, Astoria, Illinois 61501, pages 731-A to 732-AJ. and made available through the generosity of Farmer descendent Carolyn Farmer Wickens.

For Cook and Farmer genealogy: See Ellery Farmer, **A Farmer Book**, an essential source, which has been generously posted in its entirety on the web. geocities.com/Heartland/Flats/7314/Farmer/ekam.

The present review of Joshua's life relies not only on J.F. Cook's 1908 **Old Kentucky** but is indebted to the researches conducted and generously shared by J.F. Cook's first cousin, twice removed, Charles L. Cook, of Lexington, KY. Please see ancestorstories.org. Another invaluable internet-based repository is the creation of Gary Kueber. Gary's well documented archive can be consulted with profit. Gary, a first cousin of Joshua Cook, four times removed, has traced dozens of family lines. Please consult: kueber.us/.

For the life and career of the opponent of slavery and Cook relative, John Murphy: Elizabeth L Nichols, **Cook, Murphy, Hodges: Families of Early Virginia in the Ancestry of Elizabeth L Nichols** (2004, privately printed). Elizabeth Nichols, an expert and highly professional genealogist, has relied on a number of earlier sources for her John Murphy data, including (for John Murphy's 1810 letter) **History of the Rev. William Murphy and his Descendants, 1798-1818** by Alice Murphy Sturgess (1918), which has been posted at pastracks.com / Murphy /murphytoc) and Spencer's **History of Kentucky Baptists From 1769-1885** (1886, vol I, page 387).

Much of the Cook material posted by Gary Kueber (see above) was created by William L Scroggins. The narrative of the killing of Addison Cook (reproduced here) has been published on line at kueber.us/, provided by Scroggins. Bill Scroggins cites as his source, **Some Old Time History of Shelbyville and Shelby County**, Ed. D. Shinnick, (columns from the *Shelby Record*, 1916-18) reprinted by Blue Grass Press, Frankfort, 1974.

For biographical information concerning J.F. Cook's activities in Missouri: See **The Baptist Encyclopedia** (Philadelphia: Louis W. Everts, 1881, William Carthcart, Editor, p. 272) and **Hannibal-LaGrange College History** by J. Hurley & Roberta Hasgood, 1995, p. 130; both made available by the generosity of Charles L. Cook.

Additional biographical information: **History of Lewis, Clark, Knox and Scotland Counties, Missouri** (1887), Reprinted, Stevens Publishing Co, Astoria, Illinois 61501, pages 731-A to 732-AJ., and made available through the generosity of Farmer descendent, Carolyn Farmer Wickens.

Some biographical details, especially concerning Susan Good Farmer Cook, may be found in a LaGrange *Democrat* obituary of her, preserved by Betty Cook and also provided generously by Farmer descendent and skilled genealogist Carolyn Farmer Wickens.

Additional J.F. Cook biographical details taken from "Dr. Joshua Flood Cook Years, 1866-1896," **Hannibal LaGrange College History**, J. Hurley and Roberta Hasgood (Marcelene, MO. Jostens: 1995, Chapter 2, made available to me by the generosity of Charles L. Cook. See also **History of Missouri Baptists**, J. R. Douglass, Kansas City: Western Publishing Company, 1934, pages 507-09, also shared by Charles L. Cook. (See source notes, above.)

For the "Abstract of College Laws" see **Frontiers, the Story of the Missouri Baptist Convention**, J. Gordon Kingsley, Jefferson City MO: Missouri Baptist Historical Commission, 1983, page 89, available through the generosity of Charles L. Cook.

WE STILL LOVE OUR BRITISH KEN

No people were so cruel to us as were the British. They armed the Indians and made them their allies in every cruelty [. . .] the English leaders incited the Indians to every beastly crime. They even came into Kentucky, against which they had the greatest grudge, and murdered our people. [. . .] Independence was not really assured, though treaties had been made, until General Jackson settled the British at the battle of New Orleans. [. . .] George the Third had to hire Hessians, the very slaves among the Germans to fight his battles, for the English would not furnish the men, and for that reason we can still love our British ken.

J.F. Cook, **Old Kentucky**, pages 102-03

> *The mound-builders left their record, and some have been disposed to believe that the Indians are the descendents of the mound-builders. Some have supposed that they cam in after the mound-builders had occupied he country for generations and drove the mound-builders out, which opinion I incline to. [. . .] In 1876 I served as Centennial Manager for Missouri, and with Honorable Thos. Allen, a man of wealth and culture, opened small mounds in southeast Missouri and took from them almost enough pottery ware to make two wagon-loads. We could not tell the composition of the pottery, but the vessels were of various kinds and shapes, principally shapes of animals and birds. We determined these articles were put there to hold water and food for the benefit of the dead. Much of it was carried to Philadelphia, and from there it was scattered, I do not know where.*
>
> J.F. Cook, **Old Kentucky**, pages 99, 100

> *There were very few cases of typhoid fever, but one I remember well. A small boy, about ten years old, was taken with a severe chill; he was put to bed and two physicians, the best known in that part of the country, were summoned. They bled him freely, and the marks of the lance can be shown on his arms today; he was given calomel, wrapped up and kept warm. And from the time he was taken sick, the latter part of February, till he began to recover, the first part of June, he had not one drink of cool water, nor was he thoroughly bathed. He became a living skeleton, and had it not been, seemingly, for a special providence, he would not be worrying you with this foolishness today.*
>
> J.F. Cook, **Old Kentucky**, page 133

Revival Grows in Interest Daily
Dr. Cook Preaching to Increasing Crowds

Few people have a happier life than a minister has, but what is it that puts a stab into the soul? I often wonder what my people would do if they knew what I know about them. How would you feel if you saw your beautiful wife and another beginning to drift? A year or so ago I saw a bride of a few months being embraced by a college student. What does God think of a man or a woman who proves a traitor to all that is high and holy in life? And then to see a boy of 12 or 14 smoking cigarettes causes the deepest pain in the heart of any true minister of God. He knows that if the boy keeps up this pernicious habit, that he is bound to be a degenerate or a thief, stunted in body mind and soul. [. . .] We say no one knows about me. But has God died? How would you feel tonight if God would suddenly write on your forehead exactly what you are?

Cecil V. Cook Sr
The Index-Journal
Greenwood South Carolina
April 14, 1925

"HOW SHE PUNISHED ME WHEN I DID WRONG"

William F Cook
Lucy Flood Cook

Joshua Flood Cook (1834-1912)
Cecil V Cook (1871-1948)
Cecil V Cook, Jr (1913-1970)

William F ("Billy Dick") Cook (1802-1850/55) was born in 1802 in Shelby County, KY. William's parents were **Abraham Cook** (1774-1854) and **Sarah Jones** (1777-1856). William was named for his paternal grandfather, **William Cook** (1725/30-1790), whose wife was **Margaret (Jones?)** (1734-1797). (For details, please see sketches, at pages 179 and 223.)

Billy Dick Cook married **Lucy Flood** (1802-1865) on March 27, 1833 in Shelby County and lived there the rest of his life. The five children of William and Lucy Flood Cook were: Alexander (1832/38-1844?), **Joshua Flood** (1834-1912), Mary (1836-b/f 1865), Abraham (1839-?) and Joseph (1843-?).

"William F." was listed as the head of household on the 1840 Shelby County census and was again listed ("W.F.") on the 1850 Census. "W.F. Cook" also appears on the 1850 federal census for Shelby County. William died sometime after the 1850 census and before 1855, when his son Joshua went away to college. (Joshua was not then living with his parents, in any case, but in Missouri in the home of his uncle Noah Flood.) William's widow, Lucy, married Thomas Brewer in November, 1855.

William is referred to as "Billie Dick" within at least some parts of the family. But what was Billy Dick Cook's true middle name? A grandson, Homer Martien Cook, inscribed the following in his copy of his uncle Joshua's book, **Old Kentucky**: "Dr. Joshua Flood Cook is the oldest child of my grandfather - 'Uncle Billie Dick Cook.' My father Joseph Cook was the youngest child." In 1945, Homer Cook wrote to **Betty Taylor Cook** (1918-2000),

"Grandfather Cook was William Richard Cook, and had a nickname 'Billie Dick'." Homer Cook must have assumed the middle name of his grandfather was *Richard* since his nickname was "Dick." But "Dick" seems to have been used in this instance as a shortened "Fredrick." Homer's "William Richard" statement has to be discounted because of the greater evidence for "W.F." which family historian Charlie L. Cook (in a private communication) has marshaled. Charlie has pointed out that "W.F." appears in all known official records (three times in 1840, 1850 census, three times in Shelby County Marriage Records) and that "W.R." appears in no such records.

William Cook impressed his son Joshua (**Old Kentucky**, page 65) as a traditionalist of home and hearth. "It took a year's hard work to get a cook stove into my father's kitchen and to the day of his death he contended that food did not taste the same as when cooked around a great fireplace, and I am of the same opinion today."

William seems to have possessed a rowdy sense of humor, influenced by whiskey. His son reports (page 66-67) that William and William's brother-in-law Ned Flood once shot a hog to wound it and make it squeal; "there was confusion, negroes and all laughing, thinking that the men were drunk. Of course they *had* whiskey at all these affairs, but I don't remember ever to have seen a drunken negro or white man at a hog-killing or a corn-shucking."

His son Joshua recorded (page 116) William's death, in a casual aside to a remark about how Joshua spent his college vacations. "When I was in Georgetown College, from 1855 to 1858, my father being dead and the family scattered, I had no home and I spent a great part of my vacations visiting around with my college-mates through the different counties."

Lucy Flood Cook (1802-1865) the great grandmother of **Cecil V Cook, Jr** (1913-1970), Joshua's mother and Cecil Sr's grandmother, was born in Kentucky in 1802. Her parents were **Mary Bondurant** (1782-1863) and **Joshua Flood** (1772-1850). Lucy married **William F Cook** (1802-1850/55) after they each had reached the mature age of thirty-one. After William died (between 1850 and 1855) Lucy married Thomas Brewer on November 25, 1855.

As stated above, Lucy and William's five children were Alexander (1832/8-1844?), **Joshua** (1834-1912), Mary E. (1835-64), Abraham (1838-c. 1844?) and Joseph (1842/3-78). The 1850 census lists "S" as a son born in 1842-43. This might perhaps merely mean *son*. For, as just stated, a nephew of Joshua, Homer Cook, has written, "Dr. Joshua Flood Cook is the oldest child of my grandfather - 'Uncle Billie Dick Cook.' My father Joseph Cook was the youngest child." Joseph could have been the "S" [son] recorded by a hurried census taker. Some informal records list "Alexander," but not "Abraham," which is an error. *Alexander* is a name lacking a long tradition in the family, which *Abraham* certainly has. But in fact, there was both an "Alexander" and an "Abraham" in this generation of this family.

Several Cook Family genealogists have actively traced these siblings. The following information comes by way of Charlie L. Cook, who has researched and coordinated the sharing of data among a covey of family historians. The four siblings, all younger, of J.F. Cook are as follows:

Mary E. Cook (1836–1864), daughter of William and Lucy, married Nathaniel Flood (1819–1897) They were the parents of Wesley Flood (1856–1933), Joshua D. Flood (1857 – 1950), Berry O. Flood (1859-?) and John O. Flood (1861-?).

Alexander Cook (1834/8-1844?) (2nd Edition NOTE: census & tax records imply Alex' death about 1844.)

Abraham Ford Cook (1839–1903), son of William and Lucy, married Sarah Ann Judy (1852–1923) and with her, was the father of Phillip Judy Cook (1870-?), William Lucian Cook (1872-1893), Abraham Floyd Cook (1875 – 1959) and Leon Aubrey Cook (1877 – 1922).

Joseph Norman Cook (1843–1878) son of William and Lucy, married Nannette Amanda Malvina Martien (1845–1911). Their children were Homer Martien Cook (1869 -?) and Joseph Norman Cook (1870 -?).

"SHE WOULD TAKE ME OFF BY MYSELF AND PRAY WITH ME"

Joshua Flood Cook recalled his mother Lucy as a devout woman, who knew how to use prayer to instill good behavior in her young son. Joshua writes (138) that his mother "was always kind and cheerful. I do not recall that she ever struck me a blow in anger; but how she punished me when I did wrong - she would take me off by myself and pray with me, and try to instill into my very soul the principles of a beautiful Christian life."

J.F. Cook, in his **Old Kentucky** memoir, provides little information about his siblings. He generally recalls the happy home of his childhood and also reports (page 180), owing to the difficulties with mail delivery during the Civil War, "my only sister [had been dead] nearly a year before I learned of it." The only information about his brothers this reader can discover from Joshua's memoir is the suggestion that they participated in Confederate raids in Kentucky and Ohio conducted by John Hunt Morgan. Joshua writes (page 163), "my only two living brothers were with him when not on detached duty." But which brothers? Ellery Farmer in his **Farmer Book** (see Sources) states that Lucian Farmer (1848-1893), as well as Joshua's brother-in-law [George Farmer; see below] "was a soldier in Gen John H Morgan's command."

John Hunt Morgan conducted raids (see above, page 64) between Oct 1862 and July 1863, when he was captured and imprisoned in Ohio. Morgan escaped and renewed his forays in 1864, and was killed on a raid into Virginia.

NOTE 2ND Edition: Joshua had three brothers but only two "living," as he said, during the Civil War. These two were Abraham and Joseph (page 165, above); Alexander had died as a small boy. (Charlie L Cook has supplied information from census and tax records, which tend to confirm Alexander's early death.) Thus the Cook brothers who rode with Morgan were Abraham and Joseph.

Joshua states that his brothers were with Morgan "when not on detached duty." This comment indicates that the brothers took part in Morgan's unofficial raiding activities. Joshua's memory of certain details of military affiliations and actions of half a century earlier may have faded by 1908, when he published his memoirs. But his information about Morgan is accurate. Morgan seems to have conducted both formal and informal sorties. Joshua may not have recalled or even known about all of the Morgan-lead actions his brothers took part in. On October 23, 1861, Joshua's brother-in-law, Willie Farmer (1840-1862) wrote to "Dear Bro and Sis" from his Confederate billet at Camp Jackson, near Bowling Green, KY, to say, "Uncle Abe [Cook] and Geo Farmer are about 20 miles from here. They belong to Morgan's company. I want to get a permit and go and see them before long. They have been in two skirmishes."

General William Sherman, in a lengthy Dec. 17, 1863 letter to Commander-in-Chief General H.W. Halleck had much to say about the kind of men, who rode with Morgan. Sherman's remarks are found in his memoirs, under the heading, "The Young Bloods of the South." According to General Sherman, these men are *"sons of planters, lawyers about towns, good billiard-players and sportsmen, men who never did work and never will."*

Sherman is just getting started:

"War suits them and the rascals are brave fine riders, bold to rashness and dangerous subjects in every sense. They care not a sou for niggers, land or anything. They hate Yankees per se and don't bother their brains about the past, present or future. As long as they have good horses, plenty of forage, and an open country, they are happy. This is a larger class than most men suppose and this is the most dangerous set of men this war has turned lose upon the world. They are splendid riders, first rate shots and utterly reckless."

SOURCES:

William F Cook and Lucy Flood Cook genealogy, generally: Betty Taylor Cook's unpublished genealogy book, and her notes.

Additional Cook family information may be found in **Old Kentucky**, by J.F. Cook (New York and Washington: Neale Publishing, 1908).

Addition genealogical information has been established by Gary Kueber. See kueber.us/, who cites (see Gary Kueber [http://kueber.us/p58.htm#i1154]) Eula Richardson Hasskarl, *Shelby County Kentucky Marriages* Vol II (1834-1878).

Details about the lives of Joshua Cook's siblings has been generously provided by genealogist and Abraham Cook descendent Charlie L. Cook, who has cited Hasskarl (see ancestorstories.org) and descendent Pat Sengstock.

Sherman's 1863 letter to Hallack may be found in Sherman's **Memoirs** (Library of America, 1990, p. 363).

THE SON OF HOSEA COOK (abt 1769-1792)

Fifty years ago a magnificent gentleman from either Indiana or Ohio approached me and said, "We are kinfolk. Your father and I were cousins." I thought that I knew all my father's cousins, for he had only two uncles living and I knew all their sons. I said, "Sir, you are not my father's cousin, as I see it." He replied, "Have you never heard that a child was born to the widow of Hosea Cook – the Hosea Cook who was killed at the massacre at Elkhorn – three months after his death?" I said, "Yes. I have been told so." "I am that child," he said, "the son of Hosea Cook who was killed three months before I was born." J F Cook, **Old Kentucky** (1908, page 88). For Hosea Cook, Jr, see below, page 182 f., esp 199.

"HE GOT SO WARM HE SCARCELY WOULD SIT ON HIS SADDLE"

Susan Goode Farmer & Her father John Goode

John Goode Farmer (1808-1871)
Susan Goode Farmer Cook (1838-1890)
Cecil V Cook, Sr (1871-1948)
Cecil V. Cook, Jr (1913-1970)

Susan Goode (1783-1864) was the sixth daughter and thirteenth child of **John Goode** (1739-1792) and **Sarah Brown** (1745-1812). Susan (Susanna) married **Benjamin Farmer** (1783-1837) on October 15, 1807 and moved to Kentucky with him that same year. They entered land from the federal government in Franklin County, at Farmdale, a hamlet named for them.

Susan's mother Sarah Brown, was the daughter of **George Brown** (?-1805/07) and _____ **Robertson** (?-?), daughter of **George Robertson** (?-abt 1795.)

Susan was born in the Skinquarter Section of Chesterfield County, Virginia, so named a century earlier as the "quarter" where native peoples gathered to skin their animals after a hunt.

John Goode (1739-1792), Susan's father and third great grandfather of **Cecil V. Cook, Jr** was born in Virginia Colony and lived there all of his life. After a long and emotional inner struggle, he became convinced that he must become a Baptist and then a Baptist preacher. He was baptized and then ordained by pioneer Baptist preacher William Hickman, (1747-1830/34), who baptized Goode into the membership of Skinquarter Baptist Church in Chesterfield County VA, where Goode was later made the pastor.

Forty years after his death, John Goode was a figure of potent recall in the mind of the aged William Hickman (1747-1830/34). On reaching ancient years in 1829, Hickman wrote a remarkable memoir, which he titled "*A Short Account of My life and travels, by William Hickman*

For more than Fifty years; a professed Servant Of Jesus Christ. To which is added a narrative of the rise and progress of religion in the early settlement of Kentucky: giving an account of the difficulties - we had to remember." (Hickman's apparently unpublished 1829 memoir has been placed in the Appendix to the present work.)

Hickman, born in Virginia Colony, early on resisted all thoughts of joining the dissenting and illegal society of the Baptists; he could not comprehend such a thing as total immersion: "I drew the conclusion they were like Sturgeons out of the Seine, wallowing in the sand." Finally a search of the Scriptures convinced him that "dipping" was the only authorized mode of Baptism: "One evening, being alone, meditating on the right *way*. I recollected Paul's conversion in the 9th Chapter of Acts. I took the book, and thought I would search that chapter carefully. If I did not find it there I would oppose the Baptists as long as I lived, but to my great mortification, Ananias says to Paul "Why tarriest thou, arise and be baptized;" I knew he was a man not an infant; I closed the Book and thought I would oppose no longer."

Of John Goode, Hickman wrote in 1829,

"There was a fast published by Congress during the war, to be observed throughout America; I think it was the 23rd of April, 1777. I appointed a meeting on that day at a neighbor's house, and there came out a large number of people; I think my text was in Joshua, 'Neither will I be with these any more, unless you put away the accused thing from among you,' It was in an orchard; the house could not hold half of the people; I did not think I had spoke with more liberty than common. At the close of the discourse there came up a heavy rain; I led the people to the house, singing 'Lord, what a wretched land this is' etc, the hymn being long, all that could crowd in the house did so. Some went in the out houses. I finished the song in the house and spent some time in exhorting from it, and then the meeting broke. There was a middled aged man of the name of **John Goode** *in the yard who applied to Col.*

Hankins to write his will. The Col. said to him, 'What is the Matter? John, you're not sick?' The reply was, 'I shall die.' Col. Hankins laughed him out of it. He wont home, slain by the Sword of the Spirit, his conviction was sharp and severe. He told us afterwards he neither eat, drank nor slept for three days and nights, till the Lord spoke peace to his wounded spirit. . . .

"A remarkable circumstance took place with **John Goode**, above alluded to; as I went out with my little boys to drop corn, on the roadside, there came a man riding up; he called to me, and when I went up to him the first word he said to me was, to tell how a person felt when he was converted; but instead of my telling him he immediately told me; he got so warm he scarcely would sit on his saddle. I invited him to the house, he said he came on purpose--his soul was alive. He told me I need not mention baptism to him, he said blessed be God, he was baptized with the Holy Ghost, and fire, he needed no more. I told him to search the scripture, and that would teach him his duty. . .

"This was on Saturday morning the Sunday week I had an appointment at Muse school house, a few miles beyond his house. I asked him if he would go with me if I would come by and take breakfast with him, he said he would with pleasure. When I went, he was sitting on his porch with a Bible in his hand; he commenced by telling me I need not say anything about baptism, his Holy Ghost and fire baptism would do for him. I spoke to him as above, for his cup appeared to be running over; I appointed meeting that evening at his house.

"After meeting closed in the day at the school house (it was the first time I had been at that place and there being a large congregation) I missed **Mr. Goode** till the people were nearly all gone; at last he came out of the woods. I asked where he had been all the time. He told me Mr. Branch, one of his rich neighbors, a church warder, had taken him out to give him some good advice, and it was to take care of the Baptists, for they preach damnable doctrines, and that they will not rest till they dip you. **Goode** replied that Mr. Hickman had not persuaded him, *only advised to read the scriptures. Ah! he said, that is their cunning. The above he told me as we were riding along. I went to his house to dinner and about one by the sun I began worship; a large collection came out, as it was a beautiful afternoon. I took 13 of the first verses of the 3rd chapter of John; you may expect nothing very methodical; the Lord opened the hearts of the heavens, and, I hope, was with me. . . .*

"Baptists in those days could be told in any company--they loved one another. The Church was called Skinquarter, and increased, from its origin. Many other circumstances too tedious to mention and great many valuable things have slipt my memory. This Church raised three ministers, James and Josiah Rucks and **John Goode,** the same mentioned previously, who was baptized with the Holy Ghost and fire. He stood out a long time at last, having received a lashing of conscience, nothing would do but he must be baptized in water, and afterwards he was very zealous for that mode of immersion. Now there were four of us in the Church that labored in the vineyard, the neighbors joined and we had a comfortable meeting house built. . .

"To return to Chesterfield again, Satan took the advantage of the three preachers alluded to above, and sewed seeds of discord among two of them; we were fearful it would be attended with serious consequences, but providence prevented; like the disciples of old, each wanted to be greatest. One of them named Josiah, the most meek and pious at first, wished to deal with, and was willing to exclude all that were superfluously dressed, once dealt with a young lady, the daughter of Col. Haskins, for wearing stays, they being in fashion in those days. He arraigned her before the Church--she was truly a meek and pious young lamb.

"I plead her cause and saved her. She afterwards became the wife of Mr. Edward Trabue, and died in Kentucky. But the said Josiah, after while became more popular than the rest, took to traveling, became dressy, rode to different counties, and was pretty much of a fop, as I was told, when I moved to Kentucky, though I never *heard anything improper in his conduct otherwise. He moved to North Carolina and married rich, and was thought to be a good preacher. I received one letter from him after he became rich; he wrote like a good man. Brother James, his older brother, was esteemed in the Church-- but was a long time confined with the rheumatic pains, so that he had to sit down and preach. They chose* **brother Goode** *for their minister. . . After the death of* **Brother Goode***, the church selected Brother Charles Forsee as their preacher; he is still tending them, and is very old. I have known him upwards for fifty years."*

John Goode was the son of **Benjamin Goode** (circa 1700-aft. 1764) of Henrico County, Virginia Colony. Benjamin's mother was **Susanna** _____ (?-?) and his father was **John Goode** (1680-aft. 1752), who lived on Four Mile Creek, Henrico County. John was the son of **Margaret** _____ (?-b/f 1679) and immigrant **Edward Goode** (1647-aft 1708). Born in England, Edward immigrated in 1667 and lived on Four Mile Creek.

SOURCES:

Goode and Farmer genealogy, generally: Betty Taylor Cook's unpublished genealogy book, and notes.

Additional Farmer genealogical records: **A Farmer Book** by Ellery Farmer (1955), on the web at geocities.com/Heartland/Flats/7324/Farmer/farmer

Ellery Farmer created a chart of the ancestors of Susan Goode Farmer, which he gave to Cecil and Betty Cook in 1945 and which contains much valuable information, including the Goode data reproduced here. In a letter accompanying the chart, Ellery wrote (from Orlando, FL), *"One thing I liked about living in Virginia was that I was close to the old records, from which I could dig out family history."*

Additional information concerning John Goode has been found in *"A Short Account of My life and travels, by William Hickman For more than Fifty years; a professed Servant Of Jesus Christ. To which is added a narrative of the rise and progress of religion in the early settlement of Kentucky: giving an account of the difficulties - we had to remember."* Hickman's apparently unpublished 1829 memoir has been placed in the Appendix to the present work.

> *Their appearance did not add to the devotion of the young ladies.*
>
> *In the latter years of the Indian war [1780s-90s] our young men became more enamored of the Indian dress throughout, with the exception of the matchcoat. The drawers were laid aside and the leggins made longer, so as to reach the upper part of the thigh. The Indian breech clout was adopted. This was a piece of linen or cloth nearly a yard long, and eight or nine inches broad. This passed under the belt before and behind leaving the ends for flaps hanging before and behind over the belt. These flaps were sometimes ornamented with some coarse kind of embroidery work. To the same belts which secured the breech clout, strings which supported the long leggins were attached. When this belt, as was often the case, passed over the hunting shirt the upper part of the thighs and part of the hips were naked.*
>
> *The young warrior instead of being abashed by this nudity was proud of his Indian like dress. In some few instances I have seen them go into places of public worship in this dress. Their appearance, however, did not add much to the devotion of the young ladies.*
>
> Joseph Doddridge, *Early Settlement and Indian Wars of Western Virginia and Pennsylvania* (1824; reprint, Parsons: McClain Printing Co., 1960), 92-93.

"THEY CAME POOR TO KENTUCKY TO BETTER THEIR CONDITIONS"

Joshua Flood
Mary Bondurant

Lucy Flood Cook (1802-1865)
Joshua Flood Cook (1834-1912)
Cecil V Cook (1871-1948)
Cecil V Cook, Jr (1913-1970)

According to Joshua Flood Cook's memoirs (**Old Kentucky**, page 59), his maternal grandfather **Joshua Flood** (1772-1850) was born in Virginia, did not inherit any part of his wealthy father's land in Buckingham County, Virginia and came "poor" to Kentucky with three brothers and two sisters "to better their conditions." And Joshua Flood succeeded, recalled his namesake grandson, "living in great comfort and happiness" by the time little Joshua Cook was born in 1834.

Joshua Flood, a farmer of the old school, preferred oxen as beasts of burden and refused to have a mule on his place. According to his grandson, Joshua admired Thomas Jefferson, Andrew Jackson, John the Baptist and the Apostle Paul. He refused to permit a cook-stove in his house. In declining years, he would arrange for his wife to ride to church in an ox-cart, with a slave, Daniel, walking along beside.

Joshua Flood was handy with his venerable smooth bore musket. Annoyed that his son-in-law **William F Cook** had deliberately shot a hog in the snout to make it squeal, grandfather Joshua, aged about seventy-six, ran to his house, got his weapon and ran back to the hog-killing grounds. He then shot dead the wounded animal, while both rifleman and hog were on the run. His grandson reports (page 67) the old man then uttered his favorite expression, "There is no devil, if I cannot fetch him down." Which means . . . what?

Joshua Flood's fifth son (and Lucy's younger brother) was given the arresting name, Noah Flood (1809-

1873). Noah was actually named for his father's brother, Noah Flood (1763-1818), who was born and died in Buckingham County, Virginia. This first Noah Flood had married Sarah Fuqua (1763- aft 1841) on November 30, 1785 in Buckingham Co. Noah Flood of Buckingham County VA was a veteran of the Revolutionary War, suffering a disabling wound to his right hand. His wife submitted an application for a veteran's pension in 1841.

Noah Flood, son of Mary and Joshua Flood and the namesake of his venerable patriot uncle, was recalled by his own nephew Joshua Flood Cook (**Old Kentucky**, page 60) as a Baptist preacher, very well known in Missouri. This is confirmed by historian W. Pope Yeaman. (See Sources, below.) In a book published thirty years after, Yeaman cited the exact date of Noah Flood's death and added *"In August, 1873 on the eleventh day of the month, one of Missouri's greatest Baptist preachers bid a final adieu to family and friends and closed his labors for an eternity of refreshments. Noah Flood was one of nature's rare works, one of God's blessed gifts of a man to men. He was Websterian in mental frame and power of thought, Jacksonian in will, Lincolnian in generosity of heart, with the candor and unevasiveness of a Cleveland. But above all he was Christly in spirit. He was unpretentious in manor and socially jovial, yet an exemplar of moral uprightness and Christian integrity. This man, though now dead a quarter of a century, is as frequently mentioned by the living as are many living men. In the Baptist homes of central Missouri his name is a household word. His sermons, his baptisms, his conversation, his genial wit and withering sarcasms, are remembered by hundreds who love to quote his sayings and honor his memory."*

In about 1851 Noah Flood opened his Missouri home to his nephew, Joshua Flood Cook. Young Joshua was struggling to get himself an education and Noah permitted the boy to move to Missouri to live with him. The Floods at that time lived near Columbia in north central Missouri, where Noah was pastor of the Walnut Grove Baptist Church.

Mary Bondurant (1782-1863) was born Sept. 28, 1782 and lived until April 30, 1863. Mary became wife to **Joshua Flood** (1772-1850) at age fifteen. They were both from Buckingham County, VA. Her grandson remembered (**Old Kentucky**, page 59) Mary as "possessing the sweetest disposition of any woman I ever knew." She told her grandson - her husband's namesake - that her best time in life was during the early days of her marriage in their "settlement in the woods." This was a one-room cabin with a dirt floor and round log walls. At night, Mary could look out and see the stars. Mary described her wedding bed with precision to her attentive grandson. "Her first bedstead was composed of forks driven in the ground, and poles laid across to the cracks in the walls, on which were stretched boards, and over these boards was made the bed."

We are grateful to Joshua Cook for preserving the spirited recollections of a late eighteenth century bride in Shelby County, KY: a little Huguenot girl no more than a child herself, keeping house in the forest with her young man. "During the day Grandfather would cut the brush and they would burn it at night, like two children playing around a bonfire."

Writing in 1907/8, some one hundred and ten years after the events described, J.F. Cook cannot resist adding that the nuptial happiness of his grandparents surely must have extended to their slaves. "I think grandmother inherited two negroes, who had their own cabin and were as happy as their owners."

Mary was the daughter of physician, **Jeffrey Bondurant** (?-?) and **Mary Davis** (?-?). J. F. Cook identified his grandmother Mary Bondurant and her ancestors as Huguenots, French Protestants. The Huguenots were driven from France in the seventeenth century. (See the Index, and in more detail above, pages 28-40) Many Huguenots, after a generation or more looking for an asylum in England, the Netherlands or the German "*Paltz*" (Palatinate), found their way to the English colonies, primarily New York and Pennsylvania.

A great migration of "German" immigrants began after London loosened restrictions, which had limited European immigration to English America prior to the middle decades of the eighteenth century. Many of these *Germans* were *French*, the children of Huguenot refugees, who had spent a generation away from France. The children knew they would never return and elected to begin anew in America. (An example of this pattern may be found in the Dornis-Diller sketch, page 269.)

SOURCES:

Joshua Flood and Bondurant genealogy, generally: Betty Taylor Cook's unpublished genealogy book, and notes. Also **Old Kentucky**, by Joshua Flood Cook (New York and Washington: Neale Publishing, 1908).

On Noah Flood: W. Pope Yeaman, **History of the Missouri Baptist General Convention** (E.W Stephens Press: Columbia MO, 1899), especially at page 153 for Noah Flood.

For additional information on Captain John Flood's genealogy, see hill-ky.org/flood

---

Proper . . . revenge and hatred

For the hideous, unnamable, unthinkable tortures practiced by the red men on their captured foes, and on their foes' tender women and helpless children, were such as we read of in no other struggle, hardly even in the revolting pages that tell the deeds of the Holy Inquisition. It was inevitable - indeed it was in many instances proper - that such deeds should awake in the breasts of the whites the grimmest, wildest spirit of revenge and hatred.

President Theodore Roosevelt, "Kentuckians and Bordermen," from a chapter he contributed to Joshua Flood Cook's **Old Kentucky**, pages 194-95.

*"TILL HIS ANGUISH BECAME
ALMOST INTOLERABLE"*

Abraham Cook
Sarah Jones

William F Cook (1802-1850/55)
Joshua Flood Cook (1834-1912)
Cecil V Cook (1871-1948)
Cecil V Cook, Jr (1913-1970)

    Joshua Flood Cook's paternal grandfather, the father of **William F Cook** (1802-1850/55) was **Abraham Cook** (1774-1854). Abraham was born in Virginia on July 6, 1774 and died in Missouri on Feb, 10, 1854. Abraham's parents were **William Cook, Jr** (abt 1730-abt 1790) and **Margaret (Jones?)** (1734-1797). They - or perhaps Margaret alone - moved their large family to Kentucky in about 1784. In about 1787/8, Abraham, future Baptist preacher, was baptized at age 13. William, young Abraham's father died when the boy was about sixteen if not earlier. For the next five years – until his wedding day - Abraham would have remained in his mother's home, farming his father's land.
    Abraham Cook married **Sarah Jones** (1777-1857) on Sept 17, 1795 and moved with her from Forks of Elkhorn to Six-Mile Creek in Shelby County, KY. There Abraham participated in the construction of Six-Mile (now Christiansburg) Church in 1799. Sarah and Abraham had twelve children, though two of these may have died at birth or soon after birth. **William F Cook** (1802-1850/55), the future father of **Joshua Flood Cook** (1834-1912) was Abraham and Sarah's fifth child.
    The twelve children of Sarah Jones and Abraham Cook were:
        Eunice (1798-1816/19) – married her cousin Hosea
            Dunn (1791-1862)
        Elizabeth (1799-1877) – married Israel B. Christie
            (1793-1877)
        Abraham Jr (1801-1884) – married Hannah Miles
            (1802-1855)

Prudence (abt 1802-1887) – married Jesse Johnson (1808-1852)
William F (abt 1802- by 1855) – married **Lucy Flood** (1802-1865)
_____? (1805-1805)
_____? (1807-1807)
Wesley B (1809-1864) – married Sarah King (1816-1892)
Sarah Catherine (1810-1890) – married her cousin Abraham C. Cook (1802-1893), son of Wm Cook III & Katherine Crutcher
Amelia Ursula (1813-1895) – married William Miles (1805-1885)
Elenore (1815-1897) – married Daniel Boone Duncan (1806-1884)
Hannah (1818-1851)

Abraham Cook bought 558 acres of Shelby County farmland from Charles Lynch on March 24, 1807. How Abraham was able to finance this purchase is not known. The likely source was wealth inherited from his parents, William and Margaret Cook who had owned hundreds of acres of Virginia land and sold the last of it when they moved to Kentucky in 1784. Abraham's grandson, Joshua, in his 1908 memoir, remembered his grandfather Abraham had enough land to give parcels to his many children.

Abraham was ordained a Baptist preacher in 1809, having been licensed in December 1808 by Indian Fork Church in Shelby County. William Hickman (1747-1834) in his 1829 unpublished memoir mentioned that he baptized thirteen-year-old Abraham Cook in 1787 at Forks of Elkhorn, Kentucky (not yet a state). In his memoir (reproduced as an appendix to the present work), Hickman says:

"About that time [1787] the Forks of Elkhorn began to settle, Mr. Nathaniel Sanders, old brother John Major, brother Daniel James, old William Hayden, old Mr. Lindsey, and a few other families had moved down, and as there was a prospect of a large settlement Mr. Sanders named to his neighbor, Major, it

would be right to get some minister to come down and live among them, which pleased Major, he being an old Baptist.

"They consulted who they should get, and having a small acquaintance with me, Mr. Sanders named me; this was strange, as Mr. Sanders was a very thoughtless person about his soul; however they agreed among themselves to make me a present of 100 acres of land; this was unbeknown to me till afterwards . . . I went to the meeting [at Marble Creek] and stated to the brethren the circumstances; they were for awhile unwilling to let me off, but at length they said if it was my wish, and for my advantage, they would submit. I then felt free and went down instead of writing. . . About this time there was a great fall of snow, and the balance of February and all March was very cold, but not to hinder the meetings; and in the course of ten months there were twenty or thirty obtained hope in the Lord; **old sister Cook's family**, brother Major's children and several of their blacks; no weather scarcely stopped us, and we thought but little of the Indians.

"When April came it brought a fine Spring and we began to talk of becoming an organized Church. Several brethren moved down from Clear Creek to preach to us, and help us on, and as well as my recollection serves me, there was a number baptized before the constitution of the Church, for brother Lewis Craig was with us at times. We went for help from Clear Creek, South Elkhorn, and I think Marble Creek; we got together, and, after due examination we were constituted a church of Christ. This took place the second Sunday in June, 1787, and they were pleased to call me to go in and out before them. . . I think in the course of a year, I must have baptized forty or fifty; **I baptized nine of old sister Cook's children**, and among the rest that well known **Abraham**, now the Minister of Indian Fork church, in Shelby County."

Abraham was described in a near contemporary source as "over six feet, very straight rather spare, dark swarthy complexion, large dark brown eyes, and black hair. He possessed a strong constitution and was very energetic. His bearing was dignified and commanding, and his manners gentle, affectionate and persuasive. His voice was clear strong and musical and could be heard at a great distance. He usually preached two hours at a time."

Abraham Cook was chosen pastor of four churches, Indian Fork, Six Mile (later, Christiansburg), and Buffalo Lick in Shelby County and Mt. Carmel in Franklin County. He refused any pay to preach. A Baptist historian, J.H. Spencer offers an explanation why Abraham was not ordained until he had reached the age of thirty-five. Poorly educated and with "a humble opinion of his natural gifts," Abraham resisted his inner prompting to preach "till his anguish became almost intolerable."

His grandson Joshua recalled attending his grandfather's services as a barefoot boy. Joshua said (**Old Kentucky**, page 94) his grandfather Abraham was a distiller of "a great deal of whiskey and brandy" but gave it up after studying "carefully through the entire Bible nineteen times." Not eighteen. Not twenty. Nineteen.

THE 1792 COOK MASSACRE

The teenaged Abraham Cook and his family near and distant suffered a great grief in the spring of 1792. Two of his brothers, Hosea and Jesse, were murdered in their settlement near Frankfort, KY. Two of Abraham's young nephews, sons of his sister Bathsheba and her husband William Dunn, fled into the forest and were never seen again. Abraham's brother-in-law Lewis Mastin (husband of his sister Margaret), was killed (probably, shot to death) in the same incident. The Innis Bottom Massacre was one of the last recorded Indian attacks in Kentucky. (For a likely reason for the attack, see 234-5, below.)

Many stories of the Innis Bottom Massacre appeared several generations after the event. They all contain elements that go back to the earliest recollections. At the same time, there are embellishments added later. The oldest recollections were passed down through descendent family lines and purport to contain memories of survivors. Among family historians, an informal consensus exists today, more than two hundred years after the event, that the two surviving women, who fought off the attackers, were the wives of the murdered brothers: Betsy Edrington Cook (wife of Hosea) and Elizabeth Bohannon Cook (wife of Jesse). Although many of the accounts collected and examined here contradict that consensus, my conclusion is that the consensus is correct.

Of the many records of the killings at Innis Bottom, a half dozen are worthy of attention. The first narrative that we consider is not the oldest but is probably the best preserved and has reached the widest audience. This is a description reported ninety-four years after the event by J. H. Spencer, in his **A History of Kentucky Baptists** (vol. 1, page 432, 1886). Other records under review here include the recollections of a purported survivor, Rachel Cook Murphy (1753-1832), as recalled in Oregon by her aged grandson, Ira Francis Marion Butler (1812-1909) and recorded in writing by *his* grandson (by 1909). An 1843 narrative (Dillard's account) represented as being directly from Abraham Cook, brother of the murdered Cook brothers, is examined. There is, as well, a memory from Sarah Jane Herndon, who dictated (1898) a story, told to her by her grandmother, Martha Faulconer Stephens (1767-1833). We shall also examine what Joshua Flood Cook wrote about the Cook Massacre in his memoir, **Old Kentucky** (1908), an account which features "Aunt Peggy," that is, Margaret Cook Mastin (abt 1767-by 1829), the sister of Abraham Cook, Joshua's grandfather. The earliest version published in book form (Collins, 1847) is also reproduced. Finally we will consider three interviews of elderly, early settlers, one of which may contain statements first made in 1798. All of these narratives (and more) have been treasured within the family and recently collected and shared by family historian Charles L. Cook (See Sources, below).

SPENCER'S 1886 ACCOUNT:

The Spencer narrative (**bold** added) reads as follows:

"About Christmas, in the year 1791, two of her [Margaret Cook] sons, Hosea and Jesse, having married, and one of her daughters having married Lewis Mastin, the three young families, together with three or four others, settled three or four miles lower down on Elkhorn, in what was called Innis' Bottom. Here they remained undisturbed more than a year.

"But on the 28th of April, 1792, the settlement was attacked at three different points, almost simultaneously, by **about one hundred Indians**. The two Cooks were shearing sheep. At the first fire of the Indians, one of them fell dead, and the other was mortally wounded. The wounded man ran to the cabin, got his and his brother's wife, and **their two infants**, and a black child into the house, barred the door, and fell dead. The **two Mrs. Cooks** were now left to **defend themselves and their babes** against the **bloodthirsty savages**. They had a rifle in the house, but **could find no bullets**. One of them, finding a musket ball, **bit it in two with her teeth**, rammed one piece down the rifle, and, putting the gun through a small aperture in the wall, fired it at an Indian who sitting on a log near the cabin. At the crack of the rifle he sprang high in the air and fell dead.

"The Indians tried to break the door open. Failing in this, they fired several balls against it. But it was made of thick puncheons, and the balls would not penetrate it. As a last resort, they sprang on top of the cabin and kindled a fire; but one of the heroic women climbed up in the loft, and threw water on the fire till she put it out. Again the Indians fired the roof, and, this time, there was no water in the house. But when did a mothers courage or resources fail when the life of her babe was at stake? Still remaining in the loft, though an Indian had shot down through the roof at her, she had called for the **eggs** which had been collected **in the house**. These she **broke and threw on the fire till it was extinguished**.

"Once more the **baffled and infuriated savages** kindled a fire on the cabin roof. This time there was neither water nor eggs. But another expedient was soon found. The jacket, thoroughly saturated with blood, was taken from the body of the murdered man, and thrown over the newly kindled fire. At this moment, a ball from the Indian's rifle passed through a hank of yarn near the woman's head but did her no harm. The **savages** at last retired, and left the young mother [sic] to weep over the bloody corpses of their husbands. **Lewis Mastin was killed** about the same time. The Indians were pursued, but they all escaped across the Ohio River, except the **one killed by Mrs. Cook** and one other."

There is little question that four and perhaps five murders (two or three men, two boys) occurred at the time and place stated. But elements of the story, as reported here, repeated in other published reports and enlarged in family lore, have grown into mythic proportions. One hundred assailants? The biting in half of a musket ball? The successful firing of such a misshapen missile from the barrel of a "gun" (certainly not a "rifle" with a bored barrel)? The dousing of an outside roof fire, from inside, with eggs? These features resonate as a tragedy heroically retold but not necessarily recalled by any who experienced it. This is a tale in which the grief of survivors, friends and kin is supplemented by details of extra-human exertions, projected upon events by later, approving generations.

Inquisitive family historians have collected some twenty separate narratives of the Cook Massacre. Most of these, like Spencer's in 1886, were created long after the events, and are based on a handful of published accounts (Collins 1847, Arthur and Carpenter, 1854). But there are three (perhaps four) accounts, reproduced here, which may contain contemporary recollections.

RACHEL COOK MURPHY / IRA FRANCIS MARION BUTLER ACCOUNT (By 1909)

The survivor's account, apparently told many times to fascinated grandchildren, was preserved finally in writing but not before it became somewhat garbled and confused about who is who. This is the recollection of Rachel Cook Murphy (1753-1832), as told and reduced to written form, allegedly, by a grandson, Ira Francis Marion Butler (1812-1909). Ira's maternal grandparents were Rachel Cook (1753-1832) and John Murphy (1752-1818) (son of the Rev. William and Martha Hodge Murphy). Ira was the son of Peter Butler and Rachel Murphy, named for her mother.

Ira Butler is said to have heard directly from grandmother Rachel that she was present at Innis Bottom on April 28, 1792. Despite misstatements about some important details, the basic fact presented is that Rachel Cook Murphy was one of the women in the barricaded cabin. Rachel could have been visiting her brothers and their families and, significantly, her sister Margaret, wife of Lewis Mastin. (The 1886 Spencer account omits any mention of the fate of Margaret Cook Mastin, whose husband, Lewis, was killed. Margaret and Lewis Mastin had been the parents of two children: Phoebe and Lewis Jr. In 1797, the widowed Margaret married James Hackett in Franklin County KY.)

Ira Butler was said to have written his own account but we do not have that version. What we have is this:

*"In his own handwriting Ira give this account which took place in **eastern** Kentucky: His Great Grandmother: **Rachel Cook was at the log cabin** of her brother Abraham in Kentucky during the Indian hostilities. The Indians came and attacked the cabin and **killed Abraham Cook**. He fell the doorway when he was shot and **his wife and Rachel dragged him inside** and barricaded the door. The Indians then threw fire chunks on top of the house til they set it on fire, the wemen then took one **pan of milk** and with **the blood** they could wipe up from the dead mans wound put out the fire. The old **Chief** then mounted a stump in the yard and facing the house slapped his hands on his breast and said "white squaw can't shoot."*

*"One of the wemen then put the gun through the port hole and killed the Chief. They had a **pan of bullets already moulded setting under the bed** but they were **so excited they couldn't find them**. So **they cut a piece off** and while **one bit off lead the other shot the Indian** and killed him. The other Indians put their heads to the ground as they thought they heard horses coming, so they all left.*

"(Grandpa said he always thought when he was a little boy that his grandmother Rachel Cook was the prettiest old lady he ever saw. Her father may have come from England; at least she was of English descent.)"

Cook descendent and genealogist Pat Sengstock has posted a comment, suggesting that this account "might serve as a classic example of 'the telephone game' and what poor reporters we human beings can be." She pointed out that the scene of the massacre was not "eastern" Kentucky and that Abraham Cook could not have been killed. Abraham, 17 years old in April of 1792, was yet unmarried and lived on for decades, farming and preaching in Shelby County.

Ira Francis Marion Butler, grandson of Rachel Cook Murphy, confused Abraham with his killed brothers - a mistake Rachel, sister of Abraham, would not have made. But to a small child, details about who was who and who was present, would be incidental to the idea that his grandma was an actor in such exciting events. The presence of Rachel at Innis Bottom is the gist and the importance of the Murphy / Butler narrative. But is it the truth?

Ira Butler, who grew up in Kentucky and moved to Oregon, may not have known Abraham Cook personally, but knew of him and associated him with an incident, which took place twenty years before Ira was born. Rachel's story, recast by Ira, suggests a plausible series of events as recalled by a participant. Rachel's telling, as passed down by her grandson, clarifies that the women did not bite musket balls in two but rather, "cut" lead and then tried desperately to shape unmolded lead by biting. This detail contrasts sharply with Spencer (above), which states there were not bullets on hand in the cabin, requiring a musket ball to be bit in two and jammed into a "rifle." But the Murphy-Butler re-telling creates its own difficulty about bullets by stating that there were some on hand but these could not be found because of the excitement of the trapped women. Nonetheless, Rachel's narrative, recalled by Ira and recorded by *his* grandson, sticks to simple facts. There is no mention of 100 Indian attackers. The roof is fired by tossing burning brands onto it; hot fires on the roof of the cabin are doused with milk and then blood, not eggs. The attackers fled, fearing the arrival of mounted rescuers. All these features are plausible.

The Rachel survivor narrative has escaped much of the sentimental and romanticized supplements formed during the nineteenth century, an era whose stories were marked by grandiloquent ornamentation. This narrative is not free of all embellishments – there is a "chief" of the Indians; there is a shot fired true in response to a surly insult. Of course, such things *might* have happened. That is the only opening a good story teller needs.

In the stories of the early Indian wars, as retold by admiring children and grandchildren of the first settlers, the course of the events are synchronized with the sensibilities of a later era. These later generations needed to discover cravenness and inhumanity in an alien enemy and heroism and innocence in ancient relatives. The enemy was described as a bitter foe, whose inherent depravity eliminates the necessity of acknowledging actual motivations, objectives or tactics. (Of course, it would not be difficult to see cravenness and cowardice in a surprise attack on peaceful families in their isolated houses.) The message in fond remembrance: our people were killed by savages for no reason other than the murderers' depraved nature. In the nineteenth century re-telling of the Indian wars, America learned to demonize her adversaries.

JOSHUA FLOOD COOK's VERSION (1908)

To speak of the motives of story-tellers does not suggest we may casually dismiss retold stories as untrue. We should cherish the oft' told saga and discard it only with the greatest caution, if at all. Joshua Flood Cook's great uncles Jesse and Hosea Cook were killed at Innis Bottom along with Lewis Mastin, the husband of his great aunt Margaret. The two little boys of Bathsheba Cook Dunn were also murdered there. Had they lived, they would have been Joshua's uncles. Joshua, late in life, wrote it all up in his memoir, **Old Kentucky** (1908, pages 77-79). But Joshua Cook's family ties to the event do not compel subsequent readers to consider his account authoritative, and it isn't.

J.F. Cook wrote that he obtained information about the massacre from his "aunt Peggy" who lived through it. Joshua wrote, *"This is the story as I got it from my grandfather's sister and from my grandfather, who, by the way was not there at that time but knew all the circumstances."* As his narration makes clear, Joshua intends his readers to believe he is passing along information he received from Margaret Cook Mastin (Hackett), his "Aunt Peggy." But wait a minute, Joshua. Your great Aunt Peggy died by 1829 (when her second husband,

James Hackett remarried) and you were not born until 1834. (Emphasis **added** to the following 1908 J.F. Cook account.)

*How often have **I heard her repeat the story** of the attack the Indians made upon the Cook cabin, in Innis Bottom on Elk Horn, four and one half miles from where Frankfort is now situated. In some way the account of that has been confused. I have not read a history of Kentucky in twenty-five years; though I remember the account given by Collins, an account which is measurably correct, and yet there is some little confusion in that and in recent accounts. In the Courier-Journal of October 8, 1905, there is a beautiful picture of the place where the Cook family was massacred. It was one of the prettiest scenes on the Elk Horn.*

*There must be some confusion in regard to the time when the old fort was erected, for there was no fort there when my people defended their cabin. As told me, after things settled down in Kentucky so that people could leave Bryan's Station, two of the Cooks, Hosea and Jesse, with a brother-in-law named **Mastin**, concluded to settle down on the beautiful Elk Horn. **Mastin** married **Peggy Cook, who was there and knew of the circumstances. Jesse Cook** had been **out hunting** and **was shot**, but they did not know it. The other **two were shearing sheep**. It was a **charming spring morning**, and they had cleaned their guns, and **expecting no trouble had left them empty** after cleaning that they might dry, as was **often the custom with us in Kentucky**. They were old flint-lock guns, and unless the priming was kept dry they were not reliable.*

***The women were cheerily singing some old gospel song**, when all at once they heard the ringing of rifles close to the cabin. **One of the men** fell by the sheep he was shearing; **the other man was shot**, presumably near the heart or through it, but he ran and fell in the door and the women pulled him into the cabin and barred the door, which was made of heavy slabs. The cabin was made of logs closely fitted, so as to need no "chinking" as it was termed, up for about five feet; then the cracks were more open so as to admit light and air. There was no crack large enough to put a gun through* *for five feet or more, and there was no way to shoot out without climbing up that high except one place, and that was where the facing was pinned up on the logs and had sprung a few inches in one or two places. When the door was barred* **the Indians made signs as if they would be very kind to them** *if they would let them in. The one who had stayed behind to rob the dead man came up, and he could speak some English.* **Aunt Peggy** *always* **thought it was Simon Girty**, *or someone he had taught some English to. They* **fired the cabin first at the door**, *try to burn the door out, but the women* **put this fire out with what water they had** *in the cabin. The Indians then climbed up and* **threw fire through the upper cracks**. *That was easily put out when it fell to the floor; but the women's resources were very limited. Once fires were kindled so as to endanger the cabin in two places, but* **Aunt Peggy** *took the bloody shirt from* **her dead husband** *[Lewis Mastin] and put that out.* **One of the other women** *[were there more than two?] broke up a hen that was sitting, and* **rubbed the fire out with the eggs**. *In their desperation they used every available means.*

After this the Indians drew off for a consultation and the women had time to think things over. The guns were there, the old powder-horn was there, but they could not find the bullets. One of the women found **a piece of lead, bit off a piece, chewed it as round as she could** *in that short time, and they loaded the gun with this, and when it was loaded she peeped through the crack at the door-jamb and saw the Indians out in the front.* **The chief**, *with his men around him, in order to strike terror to their hearts,* **told what he would do to them** *if they did not surrender; and thereupon* **the Indian sat down upon the body of Hosea Cook**. *Having dragged it up in front of the home, and* **proceeded to scalp him**, *being directly in the range as old* **Aunt Peggy said**, *she* **thought that God managed it for them**. *The gun was put through the crack and the Indian was shot squarely through the body. Women knew how to shoot in those days.* **Aunt Peggy said** *that when the ball struck the Indian he leaped high off the ground, gave a yell, and fell down dead. Though Indians are very brave when they have the advantage, when they think they* are in danger they are veritable cowards. They took the body of the dead Indian and threw it into the Elk Horn, and it lodged down against a rock, which is called Indian Rock to this day. By this time the women had **found a saucerful of bullets**, and **Aunt Peggy said** that, strange as may seem, **they hoped the Indians would stay** long enough to get a few more of them. But they left. **She said** during the whole scene there was not a tear shed, but after it was all over they took the bodies of their husbands and washed them and prepared them for burial. And the dear old woman said it seemed as if they shed tears enough over them to wash their faces.

This is the story as **I got it from my grandfather's sister and from my grandfather** who, by the way was not there at that time but knew all the circumstances.

One feature unique to Joshua's telling is the implication that more than two women were present in the surrounded cabin. If this version is accepted then we need not make a choice about which *two* women were present. There were three, or four: the wives of Hosea and Jesse Cook, Margaret, the wife of Lewis Mastin, and Rachel Cook Murphy. Before we can embrace Joshua's suggestion that there were several women in the cabin, we note some difficulties with his narrative. For example, according to Joshua, the man who was shot and ran to the cabin where he died was "Aunt Peggy's" husband, Lewis Mastin. No other narrative has Lewis Mastin in the Cook cabin; Joshua seems not to know his first name.

Joshua Cook's account suggests that he obtained his information from one of the three sources generally available by 1900, the published histories of Collins (1847), Arthur and Carpenter (1854) (a patent reproduction of Collins) and Spencer (1886). (See Sources, below.) Joshua also cites his grandfather, Abraham Cook, as a source. However, since J.F. could not have heard Margaret Cook Mastin speak "many times" about the Innis Bottom Massacre, but says he did, it may be that J.F. Cook never discussed the details of the incident with any of his elderly relatives. However, when he got down to writing his memoirs, he wanted the readers of his book to think that he had. Joshua had no direct access to the memories of his great aunt Peggy, who had died before he was born and could never have spoken a word to him. His assertions to the contrary undermine Joshua's credibility concerning his grandfather. It seems unlikely that his grandfather, Abraham, said anything to Joshua about Innis Bottom. Had Joshua actually received the story directly from his grandfather Abraham, would he have had to invent "Aunt Peggy" as a source?

Writing in the twentieth century, Joshua wanted to make certain points about the piety of his ancient ancestors and the low qualities of their murderers. He could not do so with authority except by claiming access to special information. Invoking a participant as a source, Joshua could then write that the women at the cabin "were cheerily singing some old gospel song" when the attack occurred. He could also invoke Aunt Peggy to state that God had managed the shot which killed the "chief" at the very moment he was about to scalp the dead Hosea. He could also cite Aunt Peggy in speculating that none other than the most infamous of renegades, Simon Girty, may have been there. On a roll, he could even have his Peggy wish, incredibly, that the Indians had not left until she had killed more of them. Finally, the attackers come in for a dose of racial disdain from Joshua: "Indians are very brave when they have the advantage, when they think they are in danger they are veritable cowards."

Our exegetical investigation is complicated by the distance between our Now and the Then of the 1792 event. It is like trying to figure out which are the *original* stanzas of an ancient poem or folk tune. You can never be sure, and some of the supposedly *later* verses may actually be better then earlier ones. But it seems a valuable exercise to attempt to understand what happened, and who was there.

If passed-down stories are dismissed out of hand as not historical, we lose sight of the needs the stories are intended to fill. A perhaps wiser and certainly more interesting approach is to listen closely for hints as to the motives of the story teller. We speculate as to what might have motivated Joshua to claim an eye witness as his source and we therefore conclude that Joshua wrote as he did because he felt he must. By 1907/8, Joshua wanted to elevate the family's tragedy to the status of popular legend and pious example. He also wanted to cast himself in the role of preserver and public voice of this signal, family event.

The needs of Rachel Cook Murphy, in Ira's telling, probably included a desire to dramatize her survival to fascinated grandchildren. Rachel (or Ira, for her) may also have wished to ascribe nobility and heroism to herself and to an unnamed sister-in-law. (Margaret, her sister, is not mentioned at all in the Rachel/Ira story.) In Ira's account, Rachel and another woman had survived a murderous encounter. But three young men and two children had not. All were close family members and all of the survivors were caught up in a vortex of grief and loss.

The paradox of hope through tragedy is the theme of grandmother Rachel Cook Murphy, who *survived* (in Ira's recounting) to tell her tale to a new generation. Life, as inexpressible gift, was the possession of the little ones gathered to hear Rachel's story of Indian Times. She had been spared; new lives had been born. She could tell her story with slight need for embellishment. Rachel had lived through the event and it was dramatic enough. Her story was one of catastrophe, a tale of destruction, the blasting of every hope and dream of lost loved ones, including small children, whose young lives had been wiped away in an instant of terror. But her story ended happily in Rachel's telling. She had lived. Her family had survived. The evidence of this was in the lives of the rapt grandchildren who heard it all from her own lips.

The paradox of hope and tragedy became, in the telling of old man, J. F. Cook, an occasion for noble legend. We are not surprised that devout Joshua has his ancient female relations sing a gospel hymn on that dreadful day. But Rachel's bare narrative is perhaps a more fruitful gift, a permanent signal of a hope that transcends loss. Her spare account found its voice in the garbled memory of elderly Ira Butler, way over in Oregon, who had been her grandson back in Kentucky.

But a nagging question requires an answer: was Rachel Cook Murphy at Innis Bottom in April, 1792?

THE 1843 DILLARD ACCOUNT:

Another narrative, which brings us close to the events of 1792, is one offered to the reader from the memories of Abraham Cook, the brother of the deceased Jesse and Hosea. This account was published in a Frankfort, KY newspaper, *The Observer & Reporter,* Tuesday November 14, 1843. The article is entitled "A Fragment of Kentucky History." Its author is identified as R.T. Dillard. The opening paragraph is as follows (emphasis **added**):

*"Mr. Wickliffe:-It you deem the following narrative worthy of a place in your paper, it is at your disposal. The **facts are from the pen of Rev. Abram Cook**, of Shelby County, a venerable, minister of the Gospel, and brother of the two Cooks mentioned in the narrative. I believe it has never been published, and it is worthy a place in the history of our State."*

Dillard then writes:

In the winter of 1791, a settlement was formed on main Elkhorn about three or four miles below the juncture of the North and South forks, by the families of Jesse Cook, Hosea Cook, **Lewis Martin***, Wm. Dunn, Wm. Bledsoe, _____ Farmer and the overseer of Col. Innis, with three negro men. There was also a single man by the name of* **McAndre,** *who* **resided in the settlement***. These constituted the whole strength of this infant colony.*

Their cabins were built about three or four hundred yards apart, in the woods, interwoven with thick cane and undergrowth, so that they could not be seen from each other. Thus situated, these young beginners in the world (for they were all young families) began to think of future prosperity and domestic happiness. The winter passed away, and the spring had commenced but nothing as yet occurred to interrupt their peace or blight their hopes of the incoming year. A lonely Indian, on horseback, had passed through the settlement, whom they regarded perhaps, as a stranger from some marauding party. For after he escaped **the idea of an attack never** *entered the minds of these new settlers*. Doubtless, he was a spy, who, after noticing the position and strength of his enemy, retreated to bear the intelligence to the wigwams, of his countrymen.

The duties peculiar to early settlers were being performed, and the whole colony was commencing the preparations for the ensuing crop. Some were cutting the huge timber trees, others were spitting rails and making fences; the log pile and brush heap, yielded to the flames which enveloped them. When on the 28th April, 1792, **about one hundred Indians** made a **simultaneous attack on the whole settlement**, in the hope no doubt, of laying waste all that had been accomplished by these settlers.

When the attack was made on the cabins of the Cooks one of **these young brothers** was shearing a sheep a short distance from the house, whilst **the other was sitting** by looking at his brother thus engaged in his business. Thus situated, they were fired on by the foe, concealed behind the fallen trees and undergrowth; and the elder brother fell dead; the other was mortally wounded, ran into the cabin and **fell dead at the feet of his wife and sister-in-law**. And now commenced a conflict unsurpassed by the chivalry of Greek or the Roman, **Two females, with each an infant**, in a log cabin; the **husband of one dead** in the yard; **the husband of the other prostrated in death** upon the floor of the hut; whilst the yell of the **reckless savages** made the forest resound. This was enough to subdue the spirit of the most resolute, much less of two helpless females.

The Indians now commenced the attack on the house by firing a discharge at the door: but being made of thick puncheon, the balls did not penetrate it. Then the tomahawk was applied, but with no better success. The women seeing that their fate was sealed, now resolved to sell their lives as dearly as possible, and no longer act on the defensive. There was a rifle in the house, but it was not loaded, and a pouch with balls, but, owing to some circumstance or other, they were too large, Unsubdued in spirit, the heroines **whilst the one charged the gun with powder, the other bit a bullet in two**, and finished loading the **rifle**.

An Indian had seated himself not far from the dead body of young Cook in the yard, **perhaps with the intention of scalping him**. At him the deadly rifle with unerring aim, was leveled by one of the beseiged women, and in an instant the red **man fell dead by the side of Cook**.

The death of one of their party inflamed the rest to desperation, and instantly, two **ascended the roof** and **kindled a fire**. This was awful! Death in its most horrid form now stared these gallant females in the face; but soon they extinguished the flames with a pale of water, as soon as it commenced to burn. Thus the contest continued for awhile, until the water was exhausted. Again the enraged foe prepares the fire, and the flames commence the work of destruction. But fortunately some **eggs** are discovered, they are **broken to pieces** in a vessel, and **the flames** again **stopped**.

Determined on reducing the cabin to ashes and the feeble, but dauntless defenders with it, they again apply the torch to the boards, and **a small hole is burnt in the roof**. Confident now of triumph they descended from the house top to witness with rejoicing, the conflagration, and to hear the screams of the inmates. But the conflict is protracted by an expedient unparalleled in the history of warfare. The waistcoat, **dripping with the blood of a dead husband, and brother-in-law**, is taken from his body and thrust into the hole the fire had made in the roof.

When the attack was first made **McAndre made his escape on horseback** in sight of the Indians. And in all human probability, the preservation of the lives of these women and children is owing to this fact. The old settlement was but three miles off: the conflict had been longer than was anticipated, the Indians who attacked the other houses of the settlement **had done their work and ran off**, and those which attacked the house of the Cooks might reasonably suppose, that soon the men from the upper settlement would be alarmed, by McAndre, and would rush down upon them. So **they** bore off the dead body of their companion and **threw him in the creek**. Not yet satisfied, as they retreated, one of them fired a random shot at the upper part of the house, or gable end, where one of the women in the loft acted such a *gallant part, and the ball passed near her head, passing through a hank of yarn.*

It was fortunate for the settlement, that the most of them were absent from their houses. **Martin was killed**, *but* **McAndre**, *who was in conversation with him,* **took Martin's child and escaped** *on horseback as above stated. Dunn and two of his sons were at home. The father escaped, but both of his sons were killed.*

The cabin where Innis's overseer lived was also attacked. The overseer happened to be absent; but the negroes were at home. One was sick and, was massacred, the other two were taken prisoners - one of which some time after returned to his master. Farmer's house was not discovered at all, being built in a thick piece of woods surrounded with cane and underbrush. After the massacre the survivors returned to the old settlement.

This narrative, published fifty-one years after the event, is notable for the precision with which the cabins are located in the settlement. These details probably come from Abraham Cook, who may have helped build the cabins. Dillard's record also contains flourishes of rhetoric - "*now commenced a conflict unsurpassed by the chivalry of Greek or the Roman*" –"*the yell of the reckless savages made the forest resound*" – "*Death in its most horrid form now stared these gallant females in the face*" – "*the conflict is protracted by an expedient unparalleled in the history of warfare*" – "*the heroines whilst the one charged the gun with powder, the other bit a bullet in two.*" Such high-toned composition points us away from the farmer-preacher Abraham Cook, who probably never spoke such florid words in his life. (He is called "Abram" in this account, said to be from his own pen.)

In fact, we know that Abraham Cook was not the writer. R.T. Dillard submitted the piece to the newspaper and he accepted authorship of it. In Dillard's telling, the adversaries are "reckless savages." Eggs are used to douse a roof fire set from the outside - after the arsonists had conveniently vacated the roof. There is a biting in two of lead to make a smaller bullet, which is then loaded into a "rifle." One cannot know with certainty if these details are embellishments contributed by Abraham or by R.T. Dillard but we can safely conclude they are embellishments.

Rachel Murphy, in the narrative credited to her grandson, added few such embellishments - and she was there. Allegedly.

Family historian Pat Sengstock has written, "I have always pictured Rev. Abraham as the press man for the story and the main person who brought it into the local folklore. He was well-spoken, commanded the attention of large audiences through his church communities, and is directly referenced as the source in many of the accounts."

My money is on Dillard as the early legend-maker. He certainly got some information from Abraham but then, all on his own, added the grandiloquent prose. Dillard got wrong some important details. It is an error to refer to Mastin as *Martin*. This is a mistake Abraham Cook was unlikely to make concerning the name of his sister's husband. The Mastin family and the Cooks had known one another for decades, from their years as neighbors in the lower Shenandoah Valley of Virginia.

Dillard assumed that because the event was remembered as a massacre of *Cook Men,* then the surviving women had to have been *Cook wives.* But if Ira's and J.F. Cook's versions are credible, they were not Cook in-laws, but rather daughters of William and Margaret Cook, and sisters of the killed Jesse and Hosea. From the versions of Rachel (Ira) and Joshua, it would appear that one of the women was Margaret Cook Mastin; the other was her sister, Rachel Cook Murphy. Joshua implies there may have been three or four women present, but dramatic effect worked better if the number of embattled women was but two.

Dillard worked hard to write out an attention-getting narrative of his own confection. He uses language that seems foreign to the self-confessed ill-educated Abraham, and inserts the flowery flourishes at the very points in the telling, where the *egg* and *lead* embellishments occur. In the interests of establishing his own credibility and getting his narrative published (in 1843) under his own name, Dillard offers as his source "Rev. A Cook," a family member of the victims and an after-massacre bystander. Dillard was neither.

Dillard gets his narrative into trouble by mentioning (as he had to) that there were several cabins in the settlement, not just one. But instead of saying he had no information at all about the fate of the occupants of the other cabins, he wrote, "*the*

Indians who attacked the other houses of the settlement had done their work and ran off . . . ." What work? Did the Indians kidnap or kill people? Did they set fires? Did they steal livestock or tools? Why did these successful attackers run off and not join in assaulting the surrounded Cook cabin? If there had been Indians who had attacked other houses and then "ran off," was there no one in another cabin who could have emerged to help the embattled Cook women? None of this is resolved in Dillard's telling.

The chaos of warfare may account for many inconsistencies, but Dillard's narrative is in more trouble when he states that each of the embattled women was the mother of an infant. This is untrue. Hosea Cook and Elizabeth Edrington were married on December 3, 1791. Elizabeth was six months pregnant at the time of the attack. Their only child, Hosea Jr (1792- abt. 1860), would be born in July of 1792, three months after Hosea Sr was killed (p. 168, above). Is this a detail Abraham, Hosea's brother, would have gotten wrong? Perhaps, after half a century.

Dillard also fails to clarify why, after visiting Innis Bottom with Abraham Cook in 1837, he waited six years before publishing an account, whose "facts" he says come from the "pen" of Abraham. A storyteller will fudge the details and Dillard is writing an adventure story to mark a fiftieth anniversary. He has his heroines and villains identified and in confrontation. Facts which do not fit his tale might simply be changed.

Abraham Cook may not have gone back to Innis Bottom very often. He was busy six of every seven days on his Shelby County farm and on Sundays at one or another of the churches in his charge. This may not have left time for much travel, even in winter months, even to nearby Frankfort. After Margaret Cook, his mother, died in 1797/8, most of his family had moved into Shelby County, where Abraham lived. Historian Merlyn Cook reported in his paper, *Our Ancestors,* that by the time of the 1800 census, the only two descendents of William and Margaret Cook with a Cook surname, still in Franklin County, were (1) Hosea Cook Jr, only son of the killed Hosea, and (2) Seth Cook, son of the killed Jesse. By 1820, both of these grandsons of William and Margaret Cook had left the area. (See p. 168.)

The absence of close family around Frankfort would have given Abraham less reason to visit Frankfort or the disserted (abandoned) settlement on the Elkhorn. He might have avoided Innis Bottom, the home place that had been cut out of the forest by his brothers, Hosea and Jesse. But this modest clearing became, a few months after its founding, not the hoped for homestead but the graves for their own murdered bodies.

From the final paragraph of R.T Dillard's piece, the notion is confirmed that Abraham did not often visit this sad, destroyed settlement.

In the fall of 1837, I visited the scene of the above narrative, in company with the venerable servant of God, A. Cook. **The cabin of his deceased brothers had fallen, and was surrounded with briars**. *He walked about fifty yards from the house and* **looking with much apparent anxiety** *about, at last remarked* **I am standing within ten feet of the grave of my brothers**. *But the ploughshare had often passed over the spot, where rested the remains of his slaughtered brothers. Being on the ground himself, in two hours after the battle, he pointed out various things that had riveted themselves in his recollection, and which the scene brought back with all the vividness of the transaction itself. Mr. Cook still lives in Shelby, beloved and respected by all who know him and one of his sisters-in-law was living a few years ago, and may be still alive.*

This final note explains some of the details Dillard has offered. The fallen-in log house was a structure Abraham probably helped to build. Standing there in 1837, terrible memories would have rushed in upon him. Present within a few hours of the deaths of his brothers, their murdered bodies were his responsibility. He could not pinpoint for Dillard the location of his brothers' graves because of Abraham's shock at their deaths, a sudden and absolute loss to this teenager. The murders at Innis Bottom would have brought down upon him a sadness never to be lifted in life. Numbed with grief, he helped bury his brothers, then searched the forests in vain for his nephews, then joined in comforting his mother, two young widows, and his sister, sorrowing Bathsheba Cook Dunn, whose two sons had been killed or kidnapped. (The two young boys were never heard from again; children's bones were later found, it seems.) All of this anguish would have rushed back upon Abraham Cook as he stood upon the ground at Innis Bottom in 1837.

Visiting his brothers' unmarked graves a near half century after their deaths, Abraham would have remembered Hosea and Jesse as the pals of his youth. Young men who were present to him for guidance and counsel, for a brief span of time, in the absence of William Cook, their departed father. But now, here was Abraham, an old man himself, returning to the open air slaughter pen, where familial hope had been drowned in fraternal blood. Standing there on the ground above the unmarked graves, Abraham was moved by what Dillard describes as "much apparent anxiety." Was Abraham crying for his lost brothers? For his lost nephews? For the ruined hopes of young wives? For the ancient grief of his sisters and his mother? For himself? Yes. He was a Cook.

COLLINS' ACCOUNT (1847)

Dillard's 1843 newspaper article seems to have been the first published account of the Innis Bottom Massacre. It was soon followed by others, with pride of place as a published book going to Lewis Collins' **History of Kentucky** (1847, p. 306-307). Collins (**bold** added, here) entitled his version of events "Female Heroism."

*The **facts** in the following account of an attack on Innis settlement, near Frankfort, in April, 1792, are **derived from the Rev. Abraham Cook**, a venerable minister of the Baptist church, himself a pioneer, now upwards of eighty hears of age, and the brother of Jesse and Hosea Cook, the husbands of **the two intrepid and heroic females whose bravery is here recorded**:*

Some five or six years previous to the occurrence of the event named a settlement was commenced on South Elkhorn, a short distance above its junction with the North fork, which, though not very strong, was considered a sort of asylum from

Indian invasion. About Christmas in the year 1791, two brothers, **Jesse and Hosea Cook** and their families, their bothers-in-law, **Lewis Mastin** and family, and William Dunn and part of his family, with William Bledsoe and family, moved to Main Elkhorn, about three miles from the named place, and formed a settlement in a bottom there, known as Innis Bottom. A man by the name of Farmer, with his family, shortly after made a settlement a short distance lower down the creek; and an overseer and three negroes had been placed on an improvement of Colonel Innis a short distance above. The new settlement was between three and four miles from Frankfort, at that time containing but a few families. It was composed of newly married persons, some with and others without children. They had been exempt from Indian depredations up to the 28th of April, 1792, although a solitary Indian on horseback had passed it in the night, during the preceding winter. The two Cooks settled in cabins close together; **Mastin and Bledsoe** occupied double cabins some three hundred yards from the Cooks; the cabin of Dunn was about three hundred yards from those above named, and Farmer's about the same distance below the Cooks: while Innis' overseer and negroes were located about three-fourths of a mile above.

On the day above mentioned (the 28th of April, 1792), an attack was made on three several [sic] points of the settlement, almost simultaneously, by about **one hundred Indians**. The **first onset was made upon the Cooks**. The brothers were near their cabins, one engaged in shearing sheep, the other looking on. The sharp crack of rifles was the first intimation of the proximity of the Indians; and that fire was fatal to the brothers as **the elder fell dead, and the younger was mortally wounded**, but enabled to reach the cabin. The **two Mrs. Cooks, with three children**, (two whites and one black), were instantly collected in the house, and the door, a very strong one, made secure. The Indians, unable to enter, discharged their rifles at the door, but without injury, as the balls did not penetrate through the thick boards of which it was constructed. They then attempted to cut it down with their tomahawks, but with no better success. While these things occurred without, there was deep sorrow, mingled with fearless determination and high resolve within. The **younger Cook, mortally wounded**, immediately the door was barred, sunk down on the floor, and breathed his last; and **the two Mrs. Cooks** were left the sole defenders of the cabin, with the three children. There was a rifle in the house, but **no balls could be found**. In this extremity, one of the women got hold of a musket ball, and placing it between her teeth, **actually bit it into two pieces**. With one she instantly loaded the **rifle**. The Indians failing in their attempts to cut down the door, had retired a few paces in front, doubtless to consult upon their future operations. One **seated himself upon a log** apparently apprehending no danger from within. Observing him, Mrs. Cook took aim from a narrow aperture and fired when the Indian gave a loud yell, bounded high in the air and fell dead. This infuriated the **savages**, who threatened (for they could speak English) to burn the house and all the inmates. Several speedily climbed to the top of the cabin, and **kindled a fire on the boards of the roof**. The devouring element began to take effect, and with less determined and resolute courage within, the certain destruction of the cabin and the death of the inmates, must have been the consequence. But the self possession and intrepidity of **these Spartan females** were equal to the occasion. One of them **instantly ascended to the loft, and the other handed her water**, with which she extinguished the fire. Again and again the roof was fired, and as often extinguished. The water failing, the undaunted woman called for some **eggs**, which were broken and the contents thrown upon the fire, **for a time holding the flames at bay**. Their next resource was **the bloody waistcoat** of the husband and brother-in-law, who lay dead upon the floor. The blood with which this was profusely saturated, checked the progress of the flames but, as they appeared speedily to be gathering strength, **another and the last expedient proved successful**. [What was the "last expedient?] The savage foe yielded and the fruitful expedients of female courage triumphed. One Indian, in bitter disappointment, fired at his unseen enemy through the boards, but did not injure her, when the whole immediately descended from the roof.

About the time the attack commenced, a young man named **McAndre, escaped** on horseback in view of the Indians, who, it was supposed, would give the alarm to the older neighboring settlement. As soon as they descended from the housetop, a few climbed some contiguous trees, and instituted a sharp look-out. While in the trees, one of them fired a second ball into the loft of the cabin, which cut to pieces a bundle of yarn hanging near the head of Mrs. Cook, but without doing further injury. Soon after, they threw the body of the dead Indian into the adjacent creek, and precipitately fled.

A few moments after the Cooks were attacked, **Mastin**, in conversation with McAndre near his cabin, was fired upon and **wounded in the knee**; but not so badly as to disable him. He commenced a rapid retreat to his house, but received **a second shot**, which **instantly killed him**. McAndre escaped on horseback, and carried with him to the old settlement one of Mastin's small children. **Dunn and two of his sons**, one aged sixteen and the other nine years, the only members of the family then in the bottom, not having been observed by the Indians when the attack commenced, **escaped to the woods and separated**. The old man made his way safely to the older settlement, but **the boys were** afterwards discovered by the Indians, and both **murdered**. One of the negroes at Innis quarter, being sick was killed, and the two others taken captive, (the overseer being absent). Of the captives, one died among the Indians, and the other returned to his master. The survivors of this infant colony were taken to the oldest settlement, and found all the kindness and hospitality so characteristic of pioneer life.

The alarm was quickly communicated to the adjacent settlements, and before night-fall, a body of from seventy-five to one hundred men were in hot pursuit of the retreating foe. The main body of the Indians, however, reached the Ohio and crossed it safely, in advance of the Kentuckians. A small party who had lingered behind and stolen some negroes and horses from another settlement, were overtaken on the succeeding morning, a short distance from the Ohio, by a portion of the pursuing force, among them **the venerable William Tureman**, of the city of Maysville, then a youth. The whites fired, and the hindmost Indian fell, severely wounded. One of *the whites imprudently rushed his horse through the tall grass to the spot where the Indian fell, when the latter raised his rifle and shot him through the heart. He then rose to his feet, and attempted to reach the thicket to which his companions had retreated, but was fired upon and killed, some fifteen or twenty balls having been lodged in his body.*

By 1847, when Collins wrote this account, it is likely that all of the survivors of the events of half a century before were dead. Possibly, Collins sought out the elderly and prominent Abraham Cook and from him obtained information. This seems likely, for Collins knows Mastin as *Mastin*, not Martin. Collins had other sources, which placed other people in the settlement, including Bledsoe and a man and his family, named Farmer. Collins relates that a coordinated attack began with an assault on the Cook cabin, which gave alarm to the residents of other cabins. Collins alludes to a "final expedient" as the decisive fire retardant at the Cook cabin – but he elects not to give details. Why not? Is it possible the final solution to the roof fire was the contents of a chamber pot? Why would Collins have made reference at all to this expedient, if he decided he could not be explicit? Does this diffident detail add or detract from the reliability of Collins' account?

Collins explicitly identifies the two women in the surrounded cabin as the wives of Hosea and Jesse Cook. There are no other women. Collins writes that Mastin was killed, being wounded first by a shot to his knee. This precise detail is accompanied by the information that Mastin died at his own cabin, not at the Cook cabin (as J.F. Cook wrote in 1908).

Where in Collins' account is the widow and mother, Margaret Cook Mastin? She is the central figure for J.F. Cook. And what of Bathsheba Cook Dunn, whose husband, William, survived but whose two young sons were killed? And what of the rest of Bathsheba and William's children? Should the presence of the two Cook wives (Collins account) be added to Rachel (Ira's account) and/or Margaret (Joshua's account) or substituted for them?

It seems probable that Collins got much of his information from Dillard's 1843 newspaper article, using it without citation. He then added new information from new sources, such as a mention of a certain William Tureman, who was active in the posse organized after the event. Collins' accurate reference to *Mastin*, gives weight to the facts of his narrative. He did not get that from Dillard's account ("Martin").

THE 1898 SARAH JANE HERNDON ACCOUNT

Another significant re-telling of the Innis Bottom massacre is from a lengthy written statement (1898) by Sarah Jane Herndon, who recalled, when a very old lady, stories told her by her grandmother, Martha Faulkner Stephens (1767-1833). Martha, the ancient story teller is a relative of **Betty Taylor Cook** (1918-2000), wife of **Cecil V. Cook Jr** (1913-1970).

Martha was a daughter of **John Faulconer** (1722-c. 1790/99) and **Joyce Craig** (1732-1812), ancestors of Betty Cook through their daughter **Anne Falkoner** (1769-1834); Ann(e) was the wife of **William Juett** (abt 1766-abt 1821) and the mother of **Ellen Jane ("Nellie") Jewett /Juett** (1789-1849), who was the mother of **Junietta Gouge** (1815-1846), who was Betty's double great grandmother. Punctuation and **emphasis** have been added in this reproduction of Sarah Jane Herndon's account:

July 1898

I remember when I was a little child and that was a long time ago, as I am nearing my four score years, sitting by Grandmother's knees, Martha Faulkner Stevens, daughter of Jossa [Joyce] Falkner, fifth daughter of Tailfera Craig [Betty Cook's ancestor Taliaferro (Toliver) Craig (1704-1799)] [who] first married Martha Hawkins [and] died in 1795, as she sat at the foot of her bed and leaned her chair back against the food [foot?] board knitting and telling me of Indian times [. . .] A little more Indian news and I am through. My grandfather John Stephens and grandmother Martha Faulkner were married in 1785. Was born in Orange County Virginia. [. . .] Six miles east of Franklin on the Lees Town road [. . .] He was plowing not far from the house, and Grandmother was out near him, when the news came that the Indians had attacked the

*Cook settlement, [he] throwing off the [plowing] gear jumped on his horse, **taking his gun with shirt and pants**, told grandmother to shut up the house and take the old gray mare and go to her father's, talking her child Benjamin in [with?] her - this was in the afternoon - and went **eighteen miles** and the only [road] was **through the woods** or rather wilderness **the trees being blazed**. Grandmother [Grandfather] got to the Cooks which was near the fork of Elkhorn creek a short time after the Indians left. [O]ne of the men was killed in [and] the other one (being only two) got in the house and helped the women bar the door. [O]ne of the Mrs. Cooks could shoot a gun but **did not know how to load** it. The **other Mrs. Cook could**. [T]hen bullets began to get fewer and fewer. One of them **bit the bullets into** [in two] and **kept up the firing**. The Indians then set the house afire. [T]hey had hens setting under the house, **so tearing up the floor, they took the eggs and put [it] out with them**. The Indians, thinking the man in the house was still living, left. My grandfather helped bury the brothers side by side in one grave.*

So good bye for the present.
Mrs. S. Jane Herndon.
Grandfather volunteered when was about sixteen years old in the revolusing work and served until closed. Also at Bryans Station. [. . .]
Copied by Lockett Smith
May 12, 1936

This telling, in the form we have it, contains, according to family historian William Scroggins, corrections in hand written marginal notations. It is of course not a contemporary record, but it has a contemporaneous ring: a rescuer, arriving on the scene, prepared to fight and die for his neighbors, could do no more than bury them. The Herndon-Stephens account has picked up the familiar romantic features, such as extinguishing a fire with eggs and the biting in two of bullets. But this ancient memory strengthens the notion that lead might have been bitten and eggs might have been tossed on a fire.

There is a suggestion as to the identity of the two women, who barricaded themselves in the cabin. They were both "Mrs"

Cook and we are thus presented with some options. Should they be substituted for, or placed in the cabin joining, Rachel Cook Murphy and/or (J. F. Cook) her sister, Margaret Cook Mastin.

What of the weapons of warfare John Stephens carried in his frantic ride towards Innis Bottom? The statement we have is that he raced on horseback for eighteen miles through the woods, following a blazed (marked) trail, *"taking his gun with shirt and pants."* Shirt and pants? It seems unlikely that Stephens would have been carrying an extra suit of clothes. But it is not hard to imagine the ancient Sarah Jane Herndon, recalling the household armaments of former times, and stating that her granddad rode through the forest, carrying his musket (not a rifle with a bored barrel) and a *sheet (*of lead) and *pan* (of musket balls, in a bag). Perhaps Lockett Smith did not know what to make of "sheet and pan" when he copied out the narrative in 1936 and so wrote down: shirt and pants.

FRANCES NELSON FAULCONER, INTERVIEWED IN 1844

There is another contemporaneous recollection worthy of comment. A daughter-in-law of the previously mentioned **John Faulconer** and **Joyce Craig**, has left us her memories of the Innis Bottom Massacre. This is Frances Nelson Faulconer (?-aft 1844). Frances' husband, Joseph (1757-1833), was a brother of Martha Faulkner Stephens (1767-?), whose account we have (above) and of **Anna Falkoner** (?-?), ancestor of **Betty Huey Taylor Cook** (1918-2000) (see above). In 1844, Frances told an interviewer (**bold** added with information added [in brackets].

"The Cooks lived on two of our houses in Fayette. They had gone down to Innis' Bottom but a few weeks. **Hosea and Seth were out shearing sheep at the end of the chimney***, when the Indians came upon them and shot them.* **Seth** *got in before he* ***fell****, his feet sticking out. Betsy (***they were both Betsys***) pulled him in and shut the door.* **Lewis Maston***, (a brother-in-law of the Cooks)* **and Bohannon** *were out plowing, hadn't gotten in their corn yet.* **Maston** *rode by his cabin door, caught up his little child (all the child he had) without getting down, by the arm, told his wife* [Margaret] *to*

hide, the Indians were there, & so **rode off** without making any stop. **She hid** and Maston's family escaped. **Bohannon was killed** and **his boy lost**, but the boy's bones (as they afterwards believed them to be) were found. **Maston died, & his widow afterwards married** and is now living down by Shelby somewhere."

Apparently, before moving to Innis Bottom, the Cook brothers lived in two cabins in Fayette County, which were owned by either the husband or the father of Frances Faulconer. Her narrative is valuable as straightforward, unembellished evidence (if any is needed) that killings took place at Innis Bottom in 1792, but Frances' memory is not reliable in many significant details. Frances stated incorrectly that Lewis Mastin survived. There is no doubt that Mastin died at Innis Bottom. Family historian William Scorggins has established that the deceased Mastin's estate was inventoried in December, 1792. Frances Faulconer is inaccurate in stating that Seth Cook was killed. Seth was not present and therefore not killed. Also contrary to Frances' recollection, John Bohannon (1755-1832) played no part at Innis Bottom. John was the husband of the Cook brothers' sister, Helen (1756-1837). John and Helen went to KY from VA in Oct 1779, settling at Wilson's Station (aka Fort Liberty). They never lived at Innis Bottom and none of their children were killed there. Notably, Frances' account strengthens the identification of the embattled women as the "two Betsys." Do weaknesses in some points make Frances' brief narrative wrong in all? We think not.

The two sons of Bathsheba Cook and William Dunn were killed, although their father William survived. The mother of the two dead boys, Bathsheba Cook Dunn, is not mentioned in this or any of the narratives. We note in passing that the deaths of their two sons may have wrecked the marriage of Bathsheba and William Dunn. We suggest this, even though Margaret and William had two more children together, born in 1793 (Ruth) and 1795 (Sarah). (Altogether, they were the parents of seven, including the two young boys who died at Innis Bottom.) In 1798, William was excluded from the will of his mother-in-law Margaret (Jones?) Cook, who directed that her surviving sons,

Seth, William and Abraham, as executors, look after their sister Bathsheba, paying her directly from her portion of her mother's estate, as Bathsheba's needs required. At Bathsheba's death, any remaining portion due her "be given to her Children only." (For details, see Index and the William and Margaret Cook sketch in this volume, page 223, esp. at 240.) Family historian, William G. Scroggins has documented that the Cook brothers bought a house for Bathsheba and her children even before they had fully executed their mother's will.

Despite important errors in the details, Frances Faulkoner has enough accurate, firsthand information to give her narrative significance. The killed Cook brothers indeed were married to two "Betsys." Jesse's wife was Elizabeth Bohannon (marriage: 1791, Woodford County KY); Hosea married Elizabeth Edrington (Sept 1, 1785, Henry County VA). Neither of the two Betsys had been mentioned by name in the other accounts as present within the surrounded cabin. Other accounts do mention other women by name. Margaret Cook Mastin is identified by name in Joshua's version and Rachel Cook Murphy is mentioned in Ira Butler's version. Indeed, these women are more than mentioned; they are the central figures of these two accounts.

Mastin's child was saved because (as Collins states) *McAndre* swept the child up onto his horse and rode away for help. In the Faulconer account, Mastin himself carries his own child to safety, while his wife Margaret successfully hides herself away. But since Mastin was killed, where was Margaret? Did she hide, while two Cook wives (widows), in another Cabin, held off the attackers? Joshua Cook's late (and unreliable) narrative is the only one that places Margaret in the pivotal role within the surrounded cabin. Indeed, only Joshua mentions Margaret.

POSSIBLE EARLY EDRINGTON RECOLLECTION (1840s)

Finally, there is a snippet of a recollection which might make sense of the fire and egg conundrum and much else. Family genealogist Pat Sengstock has transcribed and shared item 13 CC 187 from the invaluable Draper Manuscripts. This brief hand written page presents special difficulties owing to ambiguities as to its provenance. But there is an undeniably authentic resonance, which cannot be overlooked. The interviewer is identified as John D. Shane. The interview date is not known, though the number "98" appears at the bottom of the single page. (It is unlikely this date, whether taken to mean 1798 or 1898, refers to the date of the interview; John D. Shane is known to have conducted interviews with old Kentuckians in the 1840s.) Perhaps "98" was someone's best guess, a half century later, as to the year of the massacre. (Emphasis in **bold**.)

"Benjamin Edrington on the line for Franklin and Anderson. **Brother to Mrs. Cook**. Innis Bottom is on Elkhorn. The **two were out shearing sheep** at the time. One was killed, the other got in, in time to bar the door. The Indians then attempted to fire the house. The one woman then **pointed the gun to keep them from coming down**. The other put out the fire, 1st with **water**, 2nd with **milk** 3, with **eggs**, and then (lastly) said there would be plenty of men there after awhile. The Indians then went down and set on a log where one was shot.

"Ambrose White (Mrs. Church) was taken prisoner, shot in the arm. Was out five years and six months. Was then living in North Carolina. Had been out here looking at the country. Was in company with five or six at the time he was taken. His horse sprang between two saplings and dragged him off. Arm undressed til he got to the towns, e&c.

"Miss Ballard."

This item appears (to me) to be an interview conducted jointly with two women, a Miss Ballard and a Mrs. Church. The interviewer was asking one person (Miss Ballard) about Innis Bottom, and the other person present (Mrs Church) added a recollection of her own. The additional commentary is unrelated to Innis Bottom. It is a memory having to do with the Indian Wars in Kentucky. Believing this unrelated recollection was nevertheless valuable, the interviewer jotted down what he heard, on the paper in front of him, which had the Innis Bottom information already written on it.

In the foreshortened notes of the interviewer, Miss Ballard is shown to have indicated her source to be Benjamin

Edrington (1770-1850), whom she identified as a Revolutionary War soldier "on the line from Franklin and Anderson" and then as "brother to Mrs. Cook." It is possible Miss Ballard confused Ben with his soldier father. Ben Edrington was too young for the war, but his father, John Edrington (1734-1808), was a soldier in the war from Virginia, before relocating to Franklin County KY. "Mrs Cook" is a reference to Elizabeth Edrington Cook, widow of Hosea Cook, Ben Edrington's sister.

In my reading of this account, the attackers are said to have attempted to set fire to the house by throwing firebrands from a distance. The women showed themselves to be armed; one pointed her weapon to keep the attackers from "coming down" to the cabin, from out of the woods. Meanwhile, "the other" (it is implied, there were but two women) worked desperately to put out the fire on the roof by climbing up inside the house (possibly onto a sleeping area, or loft) and throwing any liquid at hand upon the underside of the roof, including water, milk, eggs. This was enough to dispose of the danger created by the thrown fire brands. Meanwhile, the woman who was armed shouted out to the concealed attackers, that "plenty" of men soon would be on the scene. Perhaps to indicate a lack of fear or to get closer to the cabin, or to come together to talk things over, Indians exposed themselves and one was shot.

This report makes a coherent connection between attempts to burn down the cabin by throwing firebrands from a distance and corresponding efforts to put the fire(s) out.

There is no mention here of the death of Lewis Mastin. This omission may be explained only by our speculation. Perhaps the interviewer did not ask about anyone but the Cook brothers. Perhaps the interviewee told only what she had been told by Benjamin Edrington, a Cook in-law, who did not mention another in-law, Lewis Mastin. (Interestingly, Benjamin Edrington's wife was Lettice Hickman, daughter of Elizabeth Shackleford and the Rev. William Hickman (1747-c. 1830) who wrote in his memoir that he had baptized "nine of old sister Cook's children" at the founding of Forks of Elkhorn Church in 1787/8.)

The Ballard/Edrington narrative reminds that we ought not assume that Indians knew no English. Indians and English-speaking settlers had been interacting for generations on the volatile, expanding frontier. This centuries long exposure to one another, was time enough for a rudimentary pidgin English to have developed. (The exchanges were so constant and complex that some recent historians have referred to colonial America as a bi-cultural society. I think this is overstating facts, which point to a collision of separate, opposing cultures.)

Along the Elkhorn River in 1792, it would have made sense for someone to shout out from a barricaded cabin, that help is on the way, and for people within and outside a surrounded cabin to trade insults. This report is devoid of any smooth embellishments, which appear to have been added later for dramatic effect: the singing of a hymn, the presence of a "chief" of Indians, an attack by one hundred strong, the biting of bullets, the smothering of a mighty fire with eggs.

This report implies that Elizabeth Edrington Cook was present in the surrounded cabin. But such is not explicitly stated. Was this detail left out because it was obvious? Or was it assumed, that Elizabeth Cook must have been at Innis Bottom where her husband was killed? Or was this second hand recollection, transcribed on the fly as people were talking, lacking this degree of detail?

This narrative adds weight to the speculation that the two women in the surrounded cabin were Betsy Edrington Cook and Elizabeth Bohannon Cook. We exclude the story teller Rachel Cook Murphy and the widowed Margaret Cook Mastin. The exclusion of Margaret Mastin requires that we set aside Joshua Flood Cook's identification of "Aunt Peggy" (Margaret Cook Mastin) as a participant. Margaret was not there at all.

What about Rachel Cook Murphy? Ira Murphy's account placing her there is, like J.F. Cook's "Aunt Peggy" account, an inspiring but imaginative figment. The early accounts, which identify the embattled women as the wives of Jesse and Hosea Cook, were preserved independently and lack a clear interest (as Joshua Cook and Ira Butler had) in placing surviving female members of their immediate family, in the center of the action. If neither Margaret nor Rachel were there, then the two women who fought off the attack would have been the two Betsy Cooks.

The Cook massacre, even in its various re-tellings, is a paradigm of larger events. There was a high rate of killing in the Kentucky Indian wars in the 1780's and well into the '90's, on both sides and by all parties. In their isolated cabins, well beyond any protected frontier, European settlers were terrified, and for good reason. Many paid with their lives after having either floated down the Ohio from Pennsylvania or tramped into Kentucky through the Cumberland Gap from Virginia. They came to build subsistence farms in the hunting grounds of "the Originals" who rapidly began to lose access to the forests and their 200 foot high oaks, with buffalo and elk ranging beneath them.

In 1779, the above referenced Frances Nelson Faulconer crossed into Kentucky from Virginia over the famous Wilderness Road. Her 1844 interview includes an account of her journey sixty-five years earlier. Frances said, "The first buffalos I ever saw, there were pretty near 1,000 and the woods roared with their tramping, almost as bad as thunder." By 1800, the primordial Kentucky world had disappeared, as had its aboriginal inhabitants.

During the Revolutionary War, a handful of risk takers had come west as far as the Bluegrass; many of these had to give up and go back. The surviving Bryans, founders of the once famous Bryans' Station, returned to North Carolina. British Regulars and their Indian allies had attacked Bryans' Station and other settlements. In some cases, as in 1780, the British even brought artillery against the forted up "stations," which were little more than reinforced cabins transformed into rudimentary stockades. Historians estimate that by the summer of 1790, some 900 Kentucky settlers had been killed by Indians. This may be a low number. Judge Innis himself (for whom Innis Bottom derived its name) wrote to the Secretary of War in 1790, appealing for greater federal protection in Kentucky and asserting that 1500 people had been killed already. Was Judge Innis exaggerating just to get more help?

The Shawnee people were themselves recent arrivals to Kentucky. During the 1700s, they had been driven out of more easterly forests by both settlers and other tribes, and had relocated in Ohio. Apparently, they did not build permanent communities in the hunting grounds of Kentucky. But the Shawnee would have been no less terror stricken then the Europeans. Fighting desperately against mounting odds, the Shawnee, wanted to avoid extermination. They must have known that the demographics favored the new arrivals.

The deaths of the Cook brothers, the two Dunn children, and brother-in-law Lewis Mastin, was not made less grievous for their families by the retrospective information that their empty places on the frontier would be taken by thousands upon thousands of energetic and insistent newcomers, whose arrival into Kentucky was better timed, if by no more than a decade. One of these was **Anthony Crockett** (1756-1838), who served for decades as sergeant of arms to the Kentucky legislature in Frankfort. Anthony's great granddaughter, **Sue Farmer** (1838-1980) would marry **Joshua Flood Cook** (1934-1912), Abraham Cook's grandson. In his application for a federal pension, Anthony Crocket included a description of extensive military services rendered by him, which included the destruction of "indian towns." (For Anthony Crockett, see page 126.)

SARAH JONES COOK

Sarah Jones Cook (1777-1857) was a sister-in-law of the killed Cook brothers. She was the wife of their brother, **Abraham Cook** and therefore a great-great grandmother of **Cecil V Cook, Jr** (1913-1970). Sarah was the fourth of seven children born to **John Jones** (1733-1792) and **Mary Ren(t)fro** (1743-1793). John Jones was born in Virginia, the son of **Mary (Maria) van Meter** (1709-1796) and **Robert Jones** (c. 1696-aft. 1796). Mary was a daughter of **Sara Bodine** (1687-1709) and **John Van Meter** (1683-1745).

Sarah Jones Cook may have been named for her great grandmother, Sara Bodine van Meter. Or she might have been named for a double great grandmother, **Sarah Dubois** (1664?-1726), wife of **Joost Jans Van Meterer/Meteren** (1656-b/f June 13, 1706); Joost Jans and Sarah were the parents of John Van Meter. (See the Van Meter Sketch.)

Sarah Jones and Abraham Cook did not marry until 1795. This of course is one reason why she and Abraham had not joined Abraham's recently wedded brothers, Jesse and Hosea, at the new Cook settlement on the lower Elkhorn, on what became killing grounds in April, 1792. (Concerning the Innis Bottom Massacre, see above.)

WELCH CONNECTIONS

Sarah Jones, wife of Abraham Cook, was believed by her grandson, Joshua F. Cook to have Welch ancestors. This is correct. Sarah's father John Jones, was the son of Robert Jones (see above). Robert may have been born in Wales, the son of the first **Robert Jones** (?-?), who arrived from Montgomereyshire, Wales in 1698. In 1729, the second Robert Jones Jr is in Chester County, PA. Around 1730 Robert Jones and Mary (Maria) Van Meter were married. Not long after, Robert was appointed a constable of Monocacy Hundred, together with his father-in-law **John Van Meter** (1683-1745). The Monocacy region extended westward from about Fredrick, Maryland to Pennsylvania and Virginia, taking in the whole of western Maryland.

By no later than 1736, Robert and Mary Jones are living in the upper Shenandoah Valley, where their son John was born. The westward pull was powerful. In 1790, John Jones and his wife Mary Renfro are living and paying taxes in Woodford County, Virginia (later, Kentucky). Thus, in 1795, their daughter Sarah, born in Virginia, was living in KY with her parents by the time of her marriage to **Abraham Cook** when she was 18.

The Welch connection is doubled onto itself in the marriage of Abraham Cook and Sarah Jones if in fact, Abraham's mother was **Margaret Jones** (c. 1734-1797), a daughter of the second **Robert Jones** (c. 1696-aft. 1796), who was, Sarah Jones' grandfather, and, then also, Abraham's. Thus would Sarah and Abraham have been first cousins when they married in 1795.

GETTING DOWN WITH THE "NEW LIGHT" JONESES

Sarah's mother in law, Margaret Cook saw to the baptism of her children (page 239, 330) but it was not Margaret alone, who looked for a more fervent experience of the Holy, than the established Episcopal order offered the scattered frontier settlements in the 1700s. Sarah's father, John Jones was the same. John's wife, Mary Rentfro, had grown up in a home which followed the doctrines of the Church of England (page 224). But John, her husband, inherited the Free Church tendencies of his parents Mary Van Meter (Dutch Reformed) and Robert Jones (possibly, Welch Baptist).

Early Baptist preacher, William Hickman, knew the Cook family in Kentucky and has left us a valuable 1828 reminiscence. Hickman (whose entire account is appended, below) writes of his first exposure to the "new lights," when they made their appearance in his neighborhood, Buckingham County, VA. The "new lights" had settled in Virginia after migrating South. Some were straight off the ships that deposited them at Philadelphia. Others were down from New England, following conversion to a vivid, evangelistic style offered in the powerful, emotionally charged preaching of Jonathan Edwards or the Englishman George Whitfield.

"In the Year 1770 then living in Buckingham County, Virginia, the Lord sent these new lights near where we lived, curiosity led me to go some distance to hear these babblers; the too precious men were John Waller and James Childs, from the North side of James river; when I got to the meeting the people were relating their experiences, but I could not get sight of the preacher till they were done there was such a multitude of people. At last they broke; the two preachers sat together. I thought they looked like Angels; then each of them preached. God's power attended the word, numbers falling, some convulsed, others crying out for mercy; that day's worship ended. The next day they were to dip as they called it in those days.

"I went home heavy hearted, knowing myself in a wretched state; I informed my wife what I had seen and heard. She was much disgusted for fear I should be dipped too; she begged I would not go again, but I told her I must see them dipped. I went, and an awful day to me it was; one of those ministers preached before Baptism and then moved on to the water, near a quarter of a mile; the people moved in solemn order, singing "Lord, what a wretched land is this, etc".

"Though it was a strange thing in that part of the world, yet I think the people behaved orderly; a great many tears dropped at the water, and not a few from my eyes. The first man brother Waller led in had been a dancing master to whom brother Waller said he had given a gold piece to learn him to dance, and now he was about to baptize him in the name of the Lord Jesus."

New light tendencies are on display in a compelling if bizarre episode in which **Robert Jones** (Sarah's grandfather?) is the subject. In 1753, Robert was appointed Justice of the Peace for Halifax County. In that same year a group of twelve Moravians traveled from Bethlehem, PA to Wachovia, NC and stopped south of the Blackwater River to visit with a Welshman, Robert "Jonsen." William G. Scroggins, a genealogist of rare skill, has speculated that one of the Moravians, who kept his journal in German, identified their host and guide as "Jones' son." (If you say, "My name is Jones" it might sound like "Jonson" anyway, and perhaps even more so with a Welch accent.)

Robert Jones had occasion to speak privately to one of the Moravians, Br. Hermanus, and the Moravian diarist gave Br. Hermanus' report:

"Jonsen began to relate his own story for the last few years. At one time he had become very uneasy and could hardly bear the distress of his heart; then he had turned with all his misery to the Saviour, and He had let him feel the power of His blood and that had given him peace, and so it was with him to this day. And if at any time his heart was not quite right with God he turned again to the Saviour, and all was well. It was the same with his wife [Mary van Meter] and eldest son [John Jones]. He had spoken of this only to those in whom he felt and saw the same spirit, for the world understands as little of such things as a horse, and therefore he kept silence. For nine years he had not heard a sermon; and he begged that when one of us should pass this way again he would stop with him."

Nine years without hearing a sermon? This could have been a misunderstanding or an exaggeration. Eighteenth century

Southside Virginia was not *that* isolated. Maybe Robert Jones said: nine years without hearing a *good* sermon. Even if Robert Jones (with **Mary van Meter**?) had moved southward to an even more isolated place, he was able to function as a Justice of the Peace. It is difficult to fix the illusive data in this vignette into a coherent picture. But it seems likely that *Jonson,* the Welshman is *Jones*, the Welshman and it is beyond doubt that John Jones, Robert Jones son, joined the Virginia back country *new lights* just as his ancestors seem to have been moved to join *the people of the new light* in Wales.

Giving credit where it is due, we must elaborate a bit about the "new light" sects and the revival movement they fostered. Much of this fervor was imported just as were its colonial adherents. In England, Scotland and even in Protestant Ireland, militant Presbyterians called themselves people of the New Light and developed the practice of gathering in "field meetings" to hear preachers shout to them about "free grace" and to denounce Anglican bishops as no better than papists and priests as no more than hirlings. These convictions were carried into the back country almost as rapidly as the new arrivals could get off a boat at Philadelphia and get out of town. Relocated to the frontier, Presbyterians recruited new adherents, partly by direct missionary appeals, partly by harassing Episcopal clerics and partly by instigating sectarian conflict with other separatist sects. An Anglican missionary recorded in his journal in 1765, "Africk never more abounded with new Monsters, than Pennsylvania does with the new sects . . . One of these parties, known by the title of New Lights or Gifted Brethren (for they pretend to inspiration) now infest the whole Back Country." There is a direct line from the New Lights of 18th century PA and VA to the frontier Baptist Churches of VA and KY in the 18th and the 19th.

As stated, Sarah and her farmer/preacher husband Abraham Cook had twelve children. Their son **William F Cook** (1802-1850/55) was the father of **Joshua Flood Cook** (1834-1912). In 1851, near the end of life, Sarah moved with Abraham to Missouri from their Shelby County KY home. The move was occasioned by the earlier relocating there by their son Abraham Jr., and his wife, Sarah Miles. Abraham died in 1854, Sarah in

1856 in Mcfall, Gentry County, MO. They are buried in the Miles family cemetery in Gentry County.

SOURCES:

Abraham and Sarah Cook genealogy, generally: Betty Taylor Cook's unpublished genealogy book, and her notes.

For Abraham Cook's purchase of 558 acres from Charles Lynch on March 24, 1807: See Gary Kueber's web-posting at /kueber.us/p28.htm#552.

For Abraham's physical description and his hesitation to seek ordination: J.H. Spencer, **History of Kentucky Baptists** (vol.1 page 434) (1886).

Many details of the life of Abraham Cook, **Old Kentucky**, by his grandson, Joshua Flood Cook (1908).

Data on the Cooks and Murphys in Oregon: **The Cook Book** by Eunice Cook Konold, San Diego CA (1970, privately printed), copy provided to this writer by Charles L. Cook.

Three accounts of the Innis Bottom, or Cook Massacre, appeared relatively early in books and are examined here: **A History of Kentucky Baptists** (vol. 1, page 432, 1886) by J. H. Spencer, **Old Kentucky,** by Joshua Flood Cook (1908, pages 77-79); **History of Kentucky** by Lewis Collins (1847, p. 306-307). These and the accounts by (1) Butler (2) Dillard (3) Herndon (4) Faulconer and (5) Ballard are among more than twenty accounts collected by Charles L. Cook; please see his account at ancestorstories.org

William Scroggins' valuable genealogical research may be found posted by Gary Kueber at kueber.us/.

For Edrington genealogy: Ancestors of Curtis Edrington LEMING familyorigins.com

Additional Jones genealogical information, including the roster of Sara and Abraham Cook's children: Gary Kueber. See kueber.us/. Much Kueber data is independently researched; a significant amount is the work of William G. Scroggins, including Faulconer/Falconer data. See below.)

Many details and various accounts of the Cook Massacre, including quotations from astute Cook genealogists, Charles L. Cook, Pat Sengstock, and William G. Scroggins have been posted at ancestorstories.org by Charlie Cook or shared by Charlie with the Cook Family Research Group, which Charlie Cook himself has brought together.

The Sarah Jane Herndon Account of the massacre has been transcribed, preserved and shared by the incomparable family historian, William G. Scroggins, and helpfully posted by Gary Kueber at kueber.us – see there the Scroggins biographical sketch of John Faulconer.

Anthony Crockett material and his connection to Joshua Flood Cook has been outlined by Betty Huey Taylor Cook (1918-2000) in her unpublished genealogical book and its accompanying notes (arranged into more than 40 binders), in the possession of Betty's son, writer of the above treatment of the Innis Bottom Massacre (page 182). For a sketch of the life of Anthony Crockett, see page 126, above; see also Ellery Farmer's note, page 130).

For some of the details of the Jones, Van Meter and Du Bois lines, including a portion of John Van Meter's will and the colloquy between Robert Jones and Br. Hermanus: the Van Meter, Jones and Du Bois sketches of William G. Scroggins, on the web at the remarkably comprehensive and accessible website maintained by Gary Kuber: kueber.us/.

Additional data concerning Margaret (Jones?) and William Cook: *Our Ancestors* (no date), by Merlyn Joseph Cook (1914–1995), whose research paper, and much else, has been shared by Charlie Cook: ancestorstories.org

For Margaret Cook's will: Bill Scroggins' William Cook treatise (kueber.us/) and Charlie L Cook (ancestorstories.org)

Additional Du Bois information is available on the web at: Spicerweb.org

Anthony Crockett 1832 pension application: Betty Taylor Cook's unpublished notes.

"the Virginia back country *new lights*" - Page 219, above. For the New Light movement in Britain before its arrival in America and the quotation confirming that arrival: **Albion's Seed** by David Hacket Fischer, Oxford University Press (1989) page 617. For the New Light movement in the colonies, see Hickman's memoir (Appendix B, esp. pages 306-310). The term *new lights* may have come from John Bunyan, who wrote of *"the Christian that walketh according to his own light with God."* See Bunyan's *Differences in Judgement about Water-Baptism no Bar to Communion* (1673).

This note is connected to the question of Cook ancestry (see page 243, below). An early Cook, arriving in Virginia colony in the mid to late 1600s or early 1700s, would have been among the mass of English males, who arrived poor and indentured for a term of years. From south or central England, nominally Anglican, unskilled in any trade but agriculture, this Cook would have been a rural man, even if he had first tried his luck in London or some other town. This early English immigrant would have survived incredible physical hardships and the lethal threats imposed by disease and a semi-tropical climate, and lived long enough to procreate and perhaps even to get onto farmland he could claim for his children. This heartland Englishman would have been distinguishable from *borderers* (page 83), who were Protestants and clan-oriented, and who arrived a few decades later by the thousands, dominating the frontier settlements from Pennsylvania to Georgia in the mid 1700s, and then Kentucky, Tennessee and Alabama. This description is a summary of the results of the research of Fischer (cited above) and Bailyn (see page 277, 295).

"DISPOSED TO MOVE TO THE WESTERN WATERS"

William Cook
Margaret (Jones?)

Abraham Cook (1774-1854).
William F Cook (1802-1850/55)
Joshua Flood Cook (1834-1912)
Cecil V Cook (1871-1948)
Cecil V Cook, Jr (1913-1970)

Over two generations, the Jones and Cook families intertwine. As stated in an earlier sketch, **Sarah Jones** (1777-1857), wife of **Abraham Cook** (1774-1854), was the daughter of **John Jones** (1733-1792) and **Mary Rentfro** (?-?). Abraham's parents were **William Cook** (abt 1730-abt 1790/91) and **Margaret (Jones**?) (1734-1797), speculated to be a sister of John Jones and thus Sarah's aunt before she became her mother-in-law. If a Jones, even if not John's sister, Margaret likely would have been Welch and thus of New Light sympathies.

Mary Rentfro, Sarah Jones' mother was the third of nine children of **Joseph Rentfro** (bf 1700-1772/6) and **Mary Owens** (Randolph?) (?-?). Joseph and Mary Rentfro are believed to have lived in the south central Virginia county, Halifax. At that time, Halifax would have been included in Cumberland Parish, which was then co-extensive with Lunenburg County (est 1742).

The notion of a "parish" in England was adapted in America to the unique under-populated conditions of the vast region encompassed by Virginia colony. (At one time, in assertions powered by imagination and by fanciful ideas of ownership, Virginia Colony was said to extend all the way to the "western" Ocean.) The practice in Virginia under English colonial law was to empower the established Episcopal Church to supervise church administrative matters through the authority of the courts. Thus the colony was organized into *parishes* by the bishop just as the same territory was organized into counties by the House of Burgesses. A parish, often the exact division as a county, would be made the responsibility of a vestry of prominent local men. The vestry would see to the construction of a house of worship and the supervision of an Anglican clergyman, in the unlikely even that a cleric from England were assigned to the parish.

In 1746, the sheriff of Lunenburg County ordered the convening of a meeting to select vestrymen for Cumberland Parish. At its founding in 1742 and for some years following, Lunenburg County (Cumberland Parish) was an enormous territory, composed of what later became Mecklenburg, Charlotte, Halifax, Pittsylvania, Henry and Franklin Counties as well as most of the area of Bedford and Campbell counties. In essence, this was a region which is known today as the whole of the southern part – the Southside - of the state of Virginia. Despite the distances, some kind of gathering took place in 1746 and a vestry was convened. (A roster of the first vestrymen of Cumberland Parish has been preserved.) The vestry subsequently ordered that a church building be constructed near Lunenburg Court House on Reedy Creek. The building was raised with the costs paid by a tax on the public.

The vestry had to take into account the reality of distance across Cumberland Parish and the nonexistence of any decent system of roads. Across such a wide area, all of the devout could not gather each Sunday. How could the vestry expect the Anglican Church to serve a scattered population of a few thousand souls, with no feasible means for them to get to the church house? The solution was the development of a system of "readers." Private persons were authorized to conduct worship in their homes. This worship would entail the offering of prayers, the reading of scripture and possibly the singing of hymns, under the direction of a local resident willing to take on the task – for a fee. (As with the construction of the church building and the maintenance of a priest, the cost of paying a "reader" was covered by locally imposed public assessments.) The Sunday gatherings conducted by the Reader would not entail participation in the Sacraments of the Anglican Church, as there was not present an ordained priest.

In 1751, the homes of Mark Cole and **Joseph** and **Mary Owens Rentfro** on the Blackwater River were authorized for Sunday worship, for the benefit of neighbors near enough to attend. William Cook being a likely young man, is found enrolled in the Cumberland Parish Vestry Book as a reader at these locations. That he was an Episcopal Church reader suggests William, at about age 21, (1) was educated well enough for public reading, (2) was Church of England and (3) had sufficient self-possession and a sense of his own convictions secure enough to stand before his neighbors and direct them in worship. No doubt, he could also use the money.

When young William Cook stood to read the Bible to a gathered circle of neighbors in the yard or on the porch or under some shelter of the Rentfro home, he would have read a text we have only recently decided to discard. The King James Bible (1611), by 1751, would have been considered venerable but not archaic. It had aided in standardizing the language; it had helped make our William Cook into a speaker intelligible to our own ears. This Bible had signaled the flexibility of English, which absorbs foreign words more readily than any other language. The King James Bible was not a translation but a compilation, a compromise among existing translations, with pride of place given to the earlier translation of Catholic priest William Tyndale (1494-1536) and his helpers. Tyndale, for his trouble, was strangled and his body burnt by agents of Henry VIII. But Tyndale did, literally, have the final word, or at least most of them. Ninety percent of the text of the KJB is from Tyndale.

Read to us, young William Cook. Like the slaves standing apart from the circle of your neighbors, we would listen to you from a modest distance. Like the slaves, who would have taken special note of your telling of Moses and the Israelites on their way to freedom, we too would draw in a little closer. We would mark your cadences and your phrasings; we would know your speech as our own. Your language would flow over us like the air of the new continent your kin had come to from over the waters. Read to us, William, words we could say before you say them: *in the beginning . . . let there be light . . . land of the living . . . thorn in the flesh . . . suffer the little ones . . . salt of the earth.* In heaven, William, might we ask that you are young again? Might we ask that you read to us as you did for your neighbors, gathered from their scattered Black Water River cabins on a Southside Virginia Sunday morning? Might this be Heaven enough, listening to young William Cook read from his Bible as at the Rentfro home in 1751? A familiar Heaven, too, for the Bible read by William Cook in 1751, especially the Hebrew Scriptures, had given England and English America a sense of self as a chosen people, a mobilized people, an ethical people governed by ancient law, worshippers of no pantheon but of one God, though not the placid Heavenly Father of Jesus, but of Jehovah, Lord of Hosts.

In 1751, young William must have been attached in some degree to the Anglican establishment. By marrying Margaret (Jones?), he proved himself willing (we speculate) to permit her to instruct their eleven children in the Free Church doctrines of her Welch progenitors. This instruction would have required a sober fortitude on the part of both parents. Margaret and William would have known (we assume) that such doctrines had brought maimings, burnings, the gibbet and exile to earnest advocates of an Independent Church in ancestral England.

To speak of England and its American colonies is to speak of two different points of view about America. For the well placed in England, with secure positions and influence in London, the whole of English America was considered a dangerous, mysterious region, settled by misfits, rustics, criminals and their slaves. The coastal settlements could claim to be little more than the fringe of an enormous land mass, occupied already by God abandoned savages. But the missionary opportunity counted for little in London. The Anglican establishment had no end of difficulty finding priests willing to spend their careers in this wilderness.

The hardy settlers held to different ideas. By the mid 1700s, many looked back on a century of American ancestry. They could claim a third, fourth or even a fifth generation of collective American experience. They knew the coastline, the fields and the forests as home. They had no other country, had never seen England, would never see it, had no living relatives who had any memory of English life. These long-established colonists were regularly joined by newcomers. Throughout the 1700s, thousands of immigrants were just off the boat, some from England but many from Holland or some unintelligible German princedom, arriving unintelligible themselves.

Whether Americans for many generations or fresh immigrants, the settlers doubtless spent countless hours, over years of their lives, ruminating about how to get ever deeper into the wilderness and stake a claim to a large piece of it. They would uproot themselves for their children. Their children would do the same for themselves and *their* children.

The expanse to the south and west of Virginia spoke of a lack of restriction. This was the impulse that had brought over the ancestors of native born Virginians. This impulse continued to draw the recent arrivals. Unfolding history would prove the colonists unwilling to accept restraints imposed upon them by a distant government. This was why the established church, partnered with colonial Virginia governors, after a century and more of fitful practice in this faraway land, utterly collapsed in the span of the lives of William and Margaret Cook. (Not far into the 19th century, the old Anglican meeting house on Reedy Creek was used as a kind of community storehouse before it burned to the ground.)

The "separate" religious impulse was of a piece with the desire of many to separate altogether from the confining and coercive hand of distant authority. The powers would send a royal governor to coerce the residents and extract taxes from them, but these powers were absent from the day-to-day life struggles of colonists. The only way to make a road in eighteenth century Southside Virginia was by order of your neighbor, the justice of the peace (judge of the local court). Farmers would be assigned, with their slaves, to see to the expansion of some narrow path or the clearing of some muddy trace. You did the road maintenance work yourself; meanwhile your taxes (often collected in tobacco) went to maintain the governor and his retinue and the alcoholic gambler sent over as your priest.

The dream of getting away into "Kentucke" was shared by many. Daniel Boone, after his first visit there (1769): "I returned home to my family with a determination to bring them as soon as possible to live in *Kentucke*, which I esteemed a second paradise." Of course, Boone never said this and eventually abandoned Kentucky because of disputed land claims. Boone's statement is from his ghostwritten "autobiography," appended to John Filson's widely read **Discovery, Settlement and**

Present State of Kentucky (1784). Filson (1753-88) was a speculator in KY real estate. He died violently before reaping any benefit from his hype.

William and Margaret Cook's first home after their marriage appears to have been in the southern reaches of the Blue Ridge Mountains, in what is now (since 1785) Franklin County but what was then still part of old Lunenburg County. This county is most noted today as the location of a resort, "Mountain Lake." The Cooks lived along a trace called Fox Run on the Blackwater River. William was enrolled as a resident of this area in 1755. In 1765, as a propertied male, he voted in the Burgess election in Halifax County, also formed out of old Lunenburg.

William Cook actively bought and sold land. Between 1752 and 1765 he was involved in land transactions ("entries") in Pittsylvania County. In 1760, he received a 400 acre grant along the Blackwater River. In 1767 he bought 210 acres on the Pigg River. At about that same time, he and Margaret may have moved closer to Rocky Mount, VA, relocating to the Pigg River at Hatchet Creek, probably on his new Franklin County lands. In 1769 Margaret and William are residents of Pittsylvania County, when they sold some land to Peter Vardeman. (One wonders if William and Margaret moved or if the jurisdiction simply got a new name.) In 1767, the tax rolls (List of Tithables) of Pittsylvania County, VA included **Robert Jones Sr** and Jr, **John Jones**, **Joseph Rentfro** and **William Cook.**

Family Historian Merlyn Cook, in his unpublished (but widely circulated) history, *Our Family*, has helped to clarify the confusing nomenclature of Virginia counties in the 18th century. Basically, larger jurisdictions were subdivided as the population grew. Over time, people conducted legal business in different courthouses and clerks' offices without ever having moved.

What actually happened came about because the population was expanding and moving to the west. As this happened, large areas that had been sparsely populated were split to make additional counties. If you happened to be in the western half of the county (and the Cooks always were) you found yourself in a new county with a new county seat, even though you had not moved. The specific details of the splits from the earliest days of the colony may illustrate how the Cooks and many other families moved westward in Virginia, following the expanding frontier. Back in 1634 Virginia was first organized in shires or counties. The eight organized then were more or less the same as eight large plantations which had been acting as centers of government since 1619. From two of those original eight counties, Charles City and Isle of Wight (originally called by the Indian name, Warrosquyozke) Prince George County was formed in 1702. In 1720 an act was passed in the House of Burgesses to split off Brunswick from the western part of Prince George. But the territory didn't develop as fast as expected, so it was really 1732 before a county government was set up for Brunswick. Later in 1746, Brunswick was split to form the county of Lunenburg, which was still a large area. In fact, the original Lunenburg County, embraced all of the areas for present day counties of Lunenburg, Mecklenburg, Halifax, Charlotte, Pittsylvania, Henry, Patrick and Franklin Counties. And it also comprised the major pats of what is now Bedford and Campbell Counties and a part of Appomattox. Further splits continued to take place so that in addition to Lunenburg, where William Cook and Margaret started their married life, they lived in Halifax from 1752, Pittsylvania from 1767, and Henry from 1777. Since Franklin County was formed shortly after they left Virginia, they usually in after years identified their place of abode in Virginia as Franklin.

William was not shy about seeking vindication through the courts. Nor were his neighbors. From 1768 through '74 he brought suit and was sued in Pittsylvania County. In 1771 he objected to a survey of 41 acres, asserting the results to be an infringement upon his own lands. The case lingered until after the Revolutionary War (1776-81) and then was dismissed by Virginia's General State Court.

Local deed books and other records show that another William Cook (Lunenburg County) as well as a Benjamin Cook (Franklin County) are residents of the area where William and Margaret Cook also lived. These might have been cousins or even brothers – or no relation at all.

The eleven children of Margaret and William Cook are:

Rachel (Murphy) (1753-1832)
Bathsheba (Dunn) (1755-?)
Helen (Bohannon) (1756- 1837)
Rhoda (1 Bohannon) (2 Jamison) (abt 1760-?)
Seth (1760/70- 1840/41)
William, III (abt 1764-1814)
Jesse (abt 1765-April 28, 1792)
Margaret (Mastin) (abt 1767- by 1829)
Hosea (abt 1769-April 28, 1792)
Abraham (1774-1854)
Eunice (Miles) (abt 1775-abt 1800)

MARGARET COOK JOINS THE *NEW LIGHTS*, BUT DID WILLIAM?

There were many Joneses recorded as living at that time in the part of Lunenburg which became Franklin County; these included: David Jones (1777), **John Jones** (1777, 1784), his father **Robert Jones** (c. 1696-aft. 1796), who received two land grants in 1747 and is registered there in 1752, and Captain Thomas Jones, on the Pigg River (1777). Most likely, these Jones families were Margaret's relatives: Robert Jones was her father, John her brother. (See below.) A number of **Rentfro** family members are also enrolled (in 1747, 1769) as residents of Franklin: James (1751), **Joseph** (1747), Moses and William.

These colonial settlers were, some of them, "separates," who lived a negative. That is, they refused NOT to worship as they felt convinced they must. The first Baptists known in Virginia arrived around 1714 from England, settling in the southeast section. These may have included some Joneses from Wales, who, by the 1740s and '50s, had probably moved further west into the valley of the "Sherando" (Shenandoah). But this was not the route taken by **Robert Jones**. He and **Maria van Meter** had reached Virginia via Maryland in the 1730's, arriving with her parents. (For details, see the Index and the sketch devoted to **Sara Bodine** and **John (Jan) Joost Van Meter** & his parents **Joost Jans Van Meterer** and **Sarah Dubois**.) It is no coincidence that the first permanent Baptist Church founded in Virginia was established in old Lunenburg County.

In the 1740's a religious revival swept across the colonies. Bold, confident exhorters preached a gospel akin to that of Wycliffe and the Lollards of England 300 years before. They also sounded themes reminiscent of the Huguenots of France, Protestant exiles, survivors of pogroms in the 1600s. (See the Index.) Revivalist preachers such as the slave-owning early Methodist, George Whitefield from England and Jonathan Edwards of Massachusetts laid an exhilarating emphasis on personal conviction, personal Bible reading and the personal expression of belief by participation in congregation-centered piety. The urgent mass appeal was disconnected from any church hierarchy, which the revivalists often denounced. Congregations were to be directed by pastors (males of course), raised up from the community for this purpose. The revival momentum was centered in New England and spread to the colonies as zealous converts moved south.

With the arrival of the itinerant preacher, the back country of Virginia was gripped in a fervor unseen before in America. These zealots from New England brought the "New Light Stir" with them. Thousands of people emotionally confessed their sins in public gatherings and offered themselves up to "believer's baptism" in the nearest running water. The converted were admonished to attend regular worship, which they themselves organized, calling one of their number to be their pastor. The enthusiasm lasted a decade or more. It is known to historians as the First Great Awakening and it gave a contour to American Protestantism which remains today.

William Hickman (his memoir is appended), who became a preacher himself, commented on the novelty of the *new light* movement in rural Virginia:

> ". . . I heard talk of people called Baptists, though at a great distance; they told us they would take the people and dip them all over in the water: I drew the conclusion they were like Sturgeons out of the Seine, wallowing in the sand; that I was sure they were false prophets, I hoped I never

should see one . . . In the Year 1770 then living in Buckingham County, Virginia, the Lord sent these new lights near where we lived, curiosity led me to go some distance to hear these babblers . . . God's power attended the word, numbers falling, some convulsed, others crying out for mercy; that day's worship ended. The next day they were to dip as they called it in those days."

A decade before the arrival of the New Lights, the van Meters had moved into the north western regions of Virginia from Maryland. Their background was Dutch Reform; their goal was land acquisition; their religious future – and that of several of their children - was Baptist. Robert Jones was certainly touched by the revival drama and so was his son John and so also was his daughter, Margaret, who may have been Margaret, wife of William Cook.

In the case of Margaret, wife of William Cook, these convictions melded into an association with the dynamic Baptist movement. William Hickman said – but he may have exaggerated a bit - that Margaret, after her move into Kentucky, saw to the baptism of all of her children, adults and youngsters alike. Does this mean the William Cook family had not affiliated themselves with the Baptists back in Virginia? Or did the leaders of the newly organized Forks of Elkhorn Church require re-baptism? I suspect the Baptist connection began only in KY.

Support of a church establishment by way of taxation and fines for non-attendance was the way of life in Virginia in mid-eighteenth century. Those born and raised in that time and place were used to this arrangement. You made yourself into a criminal if you chose another way. In the wake of the "new light stir," many did. Did William Cook? We don't know. Perhaps he objected to any affiliation by Margaret but gave up his resistance after the move into Kentucky. Perhaps he resisted always. Perhaps Margaret and her children became Baptists only after his death.

In 1777, William was recommended to Governor Patrick Henry for service on the "Commission for Peace" for Henry County. The duties of the Justices of the Peace entailed presiding at sessions of the county court. William served in 1777 and 1778. Would this service have been possible if he were affiliated with the Baptists? Not likely under the colonial government of Governor Dunmore. But in 1777, the Revolution was underway and Baptists were generally enthusiastic patriots. Arguably, after 1776, William could not have expected appointment if he were a communicant of that colonial institution, the Anglican Church. On the other hand, George Washington himself was Anglican. I suspect that a locally well regarded Baptist would find no difficulty from Patrick Henry, one of the most radical revolutionaries in Virginia, in obtaining an appointment to the local court. No data has been found, which settled these issues.

Sundays at church in rural Virginia in the 1700s – and this meant, at first, the Episcopal Church - was a social and community phenomenon, as remarked by observers who could see the uniqueness of it. In contrast with Sundays in England, in colonial America, the social classes mixed freely in the church yard if not within the sanctuary. Business was done in Sunday conversation.

Philip Vickers Fithian, a young English tutor in a Virginia home, reported on worship he attended in December, 1773:

"I observe it is a general custom on Sundays here, with Gentlemen to invite one another home to dine, after church; and to consult about, determine their common business, either before or after Service—It is the Custom for Gentlemen not to go into Church until service is beginning, when they enter in a Body, in the same manner as they come out; I have known the Clerk to come out and call them into prayers. They stay also after the Service is over, usually as long, sometimes longer, than the Parson was preaching."

With much for the men to discuss and little opportunity to do so on weekdays while working their scattered farms, one may wonder if a purpose competitive with the worship of God was simply to get together once a week. Philip Fithian reinforces this suspicion in a second journal entry, from August, 1774.

"The three grand divisions of time at the church on Sundays, Viz. before Service giving & receiving letters of business, reading Advertisements, consulting about the price of Tobacco, Grain &c. & settling either the lineage, Age or qualities of favourite Horses 2. IN the Church at Service, prayrs read over in haste, a Sermon under & never over twenty minutes, but always made up of sound morality or deep studied Methaphysicks. 3. After Service is over three quarters of an hour spent in strolling round the Church among the Crowd, in which time you will be invited by several different Gentlemen home with them to dinner."

Did William Cook, by marrying Margaret (Jones?), put away from himself the social opportunities formerly open to him in the Anglican Church? Or, did so many of his neighbors in old Lunenburg affiliate with the Baptists that the advantage of Sunday social opportunities transferred to the local Baptist meetings? Or, did William retain a life long Anglican affiliation?

A William Cook(e) as well as a John Cook(e) were in Captain Buford's Volunteer Company from Bedford County, VA in 1774, in *Lord Dunmore's War*. This war was a sortie into the (now West Virginia) wilderness, sponsored by John Murray (Earl of Dunmore), Governor of Virginia Colony. Murray's objective was to provoke the Shawnee and Mingo clans into an unwinnable confrontation. The Oct 10, 1774 Battle of Point Pleasant ended this campaign and the Shawnee agreed to stay west of the Ohio River. Prior to his return to England in 1776, Governor Dunmore led the British effort in Virginia against many of the same men, who had fought under his mandate at Point Pleasant.

Owing to his age, William Cook, husband of Margaret, is not likely to have been the same William Cook, participant in Lord Dunmore's War. But the brutal aftermath of the war may have had a direct and tragic effect on the Cook family. *Lord Dunmore's War* has been called "an altogether unjustifiable war, whose bitter fruits were gathered for many years, as it had much to do with Shawnees going over to the British, in the American Revolution, and massacre hundreds of settlers [. . .] and aroused the vindictive spirit of the Shawnees, never broken until General Anthony Wayne defeated them and other western tribes at the

Battle of Fallen Timbers" in 1794. In the Spring of 1792, in Kentucky, two of William and Margaret sons, as well as two grandsons, were killed in a raid on their cabin(s). (See page 182.)

An 1890 census conducted in Wyoming County WV indicated that most county residents claimed descent from John Cook(e), who settled his family there in 1799. John Cook, Sr. and his wife Nellie occupied 92 acres in what became Wyoming County (established 1850) WV. John and Nellie were the parents of four sons: Thomas, John Jr., William, and James. Perhaps DNA evidence will show a connection (or rule one out) between the descendents of Lunenburg William Cook and John Cook Sr.

"PATRIOT, AND FRIEND, TO HIS COUNTRY"

In about 1784, after more than 30 years living in the valleys of the lower Blue Ridge Mountains, William and Margaret joined the push from Virginia into what became (1792) the Commonwealth of KY. In 1784, the Cooks sold what was probably their remaining VA property and soon joined thousands of other westward moving pioneers. A few years earlier, a floodgate had been opened and a human tide released. Thanks to their victorious Revolution against England, westward facing pioneers would no longer be considered squatters and criminals for moving beyond the eastern slopes of the Appalachian Mountains. Thanks to the victory secured by William and John Cook and hundreds of other militia men in Dunmore's War, the Shawnee and Mingo tribes had conceded Kentucky to English-speaking settlers.

In an effort to promote trade and peace with Indian tribes, England's policy since the end of the French and Indian (the Seven Years) War in 1763 had been to discourage colonial settlement to the west. In that year, a so called "Proclamation Line" had been announced – from faraway London – which forbade any person from crossing west of the summit of the Appalachian mountains. Many settlers went over anyway and a good argument can be made that their presence beyond the Appalachians caused the inclusion of these western lands within the territory of the United States, under the terms of the Treaty of Paris which ended the Revolutionary War.

Under the new, national post-revolutionary government, western settlement in Kentucky was chaotic but legal. Margaret and William moved their family, probably through the Gap in the Cumberland mountains, an opening which Daniel Boone is credited with finding. They relocated their family near present day Frankfort KY. It is thought that some of their grown children were already living nearby.

William Cook (or perhaps Margaret alone) carried into Kentucky a letter of recommendation from their former neighbors. Descendent Merlyn Joseph Cook (1914-95) reproduced the letter, signed by William and Margaret's many relatives and friends. The letter has been published on the web by descendent Charlie L. Cook (see Sources):

> *"HENRY CO., VA: This is to certify that William COOK has been a resident in this place for near thirty years; and has always behaved unblameable; and demeaned himself as a good citizen, Patriot, and friend, to his country and has faithfully Acted in the Civel department--and now being disposed to move to the Western Waters, we recommend him to the Inhabitants of that Country hoping he will meet with as warm a reception as the Merits of his Caracter Intitles him to.*
>
> *Test Joseph Anthony Jno. Rentfro, J.P. Swinfield Hill, J.P. A. Hughes, J.P.* **Robt. Jones, Sen'r** *James Calloway, Cty. Lt. Peter Saunders, Col. Robt. Jones, Jun'r Campbell Co John Dillard, J. P. Thos. Jones, Jun'r Thos. Hale, Capt'n Sam'l Hairston Henry Jones Acquilla Greer Moses Greer, J. P. Jesse Heard, J. P. Jesse Rentfro, Thos Cooper, John Hall Abraham Penn, Col. William Hall*

This letter became a treasured document to William and Margaret, who saw to its preservation by their descendents. They would have cherished every complimentary word and phrase.

Good citizen: William and Margaret had never known urban life. We could describe them as independent, small farmers and landowners, who possessed virtually nothing they did not make or bring out of the earth by their own labor - or that of their slaves. (These Cooks owned slaves, a common enough evil even on the small farms of western Virginia, well away from colonial tobacco plantations.) William and Margaret would have thought of themselves as Americans, and of their ways, language and religion as thoroughly English. But they would have known and felt their apartness from England, even before the Revolution. They would have known themselves English and yet other than English, other than citizens of any nation in Europe. They were new people on the earth and they were about something new; they were Americans, native born colonists, with the American continent laid out before them and their children. The children or grandchildren of immigrants, they would have heard family tales of the harshness of indenture in Virginia a century earlier. They would have been in the grip of a vision of land ownership that might, if only acted upon, forever protect their own descendents from such a fate.

Both before and following the Revolution, it was a commonplace that no two generations of a Virginia family had lived for long in the same place. Indeed, the records we have suggest that a couple would move several times in the course of rearing a family. No doubt some of this wandering was due to self-defeating farming methods, which ruined the soil. But the slip shod methods of home construction should not be overlooked. Many 17th and 18th century Virginia houses were no more than hovels made of green wood. Better to build anew than repair or add on to a falling-in structure, which, even if soundly constructed, would not accommodate the three or four children born since the last cabin was put up.

Our ancestors would also have had bred into them a powerful sense of migration. A willingness to up and move to improve their prospects would have been central to the outlook of these independence-minded semi-transients. It may be impossible to over-estimate the mesmerizing effect upon them of living on the edge of a limitless, unexplored, gorgeous continent – this at a time when property ownership was generally held to be the key to wealth.

Westward motion inland from the great ocean may have seemed a family tradition. But for William and Margaret Cook, there was an added factor: after so many years in the foothills and the eastern slopes of the Blue Ridge Mountains, this elderly couple would have felt the aches and pains of a lifetime on the land - Margaret had given birth to eleven children! They probably moved to Kentucky at the prompting of one or another of their children. Just one more move and they could rest; one long wagon ride to *Kentuck*. Over in *Kentuck* the children promised to take care of them.

Family unity seems to have been a powerful bond for William and Margaret Cook. Not only did they move into a dangerous wilderness, but they disposed of their Virginia lands. Their dual motive would have been to (1) keep their children close and (2) sell expensive property in Virginia so as to buy larger holdings of cheaper lands further west. The alternative (which we also see in our ancestry) is for the old folks to stay put while younger sons, lacking an inheritance of land, strike out on their own, never to return or to be seen again. William and Margaret may not have wanted this sort of separation to happen to their close knit clan. In moving to Kentucky, they took steps to avoid this. In the event, the journey into Kentucky may have been too strenuous for William, who seems to have died shortly after, if not during the trek itself – or perhaps in Virginia.

Patriot, and friend, to his country: The Colonies had just gone through a nip & tuck war with soldiers from an Empire. And had won! This elderly couple had played some loyal part, or at least their neighbors were willing so to say. Had there been any militia service by William, it would have been mentioned in this letter. But most colonists did not take up musket and powder. Some were loyalists; some did not care one way or the other. But many others, "whigs of the country" as they called themselves (see page 312), endorsed the revolt against England and contributed to the provisioning of the rebel armies. The older patriots fortified the young soldiers with food, leather goods, lead and powder and other expressions of support.

faithfully Acted in the Civel department: William Cook had served as a state-paid lay church reader, a Justice of the Peace on occasion, and had paid his taxes; his service has been documented as a Justice in the local court of Henry County (the northern portion of which went to form Franklin County). For a literate and public-spirited man, there were other services to render such as road building, for which documentation has not been located or does not exist. The government in southwest Virginia in the eighteenth century was conducted by volunteers in each small community. William had accepted his civic responsibility.

disposed to move to the Western Waters: William's old friends may have had a little fun at his expense. His best reason for leaving the Shenandoah Valley, after thirty years, was mistaken; he is in the hunt, at his age, not for good lands for his children but good water. The joke would be that William hoped to discover that legendary aquatic continental thruway that the ancient sponsors of the original Jamestown and Massachusetts Bay settlements had in the back of their minds. Or perhaps *to the western waters* is a shorthand reference for the act of moving across the mountain barrier between Virginia and Kentucky, to turn away from eastern waters (the Atlantic Ocean, the James and Potomac Rivers) and move to the region defined by the Ohio, Kentucky and Cumberland Rivers – *western waters*, as they were sometimes described.

Perhaps in the late summer or fall of 1784, this letter was read aloud midst laughter and some tears, as William said his goodbyes to lifelong Virginia pals.

In 1788, Margaret Cook - "old Sister Cook" – as Baptist preacher William Hickman wrote of her in 1829 - presented nine of her children to him for baptism at the founding of the Forks of Elkhorn Church near present day Frankfort, KY. Robert Jones, whose granddaughter would marry young Abraham, was still alive in 1797 but back in Southside Virginia. Had he heard of the baptisms, his separatist heart would have warmed to the scene in the Bluegrass: a parade of toe-headed youngsters and young adults, coming up out of the waters of the Elkhorn, singing a separatist hymn he might have learned in Wales.

Did William Cook die before his wife and children moved into Kentucky? He is not mentioned in 1788, the year of the Elkhorn baptisms or as a member of the Baptist church. Margaret is a church member, as is a William, more likely her son. In 1790, Margaret Cook is assessed taxes in Woodford County but there is no mention of her husband. In 1791, back in Virginia, Margaret is invoked in a judicial proceeding as relinquishing her rights of dower in property sold by her and her husband prior to moving to Kentucky; again, there is no mention of William Cook. In 1792, '93 and '95, Margaret paid taxes in KY, presumably as head of household.

Margaret Cook died in 1797. In that year she signed her will and her estate was inventoried. The will was recorded by court order in February, 1798. No land was devised, which suggests that title to any owned by William and Margaret had been passed either by William's will or by subsequent sales by Margaret or gifts made by her before her death.

In her 1797 will, the widow Margaret Cook made notable stipulations. Margaret had lost two sons and two grandsons at the massacre at Innis Bottom in 1792. (For details, see page 182, the Sarah Jones and Abraham Cook sketch.) Survivors of this event included William Dunn, husband of her daughter Bathsheba. William had run away through the woods when the attack commenced, which saw his two young sons murdered. For reasons unknown, Margaret showed herself inclined against this surviving son-in-law. She directed that William Dunn was to receive "one shilling" from her estate. A miniscule amount was (and is) often specified in a will to prevent a disappointed heir from being heard in court to claim that he had been overlooked.

By her will, Margaret was unwilling to put money in the hands of Bathsheba, her daughter, William Dunn's wife. Margaret directed, "Bathsheba Dunn's part is to be kept in the hands of the Executors and let to her as in their opinion she may immediately need it for own personal use and at her death the remainder of her part if any to be given to her Children only." Clearly, Margaret's son-in-law William Dunn is alive but excluded from any contact with Margaret's estate. The executors were Margaret Cook's "trusty and beloved" surviving sons, William, Seth and **Abraham**.

William G. Scroggins has speculated that Margaret may have held against William Dunn the deaths of her two young grandsons, who were William and Bathsheba Dunn's children. The boys had been killed in the woods near Innis Bottom in 1792. Their father William had survived by running through the woods; his young boys, ages sixteen and nine, also ran away but were caught and murdered.

The safe flight of William Dunn, when his sons were killed, may have told against him in the view of his mother-in-law. But can a more likely cause of estrangement be teased out of the language of the will? The phrasing suggests that Bathsheba Cook Dunn is not to be entrusted with funds which, under laws then current, became the property of the husband. Margaret may have concluded that William Dunn was a profligate. Perhaps her sons, who were her executors on the will, had pleaded with her not to give William Dunn any further opportunity to dissipate the hard won estate that William Cook had worked all his life to accumulate in Virginia and had left to Margaret for their children. In Margaret's will, do we see a family trying to come to terms with a reckless gambler or an alcoholic?

The inventory of Margaret Cook's estate was conducted on August 15, 1797. Her possessions, to be distributed among her grieving children, included a horse, mare and colt, several cows and a calf, two sows and five shoats. There are household items, pots and pans, a loom, spoons and pitchers, a bedstead and a featherbed and some farming equipment such as plow irons, a shovel, branding irons and a chopping axe. There is a standing crop. All of these items are given a value in "pounds" and, as the will directed, are then to be sold with the proceeds used to pay any lawful debts and the balance distributed to her designated heirs, children and grandchildren.

Also to be sold is an unnamed "negro boy" valued at sixty-five pounds. Not all families that moved into Kentucky from Virginia were drivers of slaves. The William Cook family was. This child may have been the son of other slaves to be found among those belonging to Margaret or to her children. (See the Index for evidence of additional slave owned by Cooks and their close kin.) He may have been a boy whose duties were light around the house of an old lady; or the duties may have been heavy. He may have stayed close by her as she became enfeebled; or he may have been sent out to work on the farms of her sons and daughters. His name is not known today. He was not recorded as living with his mother. His father is not mentioned. He is ordered in 1797 by probate procedures to be sold. This child may have been included in the tax rolls made in Franklin County KY in 1792 through 94, wherein Margaret Cook paid

A NOTE ON CURRENCY:

Margaret Cook's will specified values in "pounds." Prior to a nationally mandated standard currency that is, during the colonial period and into the early life of the Republic, all was chaos and confusion. To clarify the colonial chaos, we call upon a nineteenth century historian, Boyd Crumrine and his twentieth century counterpart, Neil McDonald. (See sources for details.) McDonald cites Crumrine: "the currency of the early days was in Pounds, Shillings, and Pence. Before and during the Articles of Confederation of 1776, and until the adoption of the Constitution of the United States in 1787, there was no supreme national authority, and therefore no national currency based upon a recognized unit." McDonald continues. "In every state there were two units of value, the State Pound and the Spanish Milled Dollar. Our people having been under the English government adopted the English pound, shilling, and penny, as the 'name' of its currency..., yet the trade with the Spanish colonies in America and the West Indies brought into the country as its only coined money the Spanish dollar and its subdivisions. Thus, the dollar of the early day was not the 'Dollar of our Daddies,' but the 'spanish Milled Dollar.'"

McDonald: "the value of the 'pound' within the 13 states varied. In PA, MD, DL & NJ it contained (in silver) 1031-1/4 grains while the value varied from 996 grains (NY & NC) to a high of 1547 grains in GA, with a value of 1289 grains in VA, MA, RI, CN and NH. [. . .] When a debt was to be paid the debt amount in pounds, shillings and pence was converted into dollars (Spanish Milled) [. . .] Due to the difference in value of the pound within the various states, to pay off a debt of 7 shillings and 6 pence in PA you would pay one Spanish Milled Dollar (coin.) Conversely, in VA, you paid a 'dollar' coin for a debt of only 6 shillings." A national currency developed over the first three or four decades after the Revolution. In 1792, the Congress pegged the U.S. dollar ($) to either silver (371.25 grams) or gold (24.75 grams). From time to time, adjustments mere made in the ratios.

taxes for the value of 70 acres of land, six horses, mares and mules, eight head of cattle, four Negro adults and three Negros under age 10. This child probably remained with Margaret after August 24, 1796, when Margaret Cook sold slaves as well as 75 acres on a stream called Dry Run, near the community of Jett. (William Scroggins has demonstrated that the stream must be "Slickway Branch," a creek appearing on modern maps of Woodford and Franklin Counties.) Apparently, sold at that time with the farm were eight Negros, four above age 16, together with 13 cattle.

The "new light" doctrines so cherished by devoted Baptist Margaret Cook, did not cast a glimmer upon the Negro child whom Margaret owned at her death. Conscientious as to the souls of her own children, Margaret was covetous of the life and the labor of this boy, whom she listed with farm animals and implements, to be sold for the benefit of one of her own. Margaret could have freed this child by her own choice but did not. Margaret Cook did not consider him a person sufficient to warrant even the listing of his name in a legal document that will sell him off to the highest bidder.

In the Heaven conjured in the imagination of Margaret and William Cook, and invoked repeatedly by their preacher son, **Abraham**, there would need to be apologies made. A paradise of endless, eternal apology made to a Negro boy surely is not the heaven Margaret Cook had in mind.

THE COOK LINE BEFORE WILLIAM COOK OF LUNENBURG

". . . if William Cook moved into Lunenburg as an adult he could have come from practically anywhere. There were Cook families all over Virginia."

William Cook's parents have been identified (on thin evidence) as **William Cook Sr** (abt 1700/10-1750) and **Ann Griffin (Griffith)** (?-abt 1725). Descendent Merlyn J. Cook reported that William Cook Sr, husband of Ann Griffin was an immigrant. In a statement preserved by family genealogist Charlie L. Cook, Merlyn wrote,

"This information is taken from a family Bible, in the possession of a cousin. Although the Bible appears to be authentic, it is hard to tell whether the information was written there as current information or some time later, thus becoming a recording of oral tradition."

The Bible in question has been identified as **Hitchcock's New and Complete Analysis of the Holy Bible**, which was printed by Roswell Dwight Hitchcock in 1872. The book's original owners may have been Isaac and Nancy Sacra Cook, or perhaps one of their children. Isaac Cook (1800-1887) was a son of William Cook III (abt 1764-1814), a son of William and Margaret Cook. Clearly, from the date of publication, the information recorded in this Bible could not have been written down in the lifetime of either William Cook (who died about 1789/90) or his son, William (d. 1814).

There is circumstantial information, which suggests that William Cook (father of William, who died 1789-90) was not an immigrant but that his great grandfather (referred to by some investigators as William Cooke II) was an immigrant from Bristol, England. Perhaps the 1872 Bible has the right name and lineage but the wrong generation. Or perhaps the Bible is correct in all details. Although no conclusions may be drawn about the parentage and ancestry of William Cook, husband of Margaret, I hesitate to discard the statement in the family Bible.

The parents of William Cook Sr (father of William, who married Margaret) have been identified, by some, as Reuben Cooke (1677-1759) and Hannah Atkinson (Gee) (?-1750). Reuben, who died in 1750, left a will which was proved in Isle of Wight County, Virginia on Aug 1, 1751. From the will, family genealogist William Scroggins has concluded: *"If Reuben Cook and Hanna Atkinson Gee were married about 1710, their son William could have been born soon afterward and old enough in 1730 to have a son William Jr., who resided in the Virginia Counties of Halifax, Pittsylvania, Henry and Franklin before migrating to Kentucky, where he died about 1790."* This conjecture may be too much for the data we have.

Just as there were several *William* Cooks, there were a number of *Reubens*. Robert W. Witt, publishing his **The Isle of**

Wight Cooks in 2007, identifies three contemporary Reuben Cooks, a father and son, in addition to the above referenced Reuben, husband of Hannah Atkinson. This *Reuben,* Witt maintains, was the father of nine children, one of whom, Witt says, was named *William.* Witt states (page 24) that this *William* (1690-1758) was the husband first of Mary _____, and the father of Daniel, *William* (1711-?), John, Mary and Henry (sic), and then husband of Naomi Knight and the father of James, Elizabeth, Elimileach, Mercurious, Lazarus, and Ephraigm. Like Scroggins, Witt states that his information relies on data from wills (Chapman, *Wills Isle of Wight*). Witt also cites: J.B. Bodie's *Births, Deaths and Sponsors 1717-1778 from the Albemarle Parish Registry of Surry and Sussex Counties, Virginia (1958)* and J.B. Grimes' *Abstract of North Carolina Wills* (1967).

Robert Witt has recorded no connection to Isle of Wight Cooks by our Lunenburg County William Cook, husband of Margaret. Clearly, the couple, William and Margaret Cook, lived in old Lunenburg County. Clearly, they were the parents of well documented children, who are found with Margaret, their mother, in Franklin County, Kentucky, by about 1784 and certainly by 1788/90. Bill Scroggins, and other researchers, notably Merlyn Cook and Elizabeth L. Nichols (see Sources, below) get us this far. Nichols questions (page 40) the Jones surname assigned to Margaret Cook. Prior to and independently of Witt, Nichols also concluded (page 41) that no reliable information exists concerning the parentage of William Cook, husband of Margaret. (See Nichols' comment in Sources, below.)

The circumstantial data assigning parentage of our Lunenburg County William Cook, to William Sr, son of Reuben and Hannah Cook, cannot be correct, if Witt's results are accurate. A relationship to Reuben and Hannah is also in apparent conflict with the statement (of uncertain provenance) in the above referenced 1872 Cook Family Bible, to the effect that William's parents were Ann Griffin (Griffith) and William Cook, immigrant. In the box below, we will trace information connecting this Reuben to a son, William, as outlined by both Scroggins and Witt but indicate why, relying on Witt's research, this line cannot be that of William Cook, husband of Margaret.

Reuben Cooke was a son of Immigrants William Cooke II (abt 1633-1698) and Joan Roper (?-?). Joan was the daughter of _____ (?) and Hugh Roper (?-?) of Burham, Somersetshire, England. Joan Roper and William Cook II had four sons: William, John, Reuben and Thomas. (Witt adds in a fifth son: Henry.) From their wills, only son Reuben could have had a son, William, who *could have married* (Scroggins) Ann Griffith. Witt states (page 9) that William and Joan were Quakers, "witnessing weddings and hosting early Quaker meetings." Witt also states (page 24) that William, son of Reuben, *died in Northampton County NC in 1758*. The clincher: Witt also states (page 43) that *William, son of William and grandson of Reuben, was the husband of Agnes Mangum, father of but one child, Christopher (1762-1842)*. Scroggins and Witt have followed Reuben's line back to late medieval England. We need not reproduce this information, as it is not relevant to the ancestry of William Cook, husband of Margaret.

The line to Abraham Cook and then to his father William (husband of Margaret) is firmly established. But this William Cook cannot be the grandson of Reuben Cook (1677-1759) of Isle of Wight County Virginia. Witt's recent results, and Nichols before him, show this connection cannot be established. There are two, separate, documented William Cooks.

The link from William Cook, husband of Margaret, to immigrant William Sr (abt 1700/10-1750) may be accepted – but only if the 1872 Bible record is accepted. Our conclusion, which is that of genealogist Bob Baird (quoting Baird, from a private communication to me): "*if William Cook moved into Lunenburg as an adult he could have come from practically anywhere. There were Cook families all over Virginia.*" For a conjecture about the immigrant circumstances of the earliest male Cook ancestor – whoever he was - see page 222.).

SOURCES:

William Cook (husband of Margaret) generally: Betty Taylor Cook's unpublished genealogy book, and her notes. Materials collected and written by Merlyn Joseph Cook (1914 – 1995), placed on the web by Charlie L. Cook: ancestorstories.org and forwarded in private correspondence. The 1767 List of Tithables for Lunenburg County: **The History of Pittsylvania County, VA**; Appendix I; First List of Tithables of Pittsylvania County, Year 1767: p. 285, on the web, variously, incl. carolyar/com/VAQuarterlies

Listing of Franklin County VA residents in the 1740s, '50. '60's and '70: **A Settlement Map of Franklin County Made for The Franklin County Historical Society**: Names and Locations of Many of the Early Settlers in the Area from 1786 to 1886, Gertrude C. Mann, & George A. Kegley, (Jan 1 1776), on the web as: "Franklin County Settler's Map" – franklincounty vagenealogy.com

Lord Dunmore's War an altogether unjustifiable war – opinion of C Hale Sipe, **The Indian Wars of Pennsylvania** (1929, 1931, 2006, Wennawoods Publishing) page 494-5.

The reference to the King James Version, integral as air, has been borrowed from Peter Ackroyd's **Albion, The Origins of the English Imagination,** (London: Chatto & Mindus, 2002, page 219). Ackroyd applied the metaphor to Shakespeare, borrowing the comparison from Gerard Manley Hopkins, who associated the atmosphere with the Blessed Virgin, *"wild air, world mothering air, nestling me everywhere."*

Cook land transactions have been compiled and placed on the web by Gary Kueber. See kueber.us/. Gary Kueber has also carefully preserved and posted the research into Cook genealogy, conducted by William G Scroggins. Much of Scroggins' findings form the basis of the 18th century Cook data relied upon in this book. In addition to his original research, Scroggins has cited the multi-volume **Southside Virginia Families**, John Bennett Boddie (Baltimore: 1966)

Bathsheba Dunn's part is to be kept in the hands of the Executors - Margaret Cook's will has been reproduced by Elizabeth L. Nichols, in her indispensible **Cook, Murphy, Hodges: Families of Early Virginia in the Ancestry of Elizabeth L Nichols** (2004, privately printed). Nichols has also reproduced the 1783 William Cook letter, and has included much valuable Murphy documentation. Nichols is skeptical of ancestral identifications, which do not bring with them solid documentary evidence. Nichols states (page 41): *"there is no indication of any connection in any records so far found of any relationship between the ancestral William Cook and any other Cook individuals, except his sons."* Nichols' stringent approach to acceptable evidence also casts doubt on the assertion that Margaret Cook's maiden name was *Jones*.

For colonial and early national currency: "The Early Currency" by Boyd Crumrine in **Annals of Carnegie Museum,** not otherwise identified by Neil McDonald, whose own work is **Notes On The Pennsylvania - Virginia Land Dispute And The Early History of Southwestern Pennsylvania**; see mcn.org/2/NOEL/Westmoreland/McDonaldTaxLists. (I wonder if Boyd Crumrine is related to the Carmean/Cremeen line; page 86.)

The Isle of Wight Cooks, Some Descendents of Richard Cook, by Robert W. Witt (2007, Heritage Books, esp. pages 3, 5, 7, 9, 13, 24, 43).

Information from and about the 1872 Cook Family Bible was first brought to the attention of this writer by Charlie L. Cook, who has shared information, including a photocopy of the birth, marriage and death records recorded therein.

Important research has been conducted and placed on the web by Bob Baird. Search: Bob's genealogy Filing Cabinet II.

"DESIROUS TO TAKE UP A TRACT ON THE WEST SIDE OF THE GREAT MOUNTAINS"

Sara Bodine
John (Jan Joost) Van Meter

& his parents

Joost Jans Van Meterer
Sarah Dubois

Maria Van Meter (1709-aft 1795)
John Jones (abt 1733-abt 1793)
Sarah Jones (1777-1857)
William F Cook (1802-1850/55)
Joshua Flood Cook (1834-1912)
Cecil V Cook (1871-1948)
Cecil V Cook, Jr (1913-1970)

DOUBLE DUTCH: DORLAND AND VAN METER

As discussed (page 21), a Dutch line, Dorland, twines with the Cook line in the marriage of **Cecil V. Cook Sr** (1871-1948) and **Blanche Dorland** (1873-1967) in Louisville, KY, 1900. Cecil however had his own Dutch ancestors, the Van Meters. The alliance of the Jones-Cook lines and the Jones-Van Meter lines preceded the marriage of Cecil and Blanche by a hundred and fifty years.
Dutch girl, **Maria Van Meter** (1709-aft 1795), married **Robert Jones**. (c. 1696-aft. 1796). Their son, **John Jones** (abt 1733-abt 1793) and his wife, **Mary Renfro** (1743-1793) were the parents of **Sarah Jones** (1777-1857). Therefore, Sarah, wife of **Abraham Cook** (1774-1854), could point to Dutch ancestors through her paternal grandmother Maria Van Meter. Her husband, Robert Jones, was a son of an immigrant Welch father.
The Van Meter family is well documented in Holland and then in Colonial America. The research identifies prominent individuals of this name without

demonstrating the specific Van Meter link to subsequent generations. The earliest mention in Holland has been said to date from a 1293 deed, wherein Van Cuick Van Meteren (two individuals?), was identified in a transfer of property. There was (is?) a village, Meeteren or Meteren, in Tielerwaard, part of a larger community, Geldermalsen. A certain Johann Van Meteren (?-by 1555), is listed in a registry of nobility in 1548 and in 1655, recorded as dead. The name *Van Metere* appears in similar listings later in the sixteenth century: Jasper Van Meteren (?-1578) in 1563 and 1578 (dead); in 1587, three others appear: Willem Van Metere, Johan Cuick Van Metere and Aert Van Metere.

Jasper Van Metere is listed as a Knight in 1570 and deserves separate mention because his seven children (five sons and two daughters) are known.

1. Cornelius Van Meteren (?-aft 1581)
2. Jan Van Meteren)?-aft 1613)
3. Jasper Van Meteren (?-aft 1610) , a justice at Deijl
4. Johan Van Meteren (?-aft 1625)
5. William Van Meteren-Van Meteren, Lord of Meteren (?-aft 1624)
6. Marie Van Meteren (?-?)
7. Cornelia Van Meteren (?-?)

Emmanuel Van Meteren (1535-1612), a prominent historian and diplomat, was an acquaintance of the Dutch-sponsored explorer of North American regions, Henry Hudson. Emmanuel was the grandson of the above named Cornelius and son of the printer, Jacob Van Meteren, who, employed the English preacher and former monk, Miles Coverdale, in the compilation of the first complete Bible in the English language, 1635. Coverdale's version was the product of a gentle temperament and has given the language sonorities - *loving kindness - tender mercy -* which will live as long as any form of English is spoken. (Coverdale's mild demeanor did not stop him from later participation, as an Anglican bishop, in proceedings which lead to the burning of heretics.) Because of his own reformist religious convictions, Jacob (Jacobus) Van Meteren was Coverdale's underwriter. In 1609 Emanuel van Meteren stated that his father Jacob was "a furtherer of reformed religion" who "caused the first Bible at his costes to be Englisshed by Mr Myles Coverdal." I know of no lineal connection between any of these Van Meteren representatives and those immigrants, who become the ancestors of **Cecil V. Cook Jr** (1913-1970).

MARIA VAN METER: from BODINE & CROCHERON, from FLANDERS TO STATEN ISLAND & BEYOND

Mary (Maria) van Meter (1709-aft 1795), wife of **Robert Jones** (c. 1696-aft. 1796), was the daughter of **John Van Meter** (abt 1683-1745) and his first wife **Sara Bodine** (1687-1709). Sarah was the daughter of immigrant **Marie Crocheron** (1660-1703) and immigrant **Jean Bodine** (abt 1662-abt 1745). Mary van Meter never knew her mother Sara, who died (perhaps in childbirth) the year Mary was born. This meant that Mary was raised by John van Meter and his second wife, Margaret Mollenauer (c. 1687-1745).

Jean Bodine, husband of Marie Crocheron, was born near Lille, Flanders (now, France) and died, probably in New York. Some say he reached America only after being smuggled out of Marseille. Jean was a son of immigrant **Jean Bodin** (John Bodine) (?-by Mar 4, 1695) and **Sara Stoff** (?-?). The elder Jean died without leaving a will. His estate was inventoried in 1695, from which it appears Jean owned property and some items of value but nonetheless died in debt. Among the property inventoried were 21 cows, steers and calves, 7 horses and colts, and 100 sheep, all valued at about 100 pounds, plus "2 negro men and a negro woman" also valued at 100 pounds.

Marie Crocheron was also born in Lille, the daughter of **Maria** _____ and **Jean Crocheron** (?-1696). From a book on the Crocheron Family (see Sources, below), we read, "Jean Crocheron removed to Staten Island where he secured title to land at Long Neck, now New Springville, where, in 1670, he erected his homestead, about one mile from the Asbury Church." In the Land Papers, volume I, p. 71, Land surveys, 1676, it is recorded that *John Crushuron* received 188 acres. *"Two lots at the North Side of the Fresh Kill on Staten Island, lying between the two runs of Karle's Neck and Long Neck. 100 rods in bredth by ye meadows Ranging NE by ye common 256 rods. Bounded NW: land of Jacob Pullion and SE: Ye commons, with 20 acres of meadow next to ye Run of Karle's Neck and 8 acres of fresh meadow."* In the New York Calendar of Land Papers, volume II, 1681-1700, on 6 April 1684, there is a description of a survey of 120 acres of land, lying upon the west side of Staten Island, to the north of Long Neck and to the south of Daniell's Neck, laid out for Jonsia Cronsoon by Phillip Welles, Surveyor. In 1685, in a memoranda in the land papers, the surveyor admits his inability to locate the land grants on Staten Island. He gives a list of names of persons to whom land had been granted and among them appears *Jousia Crousoon.*

JOHN VAN METER: from NY to NJ to MD to VA

John Van Meter (abt 1683-1745), father of Maria or Mary, and father-in-law of Robert Jones, was born in Kingston, New York; he was baptized in the Old Dutch Church in Ulster, NY on Oct 14 1683. He moved from New York to Somerset County, NJ, where he raised a family of eleven children, by his two wives. From New Jersey, John moved into western Maryland and then, some years after, into the Shenandoah Valley of Virginia. His daughter, **Maria (Mary)**, with her husband, the long living **Robert Jones** (c. 1696-aft 1796), appears always to have remained a part of John Van Meter's peripatetic extended family, at least until John's death.

In New Jersey John Van Meter recorded a number of land transactions with his mother, **Sarah Dubois** (1664?-1726) and her family, including the acquisition of 3000 acres in Salem County, in the southwest corner of New Jersey, bordering the Delaware River and Bay. On some of the transactions, John signed his name, John Vanmetere.

The acquisitions in New Jersey, as extensive as they were, turned out to be only a warm-up for much larger acquisitions in Maryland and then enormous tracts in western Virginia. In New Jersey, John developed a system of purchase and resale, which he applied time and again as he moved ever westward and onto ever larger holdings.

By April, 1724, John Van Meter acquired the first 300 of his extensive acres in Maryland. This is land upon which the city of Fredrick now is established. John was said to have been the second settler in Fredrick. He and his family lived there until 1735. John Van Meter served as the constable of Monacacy Hundred, a region extending east from present day Fredrick into present day Carroll County, north to Pennsylvania and west to (West) Virginia.

John's constabulary duties did not hinder his acquisition of holdings in Prince George's County, MD. Nor was John diverted away from his extensive explorations and trading with Indians along the western frontier, activities which gave him first hand knowledge about the prospects for settlement of the Sharundo (Shenandoah) Valley in Virginia.

In 1725, John van Meter is said to have accompanied a group of Delaware Indians, who were intent upon attacking Catawba Indians in present-day Pendleton County WV. The Delaware were themselves ambushed by the Catawba but John returned safely to Maryland and remained interested in acquiring western lands. John reported favorably to his sons and others, encouraging them to join him in seeking ownership of property in Virginia.

This family's adventures with Indians continued for generations and did not always end well. John Van Meter's brother, Isaac, may have been killed by Indians. Two of John's young granddaughters were also killed or died (apparently) after their capture by some Shawnee. Their parents (John's daughter, Magdalena and her husband, Robert Pewsy) were also taken, separated, returned home and were reunited – but not before Robert had married a Shawnee woman and fathered two children.

In 1730, John Van Meter and his brother Isaac traveled to Williamsburg, VA and made a pitch to Governor Gooch of Virginia. They expressed themselves, as the governor's proclamation stated, "desirous to take up a tract on the west side of the great mountains." The Van Meter brothers proposed that they be granted 30,000 acres on the western side of the Sharundo (Shenandoah) River, on condition they settle their families and others on the land. The Governor agreed and the patent was awarded. The following year John and Isaac sold much of this land to a relative back in New Jersey, Jost Hite.

Despite the re-sale to Hite, the Van Meter family seems to have honored the conditions of the Shenandoah Valley land patent. By 1736, John Van Meter had moved to Orange County (est 1734), VA; we note the county was named for William IV of Orange (the Netherlands), who married Princess Ann of England, also in 1734. Working with Dutch, German and French agents, John Van Meter succeeded in attracting numbers of "German" immigrants into the region. This migration included families straight from Europe but also entailed a southward migration out of Pennsylvania. The move of Pennsylvanians south across Maryland and into Virginia was doubtless triggered by many and varied reasons, including a search for larger holdings, and perhaps also a new start where slave labor could be utilized. There was also in this southern shift, a persistent quest to create communities where worship could be conducted free from the encroaching gaze of government. The old Pilgrim/Puritan quest to create a 24/7 godly community in the wilderness did not die out in succeeding generations. This objective was taken up by zealous believers of varied religious opinions. Ironically, many of the early sojourners, who moved out of William Penn's Pennsylvania were Quakers.

Which reminds me of a funny story: in 1731, a Quaker, John McKay led a group from their stopover in Maryland into the country around present day Front Royal, VA. There they settled on lands obtained "from a local Dutch fur trapper named Jan Van Meter." Describing John

(Jan) Van Meter as a trapper is like identifying Benjamin Franklin as a mere printer.

Which reminds me of another funny story: a teenage George Washington (1732-99) was commissioned to survey lands along the South Branch of the Potomac River. The year was 1747, or so. The sixteen-year-old surveyor chanced upon a community of locals and recorded the encounter in his diary: *"I really think they seem to be as Ignorant as Set of People as the Indians. They would never speak English but when spoken to they speak all Dutch."* Perhaps the settlers were suspicious of an assertive young man with survey equipment tramping through "their" property, measuring the land for Lord Fairfax. The message to young George might have been: sorry, kid, we'd love to help, but we can't make heads or tails of what you're talking about.

A visionary perspective applied to matters of land acquisition can become myopic around the kitchen table. So it seemed with John Van Meter. Making his will in 1745, John records that his son-in-law **Robert Jones** (daughter **Mary**'s husband) is to receive nothing of old John's extended holdings, unless *"Robert Jones Do not Quit Claim of or to a Pretended Right to One Hundred Acres of Land & other pretended Demand on me . . . for which he hath no right."* John Van Meter had undertaken transactions in land in three colonies, totaling some 50,000 or more acres. But near the end of his life, he is squabbling over the back forty with his son-in-law. And it's personal. If Robert does not shut up, he will get nothing. This particular beef was with Robert but John Van Meter seems to have had prickly relations with each of his daughters' husbands. Apparently he preferred to keep his holdings within the family, which meant passing land to sons, not daughters. John Van Meter was buried in a family cemetery on his farm near Martinsburg, WV.

The Van Meter acquisition and resale of Shenandoah Valley lands was the leading edge of a southbound migration from Pennsylvania into first the upper and then the lower Shenandoah Valley. This flow continued for decades throughout the 18th century. The well worn trail eventually attracted members of the **Diller**, **Slagle**, and **Keinath** families from York and Lancaster Counties, PA. A descendent of these Huguenot and German Reformed (Calvinist) and Lutheran families, Presbyterian **Blanche Dorland** (1873-1976), would marry **Cecil Cook Sr** (1871-1948), a descendent of John Van Meter. (See the Index and Dorland and Cook sketches.)

John Van Meter's career helps answer a question put to this era by Frederick Jackson Turner (1861-1932) and other historians. Were the early inland land buyers primarily settlers or speculators? The answer John Van Meter offers is: we were both. Explorers and traders – and trappers - too.

VAN METERS IN AMERICA: JAN JOOST[1], JOOST JANS[2], JAN (JOHN)[3]

John Van Meter's parents were immigrants **Joost Jans Van Meterer/Meteren** (1656-b/f June 13, 1706) and **Sarah Dubois**. (1664?-1726). Little Joost Jans arrived at New Amsterdam (New York) on the ship *Vos* (Fox) in 1662. He was the son of **Jan Joost/Joosten Van Meterer** (?-1706) whose name, in English form, he gave to his son, our John Van Meter.

The first Jan Joost, father of Joost Jans and grandfather of John Van Meter, was from Thierlewoodt or perhaps Gelderland, Holland. He brought with him to New Netherland his wife and five children. Jan Joost's wife was **Macyke Hendricksen** (Hendrygksen) (?-?) of Mappelen, in the province of Dreuth in Holland. The children were **Jooste Jans (Jansen)**, Cathrin, Geertje, Lysbeth, and Gysbert. The family settled in Wildwych (now, Kingston, Ulster County, NY).

Family historian James T. Van Meter has recorded (1978) a shocking episode which involved several members of the Van Meter-Dubois family. If the date is recorded correctly, that is, if the event occurred in 1663 and little Sarah De Bois was involved, then her date of birth, at times reported as 1664, is late. Stories of kidnapping can become embroidered as to the characters involved. It is hard to know at this late look, exactly who was there and exactly what happened. This tale, full of references to "the pioneering seed," a "friendly Indian," and a miraculous last second escape, shares aspects of romance and legend similar to re-tellings of the Innis Bottom Massacre of Cooks in Kentucky in 1792. (See, page 182, above.) Emphasis has been **added** in the following narrative.

> "Only a year after arriving in America little **Joost Jansen Van Meteren** had an adventure which set the pattern for his whole life and planted the pioneering seed which flowered in succeeding generations. He was captured by the Indians. On June 7, 1663 while the men were away working in the fields the Minnisink Indians entered several villages under the pretext of selling vegetables and. suddenly began murdering their unarmed victims. They took all they could find of value, set the villages on fire and took about 45 women and children captives. Among them were Jan Joosten's wife **Maycke** and son **Joost** from Wiltwyck and Louis DuBois' wife **Catherine Blanchan** and baby daughter **Sarah** from Esopus. Joost and Sarah were later to be married. For three months the men searched the Catskills, but had no success until on Sept. 3 a friendly Indian gave a clue to the location of the captives. A rescue party was formed led by **Louis DuBois** and Capt. Kreiger whose journal relates this event. Meanwhile, since the Indians were running short of food and winter was not far off they had decided to burn some of their Captives. Catherine DuBois and her baby Sarah were selected to be first. When the Indians were about to put the torch to her pyre she began to sing the words of the 137th Psalm. Enchanted by her voice they demanded that she continue to sing, Of course, she did. The approaching rescuers heard her, were guided to

the spot, attacked the Indians and released all the prisoners. Little Joost, too young to be much affected by the horrors of captivity, thoroughly enjoyed his three months of Indian life. Later as an adult he frequently left home to spend many weeks at a time with various tribes. In this way he was among the first whites to explore the wilderness areas to the west of the coastal settlements. He was particularly impressed by the beauty of the Valley of Virginia and urged his sons to settle there, which they eventually did."

In 1664, Jan Joost Van Meter, with wife **Maycke** and little **Joost** restored to him, is recorded as giving an oath of allegiance to England, which at that time was contending with Holland for control of the government of New Amsterdam. Apparently Jan Joost desired to learn more of his adopted nation, for in 1665 he is recorded as having purchased from the sale of an estate, the book **The Chronicles of the Kings of England**.

During the following decades and until his death, Jan was active in public affairs. He served as a magistrate in Marbleton (1673) and Justice of the Peace in Eusopus (1682). Jan was given local responsibilities under both Dutch and English governments. In 1689, after the English had regained permanent control, Jan once again swore allegiance to England.

The absence of robust patriotism among the Dutch was endlessly frustrating to the last Director General of New Netherland, the autocratic Peter Stuyvesant. Apparently many Dutch immigrants were of the same mind as Jan Joost: they would offer allegiance to either Holland or England. The seemingly casual shift was, no doubt, the result of a pragmatic assessment of the Dutch settlers' circumstances, with their main objective in mind: get along with the authority that had the biggest army in the neighborhood. Many of the Dutch were there to make money and seem to have decided there was little to be gained if hostility related to English rule flowed up from them or down upon them.

No doubt, practical minded Dutch colonists kept an eye on events back home. In 1689, the year Jan Joost swore allegiance to England, a Dutchman and his English wife, William III and Mary II, had become the king and queen of England, Scotland, etc. In New Amsterdam (already renamed New York), a question would have been asked and quickly answered: should Dutchmen in New York kick up a fuss with the English when Windsor Castle had become a homey's crib? No indeed.

Jan Joost busied himself acquiring property both in New York and in the province of New Jersey, primarily around the community of Salem and in Somerset County. On June 13, 1706, Jan's will was ratified in Burlington County, New Jersey. The estate included property he could never have claimed in Holland: six Negro slaves: a man, a woman and four children.

AN ADDITIONAL FRENCH CONNECTION

Sarah Du Bois (1664?-1726), wife of **Joost Jans Van Meterer/Meteren** (1656-1706), and mother of **John Van Meter** (1683-1745) was the daughter of **Louis Du Bois** (1626-1696) and **Catherine Blanchan** (1640-1713), the hostage who sang a Psalm and saved herself and little Sarah from being burned alive. (See above.) Catherine was the daughter of **Matthieu Blanchan** (?-?) and **Madeleine Joris** (?-?) Catherine married Louis du Bois in 1655; after Louis died, she married Jean Cottin.

Louis du Bois, Catherine's husband, was born in the Spanish Netherlands (Belgium, Luxembourg, French Flanders) and married Catherine in Mannheim, capitol of the Palatinate (*Paltz*), on the River Rhine. He immigrated with her to New Amsterdam and died in Kingston, Ulster County New York.

Much biographical data of the Cook family points often to Huguenot (i.e., French Protestant) lineage and practice. Louis Du Bois, born in a Low Country region then controlled by Spain, was called *Louis the Waloon*, thereby being identified as a denizen of Flanders, and probably a French-speaking descendent of Celtic peoples. The term

"Waloon" is Latin and may have meant that Louis Du Bois was considered either a "foreigner," a "Welshman" or merely a Protestant.

Louis was the son of **Chrétien DuBois** (1597-1655), who was a true native of French Flanders (and so, most likely, was his son) and who died prior to the marriage of his son Louis to Catherine Blanchan.

Du Bois descendents may take justifiable though ironic pride in the family ascendancy, which includes nobly-remembered Huguenots as well as some of the most powerful and sanguinary royal houses of Europe. **Geoffroi Du Bois** (?-?) was an ancestor and companion of William of Normandy, aiding William in the bloody conquest of England in 1066. Further back, the family claims descendency from Alfred the Great and Charlemagne. The absence of documentary evidence moves most medieval ancestral quests onto the ledger of legend. The Du Bois family has been called by at least one descendent, "Grand Masters of the Forests of France." The name itself gives the proof, such as it is; *bois* means *forest*.

An undocumented family connection has been made to the notable and long living W.E.B. Du Bois (1868-1963). William Edward Burghardt Du Bois wrote that he was a descendent of our **Chrétien Du Bois**, through one of Chrétien's sons, either Jacques or **Louis**. W.E.B. is perhaps the most significant Black American intellectual in the nation's history. We would claim him before we claim Charlemagne. Du Bois' best known of several notable books is **The Souls of Black Folk** (1903), whose central thesis is "double consciousness," the paradox characteristic of the Black experience in a racist society. DuBois was aware of the many paradoxical twists and turns in his own family, though perhaps unaware of the existence of his distant, contemporary cousin, Addison Cook, whose murder was the result of his association with the Ku Klux Klan (see pages 149-154). W.E.B. Du Bois was a founder of the National Association for the Advancement of Colored People (N.A.A.C.P.) and the editor, from 1910-34, of that organization's monthly magazine, *The Crisis*. His book,

Black Reconstruction (1935) ought to be required reading for anyone who thinks the Civil War ended in 1865.

SOURCES:

Cook and Jones genealogy, generally: Betty Taylor Cook's unpublished genealogy book, and her notes.

Du Bois information is available on the web at various sites; see: Spicerweb.org

"they speak all Dutch" – George Washington quoted in **The Grand Idea: George Washington's Potomac and the Race to the West**, Joel Achenbach (New York: Simon & Schuster 2004, page 93)

Bodine data has been posted very generously at DAVE'S BODINE GENEALOGY WEB SITE, freepages.genealogy.rootsweb.com/~bodine/index

David Bodine, who has conducted research in London, Holland and at the Center for Protestant Genealogy in Paris, has written: "there is a fraudulent genealogy going around that links the American Bodines to other famous Bodine-like names in France running back into the 1300's or so. There is absolutely no evidence behind this information. It appears to be the work of a 20th Century genealogist named Gustave Anjou (1863-1942). He was a Swede whose real name was Gustaf Ludvig Ljungberg. He fabricated pedigrees to please those who paid for his services. Trustworthy genealogical research on the American Bodines can really only be traced back, so far, to the Jean Bodines who came to America in the late 1600's. Anything before that is still uncertain." On the web, Dave Bodine has cited **The Crocheron Family of Staten Island, NY** by Charlotte Hix (1980), page 2, concerning Staten Island property owned by Jean Crocheron.

particularly impressed by the beauty of the Valley of Virginia: For the narrative of the kidnapping incident and much other Van Meter data: *"Van Meter Pioneers in America,"* by James T. Van Meter (1978), posted at vanmetre.com/Papers/van meter pioneers in America. For additional data: *Wonderful West Virginia* (Oct 1985), helpfully reprised by Juanita S. Halstead, *"Captured by Indians – Twice"* at hackerscreek.com/Gazette.

caused the first Bible at his costes to be Englisshed by Mr Myles Coverdal: Emmanuel Van Meteren's statement was located at wikipedia (search: *Jacobus van Meteren*).

loving kindness - tender mercy: Coverdale Bible phrasings are cited in **Albion, The Origins of the English Imagination**, Peter Ackroyd (London: Chatto & Mindus, 2002, page 296).

W.E.B. DuBois recalled his ancestry in a 1920 essay, "The Shadow of Years," in **Dark Waters: Voices from Within the Veil** (Mineola, NY: Dove Publications 1999, pages 3-11). Du Bois writes (pages 4 and 5), "Louis XIV drove two Huguenots, Jacques and Louis Du Bois into wild Ulster County, New York. One of them in the third or fourth generation, had a descendent, Dr. James Du Bois . . . who made his money in the Bahamas . . . there he took a beautiful little Mulatto slave as his mistress, and two sons were born . . . having finally gotten myself born, with a flood of Negro blood, a strain of French, a bit of Dutch, but, thank God, no *Anglo Saxon.*"

No *Anglo Saxon* "blood?" An additional note on the chaos of colonial immigration may be found on page 77.

"PROJENITORS"

Michael Keinath / Keinadt
Margaret Dillar

Catherine Keinath Slagle (1766-1855)
Margaret Slagle Fellows (?-?)
Sarah Fellows Ireland (1829-1921)
Arabelle America Ireland Dorland (1850-1895)
Blanche Dorland Cook (1873-1967)
Cecil V Cook, Jr (1913-1970)

It was at the Hill Lutheran Church in Millerstown (Annville) Pennsylvania that **Margaret Diller** (1734/44-1813) married **Michael Kainadt** (1720-1796) (surname recorded by Betty Taylor Cook as "**Keinath**".) Margaret Diller Keinath was described as small, with black eyes and hair, cheerful and fluent in her speech. Early records commemorate the baptisms of several of Michael and Margaret Keinath's children. They were each baptized by Rev. John Casper Stoever, who is remembered by Lutherans as their first minister ordained in Pennsylvania.

MARGARET DILLAR KEINATH & HER DESCENDENTS

By 1790, Michael and Margaret Keinath are recorded living in the Shenandoah Valley, in Augusta County, which had been, prior to the Revolutionary War, a great western swath of Virginia Colony. From Augusta was formed a number of smaller counties, as well as all of Kentucky (1792) and West Virginia (1863, created by Unionists during the Civil War). Michael and Margaret, and their adult children settled near Waynesboro, a portion of old Augusta, which has always remained within Virginia.

Among Margaret and Michael's 12 children, it may be helpful to recall, was **Catherine Keinath** (1766-1855) who married **George Slagle** (1761-1829) in Cumberland County, PA in 1789. Catherine and George's twelfth child was **Margaret Slagle** (abt 1795-?), named for her grandmother. Margaret Slagle became the wife of **Jonathan Fellows** (abt 1795-?). Margaret and Jonathan are believed to have been married in Virginia before moving to Indiana.

Jonathan and Margaret were the parents of the long lived **Sarah Fellows** (1829-1921). Sarah, born in Waynesboro, Virginia, lived most of her adult life in or near Columbia City, Indiana, as the wife of **Martin Ireland** (1821-1904). Sarah died in Chicago in 1921. She was the mother of **Arabelle America Ireland** (1850-1895), wife of **James E. Dorland** (1844-1915). Arabelle and James' second child and second daughter was **Blanche Dorland** (1873-1966), wife of **Cecil Virgil Cook Sr** (1871- 1948) and mother of **Cecil V Cook, Jr** (1913-1970).

MICHAEL KAINADT & "THE NEGRO WOMAN SALL"

Michael Kainadt (1720-1796) (aka Keinath / Koiner / Koyner / Coinert / Coiner) is believed to have immigrated to America from Protestant Germany about 1740, arriving in Philadelphia and settling in New Holland, Lancaster County PA. Michael was described as of medium height, well proportioned, with a straight posture and erect walk. His voice was said to have been harsh, and he was known for his hot temper. Despite this, a daughter-in-law (son Casper's wife) said of him that he was an agreeable visitor in her home.

Michael was a ship owner who made some five trading voyages across the Atlantic after his first arrival to America. On his last trip back to Germany, he persuaded his sister to sail to America with him, but she was swept overboard in a storm. Michael lost all of his cargo on this crossing and never made another. Michael is known to have served in the Northampton County PA Militia during the Revolutionary War. His four sons, Casper, Conrad, George and George Michael also saw service, with Conrad an Ensign in the Pennsylvania Navy, while the other sons were in the Pennsylvania militia.

The name Keinath/Kainadt, has traveled through subsequent centuries as Koiner, Koyner, Coinert and Coiner. Many spelling options were selected by clerks and notaries at their discretion, to say nothing of the convention of those days, which allowed you to call yourself what you pleased and spell your name as you wished.

By the fall of 1789 (the year of their daughter's marriage back in Pennsylvania) the elderly Michael and Margaret Keinadt are found in the Shenandoah Valley, Augusta County Virginia (as stated), near present-day Waynesboro, where they lived the rest of their lives. Land purchases by Michael Coinert are recorded in Augusta County in 1790. Ancient records of Bethany Lutheran Church (the old "Keinadt's Church") report that in 1794, the devout and community-minded Michael Keinadt, at 73, made the nails for the first log church, called Spindle's Meeting House (named for the first pastor).

Michael and Margaret Keinadt are buried in the cemetery at Keinadt's Church. Today, the cemetery is called "Trinity Lutheran Graveyard" and is located a few miles north of Waynesboro, VA on Route #12, Crimora, Virginia. The large monument over their graves was erected a century after their passing, to commemorate a family reunion in 1896. The inscription states: "Margaret and Michael-Projenitors of the Koiner, Coyner, Coiner, Kiner, Kyner families." To that list could have been added, by 1900, the married names of Keinadt women who, for themselves and their children, exchanged "Keinadt" for the surnames Fellows, Ireland, Dorland, and Cook.

Michael Keinath's will is dated June 15, 1796. He left considerable wealth to his children and made provision for his wife and his son, Fredrick, whose mental condition rendered Fredrick incompetent. He also left to his wife a "negro woman Sall & one cow of her choice, to have & possess during her life and to be at her disposal." A large garden was left to a son, who was to furnish his mother produce from it "provided that negro woman Sall is not be to be sold out of my Family."

The fact of human slavery is ever a mystery for descendents. This proviso in his will suggests a bond between Michael Keinath and Sall (Sally? Sarah?). Michael's enslavement of Sall is an attachment he acknowledges from the grave. It is to be maintained by his family at the cost of depriving his own wife of food and his son the ownership of a food source, the family garden.

Why did Michael do what he did in his will? Was Sall a faithful servant? If so, then why did Michael see the need to threaten his family on her behalf? Had Sal been faithful only to him? Was Sall infirm or otherwise incapable of fending for herself? This might explain why Michael did not free her before his death and also why he expressed a desire that she not be sold. Was Sall a mistress of Michael? Or perhaps his child? This might explain Michael's desire to keep her within the family circle, possibly against the wishes of his wife and son. A more thorough or fortunate investigator may solve the riddles surrounding Michael Keinath and the "negro woman Sall."

The larger context must include the possibility that Sall journeyed with the family, when they moved from Pennsylvania to Virginia. Throughout the 1700's, slavery was legal and actively practiced in Pennsylvania, though never on so large a scale as in tobacco-blessed Virginia. In Pennsylvania, by the 1760's, slavery fell into infrequent use. This change was owing to the presence of indentured German immigrants, who had begun to arrive by the thousands, in response to invitations from friends and relatives and the advertising of shipping agents. These workers, bound to service for a term of years, were in many cases skilled and literate. In the increasingly diverse, manufacturing oriented Pennsylvania economy, such workers proved to be more productive and economical to business owners than were African slaves.

The main appeal of slaves, brought in from Africa or Barbados and other English possessions in the Caribbean, was always in the uncompensated life-long labor they provided. This was a signal asset to the large scale agricultural operations, which developed in Virginia and other Southern colonies. Michael Keinath and his many sons may have moved to Virginia, as did numbers of other German-speaking Pennsylvanians, because of their desire to continue as farmers but in a more temperate climate, where large tracts of land were being made available and where slaves could be utilized more efficiently.

In the nineteenth century, much was made of the physical size of representative members of the Diller and Keinath / Kaindt / Koiner families, whose "marvelous" physical development was commented upon and then attributed to their earliest immigrant ancestors. *"Marvelous representations of the physical development and strength of some of the earlier Dillers has been related. Some of the earlier Koiners were much stouter than the present generation; so that both sides may trace their largest specimens of physical manhood to their strong-haired and robust English mother."*

This "strong-haired and robust English mother" is Caspar Diller's wife, **Anna Barbara** (1703-?). Anna Barbara may not have been English, but French, though German-speaking. (See the Diller/Dornis sketch, page 269.) A tradition has been passed down that Anna Barbara was *"of large stature, masculine development, and had a bountiful supply of hair."*

Good size, big-haired descendents of masculine development, as well as small, bald ones of female development, may make what you will of this description. And then there is another report, which commemorates, at the time of the Civil War, the simultaneous weighing of six Pennsylvania Diller brothers, whose combined weight totaled 1636 pounds. These Pennsylvania Dillers, averaging 270 pounds or so, served in the Union cause, against the interests of their Keinath and Koiner cousins in nearby Waynesboro, Virginia.

SOURCES:

For Arabelle Ireland Dorland's Kainadt or Keinath or Koiner ancestry: Betty Taylor Cook's unpublished genealogy book, and her notes.

Some helpful material may also be found on the web at "Ancestors of Linda Nicholson"

For information concerning the church and burial records of the Keinadt/Coiner family in Augusta County, Virginia: Bethany Lutheran Church History, on the web at: Bethany-trinity-trinity-va/org/history.

their combined weight was 1,636 pounds - **History of Cumberland and Adams Counties, Pennsylvania** (Chicago: Warner, Beers & Co., 1886, esp pages 352-53)

For slavery in Pennsylvania in the Eighteenth Century: "*Slavery in Pennsylvania*," by historian Douglas Harper: slavenorth.com/pennsylvania

> *Margaret and Michael-Projenitors* - A roster of the graves at the Trinity (Bethany) Lutheran Church is posted at:
> geocities.com/augcem/index.html?1018315012530
>
> The "Keinadt" graves, plus dozens of Koiners, and other related names, are listed as follows:
>
> *Keinadt, Catharina 1778 - 1825*
> *Kienadt, Margaret Diller 1734 - 1813*
> *Keinadt, Michael 1720 - 1796*
> *Margaret and Michael-Projenitors of the Koiner, Coyner, Coiner, Kiner, Kyner families*

"OF ALL SORTS OF OPINIONS THERE ARE SOME"

Caspar Diller
Anna Barbara Dornis

Margaret Diller Keinath (1734/44-1813)
Catherine Keinath Slagle (1766-1855)
Margaret Slagle Fellows (?-?)
Sarah Fellows Ireland (1829-1921)
Arabelle America Ireland Dorland (1850-1895)
Blanche Dorland Cook (1873-1967)
Cecil V Cook, Jr (1913-1970)

    Anna Barbara Dornis (1703-bef 1766) was the wife of **Caspar Elias Diller** (1696-1787) and the mother of **Margaret Diller** (1734/44-1813), the wife of **Michael's Keinath** (1720-1796). Anna Barbara's father has been recorded as **Christian Dornis** (?-?).
    Caspar Dillar's parents are said to have been **Adam Elias Diller** (?-?) and **Marie (Maria) Balliet** (?-?). However, Marie's husband has also been named as **Johnsses Tuller (Diller)** (?-?), whom she is said to have married in 1690 in the city of Hornbach, Alsace, a much disputed region where both German and French were spoken and where many towns of medieval and even more ancient vintage were given two names, one in each language. No doubt, the subject peoples of Alsace were inclined to be flexible about their own surnames, so as to accommodate more easily the clerk, notary or judge of the moment who was looking now to a German prince, now a French monarch for his stipend. In addition to Tuller, Johnsses' surname has been written as, Teller, Deller and Diller. Johnesses Tuller was said to have been a Protestant of Switzerland. The name of Adam's (or perhaps Johnsses) father has been preserved as **Michael Dellor** (?-?).
    The parents of Caspar's mother, **Marie (Maria) Balliet**, are recorded as **Anna Fruibeau** (?-?) and **Jacob Balliet** (1641-1706) of Schalbach another town of Alsace, with of course a German name, as well: Schwalbach. In

1680 Jacob Balliet is shown as a day laborer of Schalbach. On Feb 19, 1706, Jacob was listed as holding the position of *Gerichs-Schoffe*, or associate judge of Schalbach, at his death. One wonders if Judge Bailliet might have been first the victim (in 1680, a day laborer) and then a beneficiary (in 1706, an associate Judge) of the pendulant religio-politics of the day.

The surnames Fruibeau and Balliet figure in Huguenot records of the period. The family name, *Balliet* appears in the Huguenot town of Burbach in 1625. *Fruibeau* is a local Huguenot family name of Schalbach, where, in 1592, Hans Fruibeau, Qladt Fruibeau and German Fruibeau are listed as residents.

In North Annville Township, between Annville and Cleona, just west of Lebanon, Pa. is located the Hill Cemetery belonging to the Lutheran, Hill Church (*Berge Kirche*), which the Diller family helped establish in the 1730's. The present church building was constructed in the nineteenth century. The church and cemetery are located on Hill Road, two miles north of its intersection with US 422, west of Lebanon.

Caspar Diller's grave is in the Hill Church Cemetery. The writer visited this beautiful hill-top setting in April, 2006 and recorded the inscription on Caspar Diller's grave:

Hier Ruhet
Caspar Elias
DILLER
Geb. im jahr anno
d.1696 Junius den 25ten
Ist alt worden 91 jahr
& 5 monten

Translation: *Here lies Caspar Elias DILLER, born AD 1669, June 25, died at age 91st years, five months.*

The gravestone on which the inscription is found appears much younger than 1787. One assumes the epitaph is a faithful reproduction of the original. Beside the gravestone are two others, one large, the other small.

Neither of these ancient markers contains legible lettering, which has been effaced by over two hundred years of Pennsylvania winters. A reasonable inference is that the larger unmarked grave beside Caspar's is that of his wife, Anna Barbara, and the smaller is that of a child.

Perhaps not. A Mr. Brakebill has stated that "later in life, old Caspar got tangled up with a widow lady in Lebanon [PA] and married her in 1766, after his first wife had died. The court records show that he had to put up a lot of property, etc, in her name at the time of marriage." Caspar's second wife was said to be Magdalena Meyer (?-?); they married April 14, 1766 in Lebanon, PA, Reverend Stoever presiding. The minister was John Casper Stoever, Jr, Lutheran minister and pastor of the Hill Church. A large monument to John Stoever may be found in the Hill Cemetery, close by Caspar's own grave.

As in Europe where the *Diller* surname was bandied as Tuller, Teller, and Deller, so in America *Diller* has been recorded as Thaeler, Thaler and perhaps Taylor. Even though Caspar's Hill Cemetery stone is in German the Diller surname suggests French origins (de Llér, Daillé). From all that is known and reasonably surmised, Caspar's parents - like his wife's family - seem to have been French Protestants or Huguenots, the losers in the bloody wars of French religion and royal succession in the sixteenth and seventeenth centuries. The Dillers were probably driven out of France, a result of Catholic and specifically Jesuit urgings pressed upon the King. They may have received a temporary welcome in the German Palatinate (generally, those jurisdictions along the west bank of the upper Rhine). This asylum became available to the Protestants of France at about the time of Caspar's birth. Charles of Hesse-Cassel, on April 18, 1685, invited Huguenots into the Palatinate. Thousands accepted the invitation. Thus were removed from France many literate and productive subjects. (For the Huguenot Phenomenon: pages 28-40.)

The asylum proved insecure. Louis XIV endeavored to claim the Palatinate for France and so regain his delinquent Huguenot subjects. He did temporarily gain control of Lorraine (adjacent to Alsace) in 1678, which was lost to France once again nineteen years later. The territorial conflict lasted for two hundred years and more, igniting several wars. As years of uncertainty stretched into decades, settlement in America, no doubt, looked better and better.

Once in Germany, the refugee Dellor family, with their roots in a part of France containing many German speakers, would have accommodated easily to the German language. Caspar may have learned German as a child and possibly as his first language. In any case, once in the *Paltz* (German Palatine), Caspar if not also his parents, adopted Lutheran practice in preference to the French and Swiss Huguenot doctrines of their French homeland.

In America, Caspar was Lutheran, though perhaps of a reformed flavor. (The Hill Church building in Annville was shared by both a reformed and a traditional German Lutheran congregation.) If Caspar and Anna Barbara were reformed Lutherans, they would have been inclined, in contrast to Martin Luther and his rigorous adherents, to (1) view Baptism as possibly but not absolutely an occasion for the "rebirth" of the believer (2) hold to the view that the Lord's Supper invites the Christ to be present in spirit, not literally, and (3) emphasize the civil law as a tool for the criminal suppression of nonconformity. This last is a theme shared by both Calvin and Luther, which, despite the best efforts of Adams, Jefferson and Madison, crops up in the United States like the virus that it is.

Tenacious Diller genealogists have teased out of ancient Pennsylvania and German records, interesting bits of information concerning Anna Barbara and Caspar. Their arrival in America is memorialized in the passenger list of the ship *Samuel*, which brought a boatload of 200 "Palatines," to Philadelphia from Amsterdam on August 17 1733. (The *Palatinate* region of Germany includes the counties of Kurpfalz, later Bayern-Pfalz, and the more northern counties of Kraichgau, Hessen, Baden-Durlach, as well as the county of Wertheim, later Baden.) The Dillers in Germany have been associated with a village called Gauangelloch (southeast of Heidelberg), where Lutheran church baptismal records preserve the births of four boys and three girls to Casper Elias Diller and Anna Barbara Dornis.

The Diller family, arriving in Philadelphia, included Caspar Elias Diller, 37, Anna Barbara (Dornis), 30, Philipp Adam, 10, Hans Martin, 8, Rosina, 4, Christina, age 2. Other children would be born in America. The occupation of both Caspar and Anna Barbara was listed as *taylor* with Caspar also recorded as a *shoemaker*. Later records indicate that Caspar became wealthy as a farmer and land speculator in Lancaster County, PA.

In a Lancaster Co PA will book (WFT Vol. 11, #423) Caspar Diller's birthplace is given as Alsace, Kraichou District. His marriage to Anna Barbara Dornis, daughter of **Christian Dornis** (?-?) is recorded as 1719, in Gaunangrlloch, Germany. It has been reported that the family's first home in Lancaster County was Earl Town, east of Lancaster and that he sold his farm for division into lots from which was established the settlement of New Holland. Caspar is said to have moved some thirty miles north of Lancaster to the Lebanon area, settling in Millerstown (later, Annville) a few miles west of Lebanon. Other German Protestants had already settled in this part of the fertile Cumberland Valley, after moving out of crowded "Germantown," near Philadelphia.

By the middle of the eighteenth century, enough French/German immigrants had arrived in Pennsylvania (known for its promise of religious freedom) to trigger the departure for that colony of many thousands of additional European settlers. Word had gotten back to Germany that PA was good and that VA might be even better. Caspar and Anna Barbara Dillar and their children were in an early wave of this German-speaking tide. Caspar could not have imagined in 1733, the year of his immigration, that he would live to see his children (some born in Germany) and grandchildren fight to final victory in a nation-building cause, aided by Catholic France, against Protestant, English soldiers and German mercenaries. Who knew?

In America, German-speaking French Protestants such as Caspar and Anna Barbara Diller were called "Swiss Brethren" by the chattering classes. They were lumped together with other dissenting European Protestants by colonial administrators and court clerks. The lump including Mennonites, Amish, Moravians, and various Pietist and Anabaptists sects, such as Seventh Day Baptists, Unitas Fratrum, and a sect in Pennsylvania called "the Woman in the Wilderness." I am not kidding. It is possible that none of the Swiss Brethren were from Switzerland.

We should not conclude from the arrival of "Swiss Brethren" in the 1700s that immigrants exclusively from the European continent created the American religious buffet. The pious German-speaking partisans of Calvinist convictions, fresh off the boat from Amsterdam, were preceded of course by English dissenters a century before. Just as it was not all Huguenots in the 1700s, it was not all Puritans and Pilgrims in the 1600s.

Thousands of immigrants in both the seventeenth and eighteenth centuries wanted nothing at all to do with any of the contentious sects. Probably a majority of the early arrivals were indifferent to zealotry and the partisan bickering that seems to accompany it. If you don't believe me, you can take the word of one of the politicians of the day.

In 1687 (Catholic) Governor Dongan of New York reported, *"Here bee not many of the Church of England [and] few Roman Catholicks [but] abundance of Quakers - preachers, men and women especially - singing Quakers, ranting Quakers, Sabbatarians, Antsabbatarians, some Anabaptists, some Independents, some Jews, in short, of all sorts of opinions there are some and the most part, of none at all."*

All sorts of religious opinions and no opinions at all. Isn't this what an Enlightenment - unfettered intellectual activity - is all about? Octavio Paz (**On Poets and Others**, 1986) and before him, Edmundo O'Gorman (**La idea del descrubrimiento de america**, 1951) have argued that America, both North and South, was not actually *discovered* but rather was *invented* by European immigrants, hopeful, assertive *arrivists,* who created and passed on to their children utterly new societies.

For the Indians already on the land, the process of creation as carried out by Europeans was one of astonishing destruction. But this judgment should not blind us to the newness that came in the wake of the aboriginal catastrophe. In North America, the immigrants brought a Renaissance with them in the form of political and religious diversity and dissent. North American denominational variety served as the template for political enlightenment, which lead to the throwing off of coercive and highhanded European hegemony. By the middle of the eighteenth century, colonists had developed an openness to political experimentation. Everyone seemed to be carried along by the tide of humanity that was becoming the new American society.

Dissenting and divergent religious opinions stimulated the imagination. All sorts of innovation might be possible in a *new world*. Much of the experimentation, from Jamestown, Virginia to St. Mary's City, MD, to Pennsylvania, to Rhode Island, to Plymouth, and a great deal of the rhetoric everywhere was grounded in wild notions, often prompted by piety. Adams, Madison and Jefferson owed as much to John Bunyan and the Restoration pamphleteers as they did to Burke and Locke. If *Pilgrim's Progress* was not in their heads, it was in the milieu that the founders and framers took for their own.

In Latin America, unfortunately, there was no diverse religious flowering but rather the *Contra Reforma*, imported from Spain. As a consequence, without a broad-based receptivity to political innovations that could be molded by local leadership, only a series of partial and unsatisfactory top-down political revolts proved possible – and has ever proved possible.

Caspar and Anna Barbara Diller and their children would have been received in eighteenth century Mexico, Colombia, Argentina or Peru as dangerous, alien renegades, not as the flexible and industrious nation-building opportunists they were. (Brazil, a bit more free and easy, might have been a friendly exception.)

To the surprise of no one who has read this far, we have concluded from the records preserving what is known of the Diller and Keinath families, that many of the ancestors of **Cecil V Cook, Jr** (1913-1970) by way of his grandmother **Arabelle America Ireland** (1850-1895), and Belle's mother **Sarah Fellows** (1829-1921) and Sarah's grandmother **Catherine Keinath Slagle** (1766-1855), were Huguenots. The Huguenot experience is treated in more detail elsewhere (see page 28), for the same origins have been traced back from **Blanche Dorland** (1873-1967). The exiled French Protestants ancestors of Cecil Cook, like the Huey ancestors of Cecil's wife, **Betty Huey Taylor Cook** (1918-2000), settled in south-central PA. In the 1700s, the Pennsylvania Hueys, were, it seems, near neighbors of the Dillars. The Hueys are found in Churchtown, just east of Earltown (East Earl) where **Anna Barbara** and **Caspar Diller** first settled.

Here is a brief summary of the lives of Margaret Diller & Michael Keinath and of Arabelle Ireland & James E. Dorland and of Belle's parents, Sarah Fellows & Martin Ireland, taken from previous sketches. Caspar and Anna Barbara's daughter **Margaret Diller** (1734/44-1813) and her husband **Michael Keinath** (1720-1796) moved from Lancaster County, PA to Waynesboro Virginia. In 1789, probably before Margaret and Michael left PA, their daughter **Catherine Keinath** (1766-1855) married the Revolutionary War drummer boy, **George Slagle** (1761-1829). Catherine and George moved to Virginia as did her parents. Their daughter **Margaret Slagle** (?-?) married **Jonathan Fellows** (abt 1795-?) in Virginia and moved west with him to Columbia City, Indiana, where their daughter **Sarah Fellows** (1829-1921) married **Martin Ireland** (1821-1904). Martin and Sarah's daughter was **Arabelle America Ireland** (1859-1895).

Arabelle's husband, **James Emory Dorland's** (1844-1915) earliest Dutch immigrant ancestors are found first in Brooklyn, NY, in the seventeenth century, then New Jersey in the eighteenth and Ohio in the nineteenth. Meanwhile, the Farmer and Cook ancestors of **Cecil V. Cook Sr** (1871-1948), husband of **Blanche Dorland** (1873-1967) were fixed first in Virginia and by the end of the eighteenth century had moved into that western extension of Virginia Colony, which became the commonwealth of Kentucky.

SOURCES:

For information concerning Jacob Balliet and his daughter Maria and her husband: Jacob Balliet of Schalbach (1641-1706) cached on the web and word searched "Jacob balliet+Deller+Huguenot" – information based on: **The Allaman Heritage**, Durward B. Allaman / Richard J. Henry (1997).

For details about Caspar Diller's French origins and PA gravesite: **The Diller Family**, By JL Ringwalt (1877, Released February 2003) on the web at accessgenealogy.com/scripts/data/database.

For details of the territorial disputes, which engulfed Alsace, see: The *Vanguard*, a Presentation of *HightowerTrail.com*

singing Quakers, ranting Quakers, Sabbatarians, Antsabbatarians, some Anabaptists, some Independents, some Jews: The statement by Governor Dongan: **The Peopling of British North America, An Introduction**, Bernard Bailyn (Wisconsin: 1985) page 96.

For the passenger list of *The Samuel*, which brought Caspar and Anna Barbara Diller to America in 1733: The Palatine Project, progenealogists.com/palproject

For O'Gorman and Paz and the invention of America: **On Poets and Others**, by Octavio Paz (New York: Arcade Publishing, 1986).

For data concerning Caspar Diller's mention in a will book, and his second marriage: *"Early Diller History, Retrieved from various Internet sources in Spring 2002"* Edited and cleaned by Andrew C. Diller. Dillernet.com by way of a Google search: Caspar+Diller+genealogy+Pennsylvania.

For the presence of European Protestant sects in Pennsylvania in the eighteenth century: **A History of the Christian Church**, by Williston Walker, revised by Richardson, Pauck and Handy (New York: Scribner's, 1959); for the Calvin quotation: see **A History of Christianity**, by Clyde L. Manschreck (Englewood Cliffs, NJ: Prentice-Hall, 1964).

> "A MEDLEY OF NOTIONS"
>
> In drawing attention (page 275, above) to liberation rhetoric in the colonial milieu, credit must be given to Gordon S. Wood. In **The Creation of the American Republic** (Norton, 1972), Wood places emphasis (page 17) upon "a medley of notions taken from English Enlightenment rationalism and New England Covenant theology." In this medley, I would include the influence of John Bunyan, whose *Pilgrim's Progress* (1678, 1684) encouraged devout Americans to see their personal struggles as a pilgrimage toward Heaven. The medley of ideas, with Bunyan included, caused the redefinition in America of such concepts as *liberty, freedom, equality, natural rights* and *justice*. The widespread employment of these ideals allowed a vast cross section of the colonial population to believe they were all talking about the same thing - even if they were not - when these concepts were invoked in support of armed resistance against British rule by 1775/6. Joshua Flood Cook's own notion of *liberty* was limited by racial dogmas. Nevertheless, in 1908, anticipating Gordon Wood, he recognized the expansive aspects of *liberation* and *inclusion*. "The seaboard," Joshua wrote, "was settled by people who thought they knew what the word Liberty meant . . . but . . . history shows how little they knew about it . . . New England whipped men at the post for freedom of speech; Virginia imprisoned men for preaching the Gospel . . . in the fullness of time . . . it became necessary for people to . . . show what Freedom meant." (**Old Kentucky**, pages 27-28.)

A GENEALOGY OF BIBLICAL PROPORTIONS

John Flood
Agnes Payne

Joshua A. Flood (1772-1850)
Lucy Flood Cook (1802-1865)
Joshua Flood Cook (1834-1912)
Cecil V Cook (1871-1948)
Cecil V Cook, Jr (1913-1970)

Joshua Flood's father was **John Flood** (1695-1782). John was 77 when son **Joshua** was born, in 1772. This is a stemma of Abrahamic scale and must be taken on faith. Born in England, John died in Buckingham County, Virginia at age 87. A British Navy captain, John advised his sons at the advent of the Revolution "that they were Americans and to fight for their country."

John Flood married _____ Davis (?-?) in 1754, when he was fifty-nine. The couple had three sons, Henry (1755-1827), John Jr (1757-1826) and Thomas (1760-1811). The two older sons may have been born in England; Henry and John Jr died in Buckingham County, Virginia; Thomas died in Wilson, TN. John Flood and his first wife may have married in England but their great-great grandson, Joel W. Flood, wrote in 1913 that "Miss Davis" was "from Glouschester County." By no later than 1760, the year of the birth of son, Thomas, the couple is in Virginia Colony. On March 3, 1760, for the sum of thirty shillings, John Flood received a land patent in Albemarle County, Virginia Colony. The grant was 295 acres in what became (in 1762) Buckingham County.

A church is believed to have been built on land donated by John Flood from his farm near Dillwyn. This became the Buckingham Baptist Church (sometimes referred to as "Buckingham Olde Church"). John Flood was an officer of the church from 1771 to 1774, serving as Sexton. It is likely this church John Flood attended was Anglican, later becoming Baptist, after the Anglican Church was deprived of its colonial government subsidy.

This turn of fortune was the direct result of the patriot victory in the Revolution. A plaque donated by the descendants of John's son, Henry Flood, is mounted on the wall of the church and states that John and his wife were buried beside the church. A later addition was built over their graves. The church is located on U.S. Route 15 in Buckingham County, VA.

In about 1762, John Flood married **Agnes Payne** (1730?-?) in Buckingham County. Agnes may have been John's housekeeper. Such things have happened before and since. John and Agnes had six children, Noah (1763-1818), Moses (1765-1852), **Joshua A**. (1772-1850), Joseph (1774-1849), twins William (1777-1845) and Mary (1777-1853) and Benjamin (1780). The five youngest children died in Kentucky. This chronology fits what **Joshua Flood Cook** (1834-1912) wrote in 1908 (**Old Kentucky**, page 59) concerning his grandfather **Joshua Flood**. J.F. Cook wrote that his grandfather Flood, having failed to inherit any Virginia property, came, as a young man, "poor" to Kentucky with a number of brothers and sisters.

Apparently, all of the siblings who failed to inherit from John Flood were the children of John and his second wife, Agnes Payne. The Virginia land remained with the older, better established sons of their mother, _____ Davis and old John Flood. The David-Flood heirs and descendents, who remained in Virginia, achieved great political prominence there. Joshua Flood and his siblings did come poor to Kentucky, just as grandson J.F. Cook wrote it up.

SOURCES:

John Flood genealogy: Betty Taylor Cook's genealogy book, and notes; **Old Kentucky**, by Joshua Flood Cook (1908) and a Feb 20, 1913 letter from John and _____ Flood's double great grandson, Joel W. Flood (1839-1916) to "Cousin Fannie." For many details about John Flood's wives and children: *"Genealogy Report of John Flood,"* at freepages.genealogy.rootsweb.com/ ~cougar/flood/flood_john.txt.

A THOUSAND ACRE SHIRE ON "YE NECK OF LAND"

Thomas Farmer and Virginia Colony

Henry Farmer (circa 1657-?)
Henry Farmer II (1696-1753)
Elam Farmer (circa 1725-1784)
Hezekiah Farmer (circa 1760-1826)
Benjamin Farmer (1783-1837)
John Goode Farmer (1808-1871)
Susan Goode Farmer Cook (1838-1890)
Cecil V Cook (1871-1948)
Cecil V. Cook, Jr (1913-1970)

Ellery Farmer, in **A Farmer Book**, reported that **Thomas Farmer** (1586/1594-?) arrived in Virginia Colony in 1616 on the ship *Tryall*. This early immigrant, had come, as did the rest, "to found an empire upon smoke." By 1620, Virginia Colony was exporting some 50,000 pounds of *Nicotiana tabacum* – a drug which began as a fad among London dandies and quickly became the quintessential colonial cash crop.

Tobacco's addictive properties only added to its value and thus contributed to the large welcome given to slave ships, which brought the cheapest imaginable laborers to enrich émigré plantation owners - the true beneficial heirs in the Virginia Commonwealth of the English Protestant Reformation. Cancer induced by tobacco would claim the life of **Cecil V Cook, Jr** (1913-1970) some nine or perhaps ten generations and 350 years removed from Thomas Farmer's modest Jamestown beginnings.

While the English colonists got maize and tobacco, the Indians ("naturals" or "originals" as the English sometimes called them) got domesticated animals, metal weaponry, European insects such as the honey bee and the earthworm – and disease, which may have wiped out Indians in Old Virginia just as it had in New England.

"WEE HOLD NOTHINGE INJUSTE, THAT MAY TEND TO THEIR RUINE (EXCEPT BREACH OF FAITH)."

In 1623, Thomas Farmer was listed as a resident of what came to be called Farrars Island, a 1000 acre shire on the James River known as "ye Neck of Land." A year before, Thomas had survived a series of well planned Indian attacks, which killed almost 400 immigrants.

The Pamumkey were led in 1622 by a very able chief, Opechancanough, who had inherited the plenary chieftainship of a regional Indian empire known as Tsenacomoco. Scholars have concluded that Tsenacomoco was a confederation of six clans located on the western shores of the Chesapeake Bay. The clans had been brought together under the leadership of the famous Powahatan. On his death in 1618, his brother Opechancanough, had taken charge. In 1622 Opechancanough tried to wipe out the English, who had been trying since the earliest contact, to wipe out or enslave the Indians. About one third of the settlers were killed.

The approach to replenishing the founding population in Virginia Colony was simple and direct: recruit newbies from a seemingly endless supply of impoverished, English *men*. Despite the deaths of countless, anonymous, indentured newcomers, they continued to arrive in waves and restored and increased colonial numbers far beyond the local population. Meanwhile, the Indians faced extermination.

When a representative of the Virginia Company, under whose charter the Colony was governed, asked the governor and his council to observe just rules in their recharged campaign (after the 1622 attacks) to exterminate the aboriginal peoples, the council replied, *"wee hold nothinge injuste, that may tend to their ruine (except breach of faith)."* That last bit about avoiding breach of faith soon was moved over to the *nothinge injuste* column. This was after the English discovered they could wipe out an entire Indian village, if they approached, making gestures of friendliness.

JAMESTOWN: "SO FAR UP AS A BARK OF FIFTY TUNS WILL FLOAT"

The wordy instructions to the Jamestown settlers spell out why they were to establish themselves upriver, at a far distance from the coast. The two main reasons for the up-river founding were (1) greater convenience in the moving of anticipated goods out to sea from the surrounding countryside and (2) better security against an ocean-going enemy. The English knew that Catholic Spanish Colonists from St Augustine, Florida had wiped out a French Protestant settlement on the Florida Gulf Coast in 1565. The Dutch and the French themselves were also considered a threat to this tiny English settlement. Up the James the settlers were instructed to go; upriver they went.

> "But if you choose your place so far up as a bark of fifty tuns will float, then you may lay all your provisions ashore with ease, and the better receive the trade of all the countries about you in the land; and such a place you may perchance find a hundred miles from the river's mouth, and the further up the better. For if you sit down near the entrance, except it be in some island that is strong by nature, an enemy that may approach you on even ground, may easily pull you out; and if he be driven to seek you a hundred miles [in] the land in boats, you shall from both sides of the river where it is narrowest, so beat them with your muskets as they shall never be able to prevail against you."

The lives of Virginia Colony immigrants were harsh almost beyond belief and would remain so for a century and more. The settlers seem to have had to create everything from scratch. Bernard Bailyn and other historians of the colonial Chesapeake have given depressing descriptions of the living conditions of the early settlement. As late as 1697, settlers reported that Virginia *"looks like a wild desart, the high-lands overgrown with trees, and the low-lands sunk with water, marsh and swamp . . . perhaps not the hundredth part of the country is yet clear'd from the woods, and not one foot of the marsh and swamp drained."* This description reflects the aftermath of English occupation, not pre-English settlement. The Indians might have left a more orderly imprint upon the land, an imprint which vanished after the intervention of the English and the epidemics they brought to the settled, indigenous communities.

The picture of Virginia as untouched, after millennia of occupation by indigenous clans, is hard to square with recent anthropological and historical investigations. Prior to 1607, Virginia may have been occupied by thousands of inhabitants, who disappeared shortly after contact with Europeans and the diseases they introduced. The scientists of our own day have concluded - or at least, have argued - that eastern North America was home for hundreds of thousands of people of Asian origin, who were wiped out by early contact with European explorers and traders, beginning in the 1500s.

But the picture of pre-English Virginia is complicated by a lack of solid information. The present state of knowledge suggests that there were numerous indigenous settlements. But a vast indigenous population seems *not* to have been part of the history of coastal Virginia in the decades before English settlement. Surmises based on slight data gives a population of not more than 15,000 Indians along the western Chesapeake from Cape Henry north to *Anacostan*. Living in scattered villages of a few hundred people, in an area of some 5,000 square miles, 15,000 people is not a large population.

Despite modern surmises which are inclined to suggest otherwise, it still seems probable that the First Families of Virginia, the *Pamumkey* clan, had lived on the land for millennia but left little or no trace of their habitation. The absence in Virginia of signs of native occupation a hundred years after the permanent arrival of the English seems to be the result of (1) only modest changes in the landscape effected by the *naturals*, (2) the likelihood that there were not more than a few thousand Indians on the land in 1607 and (3) the withdrawal or disappearance (by warfare and disease) of the native populace not long after the first few decades of contact with the English.

Most of the evidence for a great indigenous pre-colonial population comes from New England, where dozens of European vessels dropped anchor for a hundred years prior to the founding of permanent settlements, beginning in 1620. The Northeast is also the region, as opposed to Virginia and the Old South in general, where pre-settlement signs of contagion among the native peoples have been concentrated. (Some of the early New England colonists, semi-starved and suffering from exposure, occupied Indian coastal towns, which were found abandoned, except for corpses.)

The early Virginia settlers did of course turn to the clearing of land to make room in the woods for tiny two-room cabins and equally modest cultivation. They found the going to be exhausting. As a result, no effort was expended on clean-up. Cleared land, with all the work done ax blow by ax blow, left the stumps of trees and tangles of vines on the edge of every cleared plot. After a century of pioneering effort, Dr. Bailyn has said, "there was ruin and debris all along the banks of the Chesapeake Bay and the lower reaches of the rivers that empty into it, wherever there was or had been habitation."

The homes the colonial English made for themselves in the 1600s were utterly stark and devoid of any sort of convenience. A typical farmer's cabin along the Chesapeake, even after two or three generations was, as described by Bailyn (see Sources below), "a dark, drafty, dirt-floored insect ridden, one- or two-bedroom box made of green wood and scarcely worth maintaining in good condition since it would be abandoned as soon as the few acres of farm land it adjoined were exhausted by ruthless tobacco cultivation. These ill kept, crowded ramshackle little farm houses, were so flimsy they were virtually uninhabitable after a decade unless they were substantially reconstructed." These cabins were "dribbled over the landscape without apparent design." Most were a mile or more from the next habitation, if not totally isolated.

The "great house" of a more affluent planter would be nothing more than four or seven or ten connected rustic rooms, instead of the typical two, surrounded by a scattering of out buildings. Brick construction was rare; there probably was none at all for a half century after the founding in 1607. *Greenspring*, the 1660s brick home of Governor William Berkeley (1605-1677) (gov: 1642-52, '60-'77), was ultimately modified with the increase to two stories and the addition of a pitched roof and a porch-arcade. Even so, architect Benjamin Latrobe, visiting the "mansion" a century after these additions and just before the house was taken down, described the brickwork as "crude" with the whole place giving the appearance of "solidity with no attempt at grandeur." Daniel Webster (1782-1852) is supposed to have said, "When tillage begins, other arts follow." Maybe. The arts, including architecture, were late to arrive in Virginia.

Thomas Farmer was on the muster rolls of Virginia Colony in 1624. Ellery Farmer pointed out that to be listed on the muster rolls suggests that Thomas Farmer was a man of some responsibility and not an indentured servant. Thomas Farmer was identified as a member of the House of Burgesses 1629-30 from the "Plantation of the College" and the Neck of Land. By way of context, Ellery Farmer, writing in the 1950s, added these comments:

"The writer inspected two monuments erected on Farrars Island many years ago by the Association for The Preservation of Virginia Antiquities. One of the monuments commemorates the location of a town named Henricopolis for Henry, Prince of Wales, which was established by Colonial Governor Thomas Gates in 1611. After the Indian Massacre of March 1622, the town ceased to exist. The other monument commemorates the location of the "Plantation of the College Lands" which had been set aside by the London Company in the 1620's for the

establishment of a college. The college lands extended from the falls in the James River, along the northern bank of the river southward ten miles, to 'The Neck of Land' (Farrars Island). In 1618, the colonists obtained a charter from King James I for the 'University of Henrico' It was never more than an idea; a tract of wild land and a charter from the King of England. After the Indian Massacre at Henricopolis in 1622, the plan for the University was put aside and not revived until 1692, when King William and Queen Mary established William and Mary College at Williamsburg, Va.

"Henrico County, named in honor of Henry, Prince of Wales, is the county in which Richmond is situated. Richmond is located at the falls (head of navigation) in the James River ten miles up from Farrars Island. Henrico Co., established in 1632, originally comprised the present Henrico and Chesterfield counties, but in 1749, Chesterfield was made a separate county. The James River separates the two counties. The records of 1 Thomas Farmer's descendants are Henrico Co., records until 1749, after which they are Chesterfield records for they lived across the James River from Farrars Island in the part of Henrico Co that became Chesterfield Co."

Because of the large separation in their birth years, Thomas Farmer might have been not the father but the grandfather of **Henry Farmer** (abt 1657-?). In either case, Ellery Farmer states that Mrs. A. V. D. Pierrepont, the professional genealogist working with him, noted the chronological and geographical proximity and the fact that Henry named one of his sons, Thomas and concluded that Thomas Farmer and Henry (and therefore Henry's descendents) were of the same line. This is pretty thin evidence, but what can you do?

"FAIR PLAY FROM FOUL GAMESTERS"

Ellery Farmer states that a Richard Farmer was executed for his part in the once-famous and still resonant Bacon's Rebellion in Virginia in 1676. This event was sparked by the fury of small farmers in outlying areas, who were being killed by Indian attacks and felt colonial Governor William Berkeley was indifferent to their circumstances. They were left to make their own arrangements in their own ways with their aboriginal neighbors. Richard Farmer is listed among those who were condemned for participating in the armed protest. The protest became militant when an assembly of settlers appealed to the governor to appoint a commander to see to their better protection in their isolated communities. Berkeley refused to ratify the appointment of one Nathanial Bacon, newly arrived from England and willing to take up this dangerous assignment.

When Governor Berkeley rebuffed the popular appeal for a specially designated military officer, the incensed frontiersmen made Bacon the "people's commander." The autocratic William Berkeley had served as governor for decades and had grown accustomed to his decisions receiving a pliant acceptance by a staid planter class. He declared Bacon and his followers, numbering up to 700 colonists, traitors and in rebellion. Bacon was not intimidated by the governor; he and a handful of the rebels were recently arrived from England and had probably seen worse of civil war, than what the governor threatened. They would not have hesitated to encourage English in arms against English, something that had never yet happened in America. But as a newcomer Bacon was doubtless susceptible to the semi-tropical tidewater climate. Consequently, in the middle of the crisis, Nathaniel Bacon died and his rebellion fell apart. We have a remarkable narrative of the affair from the quill of a contemporary, An Cotton (c. 1655-by 1690) who wrote a series of letters to a friend in England.

Ann (possibly Hannah) Cotton's narrative of Bacon's Rebellion recommends itself for skillfully employed literary qualities. Was this writer the wife of John Cotton (1641-1728)? Ws she Ann, a daughter-in-law to the Rev. William Cotton (1600-1640) whose mother, Joane (?-?) was an immigrant from Cheshire, England? Was this Joane an ancestor of **Elizabeth Huey Taylor**

Cook (1918-2000) through Joane's daughter, Verlinda Cotton (?-c. 1675)? Perhaps. If Verlinda *Cotton* was the wife of **William Stone** (1603-1660). But Stone's wife may have been Verlinda *Graves,* daughter of Jamestown founders, **Katherine** _____ (?-?) and **Thomas Graves** (?-by 1637). Betty Cook was of course, the wife of **Cecil V. Cook Jr** (1913-1970), the parents of the writer of this (too long) narrative. Regardless of the speculative connection to Verlinda Graves (or Cotton), Betty Cook is related in her Huey and Gaines lines to Katherine _____ and Thomas Graves. (Details of these lines may be traced in this book's companion volume, **All of the Above I**.)

For page after page, Ann Cotton sustains her dramatic tale, a reminder that letter-writing used to be an entertainment, highly prized by writer and reader. The literate An Cotton gives notice that it is not just Shakespeare who can turn out a pretty word from our mongrel English language.

Colonel Washington [George Washington's great-grandfather], him whom you have sometimes seen at your house, who, being joined with the Marylanders, invests the Indians in their fort with a negligent siege, upon which the enemy made several sallies, with as many losses to the besiegers, and at last gave them the opportunity to desert the fort, after that the English had, contrary to the law of arms, beat out the brains of six great men sent out to treat a peace; an action of ill-consequence, as it proved afterwards, for the Indians having in the dark slipped through the Legure . . . they resolved to employ their liberty in avenging their commissioners' blood, which they speedily effected in the death of sixty innocent souls, and then sent in their remonstrance to the governor in justification of the fact, with this expostulation against them, his professed friends, in behalf of the Marylanders, their avowed enemies; declaring their sorrow to see the Virginians of friends to become such violent enemies as to pursue the chase into another's dominions; complains that their messengers, sent out for peace were not only knocked on the head, but the fact countenanced by the governor [William Berkeley of Virginia] [. . .]. This was fair play from foul gamesters.

[. . .] the people formerly had for Sir W. B. [Governor William Berkeley] whom they judged too remiss in applying means to stop the fury of the heathen, and to settle their affections and expectations upon one Esquire Bacon . . . whom they desired might be commissioned general for the Indian war, which Sir William, for some reasons best known to himself, denying, the gentleman, without any scruple acceptance of a commission from the people's affections, signed by the emergencies of affairs and the country's danger, and so to advance with a small party, composed of such that on his authority, against the Indians, on whom, it is said he did signal execution.

In his absence he, and those with him were declared rebels to the state [. . .]. Bacon, some few days after his return home from his Indian march, repaired to render an account of his services, for which he and most of those with him in the expedition, were imprisoned; from whence they were freed by a judgement in court upon Bacon's trial [. . .].

Bacon "smothers his resentments and begs leave to visit his lady, now sick, as he pretended, which being granted, he returns to town at the head of four or five hundred men, well armed and resumed his demands for a commission [. . .]

The general for so he was now denominated, had not reached the head of the York river, but that a post overtakes him and informs him that Sir W. B. was raising the train bands [militia] in Gloucester, with an intent either to fall into his rear, or otherwise to cut him off when he should return, weary and spent from his Indian service. This strange news put him and those with him shrewdly to their trumps, believing that a few such deals or shuffles, call them which you will, might quickly ring both cards and game out of his hands; he saw that there was an absolute necessity of destroying the Indians, and that there was some care to be taken for his own and the army's safety, otherwise the work might happen to be wretchedly done, where the laborers were made cripples, and be compelled instead of a sword to make use of a crutch.

It vexed him to the heart, as he said, to think that while he was a hunting wolves, tigers, and bears which daily destroyed our harmless and innocent lambs, that he and those with him should be pursued in the rear with a full cry [. . .] he countermarched his army, about five hundred in all, down to the middle plantation, of which the governor being informed, ships himself and adherers for Accomack (for the Gloster men refused to own his quarrel against the general), after he had caused Bacon, in these parts to be proclaimed a rebel once more, July 29th.

[. . .] the general once more sets out to find the Indians: of which Sir William having gained intelligence to prevent Bacon's designs by the assembly, returns from Accomack with about one thousand soldiers, and others, in five shipss and ten sloops, to Jamestown, in which were some nine hundred Baconians, for so now they began to be called [. . .].

Bacon, by a swift march before any news was heard of his return from the Indians, in these parts, comes to town, to the consternation of all in it, and there blocks the governor up [. . .] he fetcheth into his little Leagure all the prime men's wives, whose husbands were with the governor, as Colonel Bacon's lady, Madame Bray, Madame Page, Madame Ballard, and others, who the next morning, he presents to the view of their husbands and friends in town, upon the top of the small work he had ast up in the night, where he caused them to tarry until he had finished his defense against his enemies' shot [. . .].

[. . .] the governor understanding that the gentlewomen were withdrawn to a place of safety, he sent out some six or seven hundred of his soldiers, to beat Bacon out of his trench. But it seems that those works, that were protected by such charms while raising, that plugged up the enemy's shot in their guns, could not now be stormed by a virtue less powerful when finished, than *the sight of a few white aprons, otherwise the service had been more honorable and the damage les, several of those who made the sally being slain and wounded, without one drop of blood drawn from the enemy.*

Within two or three days after this disaster, the govenernor reships himself, soldiers, and all the inhabitants of the town, and their goods, and so to Accomack again, leaving Bacon to enter the place at his pleasure, which he did the next morning before day, and the night following burned it down to the ground, to prevent a future siege, as he said, which flagrant and flagitious act performed, he draws his men out of town [. . .] Bacon . . . while he was a contriving, death summoned him to more urgent affairs, into whose hands, after a short siege, he surrenders his life [. . .].

Vindictive Governor Berkeley hanged several dozen of the Baconians, including, as mentioned, one Richard Farmer, who may have been a relative of **Thomas Farmer** (1586/94-?) and his descendents. Enough executions were ordered, Ann Cotton reported, "to outnumber those slain in the whole war on both sides, it being observable that the sword was more favorable than the halter [imprisonment]."

Several features make Bacon's rebellion notable even today. This was warfare in America by colonists against colonists. (But not the first, as I said in the 1st edition of this book, forgetting Maryland in 1655, when Puritans defeated Catholics in a brief but bloody battle, which led to executions and imprisonment. See **ALL OF THE ABOVE I**, pp. 373-4). Bacon's rabble militia and their bloody assaults against the Indian population, demonstrated the terrible inevitability, which marked the fate of the native peoples. Later colonial regimes, free of the contempt Governor Berkeley felt for his own subjects, realized they could enlist companies of ill-trained and undisciplined colonists on the mere promise of lands, further west. This sort of *Indian policy* became the norm in Virginia and Massachusetts, less so in Pennsylvania and New York. PA and NY generally experienced more civil relations between colonists and natives, until the deluge of newly arriving European settlers, by the 1750's, put terrible pressures on frontier relations generally.

The 1676 burning of Jamestown by rebellious colonists is evidence of the depth of alienation felt by the neglected, poorer classes. They showed patience until they became finally and utterly hostile in seeking their own redress. Exactly one hundred years after Bacon's Rebellion, the colonists, better led and for better reasons, rose in town-sponsored militias to destroy English rule over them.

After the 1670s strife, the long tenured Governor William Berkeley was recalled to England in disgrace. King Charles II, son of the beheaded Charles I, said of the intemperate Berkeley, "The old fool has killed more people in that naked country than I have done for the murder of my father." The next royal governor, and many that followed him, along with the planter class, saw the dangers of ignoring the demands of small landowners. It was realized that these were the very people needed to settle and expand the western colonial frontier. As a result, a limited vote was opened up to include more of the male population. The enlargement of the franchise, an implicit and latent trend in all the colonies, got a genuine push forward by Bacon's Rebellion.

In the colonial era, the Farmers were respectable Anglicans. Ellery Farmer reports that **Elam Farmer** (abt 1725-1784), grandfather of **Benjamin Farmer** (1783-1837) - ancestors of Ellery - served on a Grand Jury which, in May, 1772, indicted the Rector of Dale Parish, *"The Rev. Archibald McRoberts for making use of hymns or poems in the church service, instead of David's Psalms, contrary to law within twelve months past."*

The Rev. Mr. McRoberts was the Episcopal priest known to **John Goode** (1739-1792) when Goode became estranged from the established church in Virginia. Goode objected to the prosecution of Baptist preachers and the imposition of a tax upon colonists who did not attend Episcopal services. John Goode was, as stated previously (page 169; see also page 316, ff.), eventually ordained a Baptist pastor. At the Revolution, McRoberts, it is believed, immigrated (or returned) to England. And no wonder. He was denounced by the "new lights" as oppressive and misguided (and worse) but was also prosecuted by the Anglican establishment for the smallest variation from rigid traditionalism. **Susan Goode** (1783-1864), daughter of John Goode, would become the wife of Elam Farmer's grandson, **Benjamin Farmer** (1783-1837). The couple moved to Kentucky, with Susan remembered as carrying her father's *new light* principles with her. The Goode's Baptist zeal would prevail over the Anglican practice of the Farmers; emersion and public contrition were substituted for the sprinkling of infants and confirmation.

Elam Farmer's influence would be felt by the family in that all-important economic and social aspect, the practice of race slavery. In his 1784 will, Elam included the following provisions:

- *I give & bequeath to my daughter Martha Lewis one negroe woman called Doll*
- *to my son Elam Farmer all that is now in his possession except a negro fellow called Beather & at the division of my estate he is to be brought in and divided with the rest of the negroes after mentioned.*
- *to my daughter Mary Russell one Negroe called Nancy*
- *to my daughter Judith Russell one negroe called Sharper*
- *to my daughter Rhoda Boles one Negroe called Peter*
- *to my daughter Salley Farmer one Negroe called Lettey*
- *to my daughter Phebe Farmer one negroe called Fanny*
- *to my son Henry Farmer at the death or marriage of my said wife two negroes that I have lent her called Tom & Amey*

In 1826 and 1837, each in their turn, Elam Farmer's son and grandson, **Hezekiah** and **Benjamin**, would make similar devises to their heirs.

SOURCES:

Thomas Farmer and Farmer genealogy, generally: Betty Taylor Cook's unpublished genealogy book, and notes.

empire upon smoke: quotation found in **White Over Black**, Winthrop Jordan (Norton: 1968 [1977], page 71)

wee hold nothinge injuste, that may tend to their ruine: early history of Virginia and Jamestown is well treated in **American Slavery, American Freedom, The Ordeal of Colonial Virginia**, Edmund S. Morgan (New York: Norton, 1975, 2005*).*

so far up as a bark of fifty tuns will float: a command to settle upriver at what became Jamestown: *Instructions for the Virginia Colony* (1606).

An arresting though perhaps a too sweeping treatment of conditions in North America prior to European settlement: **1491: New Revelations of the Americas Before Columbus**, by Charles C. Mann (Vintage: 2006); this writer described Virginia conditions in 1607 in the *National Geographic* (May 2007, pages 34-53).

after the Indian Massacre of March 1622, the town ceased to exist: **A Farmer Book** Ellery Farmer (1955), an excellent volume; reproduces Farmer wills. On the web at geocities.com/heartland/Flats/7314/314/Farmer/farmer

a dark, drafty, dirt-floored insect ridden, one- or two-bedroom box: Living conditions in Virginia Colony and the attendant quotations: **The Peopling of British North America, An Introduction**, Bernard Bailyn (Random House, Vantage, 1988, pages 103-04)

For details and the context of the Indian raids in Virginia Colony in the 1620's, and later, see **Facing East from**

Indian Country: A Native History of Early America,
Daniel A. Richter (Harvard University Press, 2001)

whom they judged too remiss in applying means to stop the fury of the heathen: An(n) Cotton's narrative of Bacon's Rebellion: the *Richmond (VA.) Enquirer*, Sept, 12, 1804, subsequently printed by Peter Force (1835); see the Virtual Jamestown Project, on the web at: jeffersonvillege.virginia.edu/vcdh/jamestown

The old fool has killed more people in that naked country than I have done for the murder of my father: Charles II, quoted regarding Gov. William Berkeley: **A Basic History of the United States**, Charles A. and Mary R. Beard (Doubleday, 1944, page 77).

It would have been impossible to compile this record without the assistance of Mrs. W S Farmer of Frankfort, KY., who was widely acquainted in the family and had done considerable research of the Farmer family and her own Lillard family. Much help was also obtained from Mrs. AS Lillard, Frankfort, KY; Richard W Farmer of Chicago, Ill; Mrs Charles (Corrine) Lucas; Mrs George L Farmer, Louisville, Ky; Mrs. Edward C Farmer of Louisville, Ky; Mrs. Thomas A Cannon of Ashland, Ky; Miss Stella Bass, Archivist, Va. State Library, Richmond, Va; Mrs. G B McClure, Richmond, Va; Mrs Stephen W Dunwell, Poughkeepsie, NY and **Mrs. Cecil V Cook, Jr**. Bluefield, West Virginia, and many others.

Ellery Farmer
Col US Army, retired
***A Farmer Book** (1955)*
Introduction

Appendix A

DEATH OF A HUSBAND

Betty Cook (1982)

What could be more depressing than a hospital admitting room on Christmas Day? Cold. Empty. Devastating. Our family waited, trying to find a laugh to cover the fear we felt. Cecil, my husband, was to be tested for possible lung cancer. I kept saying, sometimes aloud, sometimes to myself, "Just a precaution; he's too healthy for this to be serious." These thoughts, like the beads of a rosary, kept crossing my mind.

The patient was admitted and the tests began. The results left no doubt. There was a growth and it had to be removed. Surgery took place the last day of the year, a day past our twenty-seventh wedding anniversary. The year 1968 had begun with such promise for us. Cecil's promotion as vice-president of his company and a move to a new and beautiful home in a different city made me feel secure and happy. I was to learn again a lesson that I should have mastered long ago. There is no guaranteed security or happiness apart from the security of faith in our Heavenly Father.

The surgery was "successful" in that the cancer was removed; the lymph glands around the vocal cords were excised, and radiation was scheduled. It all seemed like a very bad dream. I found myself going through all of the motions of being a good Christian. I was strong and brave. Keeping my tears to myself, I covered very well the anger I felt-not toward God, but toward Cecil. Why had he continued to smoke in the face of mounting evidence linking smoking and lung cancer? As the days passed my anger changed to compassion and love. Cecil, who had been my strength through our lives together, now had become so vulnerable and so in need of strength from me. I learned that the best prayer is one for courage to meet life's crises. I learned that I am never utterly alone and abandoned, although I have to battle these two feelings constantly. Words from Isaiah were of comfort to me, "When you pass through deep waters, I will be with you; your troubles will not overwhelm you." The picture of passing through and not staying in deep waters was of great encouragement to me. To see an end is a blessing.

Spring brought beauty in new life all around and in our family as we welcomed our first grandchild, Matthew Mitchell Cook. We returned to normalcy in our lives. We did the necessary chores to "set our house in order." We made new wills and set up a new trust agreement, which was a necessity in any case with a move to a different state. We had always tried to live in a stance that indicated we knew this life was not permanent. This knowledge served as a grounding for the time when death seemed a very real possibility.

Summer found us busy taking up new jobs in our church and learning new skills in our lives. Cecil took a course in speed reading, and I took a course for women who had been out of the job market and wanted to return. We watched men land on the moon and were thrilled by this achievement. But I was disturbed that so much was so easily spent on space exploration while so little was spent on cancer research.

Cecil had always had the joy of life, which made everything seem like fun. Now this spark was gone from his personality, and death seemed to hang over our spirits. We tried to go about our daily lives as if the "invader" had not come into our home. Our five sons were grown, with the exception of our youngest, who was a junior in high school.

Our oldest son was working on the west coast; our second son was in his last year at Union Seminary in New York; our third son was serving as a conscientious objector in a hospital in New England; and our fourth son was in the Peace Corps in Sierra Leone, West Africa. We found enjoyment in their lives and interests. But it was difficult for the family to be so far away from each other. There is strength in being together.

We read all we could about cancer and nourished our hopes with cases like Arthur Godfrey and John Wayne. They had survived lung cancer for many years. The following spring Cecil's cancer had spread, and there was involvement of his liver. He was hospitalized and my days were spent with him. We were as optimistic as we dared to be, but we were working against tremendous odds. We talked about my future alone, and we both knew in our heart of hearts that this was a certainty.

The last day of Cecil's life is a painful memory. I had stayed with him until visiting hours were over. As I left I told him, "I love you and I'll see you in the morning." I asked the nurses to notify me at any time, day or night, if there was a change. I would have stayed all night if he had been in a private room.

The next morning when I reached Cecil's, room, I noticed a sign on the door. "Please check with the desk before entering Mr. Cook's room." I knew the moment I saw the sign that he was gone. I checked with the nurse and she went in and came out immediately. He had just died. I went in and saw him propped up in bed, eyes open, hands gently resting on his lap. He did not look as though death had been a struggle; it seemed only that he had quietly left this house that had become such a miserable dwelling for him. I closed his eyes, sat beside him, and held his hands. I was thankful that he had been released from so much misery.

Gathering up his few small belongings, I put them in his suitcase and started to leave. But a nurse and an intern took me aside to a small conference room and began asking factual questions about Cecil for hospital records. I'm sure this was necessary, but at the time it seemed an intrusion. I made my way down the hall. The elevator seemed so foreign, and I wanted to shout to the people: "Something terribly sad has happened to me."

It was a lonely walk as I crossed the familiar parking lot to the empty car. One should never take this walk alone. It seemed so unfair that after all of these months with Cecil, he died alone. It still seems so to me after all this time. I drove home on that beautiful morning; and though I had known Cecil's death was imminent, I still felt numb.

I went through the final activities with a studied peace and quietness. I had lived with death as an intruding presence for a year and a half. Death was a release from the prison that held the bright and happy spirit of Cecil Cook.

The days following his death were filled with the minutiae of legal obligations. It was necessary, I am sure, but what a lot of paperwork and activity! Our wills were in order, and this simplified the settling of the estate. My days were filled with meetings with lawyers and appraisers. Our home had to be appraised by three people, despite the fact that it was mine by a survivor's right. I felt both put upon and grateful for all of the people who guided me through the maze of chores that had to be done.

Early on I had a call from the Internal Revenue Service which filled me with apprehension. I knew I was not guilty of tax evasion, but the feeling was akin to being called into the principal's office. Armed with all of my records I made my way to the IRS office. Even finding the office and a parking place was difficult. What a delightful surprise awaited me! The agent I saw was businesslike, kind, and helpful. He was a Christian and was satisfied that we had really given what we claimed.

Knowing that our home was the last one Cecil and I had shared, I nevertheless put our dream house on the market. I had always read that one should wait a year before making any decision to change residence. After a year passed, I decided to return to Louisville Kentucky, where we had lived for many years.

Buying a home alone is a responsibility, but also a challenge. It was a help to have realtor friends to sell my house and to help me relocate. Having to scale down was wise but not enjoyable. My selection pleased me. And the house I bought really suited my own personality better than any house I've ever lived in. I was encouraged by my ability to make a change, which was not only wise but acceptable to my spirit.

The next decision I faced was employment. I knew it would be better for me physically, mentally, and financially to work. Realistically, I knew I was in for a difficult time. I had tried to find a job before returning to Louisville. I thought I was tough enough to face rejection, but it taxed my self-worth. I had been out of the job market for thirty years, and being a homemaker and a volunteer worker counted for little in marketable skills. I had taken several courses in library science, a refresher course in typing, and a class on writing resumes. My search led nowhere. The most affirmation I received was from the director of a kindergarten who said, "We almost hired you!"

Upon my return to Louisville, I was offered two jobs. One was with the University of Louisville Medical School library, the other with a bookshop. I chose the latter because I needed to be with people. It was a stimulating job. I loved being around all of the new books and bringing buyer and book together in a perfect mating.

I worked in the bookshop three years before taking a job with the American Printing House for the Blind. I presently serve as receptionist and tour coordinator there. We have visitors from all over the world. I take pleasure in meeting each one.

Employment has enabled me to travel. Being alone has a few compensations, one being the ability to act upon impulse. For instance, one day driving home from my work, I decided I would apply for a passport. This set in motion a joy that has filled my life with the pleasure of seeing new places. The four trips I have made to Europe have given me three different pleasures: the joy of anticipation, the beauty of realization, and the retrospective pleasure of reliving the trip. Trips to the southwest and Mexico, to the northwest and Canada, and to New England have made my life glow. The beauty, the sights, the mental stimulation, and the history surrounding each one excite me. There is always another place to visit and another horizon to explore.

The thought of a second marriage filled my mind during the first year of my widowhood. I was terribly lonely. I am sure if I had met the right person at that time, my answer might have been yes. The longer the time I've had to "go it alone," the more reluctant I would be to surrender independence. This is an option I keep open but would consider carefully.

My church fills an important place in my life. I have taught a class of young women, and together we have worked through many of the problems today's women face. Our church decided to elect women deacons, and I was among the first three. To be set apart by ordination for service is a sobering experience. It was one of the high points in my Christian pilgrimage. I have also had the awesome experience of serving on the pulpit committee, a responsibility of far-reaching proportions.

During all these changes my family has been encouraging. They have given me love and support, and they have had unswerving confidence in my ability to meet life's demands. Their confidence in my independence is a blessing, but at times I want to be cared for.

I have enjoyed seeing grandchildren grow and develop and regret the fact that their grandfather missed all the fun of being the special person a grandfather is in the life of a little child. I am so sorry he never met Sarah Taylor Cook, the first Cook girl in three generations. How he would have loved her! He would have been foolish over our twins, Taylor and Andrew. It is sad that he only barely met two little baby boys, Matthew and William. I am sorry he didn't get to know Ben and Jon and Bill's lovely stepdaughter, Kris. I feel I must enjoy them twice as much for him.

I have experienced widowhood with many mixed emotions. I feel at times like the flip side of a good recording, just there to fill up the space. Sometimes I feel crippled by a loss of a part of me not seen by the world. In the final analysis I feel that life is a gift from a loving Father who wants me to live it well and with joy. A lack of joy in the events of each day is a supreme waste. We have been created to live and to take the events over which we have no control and weave them into a tapestry. This tapestry of our lives is made up of bright and vivid colors as well as some which are muted and dark. All are woven together to make a pattern of beauty.

My walk is still not entirely free of shadows; but I continue my forward motion. The shadows are less deep and the darkness far less penetrating. I am aware of companions along the way who have shared in the shadowed paths. Together we walk with Christ our elder brother and Savior. He has known the deepest darkness and has come through it. His victory promises that the darkness can be the beginning of light.

"Death of a Husband," by Betty Cook, in **Women on Pilgrimage**, Sherden, Nutt, Dinwiddie, McEwen, eds. (Nashville: Broadman Press, 1982). Used by Permission. All rights reserved.

ELIZABETH HUEY TAYLOR COOK

Appendix B

A Short Account of My life and travels
by William Hickman
For more than Fifty years; a professed Servant Of Jesus Christ. To which is added a narrative of the rise and progress of religion in the early settlement of Kentucky: giving an account of the difficulties-we had to remember.

HIS EARLY LIFE

    If I had something better to leave behind me, it would be a greater satisfaction to my own heart, but such as it is, you may examine it; it is principally intended for my rising large family, when I am no more in this world of trouble. I have been solicited by my brethren and friends to leave something behind me; if my children and friends think it worthy to go to the press, they may do as they please. I have no money object in view; a small pamphlet will contain the whole I shall give you, which is a brief sketch of my life from my youth up to the present date.
    I was born in the county of King and Queen, Virginia on the 4th day of February 1747; my father, of the name of Thomas Hickman, my mother's name was Sarah Saunderson before marriage. They died young, leaving only myself and a dear little Sister; the youngest child, a son, died in infancy. My Sister and myself were taken by a loving old grandmother, that did her best for us and tried to impress our minds with a solemn sense of eternal

happiness, or the torments of hell. These things bore heavily on my mind, and more so on the death of our parents; the thought of my father, fearing he was miserable, deprived me of hours of sleep; my mother, I hoped was in the glory. With these thoughts I determined not to be wicked, especially to keep from evil words.

My chance of learning was very small, having little time to go to school, I could read but little, and barely write any; my sister, also, had very little chance of learning, for we were two little orphans; but our God has been our protector and we have lived to a great age. At about fourteen years of age, I was put out to a trade; the family I had lived with since the death of my parents were orderly without any real knowledge of true Godliness, all [substitute "or"] upon works to save their Souls, none of us knew any better in those days. When I went to the place about twenty miles off, I thought if they were wicked and profane I could not live there. I found them notoriously wicked, and I thought I could not stay there. My Sister was now nearly grown. She married young and we were little acquainted for near thirty years.

I had not lived long at my new habitation before I fall in with evil habits, for master, mistress, children, apprentices and negroes were all alike in their wickedness; "evil communications corrupt good manners," I may speak with Shame, it had not been three months before I fell in with their customs and evil habits though my dear old grandmother gave me a Bible, with a charge not to neglect reading it as I was accustomed to do when with her; after awhile I neglected it. I left off saying prayers, and I learnt to curse and swear, for sinning will make us leave off prayer, or real prayer will make us leave off sinning. I lived at this place seven years.

I often went to church to hear the parson preach, when he was sober enough to go through his discourse; but no longer pipe, no longer dance. Toward the last of the seven years, I heard talk of people called Baptists, though at a great distance; they told us they would take the people and dip them all over in the water: I drew the conclusion they were like Sturgeons out of the Seine, wallowing in the sand; that I was sure they were false prophets, I hoped I never should see one, neither did I for several years after that.

HIS MARRIAGE AND CONVERSION

In the ninth year I married my master's daughter, both of us poor careless mortals about our poor immortal souls; my wife was fond of mirth and dancing, etc. In the Year 1770 then living in Buckingham County, Virginia, the Lord sent these new lights near where we lived, curiosity led me to go some distance to hear these babblers; the too precious men were John Waller and James Childs, from the North side of James river; when I got to the meeting the people were relating their experiences, but I could not get sight of the preacher till they were done there was such a multitude of people. At last they broke; the two preachers sat together. I thought they looked like Angels; then each of them preached. God's power attended the word, numbers falling, some convulsed, others crying out for mercy; that day's worship ended. The next day they were to dip as they called it in those days.

I went home heavy hearted, knowing myself in a wretched state; I informed my wife what I had seen and heard. She was much disgusted for fear I should be dipped too; she begged I would not go again, but I told her I must see them dipped. I went, and an awful day to me it was; one of those ministers preached before Baptism and then moved on to the water, near a quarter of a mile; the people moved in solemn order, singing "Lord, what a wretched land is this, etc".

Though it was a strange thing in that part of the world, yet I think the people behaved orderly; a great many tears dropped at the water, and not a few from my eyes. The first man brother Waller led in had been a dancing master to whom brother Waller said he had given a gold piece to learn him to dance, and now he was about to baptize him in the name of the Lord Jesus. I think eleven were baptized that day, among the rest was that very valuable minister of Christ, Rana Shasteen, who labored faithfully, I suppose half a century, but has lately gone home to rest; William Johnson, a worthy man and a good minister, baptized that day, moved to the back parts of Virginia.

In the fall of the next year I moved down to Cumberland County; there I shook off the awful feelings I have named above, and yoked in with a parcel of ruffians and took to dissipation, but with a guilty conscience. The Lord sent his servants in that part, as under Shepherds, to hunt his lost sheep, and pretty soon a number of our dear neighbors were converted to God; brother Bondurant, his wife and most of his children; brother Maxey and wife, the Eppersons, etc. and among the rest, my wife, though she once opposed me. She was the first effectually called of God. This set me to serious thinking; I began to lop off my worst sins; it was difficult to give up my old comrades, but I thought soberly about the worth of my soul and eternal hell; I could have no solid rest and began to think I must pray. I tried, but I was ashamed, I feared somebody would see me; however, I had left off my wicked course and continued saying prayers till I had got very good as I thought nearly good enough to go to heaven.

My wife enjoyed a great deal of the life of religion, she offered to the church in my absence. The spirit of the bond woman and her son was prevailing in me to persecute the son of the free woman. Down came all my goodness, with shame I kept her from being baptized for months, but went with a guilty conscience. I advised her to converse with Parson McRoberts, that appeared to be a zealous Episcopalian minister, he would convince her that infant baptism was the right mode; She replied that she was fond to hear him preach, but she could not pin her faith to his sleeve; all my goodness was like the morning clouds that vanished away.

One evening, being alone, meditating on the right *way*. I recollected Paul's conversion in the 9th Chapter of Acts. I took the book, and thought I would search that chapter carefully. If I did not find it there I would oppose the Baptists as long as I lived, but to my great mortification, Ananias says to Paul "Why tarriest thou, arise and be baptized;" I knew he was a man not an infant; I closed the Book and thought I would oppose no longer. After this I submitted, and saw her buried with Christ in baptism; from that day to the present my mind was made up, but, God help me, I had no evidence from God; but my mind was in foment, still striving under the law, still had little hope to get to heaven that way.

There was a certain preacher of the name of David Tinsley, who my wife was fond to hear preach; the son of the bondwoman was not killed in me I disliked him in my heart, for no other reason than his faithfulness and candor. The devil was very unwilling to give me up, but, blessed be God, though the Devil is strong, the Lord Christ is stronger than him.

I shall now proceed to give you some account of what the Lord has done for my poor soul. That same preacher last alluded to, had meeting in the neighborhood; I concluded to go with my wife to meeting and after singing and prayer, he took his text, which is found in the 5th chapter of Daniel, 27th verse, "Thou are weighed in the balance and found wanting". It was a glorious day to me, for God made use of it to show me what a wretch I was.

By a metaphor he made use of supposing a man to go in debt five hundred pounds to a merchant and he proved insolvent and had nothing to pay, he would say to the merchant, I can't pay the old debt, but I want more goods, I will now pay as I go; he stormed out, for he was a son of thunder, says the preacher, would that satisfy the merchant? No, he would take him by the throat, say "pay me what thou owest" then calmly let us know how we were indebted to God's righteous law, and now if we could live as holy as an angel in Heaven to the end of our days, how were we to atone for all our past sins? God, by his holy spirit I trust, sent it home to my heart.

That night I withdrew in secret prayer; there I found the wretchedness of my wicked heart. I could not pray, but sin and evil thoughts were in my best performance; considering that God was holy, and how I was to stand before Him, condemnation seized my troubled soul; from that time I thought I grew worse and worse, for I saw sin enough in my best performance to sink me to hell; when I heard the truth preached it all condemned me. I often wished I had never been born, or that I had been a brute, that had no soul to stand before the holy God; for months I tried to pray, but thought I grew worse and worse, till all hopes of happiness was almost gone; when I heard preaching I was condemned, I often went to meeting to get converted, I heard the gospel was free, but not for me, I was such a wretch, and condemned.

One cold and gloomy afternoon, the 21st of February, 1773, I went over a hill to try to pray, my heart appeared to be hard as a rock; when I got to the place I put myself in every position of prayer. I must have been an hour in that dismal condition, it was so cold I had to return to the house and sit awhile before the fire; I thought that hell was my portion. There was a young woman that lived in the house at that time, a professor of religion, in passing by where I sat, and in a kind of ecstasy, said I was converted; I thought she spoke unguardedly, but said not a word; I got up immediately and went out and walked about fifty yards, about the setting of daylight, all at once the heavy burden seemed to fall off, I felt the love of God flow into my poor soul; I had sweet supping at the throne of grace; my sins pardoned through the atoning blood of the blessed Savior; I heard no voice, no particular scripture applied; I continued there sometime, I went back to the house. Made no ado for fear of losing the sweet exercise; the same woman cried out and praised God; I kept still. That was one of the happiest nights I ever experienced in all my life; the next morning when I arose and looked out, I thought everything praised God, even the trees, grass and brutes praised God; I thank God for all his favors.

In the month of April I was baptized by that worthy old servant of God, Reuben Ford, who baptized my wife the fall before; we both joined the church after my being baptized as above written. It being a time when preachers were very scarce, traveling preachers would pass once in every two or three months, a number of us were the two Dupuys, the two Smiths, brother Edward Maxey, brother Jeremiah Hatcher, and my poor self we would meet, sing and pray and exhort one another. We continued in this way near three years; we then esteemed others better than ourselves, till brother John Dupuy was ordained. A large church arose and lived in harmony. After a few years the whole above written preachers became ordained; many of then, are now gone to their long, eternal homes.

KENTUCKY LOOMS IN THE DISTANCE

In the beginning of the year 1776, I heard of a new country called Kentucky, my circumstances being low in this world, and having a young and growing family of children I concluded, like Abraham of old, to go and see for myself, although it was a great undertaking. On the 23rd of February 1776, I started from home with five others, to wit: George S. Smith, Edmund Woolridge, William Davis, Thomas Woolridge and Jesse Low, and in the back parts of Virginia we were joined by three more: Peter Harston, Christopher Ervin and James Parberry. We came to the resolution, three of us professors to go to prayer every night; our new companions in their hearts opposed it, but submitted and behaved well. It is too tedious to name everything that transpired in our disagreeable journey; we had to travel in small and miserable tracks, over mud and logs and high waters; before we got to Cumberland River we met three or four men turning back, like poor cowards, and no doubt like the ten spies of Cannan, carried back an evil report; but one of the name of Harrod fell in with us and went on; we thought him much of a coward though he boasted very much; we went on and crossed the river, saw no Indians or signs.

It was on Sunday, early in March one of the company killed a buffalo, which suited us for provisions, and we prepared it by jerking, which made it necessary for us to stay all night; it being on the Indian war road, there was abundance of cane, two large log fires were made. Late in the night a dreadful alarm was made, the dogs broke out like they had seen something; poor Harrod rose up scared half to death, to appearance, cursed and damned the Indians, and said there they are; the men rose and flew to trees. I did not believe there was an Indian there, or that Harrod saw any; I did not think that I was to be killed by an Indian. I therefore kept my station by the fire; no doubt the wolves smelt the beef, and the dogs were after them; after a little they left the trees and came to their rest again. Probably readers think my behavior at the fire was foolhardy, but I could not believe I should be killed there; I am that kind of a man who never believed anything could happen by chance - however, we were all spared.

Next morning we all started on our way, and nothing of moment transpired till we came to the Crab Orchard; there we discovered a wonder. Part of the company went on to Boonesborough and the rest of us went on to Harrodstown, near Harrodsburg. When we came to the beauty of the country, I thought of the Queen of Sheba, that came from the uttermost parts of the earth to hear the wisdom of Solomon and she said the half was not told. So I thought of Kentucky; I thought if I could get but ten acres of land, I determined to move to it. I have ever been a true whig of the country. God never intended me to own much of It; my thoughts were if I could get my children in this rich new country, it might be to their advantage, which I hope it has been.

We got to Harrodstown the 1st day of April, and a poor town it was in those days, a row or two of smoky cabins, dirty women, men with their britch clouts, greasy, hunting shirts, leggings and moccasins. I there ate some of the first corn raised in the country, but little of it, as they had a very poor way to make it into meal; we learnt to eat wild meat, without bread or salt. Myself, brother Thomas Tinsley, my old friend Mr. Morton took our lodgings at Mr. John Gordon's four mile from town. Mr. Tinsley was a good old preacher, Mr. Morton a good pious Presbyterian, and love and friendship abounded among us. We went nearly every Sunday to town to hear Mr. Tinsley preach; I generally concluded his meetings.

One Sunday morning, setting at the head of a spring at this place, he laid his Bible on my thigh and said to me, you must preach today; he said if I did not he would not. It set me in a tremor. I knew he would not draw back. I took the book and turned to the 23rd chapter of Numbers, 10th verse: "Let me die the death of the righteous, and let my last end be as his." I suppose I spoke fifteen or twenty minutes a good deal seared, thinking if I had left any gaps down, he would put them up; he followed me with a good discourse, but never mentioned any blunder.

Our tour of the country answered us, but little good or advantage, for the rights of land and how it was to be got was uncertain; whether Henderson's rights would stand good in the law, whether the cabin rights would stand, between those few that were already here, such disputes were raised among them that we did nothing.

THE RETURN TO VIRGINIA

The first day of June we started back--we three alone--trusting alone upon kind providence to bring us safe to the bosom of our dear family. Our journey back was distressing; on going up the Cumberland river, we discovered moccasin tracks. We had a long and hot day's travel; we passed three men, expecting they would overtake us at night, but they failed until the next night. We came to the place we intended to encamp, and just as we were taking off our saddles those men rode up and said they saw Indian tracks on ours, which caused us to move off, which was much against my will. I would have been willing to have stayed there, and trust in Providence, but I soon found if I did I must stay alone; we moved off, traveled as long as we could keep the tracks, until we entirely lost it. We concluded to get down and tie to trees, keep the bells stopped, and have no fire.

I let my mare loose, knowing the Indians could not catch her for I knew she would not leave the other horses. Late in the night (we had our guns under our heads) I awoke, rose and saw a man hold of Mr. Morton's horse, leading him off. I raised my rifle to my face, the man stopped between me and a very large tree. I thought as he moved off from the spot that I would give him the contents of the gun, but a kind Providence so ordained that as he moved by a glimpse through the boughs of the trees, I saw his white hat; I spoke, Mr. Morton, is that you? I told him I had my gun up to kill him; you have acted very imprudent, said I; he acknowledged it, but did not think of it; he said he would not sleep, and thought he would lead his horse to pick cane. This circumstance I named to the other three men that laid at the root of another tree; they were old hunters, one said if he had seen what I did he would have fired in a moment; but blessed be God we were all spared.

In the morning about 10 o'clock we crossed Cumberland mountain. Previous to our crossing, the Indians had killed a man near the top of the mountain, his remains were discovered -- what the wolves had left. From the foot of the mountain was a station called Owen's Station; we thought when we got there we should hear who was killed, but when *we* arrived there was no person there, they had fled. We could get no intelligence. We went to Martin's Station, thinking they had all got together but when we got there the sun was about an hour high, and we had allotted all day to stay there that night; when we arrived they had also fled. We know of but one more station in the valley, which was fifty miles long. We still went on as long, as we could, our horses and ourselves much fatigued. We lay, as the night before, hard lodging and poor fire.

In the morning we aimed for the last station, which was called Pittman's and when we arrived, no human creature was there. I suppose we stayed there two or three hours, found plenty of vegetables, and corn in the loft; chickens plenty; rested ourselves and horses; took several pecks of corn, expecting to find the owners and settler with them. The next night was the most gloomy of all; we started on at time could hear the fire of guns; we were confident it was Indians, for there was no white people in the valley. As we went on, we could find a bed emptied in one place, shoes in another, pails and piggins in another. This put me in mind of the Syrians, when they fled and left their tents, etc. We came to the foot of the first mountain, called William's Ridge in those days.

The three men spoken of above, directed us not to start till they could get to the top on foot, and left their horses and baggage in our charge; but I did not obey their order; as soon as they were out of sight, I started on, the others followed; we thought they could hear the horses over the rocks. We got safe over, but did not see the spies. We had to go through a long valley near four miles and got to the foot called Powell's Mountain. We consulted whether we should go up or over it that night. We still heard guns firing at a distance, and were afraid our spies were killed; we could see nothing of them, but having their horses and baggage, we concluded to go over the mountain that night, not knowing but our men were on ahead. We got over, I suppose, an hour in the night; it was so dark that we lost the trace and the loose horses. As we had some corn, as named above we dropped down where we were, and passed the most gloomy and uncomfortable night I ever witnessed; our men lost their horses and baggage in a great canebreak; my old two companions slept none; they said a little before day I fell asleep. The sun was shining when I awoke, and my two companions gone, and I left alone. About an hour by sun, our spies and all got together, the horses found, but the baggage and corn lost; we all felt thankful. Our three men companions parted with us that morning; they took another route.

I now began to think of seeing home once more, We went up Church River (Clinch) to the first settlement, and arrived at Capt. Blackmore's public house where all the Powell's Valley run-aways were sporting, dancing and drinking whiskey. We lodge there all night. The next day we went twenty miles up the river, and providentially got to hear brother Micajah Harris preach. The next day we went on to another meeting and then took a start for home.

BACK HOME AGAIN - AT WORK FOR THE LORD

I think about the 24th of June I got home I got home safe, and found my family all well, through the great goodness of God all may neighbors and friends glad to see each other. When I returned home from my long journey, I continued to speak with my brethren and sisters. And in my poor preaching way from that time to this. The fall of the same year, I removed upon Appomatox River quite in a new settlement, where I kept up constant meeting near home, as well as in Amelia County -- as none told me to stop, but rather bid me to go on.

After a few months, I was invited to an arbour about three miles off in the bounds of Parson McRoberts church. Though he had just moved away, and Methodist had a stout society among them, no doubt a number of Christians, I continued preaching at the arbour mentioned above for sometime; the people came out well, and behaved well, but as there were no new conversions, I felt disposed to quit them; but my wife urged me to continue saying the people came out well, and we could not tell what the Lord would do in that place.

There was a fast published by Congress during the war, to be observed throughout America; I think it was the 23rd of April, 1777. I appointed a meeting on that day at a neighbor's house, and there came out a large number of people; I think my text was in Joshua, "Neither will I be with these any more, unless you put away the accused thing from among you," It was in an orchard; the house could not hold half of the people; I did not think I had spoke with more liberty than common. At the close of the discourse there came up a heavy rain; I led the people to the house, singing "Lord, what a wretched land this is" etc, the hymn being long, all that could crowd in the house did so. Some went in the out houses. I finished the song in the house and spent some time in exhorting from it, and then the meeting broke.

There was a middled aged man of the name of **John Goode** in the yard who applied to Col. Hankins to write his will. The Col. said to him, What is the Matter? John, you're not sick? The reply was, "I shall die." Col. Hankins laughed him out of it. He went home, slain by the Sword of the Spirit, his conviction was sharp and severe. He told us afterwards he neither eat, drank nor slept for three days and nights, till the Lord spoke peace to his wounded spirit. At the same meeting, an old man of the name of Thomas Boles stated that his awakening started at the orchard; this was the beginning of a blessed harvest of souls in the Christian field; almost every door was opened for preaching; I scarcely had time to get my natural rest, and the preachers from a distance hearing of the blessed work of God, came down. I was not ordained. Brother George Smith and Brother John Dupuy came often, and I hope their labors were blessed of God, and baptized a number of young converts.

A remarkable circumstance took place with **John Goode**, above alluded to; as I went out with my little boys to drop corn, on the roadside, there came a man riding up; he called to me, and when I went up to him the first word he said to me was, to tell how a person felt when he was converted; but instead of my telling him he immediately told me; **he got so warm he scarcely would sit on his saddle**. I invited him to the house, he said he came on purpose--his soul was alive. He told me I need not mention baptism to him, he said blessed be God, he was baptized with the Holy Ghost, and fire, he needed no more. I told him to search the scripture, and that would teach him his duty.

This was on Saturday morning the Sunday week I had an appointment at Muse school house, a few miles beyond his house. I asked him if he would go with me if I would come by and take breakfast with him, he said he would with pleasure. When I went, he was sitting on his porch with a Bible in his hand; he commenced by tolling me I need not say anything about baptism, his Holy Ghost and fire baptism would do for him. I spoke to him as above, for his cup appeared to be running over; I appointed meeting that evening at his house.

After meeting closed in the day at the school house (it was the first time I had been at that place and there being a large congregation) I missed Mr. Goode till the people were nearly all gone; at last he came out of the woods. I asked where he had been all the time. He told me Mr. Branch, one of his rich neighbors, a church warder, had taken him out to give him some good advice, and it was to take care of the Baptists, for they preach damnable doctrines, and that they will not rest till they dip you. Goode replied that Mr. Hickman had not persuaded him, only adviser to read the scriptures. Ah! he said, that is their cunning. The above he told me as we were riding along. I went to his house to dinner and about one by the sun I began worship; a largo collection came out, as it was a beautiful afternoon. I took 13 of the first verses of the 3rd chapter of John; you may expect nothing very methodical; the Lord opened the hearts of the heavens, and, I hope, was with me.

I suppose meeting lasted about three hours, and you may expect a great deal of repetition and some wild zeal. Numbers crying out what should they do to be saved. From that blessed night, six stated their awakening and never rested till they found it in the Lord Jesus--some mocking, some crying for mercy, the devil mad, trying to keep his palace; but poor devil got defeated and lost some of his faithful servants, both male and female, old and young, the greater number youths--most of whom, I hope, are now in heaven.

In those times I was called upon to preach a funeral sermon on the death of an old lady of the name of Reed. I was applied to by her son-in-law, and gave the appointment and attended. The old lady was buried on the Church acre, and when I went I was not permitted to preach on the holy ground; I had to go out of the lot, but ventured near the Church wall to make a finish of the grave. I then stopped to the spring to get a drink, and when about to start home the gentleman that invited me met me and told he was obliged to me. I told him he was welcome. He handed me a six dollar bill. I told him I never charged in my life. He said he knew that but wished me to accept it as a gift. I took it and he handed out another; it was the first penny I ever received in my life that way, and I was particular to let him know if I took it at all it was a gift, and not a charge, though it did not count so much. I went home with many thoughts--What! A money preacher! I looked and felt so little like it.

Soon after, a poor young man spoke to me to preach his father's funeral; I told him I would and set the time, previous to which I had a night meeting, in the same neighborhood, where I saw the same young man; he took me out; and told me he had heard I charged five pounds for preaching funeral sermons, and he was not able to give it. I asked him for his author, but he did not give it to me. I told him I had never charged a penny in my life, and then mentioned the above circumstances; well, he said if I did not charge, I might preach it; which I did, but was compelled to go off the church lot. This was the case of other buryings at the same place.

The Baptists, in those days, were much despised, which caused Christ's sheep to huddle closer together, and love each other better than when there was no opposition; for the children of the bond woman will persecute the children of the free woman. That was much the case in that country. A little before this date, about eight or nine ministers were imprisoned at different times; but to stop the work of the Lord was not in the power of the devil--the word was preached through the iron gates, and God blessed his word to the conversion of hundreds, so the wicked got their designs defeated.

But to return to my own neighborhood. It was not in my power to attend half the calls-I had, there being no preachers nearer than ten or fifteen miles, yet when they heard of the work. brother George Smith and his brother, G.S. Smith and brother John Dupuy, came and preached the word with power; the Lord attended his word. By this time it was necessary to form a church, chiefly of young converts the number at this time my recollection don't serve, but it was considerable.

After this it was thought expedient to ordain me, as unworthy as I was; they appointed brother Smith and Brother James Dupuy to perform the work. The same afternoon I baptized, I think it was in the date 1778, there was a young lady in the midst of the work sorely wrought upon, and at length she found peace; her father one of the greatest opposers in all the parts. Yet nothing would do but she must follow the footsteps of her dear Master, and after she was baptized never dared to put her foot in her father's house. He cursed and swore and wished her in hell; but she had friends enough, and homes enough.

One day her poor old mother came to my house, and asked me what I would do if she told me an experience that satisfied me and demanded baptism, I told her I should have to baptize her; she said I expect to put you to it in a short time, but my husband must not know it, if he does I know he will kill me; I told her I did not think so; she replied, "I know him better than you."

In a short time after this, the old man went from home and the old lady came to my house with her bundle under her arm; the expelled daughter was at my house at the time; the old lady related her travels, it was satisfactory, and my wife, the old lady and myself went alone to the water, which was near; her daughter would not go, for fear she would be interrogated on the subject. She came out of the water praising and glorifying God. I informed the church of this Transaction, and they were pleased with it; her husband did not find it out. I directed the deacons in time of the Supper to convey the elements to her. She being in some by-corner covered with a large handkerchief; the old man never found it out for some four years afterwards, when the worst of his rage was over.

He had a single son that lived with him, a man grown, he had a wish to join the church, but was afraid of his father; one night at meeting the members got very lively under religious exercise. Abram, for that was his name, came forward and related his experience, and I took him the same hour of the night and baptized him, Paul like. I saw the old lady, his mother, next morning, it was monthly meeting time. She says to me, "brother Hickman, did you baptize Abram last night?" I told her I had, and she appeared much rejoiced, some one told his father on Monday morning, the old man drew his cane on him and ordered him off, but did not strike him; he got out of his way and when the old man's fury got a little abated he returned, and they lived together till he married. So ends that tale.

Baptists in those days could be told in any company--they loved one another. The Church was called Skinquarter, and increased, from its origin. Many other circumstances too tedious to mention and great many valuable things have slipt my memory. This Church raised three ministers, James and Josiah Rucks and **John Goode**, the same mentioned previously, who was baptized with the Holy Ghost and fire. He stood out a long time at last, having received a lashing of conscience, nothing would do but he must be baptized in water, and afterwards he was very zealous for that mode of immersion. Now there were four of us in the Church that labored in the vineyard, the neighbors joined and we had a comfortable meeting house built.

About 1779 or 1780, there was a Church called Tomahawk, not very numerous, but some very worthy members, male and female; this church never had any stated minister to live among them, but was attended by ministers at some distance, occasionally by John and James Dupuy, George Smith and Eleanor Clay. After the ordination of Brother James Rucks they applied to him to attend them, which he did till he was so debilitated by the rheumatic pains that he was unable to attend any longer; they then applied to me, I consented and labored and tried to serve them for about three years. I lived about three miles from them and often had meetings between our church and that. In the three years I attended, I think there was no great increase or decrease, but a comfortable, happy people.

One gloomy circumstance happened in the time I attended; a man of good family and connection, who was taught by his friends and myself to be Christian having a great deal of talk with him, got and under sore temptation to curse God; he had often to jump out of bed and fall upon his knees to pray to God, to keep him from cursing him; we lived some distance from each other, and when he could get an opportunity to be with me, I could scarcely get away from him; he never was in society. The last talk we had together was in the meeting house on a Saturday. He told me, laying his hand upon the top of the head, that it appeared to him there was a burning fire there, and he was sorely tempted to drown himself; I told him that God was above the devil, and I hoped he would not, but on Wednesday following he blowed out his brains with a gun.

I was called upon to preach his funeral, which I did, to a crowded audience from these words "What I say unto you I say unto all, watch." His family and friends were much distressed.

While attending this church, there lived near a neighbor that was thought to be a Christian, but had not joined society; I said to him one evening, going from meeting, "Mr. Flournoy, when I come again, I intend to have meeting at your house, on Saturday night, hear your experience, and baptize you the next day." He asked if I was in earnest, I told him I was.

The same week there was a meeting at the meeting house for a strange minister. I went to meeting, the same afternoon the preacher, his father and mother-in-law and myself went to his house to dinner, after dinner he told me he could not stay until next meeting before he was baptized. I told him he had stayed seven years and could he not stay one month. I told him I should do as I told him that next morning he came to my meeting house, ten miles off, brought his clothing, his wife and children, mother and brother to be baptized. I told him I should do what I first told him, his cup appeared to be running over with the love of God. They went back after worship, and the next monthly meeting, as I told him I would, I baptized him in his own neighborhood.

When I left there to come to Kentucky, I left him the minister of the Church at Tomahawk. According to my recollections in six years there were but three excluded, and one of them returned and gave satisfaction; we endeavored to keep up strict discipline, but we had one male member who was a good deal of trouble to us, though often dealt with, he was one of the best men to repent and promise I ever saw, but as bad to perform; those members are a pest to society, and are too numerous in all churches.

A short account of the leading families in that blessed revival, which was the first fruits of the work--**The Goodes**, the Browns, the Baileys, the Ruckers, the Rudds, etc, etc. They, with their offspring, were early members. Old Father Brown and his lady were very old when they came in; and I believe all their children but one became members--two at a distance the rest with us. Among them was a daughter named Obedience; she was baptized quite young and married my oldest son, William she is yet alive and has been an ornament to religion ever since. Brother Bailey and his wife, a sister to my daughter-in-law, are the only three of our old members in Kentucky, they are quite old; it will not be long, before the Lord will take them home to that house not made with hands.

To return to Chesterfield again, Satan took the advantage of the three preachers alluded to above, and sewed seeds of discord among two of them; we were fearful it would be attended with serious consequences, but providence prevented; like the disciples of old, each wanted to be greatest. One of them named Josiah, the most meek and pious at first, wished to deal with, and was willing to exclude all that were superfluously dressed, once dealt with a young lady, the daughter of Col. Haskins, for wearing stays, they being in fashion in those days. He arraigned her before the Church--she was truly a meek and pious young lamb. I plead her cause and saved her. She afterwards became the wife of Mr. Edward Trabue, and died in Kentucky. But the said Josiah, after while became more popular than the rest, took to traveling, became dressy, rode to different counties, and was pretty much of a fop, as I was told, when I moved to Kentucky, though I never heard anything improper in his conduct otherwise. He moved to North Carolina and married rich, and was thought to be a good preacher. I received one letter from him after he became rich; he wrote like a good man. Brother James, his older brother, was esteemed in the Church-- but was a long time confined with the rheumatic pains, so that he had to sit down and preach. They chose brother Goode for their minister.

I preached and served them about six years, the beat part of my life. The church was composed of children of one family, no rents nor party spirits; we tried to look to the Lord for direction and protection. After the death of Brother Goode, the church selected brother Charles Forsee as their preacher; he is still tending them, and is very old. I have known him upwards for fifty years.

ON TO KENTUCKY

About this time I began to think of moving to the new country, Kentucky, which I had soon, and I was walking one evening among my little corn, on a poor spot, having nine children, I made up my mind to move to that country, as I had an idea of it for years. I knew it would be a killing stroke to my wife when she heard of my determination, for she was so attached to the church and neighbors that she could not give then, up. This was in June. However, when I returned to the house I met her between the two houses, after sunset; I told her what I had concluded on, when she burst in tears, and begged me to decline but it was in vain. I then fixed on the day to start, which was the 16th of August, twelve months. I wound up all my affairs, and started on the 16th of August, 1784. I sold my little place--it was small and poor, but there was a good framed house and orchard on it. The purchaser paid me the money down for it; or I should not have been able to move.

I attempted to preach my last sermon, but in vain, I was entirely unmanned; there were a number of preachers there, and weeping time it was, indeed. When we began our journey, Brother George Smith, was with us, and assisted us in our packages. Several of our friends followed us a day or two, but brother Smith went with us to help us along, for at least one hundred miles; my oldest son about seventeen years old, very strong and active, was the best hand we had; I was good for but little; the other boys did their part as well as they could, The next oldest, Thomas got kicked by a horse the second morning, which laid him up several days; after he recovered he went on tolerably well. After our friend Smith left us we felt more lonesome, and missed his advice and aid. We took plenty of provisions with us, and drove two (milk) cows that gave milk for the children and my wife's coffee.

The fatigues of the journey were too tedious to mention. We proceeded to the wilderness; it rained almost every day, which made it dreadful traveling; the waters were deep and no ferry boats, the children and myself wet both day and night. There were also vast crowds in the wilderness, largo droves of cattle, and the trace small; provisions, with a number, run out, but we, as poor as we were, had plenty.

I had written to brothers G.S. Smith to meet us, but he failed to get the letter as soon as I expected. The night before we got in we concluded to stop and rest; there were 500 in company. My friend Smith rode up, inquiring for Hickman's camp. He came loaded with bread and meat. The next morning we started and got to his cabin about and hour by sun, which was the 9th of November, 1784; wet and dirty, poor spectacles we were but thank God, all in common health; the Lord was with us through the whole journey.

The next day, which was Sunday, there was a meeting at Brother Smith's, and, unprepared as I was, I had to try to I preach, though there were three other preachers there, I spoke from the fourth Psalm, "The Lord hath set apart him that is Godly for himself." I was followed by a Methodist preacher, Mr. Swope, old brother W. Marshall was there, and invited me to where he lived a place called the Knobs. Some time afterwards I went to see him and we then got acquainted; he appeared to set some store by me, but thought I was tinctured with Armenianism. I thought he was strenuous on eternal justification, but never disagreed so as to have hard thoughts.

There was a church at Gilberts Creek, but I had no inclination to join so soon after I moved there. We lived in brother Smith's family. Brother John Taylor came from the north side and preached at a Brother Robert son's. William Bledsoe was there; brother Taylor took his text which was, "Christ is all in all." I fed on the foods it was like the good old Virginia doctrine.

We built a cabin near Brother Smith's where our families lived very agreeable together. On the 11th day of January 1785, my daughter Mary, was born. Brother Edmond Woolridge had purchased a large ["a large" is repeated] tract of excellent land of Col. Campbell, near

Lexington, where we concluded to move. I agree to acres of him, and sent my two oldest sons to build a cabin as it was customary in those days to help one another, with help, the boys finished one room; we moved over the 5th day of April, without accident. My wife never appeared satisfied until now. The Spring came on and everything appeared so beautiful and rich that it seemed we once more had got home.

The fourth Sunday in that month was monthly meeting at brother Louis Craig's, within two miles, where we went to meeting, We found a people whom we thought we could live happy with; we gave in our letters and was cordially received in the church. My wife was soon reconciled to the Country and Church and would not have gone back on any condition. We lived hero near three years, in love and friendship.

I shall here give some account of what transpired in that time. The next year we had a severe affliction with what is called the scarlet fever, or French measles, eight of the family were down at once, and myself among the rest, we lost a young daughter, the first of the family that died, the Lord raised the rest, but myself and several of the children wore afflicted with rheumatic pains, and it was long before we recovered--the Lord's ways are the best, but we are too apt to murmur at it.

After joining the Church as above, Brother L. Craig's and myself *were* yoke follows in the ministry. After some time, brother S. Smith moved over and joined the Church with us, where we labored together in friendship and in the fall of the same year the Elkhorn association was formed at brother John Craig's on Clear Crook. The Gospel began to spread in different parts, a church was established at Clear Crook, brother Taylor was the successful minister; a blessed work of God was produced by his labors. Some time after a church was established, now called Mount Pleasant, brother Smith served them until the Lord took him home.

I was invited another course to Boone's Creek, by two old brethren, to come and preach the word; I went down, and I hope not in vain, a church was established previous to my going by that name; there was a part of the Church attached from the body that lived on what was called Marble Creek.

I was once called to Boone's Creek to preach and baptize. I went, there was no meeting house and we met in the woods. When I got to the place there was a large collection for those days; brother John Tanner was preaching; I went on the stand, and when he concluded, I closed the meeting. Knowing the Church was to set and hear experiences, I insisted on brother Tanner to take the seat, as he was the oldest man, but he utterly refused; I was compelled to take it myself. The first man that came up was a raw Irishman of the name of Watson, he came trembling, and if I am any judge, he related a good work; I asked him all the questions necessary, and when we were about to receive him brother Tanner rose up and said he did not believe he was a Christian; I desired him to ask him questions; there was another old man who backed Tanner; however he asked him some deep questions on eternal decrees; I replied I did not (think) they were proper questions to be put to a child; then he said he would talk with him when Church broke, he was set aside; others came up until he had received seven or eight; it became dark, and we had to adjourn to the cabin; after getting a little refreshment the Church formed again; in the interval, Tanner had conversed with Watson and became satisfied; when forming again I still insisted that brother Tanner should act, but he still refused. We received after night to the amount of eleven in all.

The next day was Sunday, when they were to be baptized; we tarried together that night in conversation, some expressions from Tanner hurt my feelings; we had just heard of the work of God in Virginia and North Carolina, he spoke light of it, and said he feared it was the work of the devil; young converts by, who, hearing his remarks, appeared very much discouraged We repaied [repaired?] to the water, near the mouth of Boone's Creek, where we intended to preach and baptize; I urged him to administer the ordinance, but he still refused; I went forward, it was the first time I had baptized in the country-

-we both preached and concluded; at last, that detached part of the Church appointed preaching [preachers?] among themselves and I attended them, until at length they became a church to themselves. The most of the young converts fell in with the young church called Marble Creek, a growing young church, living in peace and harmony; I baptized the greatest part of them, in consequence of which, an attachment subsisted between us--they wished me to live among them, but Providence said no.

I shall here call my reader's attention to South Elkhorn Church, where our memberships were in 1787; the Lord began a blessed work among us, and a number of precious souls were born again among the rest four of our children. We now concluded to build a meeting house. which was the first that was built on the north side of the Kentucky River. I was called by the Marble Creek church to live with them; my inclination let me do it, and they proposed to give me 100 acres of land--the price was subscribed for, but no money paid.

THE RISE [OF] FORKS OF ELKHORN, 1787

About that time the Forks of Elkhorn began to settle, Mr. Nathaniel Sanders, old brother John Major, brother Daniel James, old William Hayden, old Mr. Lindsey, and a few other families had moved down, and as there was a prospect of a large settlement Mr. Sanders named to his neighbor, Major, it would be right to get some minister to come down and live among them, which pleased Major, he being an old Baptist.

They consulted who they should get, and having a small acquaintance with me, Mr. Sanders named me; this was strange, as Mr. Sanders was a very thoughtless person about his soul; however they agreed among themselves to make me a present of 100 acres of land; this was unbeknown to me till afterwards. On a very cold night brother Major came to my cabin, about 20 miles from residence. When he came in, upon being asked to sit down, he said no, "Like Abram's servant I will not sit down till I have told my errand." He then told what had brought him to see me, and give me till the next morning to return him an answer. We passed a night of prayer. It was a night of deep thought with me, for I wished to do right. I was halting between two opinions, and when I reflected that the Forks of Elkhorn was exposed to the savages, and as there was no settlement from there to the Indian town, I thought it would frighten my wife and children; however, I consulted them about what I should do and they being willing to go, in the morning I answered brother Major this way: "I have an appointment in Marble Creek. I will name the thing to them, and if they will give me up and let me off, I will write to you, or come down and see you and we will conclude upon it. "I went to the meeting and stated to the brethren the circumstances; they were for awhile unwilling to let me off, but at length they said if it was my wish, and for my advantage, they would submit. I then felt free and went down instead of writing.

I first went to brother Major's and from there to Mr. Sanders. I was astonished; his wife was an old professor of religion, and he walked with me to the very spring I now live at, on his own land, and showed me where I was to settle; I said to him, Sir, you don't care about religion; I want to know why you want me to come. His reply was, if it never is any advantage to me, it may be to my family. It started tears to my eyes, not knowing the [what?] Providence had in view.

I however concluded to move as soon as possible, and my son William being married, he came down and built a cabin, between Christmas and New Years, 1787. Between this and my moving, I visited my old church, and Marble Creek, and other churches, and I do hope my poor labors were not in vain. On the night of the 17th we arrived at my son William's cabin. I had sent down an appointment to preach on Sunday at brother Major's where almost the whole inhabitants came. I suppose about thirty whites and a few blacks. I hope I was looking to the Lord I took this subject, "let me die the death of the righteous, and let my last end be as his."

It was a blessed day; I think four or five experiences came from that day's labor, and, among the rest, Mr.

Sanders. The sword of the spirit pierced him to the heart; for weeks he could find no rest; at length he found it in the Lord. I was by when he met with his deliverance; we held meetings day and night.

About this time there was a great fall of snow, and the balance of February and all March was very cold, but not to hinder the meetings; and in the course of ten months there were twenty or thirty obtained hope in the Lord; **old sister Cook's family**, brother Major's children and several of their blacks; no weather scarcely stopped us, and we thought but little of the Indians.

When April came it brought a fine Spring and we began to talk of becoming an organized Church. Several brethren moved down from Clear Creek to preach to us, and help us on, and as well as my recollection serves me, there was a number baptized before the constitution of the Church, for brother Lewis Craig was with us at times. We went for help from Clear Creek, South Elkhorn, and I think Marble Creek; we got together, and, after due examination we were constituted a church of Christ. This took place the second Sunday in June, 1887, and they were pleased call me to go in and out before them. The dear man I so much dreaded I baptized, and the church chose him as one of her deacons; he was a member four or five years when he wandered out of the way, and we had to exclude him; he is now gone to his long home. I think in the course of a year, I must have baptized forty or fifty; **I baptized nine of old sister Cook's children**, and among the rest that well known **Abraham**, now the Minister of Indian Fork church, in Shelby County. The same year I baptized Philemon Thomas and his brother Richard, the latter a minister of the Gospel, the former a statesman. My meeting was at Philemon's house; Richard had a great appearance of a fop, finely attired, but God sent the word home to his heart and he never found rest till the Lord gave it to him.

I have often wished I had taken notes in those days, as my memory does not serve me; I know I have neglected giving an account of several things that might have been satisfactory to the reader, but must omit them for want of notes.

BRASHEAR's CREEK (1785) REVIVED

About this time in the midst of the work, two young gentlemen were often with us, sons of Mr. Bracket Owen living in Jefferson County, now Shelby, and solicited me to come down to their father's and preach as their mother was an old professor; I first thought it a kind of compliment, being decent young men, and as they were old neighbors with brother Major's family, and often came on friendly visits, I concluded to go. I gave them an appointment, but before the day came that I was to start, there was a cold season, so much so that every thing froze up, and I thought it impossible to got there; William Major, Benjamin Hayden, and a lady were to go, to visit two of her brothers who lived there; when the morning came that we was to start I had declined going, as there was no way to cross the river but in a little totering canoe; Mr. Major was very intent to make the attempt. Although I had declined early in the morning, as they were so anxious I concluded to go.

We started about the middle of the day to go by for Mr. Hayden, who was to be our pilot; when I got to his father's he was not at home, having gone over the river to hunt his horses, than I thought the journey was at an end but I desired his mother to give me his clothes and I would take them to Frankfort, where the woman lived that was to go with us; at that time it was a perfect forest, there being only two little cabins in it. When I went to Mr. Pulliam's whose wife was to go, she had a fine turkey before the fire. I told her to have it done, and in the meantime be ready to start, and I would go to the bank of the river and call Mr. Hayden; after some time he answered, a long ways off; when he came he had no horse; now I thought it was all over, as ha was our guide; but Providence had a hand in it, and a relation of Pulliam's was there, who told Benjamin rather than the journey should be stopped, he would lend him his mare; we dined on the turkey and crossed the river one at the time, and swam our horses by the side of the canoe, when we all got over and put our saddles on, the moon shone. We than had twenty miles to go, in the night, sometimes it was snowing and then the moon shining; we crossed Benson nineteen times, at some fords the ice would bear us over, at some fords some steps would bare us, the next stop break in; we continued this disagreeable road until we fell on the waters of what was then called Tick creek; we passed a number of evacuated cabins--the owners had either been killed or driven off by the Indians; it was a very cold night. We had no watch along, but we judged it must have been two o'clock in the morning when we called at the fort gate for admittance--the old gentleman was not at home, and the old lady - had all bared up--it was some time before we could convince her, who we were as she was afraid of a decoy, but at last she let us in, the weather being so cold, she had given me _____ [?] but she soon had a good fire raised and got us a warm supper, or, rather breakfast, put all to bed and covered us warm, early in the morning she sent out rumors (runners) to the different forts and about noon collected one of the rooms nearly full of people.

  About two years before, a small church was constituted by two old ministers brother, William Taylor, of Nelson, and John Whittaker, of Jefferson, I believe eight in number, the Indians wore so very bad among them that they scattered and kept up no government; they could not most together, and nobody preached to them till I went as above named.

  I preached on Saturday night and Sunday to nearly the same people, and know none of them, but what went with me. On Sunday night I went about a mile to another fort and I hope the Lord did not send me there in vain; on Monday morning I was to start home, this short visit attached our hearts to each other; they insisted very hard for me to leave them another appointment before I left them; at last I consented to come in again; I set a time in March, but it was with difficulty I could leave my people at home, but I went to the time on Friday, and continued with them till Wednesday, day and night, at three or four different stations; they still urged harder for a continuation of my attendance; they promised if I would they would send me several loads of grain, and would every time send a guard to the river to meet me and guard me back. I thought I would consult my wife and family and the church whether it would meet their approbation, and I would send them word. I did so, they had no objection.

    I sent word, and in May I went down and stayed longer; in that tour they came together and agreed to stand as a church on the old constitution, and I baptized one member; the next month I baptized another; brother Jaime McQuade stood by me from the first, was my singing clerk; a little after brother Gano baptized him and two or three others.

    I repeated my visits to there and baptized a number--the church grew. While going from meeting to meeting, sometimes twenty or thirty in a gang, we were guarded by the men, it looked more like going to war than to meeting to worship God. They urged me hard to move among them. I told them that request could not be granted; I had not long been moved to Elkhorn. I was attached to my people there, I could not leave them, besides all, they had given me a little home; I felt bound to them as long as I lived; buying and selling never was my object; then they told me if I could got some good minister to come and live with them it would be what they wished; I told them I would do my best for them.

    Brother Joshua Morris had just moved to the country and I thought he would suit them; I saw brother Morris, told him the situation of that people, and their wish, he consulted himself and family. I told him if he would take a tour there I would go with him; we both went, himself and people were pleased with each other. Soon after he moved and his labors were much blessed, the church grow and flourished, but many a tour I took with him, long circuits around, till at last I concluded they were well supplied. I gave out going so often; but now I knew of no country in the state so well supplied as Shelby, flourishing churches and good ministers.

    Great changes have turned up in thirty odd years; I went in front there, through cold and heat, in the midst of danger, but my God protected me till now, blessed be his name. We continued sometime after the first heavenly visits, though rather a declension seemed to take place.

A RETURN TO VIRGNIA

Having made up my mind to visit my old native land, in June, 1791, I started to Virginia; while there I visited the church I left we met with Joy and comfort, though we found a great change, a number of dear old brethren had gone to their long eternal home; but as there was a number of now members added to the church, the face of things changed.

l preached a great deal with them and traveled to different counties, and in the church where I was first born and lived three years, where I first began my labors; I also traveled through Henrico, Hanover, King and Queen, and King William, and was treated as a friend everywhere, for I had not a penny to settle with any person. I visited a number of churches, and traveled a great deal; the friends manifested their love by throwing presents in my way, for which I was thankful to God and them. I was a good deal with my old yoke fellow, brother George Smith, whom I dearly loved; he accompanied me back to Kentucky where we arrived the first of November, and found my family and brethren well.

BACK HOME IN KENTUCKY AGAIN

About this time, brother John Scott, from Scott county, come to one of our meetings and invited me to come to his neighborhood and preach, which I did. I preached in a barn of Mr. Ficklin's and I hope not in vain. After this I attended many times, at his own house, some old baptists living near, together with the new converts, they formed a very respectable and able church (McConnell's Run (1794) - now Stamping Ground) for business, under the care of brother Elijah Craig, as he lived in Georgetown, and was good deal of his time under bodily complaints, he advised the church to get some preacher to attend them steadily and he would come as often as he could; they called upon me to attend them one year. I consented, they being a people I was attached to; after my poor manner. I labored with them one year, and at the end of the year, nothing being said, I continued until the end of the second year; all being satisfied, I continued for ten years; in those years I baptized a number of precious members, and I never repented going there.

At length I thought it would be best for the church to get a minister, to live among them, and advised them to do so, as I lived about nine or ten miles from them; they at last called brother Creath, who lived fully as far as myself; he served them about four years, and quit them; they then called brother Suggett, he served them two or three years and he quit; in the time they called brother Trott, he moved among them for a short time, everything did not go right and he quit; they then called me the second time; I attended them about four years more and brother Suggett having moved near them, they moved their meeting house from their former ground, and built them a fine meeting house at the Stamping ground, and changed the name of McConnell's Run to Stamping Ground, but continued the same church. Brother Suggett attended them, being high in the esteem of each other, till he moved to a foreign land; then they called Brother Theo Boulware, he attended one year and gave up; then they called Brother S. M. Noel; they now have two preachers in the church, brother Jame Black and brother Mareen Duvall. My attachments are great to them; I hope my labors Fifth then have not been in vain; I hope the time will come when we shall meet to part no more.

SERVING FORKS OF ELKHORN

I shall now return to my own church, which I have lived with from 1788, and which I have given some account of. About the year 1800, for previous to that date the church gas under a decline, Zion had got Into her slumbers; I well recollect, at a meeting at my house on Sunday afternoon, several preachers were there, there came a young married lady to meeting who I had never seen before, she had just moved into the neighborhood; I observed in the time of preaching the tears flowing from her **eyes,** which gave me an uncommon feeling; I thought she was pierced with the Sword of the Spirit. I think it gave me a travailing soul for the cause of God. She became an humble penitent and is now I hope in glory.

Very shortly after this I heard of three females under trouble and inquiring the way to Heaven; I started out to hunt the lost sheep, and the first I went to see was a married lady; I conversed with her and she satisfied me that she was born again; I than went to two more the same day, the first was not at home, she had gone to where the other lived. I called and found them both; we walked in the garden, neither of them professed to be satisfied, but appeared humble beggars at the throne of grace; our monthly meeting near at hand, the first visited came forward and told us what the Lord had done for her; she was cordially received; my dear brother Gano though in a debilitated state, like old Jacob Caning (leaning ?) on the top of his staff, spoke at the water, and I baptized her in the name of the holy Trinity,

The next morning the other two alluded to above also come forward and I baptized them. Blessed be God the glorious work of the Lord went on and prospered in abundance; every meeting was crowded and many converted to God. By this time the work spread throughout the state; for two or three years great additions to the churches not only in Kentucky, but in Virginia and other states; such times I never expect to see again, but God is able, I suppose I baptized more than five hundred in the course of two years, though at different places; our Church increased to three or four hundred in numbers.

About this time the charges [churches?] began to branch off; we dismissed members to constitute Glen's Creek church, South Benson Church, North Fork Church, and mouth of Elkhorn Church. I attended to all these young churches at that time, they being destitute of ministers and baptized a number of members in each till they were supplied.

In those days I went down and visited my friends at Gaye Creek, and baptized a number there. Soon after that a large and respectable church arose there, and brother John Scott moved among there, and has long bean their pastor; but they, with us, have had their ebbing and flowing; the work of God prospered for several years; a number of young ministers came out as burning and shining lights, to fill the places of the old worn out servants when they are gone to rest. We have now to lament the barrenness of the times; for a number of years we have had but small in gatherings, though we still wish to wait on the Lord, hoping to see better days.

The old Mother Church at the Forks of Elkhorn is getting naked and bare, the Lord has taken a number of the leading members home to glory; within a few years back three other churches in our parts took places--viz; at the Big Spring, we dismissed a number of respectable members to form that church. About this time brother Taylor moved among us; being an enterprising good servant of Christ, and famous for planning new churches, a church was planned at Frankfort, we dismissed about a dozen to form that. After some time they contemplated a church at Buck Run, we dismissed some very valuable members to form that; from all these circumstances we are left poor and few in number, as we have had but few small increases for several years, though we are not yet out of heart, "Joseph lives and Jesus reigns." We hope the Lord will visit us yet.

For several years we have set apart every Sunday and Wednesday night for Prayer meeting and have attended so far, and hope to keep on; brother Graham and brother Gibbs, though members of Frankfort and sometimes other brethren from different churches, meet, with us, unite with us, and go forward in our petitions to Almighty God, in prayer for revival among us.

Dear Brethren, don't neglect us, as poor as we are, who knows but the Lord will still remember in mercy and we may yet enjoy better days; we fear this poor little world has got too much possession in our heart--the Lord have mercy on us. But, thanks be to God, the Lord has put it in the hearts of the people to build a good brick meeting house for the worship of God, and friends not in the society have been the greatest subscribers. We hope the hand of the Lord is in it.

GOING TOWARD THE SUNSET OF HIS EARTHLY PILGRIMGE

I am now in my eighty first year (1828) and have a greater charge on me than ever I had; I am called upon to attend three other churches besides our own, which takes up all my time; but I want to spend my latter moments to God's glory. I enjoy common health, through the goodness of God. I have nearly come to the close of my poor pilgrimage, I do believe in the true evangelical doctrines of the cross of Christ, and that I am a poor sinner of Adam's fallen family--believing the great God knew me from eternity, and included me as one of this purchase; in time he called me by his spirit and made me willing in the day of his power, for it is by grace I am saved through faith, and not of myself; therefore, he deserves all the glory.

The doctrine of election, so much trodden under foot by numbers of the human family is the life of the Church of God for we never should have chosen him if he had not chosen us, and called us and made us willing in the day of his power.

When I think back, I find I have left out hundreds of things that might have been profitable and somewhat entertaining but from a wish to reduce it as much as possible and not to make it too large, I have left out many things.

I have after my poor manner, to serve Mount Pleasant church, the North Fork, and Zion, once called the [s]outh of Elkhorn; our monthly meeting has steadily been at Forks of Elkhorn on the second Saturday and Sunday of each month, for near forty years--that I hope to serve until I am laid in the dust, for they have ever manifested their love and esteem to me, they lay near [my] heart; I wish to live and die with them, and hope to spend a blessed eternity with them, when parting is no more.

Having closed my short and imperfect narrative, I shall touch on my family affairs. My first wife was the daughter of John Shackleford of King and Queen [County, VA], as has been previously stated; by her we had thirteen children, seven daughters and six sons; there are but three of the daughters and two of the sons now living of the first children, and I hope they are doing well. My first wife died the 9th of June 1813; sorely distressed in mind about the massacre of her son, Pascal, at the river, Raisin, she pined away and died.

On the 25th of December 1814, I entered into the second marriage with Elizabeth Abbott, in Scott County; she had three children, a son and two daughters. She was the daughter of Benjamin Dicken, we lived together about twelve years and had five sons; the second we called John Gano [?], he died while young. My wife died the 25th of September, 1826 her oldest daughter is married to Thomas K. Horn, and are living with me. My four young sons are promising children; I can't expect to see them raised, but hope my surviving friends will not let them suffer but will give them good advice and endeavor to keep them from dissipation and bad company, for we know that youth is apt to go astray.

I have already named my dear and only sister, Elizabeth Broaddus, she is now living in the lower part of this state. She has been twice married first to Mr. Mitchell, who I never saw, by him she had about four children though they are not all living--but those that are doing well I hope. After his death she married Mr. Edward Broaddus in Carolina; by him she had two daughters; they are both married, and I hope are doing well. She has been a widow for twenty odd years, she is now seventy eight years of age and is "an old soldier of the Cross;" we have been, but little acquainted, since we were children, living at such a distance, but we hope to live together in the world of immortal glory.

I shall now close the few remarks I have so hastily and carelessly thrown together. If, hereafter, they should be worthy to go to press; that my connections and friends may see the difficulties and troubles I have passed through, and that, with some corrections and additions, they may be thought interesting, they are at their services. They will discover that I am a plain man, and not in the habit of writing, it is the plain and old fashioned style of its author

William Hickman

Typed from a typed copy, August 23, 1967
Fran Thompson, Kentucky Historical Society

ILLUSTRATIONS

Cecil Virgil Cook, Jr	Page 10
Cecil Cook, Jr,	Page 12
Cecil Virgil Cook, Jr	Page 14
Cecil and Matthew Mitchell Cook	Page 19
Blanche Jeannette Dorland	Page 22
Blanche Dorland Cook	Page 27
Cecil Virgil Cook, Sr	Page 44
James Emory Dorland, USA,	Page 56
Arabelle America Ireland	Page 61
James Emory Dorland	Page 65
Lucinda Haley Dorland (Lash)	Page 74
Martin Ireland	Page 80
Sarah Fellers Ireland	Page 90
Sarah Fellers Ireland	Page 92

Susan Goode Farmer Cook	Page 98
William Hawkins Farmer - Willie	Page 105
Joshua Flood Cook	Page 135
Joshua Flood Cook	Page 156
Elizabeth Huey Taylor Cook	Page 304
James E. Dorland	Page 362

INDEX

_____, 3 adult Bodin(e) slaves, 251
_____, Amery, Farmer Family slave, 294
_____, Beather, Farmer Family slave, 294
_____, Charity, Farmer family slave, 116, 117, 118, 119
_____, Daniel, Flood family slave, 175
_____, Doll, Farmer Family slave, 294
_____, Fanny, Farmer Family slave, 294
_____, female, Van Meter family slave, 259
_____, Grayless slave, 85
_____, Letty, Farmer Family slave, 294
_____, male, Van Meter family slave, 259
_____, Nancy, Farmer Family slave, 294
_____, Peter, Cook family slave, 144
_____, Peter, Farmer Family slave, 294
_____, Sall, Keinath family slave, 265, 266
_____, Sandy, Cook family slave, 144
_____, Sharper, Farmer Family slave, 294
_____, slave couple, Bondurant, Cook family, 177
_____, Tom, Farmer Family slave, 294
_____, four children, Van Meter family slaves, 259
Adams, Mary, 86
Aister, Anna Maria, 91
Akin Family, 112
Alabama, 41, 45
Albany, GA, 23, 46
Albemarle County VA, 279
Alexandre(er) Hamilton (1755-1804), 38
Alfred the Great, 260
Alsace, 269, 271, 273, 277
Anne Arundel County Maryland, 73, 75
Apollos Rivoire (Paul Revere), 38
Assoc for Preser of VA Antiquities, 286
Assoc for Preservation of VA Antiquities, 286
Augusta County, VA, 91, 95, 263, 265, 268
Bagby, Paul, 48
Baggott, James L., 51

Balliet Family, 88, 269, 270, 277
Balliet, Jacob, 269, 277
Balliet, Marie (Maria), 88, 269
Banister, H.L., 48
Baptist, 9, 11, 15, 21, 23, 28, 39, 41, 42, 43, 45, 46, 47, 48, 49, 50, 51, 52, 53, 58, 62, 64, 97, 99, 100, 106, 107, 108, 109, 111, 113, 121, 122, 123, 124, 131, 132, 133, 134, 138, 139, 140, 141, 146, 147, 148, 159, 160, 169, 175, 176, 178, 179, 180, 181, 182, 銳201, 217, 219, 231, 232, 233, 234, 239, 243, 279, 293, 328
Baptist Training Union Department, 51
Baptist World Alliance, 48
Barnwell, SC, 48
Barton, Isaac, 148
Basket (Baskett) Nannie, 119, 120
Basket(t) Family, 119, 120
Basket, Thomas, 119
Bassett, Wallace, 48
Baylor University, Waco, TX, 133
Beagle, J. W., 49
Beauchamp, Elizabeth, 86
Beauchamp, John, Jr, 86
Beaver County PA, 73
Berkeley, Wm. (1605-1677), VA Gov., 286, 288, 290, 292, 293, 296
Berwick, York County PA, 89, 91
Bethlehem, PA, 218
Blackwater River (VA, NC), 218, 224, 228
Blanchan Family, 257, 259, 260
Blanchan, Catherine, 257, 259, 260
Bledsoe, William (1792 Massacre), 194
Bluefield Bookshop, 18
Bluefield, WV, 11, 13, 15, 17, 18, 296
Bodine Family, 1, 2, 4, 5, 215, 230, 249, 251, 261
Bodine, Jean, 251, 261
Bodine, Sara, 4, 215, 230, 249, 251
Bondurant Family, 3, 119, 120, 164, 175, 177, 178, 308
Bondurant, Jeffrey, doctor, 177
Bondurant, Mary, 3, 164, 175, 177
Bondurant, William S., 120
Boone, W.C., 49
Bragg, Braxton (1817-76) Gen. CSA, 101
Braudel, Fernand, 39, 40
Breckenridge, John (1821-1875) Gen. CSA, 101
Brewer, Thomas, 132, 163, 165
Briggs John E., 49

Brown, George, 169
Brown, John (1800-1859), 145
Brown, Sarah, 108, 169
Buckingham County VA, 175, 176, 177, 217, 232, 279, 280, 307
Burgoyne, John, British Gen. (1777), 126
Butler, Ira Francis Marion, 183, 185, 187
California Gold Fields, 76
Calvin, John (1509-1564), 28, 29, 31
Calvinist, Calvinism, 39, 58, 88, 256, 272, 274
Camp Jackson, Bowling Green, KY (1862), 167
Carmean, Elizabeth, 82, 84, 86
Carroll County MD, 253
Cemetery, cemeteries, 52, 60, 68, 72, 82, 85, 119, 220, 255, 265, 270
Charlemagne (747-813/14), 260
Charles of Hesse-Cassel, 271
Charlottesville, VA, 9, 21, 23, 25, 26, 41, 45, 47, 52
Cheatham Family, 1, 2, 112
Cheatham, Benjamin, 112
Cheatham, Elizabeth, 112
Cheatham, Stephen, 112
Cheney Family, 1, 2, 73, 75
Cheney, Ann, 73, 75
Cheney, Charles, Jr, 75

Cheney, Charles, Sr, 75
Cheney, Mary Ann, 73, 75
Cheshire, England, 288
Chester County PA, 216
Chesterfield (VA) Court house, 9, 97, 108, 111, 112, 132, 169
Chesterfield County VA, 9, 97, 111, 112, 132, 169
Childs, James, 217, 307
Christiansburg, Shelby Co KY, 114, 118, 119, 120, 132
Church, Mount Tabor Baptist, Barren County KY, 148
Church, Baptist, Eminence, KY, 133
Church, Bellefonte Presbyterian, Concord, NC, 71
Church, Belmont Baptist, Roanoke, VA, 50
Church, *Berge Kirche*, (Hill Lutheran), 270
Church, Bethany (Trinity) Lutheran Crimora, VA, 95, 265, 268
Church, Buckingham Baptist (Buckingham Olde Church), 279
Church, Buckingham Olde Church, 279
Church, Buffalo Lick Baptist, Shelby Co KY, 182
Church, Clear Creek Baptist (1787), 181, 330
Church, Cliff Temple Baptist, Dallas, TX, 48

Church, Cumberland
   Parish, VA, 223, 224,
   225
Church, Dale Parish,
   Henrico (Chesterfield)
   Co VA, 293
Church, Dover Baptist,
   Pike County, MO, 138
Church, Dutch Reformed,
   39, 58, 66, 68, 70, 217,
   232
Church, First Baptist,
   Bluefield, WV, 15
Church, First Baptist,
   Danville, VA, 50
Church, First Baptist,
   Oxford, NC, 48
Church, Indian Fork
   Baptist, Shelby Co KY,
   180
Church, Keinadt's
   (Bethany, Trinity)
   Lutheran, Crimora,
   VA, 89, 265
Church, Louisburg
   Baptist, Louisburg, NC,
   48
Church, Mt. Carmel
   Baptist, Franklin Co
   KY, 182
Church, Old Dutch,
   Ulster, NY, 252
Church, Second-Ponce de
   Leon Baptist, Atlanta
   GA, 49
Church, Six-Mile now,
   Christiansburg (KY)
   Baptist, 179
Church, Skinquarter
   Baptist, Chesterfield
   County VA, 172, 320
Church, South Elkhorn
   Baptist (1787), 181,
   201, 328, 330
Church, Stamping
   Ground (McDonnell's
   Run, 1794), 334, 335
Church, Temple Baptist,
   Washington, DC, 49
Church, University
   Baptist, Charlottesville
   VA, 47, 52
Church, Walnut Grove
   Baptist, Columbia MO,
   176
Church, West Lynchburg
   Baptist, Lynchburg,
   VA, 47
Church, West Park
   Baptist, St Louis, MO,
   21, 23, 43
Church, West Park
   Mission, St Louis, MO,
   48
Civil War Battles
   Adairsville, 57
   Atlanta, 57
   Chattahoochee, 57
   Dallas (MO), 57
   Franklin, 57
   Jonesboro, 57
   Kenesaw Mountain, 57
   Lookout Mountain, 57
   Missionary Ridge, 57
   Nashville, 57
   Orchard Knob, 57
   Resaca, 57

Ricetto Mills, 57
Shiloh, 64, 97, 100, 120
Civil War. American (1861-65), 5, 45, 55, 63, 64, 72, 87, 99, 100, 106, 118, 119, 132, 142, 143, 144, 146, 149, 166, 261, 263, 267
Clark, Champ, 140
Clark, Geo Rogers (1752-1818), Gen, 126
Cleona, PA, 270
Columbia City, IN, 21, 59, 60, 79, 81, 82, 93, 95, 264, 276
Conewago (Conowago) Colony, PA, 69
Cook Family, 1, 2, 3, 4, 5, 7, 8, 9, 10, 12, 14, 15, 17, 18, 19, 20, 21, 23, 24, 25, 26, 27, 39, 40, 41, 42, 43, 44, 45, 46, 49, 51, 52, 53, 54, 55, 57, 58, 62, 63, 64, 68, 70, 71, 75, 79, 82, 93, 94, 95, 97, 98, 99, 100, 101, 102, 103, 104, 106, 107, 108, 109, 111, 112, 118, 119, 120, 121, 122, 123, 125, 126, 127, 128, 129, 131, 132, 133, 134, 135, 136, 137, 138, 139, 140, 142, 143, 144, 146, 147, 149, 150, 151, 152, 153, 154, 155, 156, 157, 158, 159, 160, 162, 163, 164, 165, 166, 168, 169, 173, 175, 176, 177, 178, 179, 180, 181, 182, 183, 184, 185, 186, 187, 188, 189, 190, 191, 193, 194, 196, 197, 198, 199, 200, 201, 202, 203, 204, 205, 206, 207, 208, 209, 210, 211, 212, 213, 214, 215, 216, 217, 219, 220, 221, 222, 223, 225, 227, 228, 229, 230, 232, 234, 235, 236, 237, 238, 239, 240, 241, 243, 244, 245, 246, 247, 248, 249, 251, 256, 259, 260, 261, 263, 264, 265, 268, 269, 276, 279, 280, 281, 289, 295, 296, 297, 298, 299, 300, 302, 303, 330, 341, 342
Cook, Abraham, 3, 9, 144, 147, 154, 163, 168, 179, 180, 182, 183, 186, 187, 191, 194, 197, 198, 199, 201, 205, 215, 216, 219, 220, 221, 223, 240, 249
Cook, Addison (1846-1871), 150, 151, 152, 153, 154, 159, 260
Cook, Bessie Hughes (?-1894), 139
Cook, Blanche Jeanette Dorland, 3, 15, 17, 18, 21, 22, 23, 25, 26, 27, 28, 39, 42, 47, 49, 52, 55, 58, 62, 63, 71, 75, 79, 82, 93, 157, 249, 256, 263, 264, 269, 276, 341

Cook, Cadmus
(Gadmus?), 99, 104,
113, 119
Cook, Carrie Mays
(Dorland's wife), 25,
26, 52
Cook, Cecil V. Jr, 1, 2, 3,
9, 10, 12, 14, 21, 25, 41,
55, 57, 75, 79, 93, 111,
112, 123, 131, 144, 163,
164, 169, 175, 179, 215,
223, 249, 263, 264,
269, 276, 279, 281,
296, 341
Cook, Cecil V. Sr, 3, 9, 15,
41, 44, 131, 169, 235,
341
Cook, Charles L, Cook
family historian, 109,
123, 158, 159, 160, 164,
165, 168, 183, 220, 221,
222, 236, 243, 247,
248
Cook, Charlie L.,
genealogist, 109, 123,
164, 165, 168, 221, 222,
236, 243, 247, 248
Cook, David H., 82
Cook, Elizabeth (1799-
1877), 179
Cook, Elizabeth Huey
Taylor Cook, 4, 8, 9,
46, 57, 68, 71, 99, 112,
126, 127, 128, 144, 160,
173, 206, 289, 297, 303
Cook, Eunice (1798-
1816/19), 179
Cook, Hannah (1818-
1851), 180
Cook, Howard Elliott, 140

Cook, Isabella
Henderson, 17
Cook, James Dorland
(bro, Cecil Jr), 23, 25,
27, 39, 52, 55, 71, 75,
79, 93, 94, 263, 269,
341
Cook, John Ernest, 9, 53,
108, 112, 122, 133, 140
Cook, Joshua Flood, 3, 9,
21, 24, 41, 63, 64, 99,
100, 101, 102, 106, 109,
111, 119, 120, 121, 123,
131, 133, 135, 136, 137,
138, 139, 140, 143, 146,
147, 154, 156, 157, 158,
159, 160, 163, 165, 166,
168, 175, 176, 177, 178,
179, 183, 188, 191, 198,
205, 213, 215, 219, 220,
221, 223, 249, 279,
280, 342
Cook, Julia West, 53, 59
Cook, Lucy Flood, 163,
164, 168, 175, 279
Cook, Lula, 99
Cook, Matthew Mitchell,
19, 298, 341
Cook, Sarah Catherine
(1810-1890), 180
Cook, Susan (Sue)
Farmer, 3, 21, 24, 41,
48, 53, 97, 98, 99, 100,
102, 104, 106, 107, 108,
109, 111, 113, 118, 119,
120, 123, 132, 133, 137,
138, 139, 158, 160, 169,
173, 215, 281, 294, 342
Cook, Wesley (1809-
1864), 180

348

Cook, William, 4, 163, 210, 223, 225, 226, 232, 235, 236, 240, 241, 243, 247
Cook, William, III (abt 1764-1814), 230
Corinth, MS, 100
Cotton Family, 1, 2, 5, 73, 75, 288, 289, 292, 296
Cotton, An (Ann), 289, 292
Cotton, Joane (?-?), 288
Cotton, John, 73, 288
Cotton, Rachael, 73
Cotton, Verlinda (?-c. 1675), 289
Coverdale, Miles (1488-1568), 250
Craig, Lewis (KY, 1787), 181, 330
Cremeen, Jacob (1731-1790), 86
Cremeen, John, III (1720-1754), 86
Cremeen, John, Jr (1691-1749), 86
Cremeen, John, Sr (1656-1713), 86
Crener, John Dorland, Genealogist, 68, 70, 75
Crestline, OH, 66
Crimora, VA, 89, 265
Crocheron Family, 251, 261
Crocheron, Marie, 251
Crocketagne, (Crosketagne) Antoine, 126, 128, 130
Crocketagne, Gabriel Gustave Gaston de, 128

Crockett Family, 1, 2, 3, 111, 123, 124, 126, 127, 128, 129, 130, 215, 221, 222
Crockett, Joseph Lewis, 128, 130
Crumrine, Boyd, historian, 248
Cumberland County, PA, 89, 93, 263, 308
Curtis, Mary, 86
Cynthiana, KY, 49
Dallas, TX, 48
Danville, KY, 9, 23, 43, 50
Darnell, Ermina Jett, genealogist, 129
Davis Family, 101, 177, 279, 280, 311
Davis, Mary (?-?), 177
de Saix, Louise, 128
Denmark, 38
Detroit, MI, 127
Dillard, R.T. (1843 narrator, 1792 Massacre), 194, 197
Diller (Dillar) Family, 4, 88, 89, 91, 93, 95, 178, 256, 263, 267, 269, 270, 271, 272, 273, 275, 276, 277
Diller (Dillar), Margaret, 4, 89, 93, 263, 269, 276
Diller, Adam Elias (Johnsses?), 88, 269
Diller, Anna Barbara Dornis, 4, 88, 89, 91, 93, 95, 267, 269, 271, 272, 273, 275, 276, 277

Diller, Caspar, 4, 88, 93, 95, 267, 269, 270, 273, 276, 277
Diller, Hans Martin, 273
Diller, Philipp Adam, 273
Diller, Rosina, 273
Dillwyn, VA, 279
Dongan, Thomas (1634-1715) Gov. New York Province, 274, 277
Dorland (Lash), Lucinda Haley, 55, 59, 66, 71, 72, 73, 74, 75, 341
Dorland (Van Dorland), Robert and Eric, Genealogists, 67
Dorland Family, 3, 5, 13, 15, 18, 21, 22, 23, 24, 25, 26, 27, 39, 42, 47, 49, 52, 55, 56, 57, 58, 59, 60, 62, 63, 64, 65, 66, 67, 68, 69, 70, 71, 72, 73, 74, 75, 76, 77, 78, 79, 82, 93, 94, 157, 249, 256, 263, 264, 265, 268, 269, 276, 341
Dorland, Charles Johnson, 70
Dorland, Cornelius, 72
Dorland, Eleanor (Aulche), 69
Dorland, Ezekiel, 55, 59, 66, 71, 72, 75
Dorland, Garret, 72
Dorland, James (1781-1858), 58, 59, 64, 66, 69, 70, 71, 72
Dorland, James Emery, 3, 18, 21, 55, 56, 58, 59, 60, 62, 63, 64, 65, 66, 67, 68, 70, 71, 72, 75, 78, 79, 264, 276, 341
Dorland, Lucas (Luke), 69
Dorland, Luke (1815-1897), 59, 70, 71
Dorland, Richard, 55
Dorlandt (Dorland), Gerret (Garret), 58, 68
Dorlandt Van Nyjenrode, Ghysbrecht, 67, 68
Dorlandt, Claes, 67
Dorlandt, Dorlant Family, 58, 67, 68, 69, 76
Dorlandt, Gerret Janse, 68
Dorlandt, Jan Gerretse, 68
Dorlandt, Lambert Janse, 68
Dorlon (Dorland, Dorlan, Durland, Durling), 68, 76
Dornis Family, 4, 88, 93, 178, 267, 269, 273
Dreuth, Holland, 256
Du Bois Family, 221, 222, 256, 259, 260, 261, 262
Du Bois, Geoffroi, 260
Du Bois, Louis, 259
Du Bois, W.E.B. (1868-1963), 260
Dunn, William (survivor 1792 Massacre), 194
Durrett, Reuben T., 140
Earl Town, Lancaster County PA, 273
England, 32, 38, 70, 83, 87, 113, 125, 127, 130,

141, 147, 173, 177, 186, 217, 219, 223, 225, 226, 230, 231, 233, 234, 235, 237, 238, 244, 246, 254, 258, 259, 260, 274, 279, 281, 285, 287, 288, 293, 299, 302
Fairfield County OH, 73
Farmer Family, 3, 4, 5, 21, 24, 41, 54, 97, 98, 99, 100, 102, 105, 108, 109, 110, 111, 112, 113, 114, 116, 117, 118, 119, 120, 121, 122, 123, 124, 126, 128, 129, 130, 132, 133, 137, 139, 146, 149, 158, 160, 166, 167, 169, 173, 194, 197, 202, 205, 215, 276, 281, 282, 286, 287, 292, 293, 294, 295, 296, 342
Farmer, Benjamin, 111, 112, 113, 169, 281, 293, 294
Farmer, Elam, 112, 113, 281, 293, 294
Farmer, Ellery, genealogist, 54, 100, 109, 110, 112, 113, 122, 128, 129, 130, 138, 158, 166, 173, 281, 286, 287, 293, 295, 296
Farmer, Henry, 112, 113, 281, 287, 294
Farmer, John Goode, 3, 97, 111, 116, 119, 120, 121, 122, 123, 132, 146, 169, 281

Farmer, Katherine Spencer Hawkins, 113, 117, 119
Farmer, Thomas, 4, 112, 113, 281, 282, 286, 287, 292, 295
Farmer, William G, 64, 97, 100, 102, 109, 167
Farmville VA, 9, 23
Farrars Island, 282, 286, 287
Fellers, Amunuel, 91
Fellers, John G., 91
Fellows, Jonathan, 264, 276
Fellows, Sarah, 3, 79, 91, 93, 263, 264, 269, 276
Fellows/Fellers Family, 3, 79, 81, 82, 90, 91, 92, 93, 94, 95, 263, 264, 265, 269, 276, 341
Fisher, Sarah, 16 (1870), domestic servant, 118, 137
Fithian, Philip Vickers, 233
Flanders, French Flanders, 251, 259, 260
Flood Family, 3, 4, 5, 9, 21, 24, 41, 63, 64, 99, 111, 119, 121, 123, 131, 133, 134, 135, 139, 144, 147, 153, 154, 156, 157, 160, 163, 164, 165, 166, 168, 175, 176, 177, 178, 179, 180, 183, 188, 213, 215, 219, 220, 221, 223, 249, 279, 280, 342
Flood, John, 4, 178, 279, 280

Flood, Joshua, 3, 144, 163, 164, 175, 177
Flood, Noah (1763-1818), 176
Flood, Noah (1809-1873), 9, 131, 134, 157, 163, 175, 176, 178
Ford, Reuben, 310
Forks of Elkhorn, KY, 124, 129, 179, 180, 212, 232, 239, 328, 329, 337, 338
Forsee, Charles, pastor, Skinquarter Baptist Church, 173, 323
Four Mile Creek, Henrico Co VA, 173
France, 7, 29, 30, 31, 32, 33, 35, 36, 37, 38, 39, 88, 126, 128, 130, 177, 178, 219, 231, 251, 260, 261, 271, 272, 273
Frankfort, KY, 113, 126, 127, 128, 130, 159, 182, 189, 194, 199, 200, 201, 202, 215, 236, 239, 296, 331, 337
Franklin County KY, 111, 115, 123, 124, 125, 126, 130, 169, 182, 186, 199, 212, 228, 229, 230, 238, 241, 245, 247
Franklin County VA, 111, 115, 123, 124, 125, 126, 130, 169, 182, 186, 199, 212, 224, 228, 229, 230, 238, 241, 243, 245, 247
Franklin, Jim, 48

French Protestants, Huguenots, 28, 29, 38, 88, 177, 271, 273, 276
Front Royal, VA, 254
Fruibeau Village, 269, 270
Fuqua Family, 176
Gaffney, SC, 23, 45
Garnett, _____, 106
Gauangelloch, near Heidelberg, 272
Gaventa, Wm. M.D., 17
Gelderland, Netherlands, 256
Geneva, 28, 29, 33
Gentry County MO, 220
Georgia, 45, 46
Germany, 31, 32, 91, 264, 272, 273
Goode Family, 3, 9, 21, 41, 97, 98, 105, 107, 108, 109, 111, 116, 119, 120, 121, 122, 123, 132, 139, 146, 169, 170, 171, 172, 173, 174, 281, 293, 316, 317, 321, 323, 342
Goode, John, 3, 9, 97, 107, 108, 111, 116, 119, 120, 121, 122, 123, 132, 146, 169, 170, 171, 172, 173, 174, 281, 293, 294, 316, 317, 321
Goode, Susan, 3, 21, 41, 97, 98, 108, 109, 111, 123, 132, 139, 160, 169, 173, 281, 294, 342
Goodfellow, Juliette E., 70
Graves, Katherine, 48

Graves, Thomas (?-by 1637), 289
Grayless (Gradeless) Family, 5, 85, 86, 94
Grayless (Grailey?) Jesse (1733/37-1799), 85
Grayless, Philadelphia (1760-1854), 84
Great Awakening, First, 231
Grimma, Saxony (Germany), 91
Guzman, Sarah Taylor Cook, 42, 302
Haley (Healy) Family, 55, 66, 71, 73, 74, 75, 341
Halifax County VA, 218, 228
Hankins, _____ Col. Skinquarter section, Henrico Co VA, 171, 316
Hannibal, MO, 133
Hannibal-LaGrange College, 109, 133, 159
Hanover, Lancaster County PA, 89
Harlingen, Somerset County, NJ, 68
Harmon, P.T., 47
Hawkins Family, 1, 2, 3, 97, 111, 119, 120, 121, 123, 124, 125, 126, 129, 132, 206
Hawkins, William, 123, 124, 125, 129
Hayden, William (KY, 1787), 180, 328
Healy (Haley?) Richard, 73

Healy, John, 73
Hendricksen, 256
Henrico County, 108, 113, 173, 287
Henricopolis, 286
Henry County, VA, 236
Hickman, William (1747-1830/34), 4, 108, 147, 169, 174, 180, 212, 217, 231, 232, 239, 305, 340
Holland, 38, 67, 68, 76, 77, 226, 249, 256, 258, 259, 261, 264, 273
Holmes County, OH, 72, 73
Holy League, 28, 36
Hornbach, Alsace, 269
House of Burgesses, 223, 229, 286
Huey, James Addison (1862-1961), 18, 49
Huey, Sara Crouch (1861-1956), 18
Huguenot (French Protestant), 7, 28, 29, 36, 37, 38, 39, 40, 88, 89, 91, 130, 177, 178, 219, 256, 259, 270, 271, 272, 276, 277
Huguenot Synod of 1559, 34
Ireland Family, 3, 5, 21, 55, 58, 59, 60, 61, 62, 75, 79, 80, 81, 82, 83, 84, 86, 87, 88, 90, 91, 92, 93, 94, 95, 130, 219, 263, 264, 265, 268, 269, 276, 341
Ireland, Arabelle America, 3, 21, 55, 58,

59, 60, 61, 62, 75, 79,
81, 82, 88, 91, 93, 94,
263, 264, 268, 269,
276, 341
Ireland, Augusta, 81
Ireland, Franklin S., 81
Ireland, Homer A., 75, 81,
94
Ireland, John M., 81
Ireland, Martin, M.D., 3,
79, 80, 81, 82, 84, 93,
95, 264, 276, 341
Ireland, Sarah J., 81
Ireland, Wooster M., 81
James River, 282, 287
James, Daniel (KY, 1787),
180, 328
Jamestown, VA, 239, 275,
281, 283, 289, 291,
293, 295, 296
Janse Peters, Hermina
(Hermptje Janse
Pieterse), 68
Jansen Schenck,
Jannetje, 68
Jefferson County KY, 331
Johnson, Trephina, 85
Jones (Jonsen?), Robert,
218
Jones Family, 3, 4, 47,
48, 75, 147, 163, 179,
183, 210, 215, 216, 218,
221, 223, 226, 228,
230, 232, 234, 236,
239, 240, 243, 245,
248, 249, 251, 252,
255, 261
Jones, Anne, 75

Jones, John, 215, 216,
217, 218, 219, 223, 228,
230, 232, 249
Jones, Margaret, 4, 147,
163, 179, 183, 209, 216,
221, 223, 226, 230,
234, 239, 243, 245
Jones, Robert (?-?) (Sr ?),
216
Jones, Robert (c. 1696-
aft. 1796), 215, 216,
217, 218, 219, 221, 228,
230, 239, 249, 251,
252, 255
Jones, Sarah, 3, 163, 179,
215, 216, 223, 240, 249
Judson, Adoniram, 134
Kansas City, MO, 52
Kaskaskia, 126, 130
Keinath (Coiner)
Catherine, 89, 93, 263,
269, 276
Keinath (Coiner) Family,
4, 5, 88, 89, 91, 93,
256, 263, 264, 265,
266, 267, 268, 269,
276
Keinath (Keinadt),
Michael, 4, 89, 93, 263,
265, 266, 276
Keinath/Kainadt, Koiner,
Koyner, Coinert,
Coiner, 265
Kentucky, 5, 6, 15, 25, 41,
45, 53, 64, 66, 69, 97,
99, 100, 101, 102, 103,
106, 111, 113, 114, 117,
118, 121, 126, 127, 128,
129, 130, 131, 132, 133,
137, 140, 141, 142, 143,

144, 146, 147, 148, 149, 155, 157, 158, 159, 163, 164, 166, 168, 169, 170, 172, 174, 175, 176, 177, 178, 179, 180, 182, 183, 186, 187, 188, 189, 193, 194, 201, 211, 214, 215, 216, 217, 220, 227, 232, 235, 236, 238, 239, 241, 244, 245, 257, 263, 277, 280, 294, 300, 305, 311, 312, 322, 323, 324, 328, 334, 336, 340
Kingston, Ulster County New York, 252, 256, 259
Klein (Kelin?) Mary Catherine, 89
Knight, Ryland, 49
Ku Klux Klan, 150, 151, 154, 260
Kueber, Gary, family genealogist, 159, 168, 220, 221, 247
La Rochelle, 33
LaGrange College, 41, 48, 50, 52, 97, 99, 106, 107, 109, 118, 119, 131, 133, 136, 137, 138, 139, 140, 145, 155, 158, 159, 160
LaGrange, MO, 41, 106, 118, 119, 131, 133, 136
Lake, John, 51
Lamb, Charles (1775-1834), 99
Lancaster County PA, 89, 91, 93, 256, 264, 273, 276

Lebanon, PA, 88, 271
Lewis, W.O., 48
Lindsey, David (?) (KY, 1787), 180, 328
Lisbon, (New Lisbon Village), OH, 66
Lorraine, adjacent to Alsace, 271
Louis XIV, 130, 262, 271
Louisville Baptist Orphans Home, KY, 49
Lousiville, KY, 9, 15, 21, 41, 42, 47, 48, 49, 50, 51, 58, 59, 62, 63, 75, 76, 128, 131, 140, 146, 153, 249, 296, 300, 301
Lowe, Margaret and John, 50
Lunenburg County VA, 223, 224, 228, 229, 231, 245, 247
Luther, Martin (1483-1546), 272
Lutheran, Lutheranism, 39, 42, 58, 60, 62, 82, 88, 89, 91, 95, 256, 263, 265, 268, 270, 271, 272
Lynch, Charles, 180, 220
Lynchburg, VA, 47
Mace, Nicholas, 86
Mace, Susanna (1656-1734), 86
Major, John (KY, 1787), 180, 328
Mannheim, on the River Rhine, 259
Mappelen, Holland, 256
Marble Creek, KY, 181, 327, 328, 329, 330

Massacre (Innis' Bottom, 1792), 182
Massacre of 1622, VA, 286, 295
Mastin (Martin?), Lewis (killed, 1792), 182, 183, 184, 186, 188, 190, 191, 202, 209, 210, 212, 215
McAndre, _____ (survived 1792 Massacre), 194, 196, 197, 204, 210
McAndre, _____ (survived 1792 Massacre), 194, 196, 197, 204, 210
McDonald, Neil, family historian, 248
Mcfall, Gentry County, MO, 220
McLean County, Ill, 79
McRoberts, Archibald, Rector, Dale Parish, Henrico Co VA, 293, 308, 316
Mercer County KY, 127, 130
Merlyn Joseph Cook (1914–1995), family historian, 199, 221, 228, 236, 243, 245, 247
Mexico City, 11, 42
Meyer, Magdalena, 271
Middle River Baptist Assoc of Virginia, 107, 122
Millertown (Annville), Cumberland Co (formerly Lancaster CO) PA, 93
Minnisink Indians, 257
Missouri, 5, 9, 21, 41, 42, 45, 47, 50, 52, 53, 66, 79, 97, 99, 106, 109, 118, 119, 131, 132, 133, 134, 137, 138, 139, 140, 142, 144, 146, 148, 149, 157, 158, 159, 160, 163, 176, 178, 179, 219
Mollenauer, Margaret (c. 1687-1745), 251
Monocacy Hundred (MD), 216
Moore Family, 1, 2, 5, 64, 66, 69, 70, 71
Moore, John, 66, 71
Moore, Mary, 64
Moravian Br. Hermanus, 218, 221
Moravians, 218
Morgan, Daniel (1736-1802), 126
Morgan, Edmund S., 129, 295
Morgan, John Hunt,, 64, 166
Mountain Lake, Franklin Co VA, 228
Murphy, John (1752-1818), 147, 148, 149, 159, 185
Netherlands, 177, 254
New Amsterdam, NY, 5, 68, 76, 256, 258, 259
New Jersey, 5, 38, 68, 69, 72, 126, 130, 252, 253, 254, 259, 276

New Liberty College, New Liberty, KY, 99, 133
New Liberty Female Seminary, KY, 99, 132, 133
New Lisbon Village (Lisbon), OH, 66
New Netherland, 38, 256, 258
New Orleans, LA, 21, 23, 42, 133, 139, 146
New York, 5, 11, 16, 38, 40, 45, 48, 59, 60, 68, 69, 77, 121, 122, 126, 129, 130, 168, 177, 178, 251, 252, 256, 259, 261, 262, 274, 277, 278, 292, 295, 299
New York City, NY, 11, 16, 59
Nichols, Elizabeth L, family historian, 148, 159, 245, 248
Nicklisson (Nicholson), Rebecca, 73
Nicklisson, John, 73
North Annville Township, Lancaster County PA, 88, 270
Northampton CO PA Militia, 264
Norton, N.S., 50
Norway, 38, 52
O'Gorman, Edmundo (1906-1995), 274
Okalona, KY, 50
Orange County, VA, 124, 125, 206, 254
Palatine States, 88, 177, 259, 271, 272

Pamumkey, 282, 284
Paris, 31, 32, 33, 35, 36, 235, 261
Payne Family, 1, 2, 4, 152, 279, 280
Payne, Agnes, 4, 279, 280
Paz, Octavio (1914-1998), 274, 277
Pershing, John, J., (1860-1948) Gen., 82
Pierrepont, Mrs. A V D, genealogist, 287
Piqua Indians, 127, 130
Pittsylvania County VA, 228, 229, 247
Poe, E.D., 50
Posey's (VA) Regiment (1776), 126, 130
Powell, Mary, 75
Powhatan County VA, 38
Presbyterian, 21, 23, 28, 39, 58, 59, 62, 66, 70, 71, 83, 256, 312
Presbyterian Church, 59, 66, 71
Prince George's County MD, 73, 229, 253
Qualey, Ethyl Barnes Dorland, 21, 58, 59
Qualey, Joe, 59
Randolph Family, 223
Réformée (French Protestantism), 36, 38, 39
Renfro, Mary, 216, 249
Renfro/Rentfro Family, 1, 2, 216, 217, 223, 224, 225, 226, 228, 230, 236, 249

Revolutionary War (1776-1781), 89, 95, 126, 128, 176, 212, 214, 229, 235, 263, 264, 276
Rhine River, 259
Richmond, VA, 48, 50, 53
Ricketts Family, 73, 75
Ricketts, Cheney, 73
Ricketts, Edward, 73, 75
Ricketts, Mary, 73
Ricketts, Thomas, 73
Roanoke, VA, 50
Robertson Family, 126, 169
Ross County OH, 79
Rucks, James & Josiah, Baptist Preachers, Chesterfield County VA, 172, 321
Saix, de Saix Family, 128
Salem County, NJ, 252
Saline County MO, 139
Salt River Township, Wayne County OH, 55
Sampey, John, 48, 53
Sanders, Nathaniel (1787), 180, 328
Sawyer, Elbert H., 52
Schalbach / Schwalbach, Alsace, 269, 270, 277
Scroggins, William G., genealogist, 153, 159, 207, 210, 218, 220, 221, 222, 240, 243, 244, 245, 246, 247
Sengstock, Pat, genealogist, 186, 198, 210, 221

Sharundo (Shenandoah) Valley, 253, 254
Shelby County KY, 53, 70, 99, 100, 102, 106, 111, 113, 117, 119, 123, 132, 141, 153, 154, 159, 163, 164, 168, 177, 179, 180, 181, 182, 187, 194, 199, 219, 245, 330
Shenandoah Valley, 89, 95, 198, 216, 239, 252, 254, 255, 263, 265
Sherman, William T, Gen (USA), 57, 64, 167, 168
Shilburne, James M., 50
Ship, *Bomekoe* (Spotted Cow), 68
Ship, *Samuel*, 88, 272
Ship, *Vos*, (Fox), 256
Six-Mile Creek, Shelby Co KY, 179
Slagle Family, 5, 89, 91, 93, 95, 256, 263, 264, 269, 276
Slagle, Christoph Friedrich, 91
Slagle, George, 89, 93, 95, 263, 276
Slagle, Jacob, 89
Slagle, Margaret, 91, 93, 263, 269, 276
Slavery, Race Slavery, 6, 64, 85, 87, 116, 118, 119, 144, 146, 148, 149, 175, 231, 241, 254, 262, 281
Somerset County, NJ, 68, 252
South Africa, 38

South Carolina, 38, 45, 62, 162
Southern Baptist Theological Seminary, 15, 41, 47, 48, 62
Spencer Family, 97, 111, 121, 123, 132, 148, 159, 182, 183, 185, 186, 187, 191, 220
St Louis, MO, 23
St. Augustine, FL, 37, 283
Stewart, Mary, 128
Stoever, Rev. John Casper, Jr, 263, 271
Stone, William (1603-1660), 289
Sturgess, Allice Murphy, family historian, 148, 149, 159
Stuttgart, Neckar, Wuerttemberg (Germany), 91
Stuyvesant, Peter (?-1672), 258
Summit, MS, 120, 133
Sunday School Board, 50
Swiss Brethren, 273, 274
Switzerland, 31, 38, 269, 274
Tarbue, Edward, 172, 323
Tarrant, Carter, 148
Taylor, Nan Elizabeth (1893-1993), 16, 18
Thaeler, Thaler, Diller Taylor, de Llér, Daillé, 271
Thames, Battle of, 127
The Great Depression (1929-41), 45
Theodore Roosevelt, 140

Thoreau, Henry David (1817-1862), 38
Toulouse, 31
Trippet, Alice, 86
Tuller (Tuller, Diller, Teller, Deller, Dellor), 269, 271
Turner, Fredrick Jackson, 256
Tyndale, William (1594-1636), 225
Universidad Autónoma Nacional de México, Mexico City, 42
University of Henrico, 287
Van Arsdalen, Hilitie (Matilda), 68
Van Lejenburg, Bella, 67
Van Meter (Van Meteren) Family, 4, 5, 7, 215, 216, 217, 221, 230, 249, 250, 251, 252, 253, 254, 255, 256, 257, 258, 259, 262
Van Meter, James T., 256, 262
Van Meter, John (Jan Joosten van Meteren), 4, 215, 216, 221, 251, 252, 253, 254, 255, 256, 259
Van Meter, Mary (Maria), 215, 251
Van Meteren, Cathrin, 256
Van Meteren, Geertje, 256
Van Meteren, Gysbert, 256

Van Meteren, Lysbeth, 256
Van Meterer (Van Meter) Family, 215, 230, 249, 256, 259
Van Nijendode, Jan, 67
Van Nyjenrode Family, 67, 68
Van Nyjenrode, Ghysbrecht, 67
Virginia, 4, 5, 6, 9, 15, 38, 45, 46, 47, 53, 81, 89, 91, 95, 96, 97, 107, 111, 113, 115, 121, 122, 125, 126, 127, 129, 130, 132, 143, 147, 159, 166, 169, 170, 173, 175, 176, 179, 180, 198, 206, 212, 214, 215, 216, 217, 219, 222, 223, 224, 225, 227, 228, 229, 230, 231, 232, 233, 234, 235, 237, 238, 239, 241, 244, 245, 246, 248, 252, 253, 254, 258, 261, 263, 264, 265, 266, 267, 268, 275, 276, 279, 280, 281, 282, 283, 284, 285, 286, 287, 290, 292, 293, 295, 296, 305, 307, 308, 311, 325, 327, 334, 336
Virginia Colony, 4, 5, 38, 126, 169, 170, 173, 223, 234, 263, 277, 279, 281, 282, 283, 286, 295
Wachovia, NC, 218
Waller, John, 217, 307

Walter Reed Army Hospital, 82
War of 1812-14, 127
Wars of Religion (1562-1598), 36
Washington, D.C., 82
Washington, George, 126
Washington, George (1732-99), 6, 49, 233, 255, 261, 289
Watts, Patricia, Ohio genealogist, 72, 75
Wayne County OH, 55, 59, 60, 72, 73, 76
Webb City, MO, 21, 42, 139
White Marsh PA, 126
Whitley County IN, 59, 79, 81, 91, 93, 94
Whitman, Walt (1819-1892), 91, 96, 121, 122
Wickens, Carolyn, genealogist, 109, 122, 124, 129, 158, 160
Wicomico County MD, 86
Wildwych, (Kingston, Ulster County NY), 256
William of Normandy, 260
Williams, Grace, 112
Williams, Harry (W. Harrison), 50
Williams, Jerome O, 50
Wilmington, DE, 115
Wilson, Sarah, 73
Woodford County VA (later, KY), 210, 216, 239

Wooster Medical University of Cleveland, 81
World War I, 53, 82, 140
Wyanconda Baptist Assoc., MO, 139
Wycliffe, John, 231
Yates, Kyle M., 51
York, PA, 89, 91

Supplement to **ALL OF THE ABOVE II**

DORLAND – pages 55, 58-60, 66

The first and second editions of **ABOVE II** lack details of the life of **James E. Dorland** (1844-1915), which he himself supplied for the book **A History of Kentucky and Kentuckians** (Johnson, 1912). Here (vol 2, 902-03) we learn that during James' service in the Civil War (August, 1862-June 1865), his widowed mother **Lucinda Haley Dorland** (1818-1893) moved, with her son Richard, from Maysville, Wayne County, Ohio to Columbia City, Whitley County, Indiana and that James joined her there after his discharge, having served in Company C, Forty-first Ohio Volunteer Infantry.

In Columbia City James completed his high school education, which had been interrupted by the War. (James volunteered and became an infantryman at age 17.) He attended high school in Columbia City for one year and then taught school for two winters, after which he obtained a "first grade" teacher certificate and was "elected" (Johnson, p. 902) assistant principal of the Columbia City High School. James served in this position for three years. James lived in Columbia City for a total of eight years and was deputy clerk for Whitley County. According to a history of the county was also a surveyor during this period.

In 1873, he became a traveling salesman for the publisher A.S. Barnes of New York and Chicago, selling and placing text books in the public schools of Indiana and several neighboring states. In 1874, a promotion to general agent prompted a move to Nashville, TN and, in 1876, to Indianapolis, IN. In 1878, James was ordered to move to Chicago but resigned from Barnes and moved to Louisville, KY, employed as the general agent for the textbook publisher Antwerp, Bragg and Company of Cincinnati, Ohio, a position he held for 12 years. In 1890, his employer and four other publishers merged to form the American Book Company and James became the ABC general agent for Kentucky and surrounding states. Johnson's **History** (page 903) credits James E. Dorland with helping to shape the laws governing Kentucky public schools. The annals of the American Education Association record James E. Dorland as an active member for many years. NOTE: The photo of James E. Dorland, on page 362, is from Johnson's **History,** digitized by Google.

James E. Dorland's grandmother **Mary Moore Dorland** (1785-1869) was born in New Jersey. James told (Johnson, p. 902) that Mary's father **John Moore** (?-?) was from Ireland. What is meant here (confirmed by Cremer, p. 206) is that John Moore was from Northern Ireland and of Scot heritage. (See **ABOVE II** pp. 66, 75). Cremer lists the thirteen children of Mary Moore and James Dorland: Eleanor, John Moore, Cornelius, James Jr., **Ezekiel**, Luke, William M., Sussana, Jane, Hilley, Archibald, Garrett, and Alexander Moore.

James E. Dorland told Johnson (page 902) that the first immigrant in his Dorland line was his great-grandfather, **Lucas (Luke) Dorland** (1748/9-aft 1787). However, this Dorland line had been in America for a century prior to Lucas' birth. Lucas' great grandfather, **Lambert Janse Dorlandt** (1639-1720) emigrated from Holland in 1663 (see **ABOVE II,** pp. 68-69). Lambert served as constable of Brooklyn (1671), magistrate (1673) and Richmond County colonial assemblyman (1690-91).

James E. Dorland told Johnson that his great grandfather Luke Dorland had fought in the American Revolution. Cremer lists (pp 283-86) Dorlands who fought on both sides (16, American, 5, British) and lists *Linus*, not Lucas Dorland.

During the American Revolution, many Dorlands on Long Island were British loyalistss; others joined their neighbors in an effort to chart an impossible middle course. All of these earned threats of violence from committees of Liberty elsewhere in New York and hostile resolutions from the Congress. The British occupation of New York and Long Island lasted for seven years (1776-1783), ending only with final British defeat. After the Revolution, facing the prospect of prosecution and property confiscations, one third of the population of Long

Island moved to Canada. The 1780s Upper Canada exodus included Dorlands.

COOK – pages 140, 223, 235

Howard Eliott Cook, son of **Joshua Flood Cook** (1834-1912) and Drucilla Hirons (?-1962) was not a soldier during World War II. Rather, Howard was an employee of Morrison-Knudson of Boise Idaho, on Wake Island, when Wake was overrun by the Japanese Army on Dec. 31 1941. Howard spent three and a half years as a prisoner of war and is believed to have suffered terrible physical and mental abuse on Wake Island and then in China and Japan, where many of the civilian prisoners and Marine POWs were taken.

The Cooks of Wyoming County, WV are unlikely to be related to **William Cook** (c. 1730-c 1790/91), husband of **Margaret Jones** (?) (1734-1797). The following statements are from *Oceana Community History*, by Warner Walker (1926) – posted on line at "West Virginia Archives & History": *In 1750 -the year in which Franklin made his discoveries in electricity, John Cook was born in London, England. The boy who was the son of a well to do native of London grew up among the people of the crowded streets of the city. He secured a moderate education. When fifteen years old he fell in love with a young lady and was married. In 1770 he and his wife set sail for America and landed at Norfolk, Virginia. In a short while they made their way through to Giles County, Virginia where they settled and raised a family of four boys, Thomas, John Jr., William and James.*

In 1798 John Cook Sr. made his first trip to what is now Wyoming County. He found a large area of level land which now comprises the farms below Oceana, West Virginia. He returned to Giles County, Virginia and told Edward McDonald about this fine tract of land which he had seen on his trip west. McDonald secured a patent from the governor of Virginia for this tract of land and sent Cook down to take charge of it for him. John Cook Sr.

with his family came to what is now Wyoming County and made the first settlement in 1802. Their log cabin, which was the first in the county, stood until the fall of 1923. It was torn down when the new village of Oceana Junction was being laid off.

But few years had elapsed when more settlements were made. The Stewarts settled in an adjoining community and intermarried with the Cook's. In 1890 two-thirds of this county were descendants of John Cook Sr. He is called the father of Oceana Community.

Re: the death date of William Cook, husband of Margaret (Jones?) (See **ABOVE II**, pp. 223, 239):

In 1901, a brief biography of **Abraham Cook** (1774-1854) stated that Abraham's father died shortly after the family moved to Kentucky in 1780. See the *National Cyclopaedia of American Biography*, by George Derby, James Terry White (J. T. White, 1901) vol 11, p. 498. The 1780 date is too early for the move to Kentucky. Therefore, this source is unlikely to be accurate as to the year of the death of **William Cook.** William had died by 1790 (wife listed alone on the tax rolls) and perhaps as early as 1784, when Wiliam sold his land in Virginia. Therefore, 1784 is the probable year, when his wife **Margaret** (1734-1797) moved their large family into Kentucky.

www.ingramcontent.com/pod-product-compliance
Lightning Source LLC
Chambersburg PA
CBHW022100150426
43195CB00008B/212